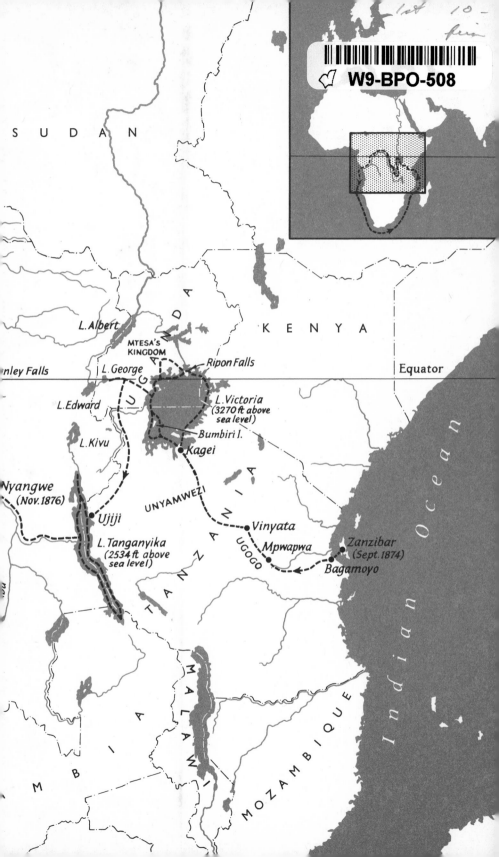

SUDAN

L. Albert

MTESA'S KINGDOM

Ripon Falls

KENYA

nley Falls

L. George

Equator

L. Edward

U G A N D A

L. Victoria
(3270 ft above
sea level)

L. Kivu

Bumbiri I.

Kagei

Nyangwe
(Nov. 1876)

Ujiji

UNYAMWEZI

L. Tanganyika
(2534 ft above
sea level)

Vinyata

UGOGO

Mpwapwa

Zanzibar
(Sept. 1874)

Bagamoyo

T A N Z A N I A

I n d i a n   O c e a n

M A L A W I

MOZAMBIQUE

M B I A

Stanley

STANLEY

An Adventurer Explored

RICHARD HALL

WITH ILLUSTRATIONS
AND MAPS

Houghton Mifflin Company Boston

1975

First American Edition 1975

Library of Congress Cataloging in Publication Data

Hall, Richard Seymour, 1925–
  Stanley: an adventurer explored.

  Bibliography: p.   Includes indexes.
  1. Stanley, Sir Henry Morton, 1844–1904.
DT351.S9H27 1975   916.7'04'0924[B]   74-30393
ISBN 0-395-19426-1

Printed in the United States of America

C 10 9 8 7 6 5 4 3 2 1

For
Jeremy Andrew Buchyzia

Contents

CONTENTS

PART THREE: POWER AND ILLUSION

Illustrations

LIST OF ILLUSTRATIONS

Foreword

I had always been ready to accept the conventional view of Stanley. His character seemed cold and barren, so that any prospective biographer would surely turn aside in dismay, like a climber from a sheer granite cliff. It would explain why few attempts had been made to tell the story of his life, although he was undoubtedly the boldest of the nineteenth-century explorers.

For all that, it was impossible not to respect his achievements. As a newspaper correspondent in the troubled Congo of the early sixties, I had gazed at his monument, that massive bronze statue (now demolished) beside the Stanley Pool; I realised that his true monument was the Congo State itself, the biggest territory carved out of Africa during the age of imperialism. Perhaps my lack of sympathy for Stanley was influenced by this very fact: he had been the empire-builder for King Leopold, and so his image was stained by the bloody horrors of the Congo, most hauntingly conveyed in Joseph Conrad's novel, *Heart of Darkness*.

My opinions began to alter during a journey over the route Stanley had travelled in his search for Livingstone. Not only was I made aware of the tenacity that would have been needed on that 1,500-mile march a century ago, but I also gained some insights into Stanley's character. With me I took a copy of *How I Found Livingstone*, and it left an impression of a lonely and complicated young man, hiding his true self behind a façade of bravado.

In writing his biography I have been able to make many discoveries about Stanley, but one of the difficulties has been to sift fact from fantasy and falsehood. His personality led him to conceal his 'shameful origins' and romantic attachments to such an extent that his own account is untrustworthy. Previous biographers have been far too ready to take him at his own word.

Readers who study the postscript to this book will realise how indebted I am to the countless people in Britain and America who have enabled me to establish, once and for all, the truth about Stanley and his background. By an irony he was his own worst enemy, for his concealments have tended only to depreciate the magnificence of his achievements.

I hope that even if some of my interpretations are open to argument, this book destroys for ever the image of Stanley as a ruthless *conquistador* and reveals him as one of the most fascinating of the Great Victorians.

RICHARD. HALL

A Note on African Names

In general, this book follows modern usage in African names. Thus the domain of King Mtesa was generally known as Uganda when Stanley first reached there, but is identified as Buganda to distinguish it from the modern – and much larger – State. The plural prefix has been omitted on tribal names; for example, the people of Buganda are identified as the Ganda.

The name Congo has lately been altered to Zaire in what was the Congo Democratic Republic. It is retained, however, by the neighbouring Congo-Brazzaville. Stanleyville has become Kisangani, and Leopoldville is called Kinshasa. A proclamation by President Mobutu changed Lake Albert to Lake Mobutu Sese Seko.

Almost all of the names bestowed by Stanley on lakes, rivers and mountains to honour his friends and employers have long since vanished.

Stanley's Travels in Central Africa

1871-72
Expedition to Lake Tanganyika for the *New York Herald*, to find Dr Livingstone

1874-77
Journey of discovery from Zanzibar to the Atlantic. Stanley becomes the first white man to explore the River Congo

1879-84
Systematic investigation of the Congo region, while opening up the interior of Africa for King Leopold of Belgium

1886-89
Stanley answers Britain's call for the rescue of Emin Pasha, and makes a second crossing of the continent

PART ONE

Hero of the Hour

1. Pledge in Fifth Avenue, Appointment in Africa

During the summer of 1874, Henry Morton Stanley made ready to venture once more into Africa. He was already famous for having rescued the most honoured of Africa travellers. 'Dr Livingstone, I presume?' was a greeting that had rung around the world. But it was not enough for Stanley to be the journalist who had achieved an unparalleled scoop and written a bestseller about it. He now wanted to show that he was an explorer in his own right, fit to be ranked with men such as Burton and Speke, or even Livingstone himself.

The journey he was planning staggered the imagination: a march of 5,000 miles across Central Africa from east to west, from the Indian Ocean to the Atlantic. He meant to settle every outstanding question about the source of the Nile, and chart all the great lakes in the heart of the continent, before plunging into the unknown land to the west of Lake Tanganyika and the fabled Mountains of the Moon. The only white man who had dared to set foot in that *terra incognita* was Livingstone, and he had been forced to turn back. Stanley hoped to emerge from his odyssey at the mouth of the Congo. The volume of water the Congo poured into the Atlantic showed that it was one of the biggest rivers in the world, but its course through the interior was unknown. Stanley intended to solve that mystery as well.

It was widely assumed that the reward for such arrogant ambition would be death. The luck that had so often saved Stanley on his Livingstone adventure would surely desert him this time. There was no lack of people who secretly hoped that the correspondent of the flashy *New York Herald* was about to be swallowed up in the Dark Continent for good. Stanley understood very well why his enemies thought he aspired above his station. In an age when explorers were generally well-born officers or wealthy sportsmen, he was looked at askance. It simply made him more determined than ever that the world should accept and respect him.

There was, however, one distraction that Stanley had not reckoned on. He had fallen in love. On Sunday, 12th July, 1874, he signed a marriage pact with a Miss Alice Pike at her home in Fifth Avenue, New York: 'We solemnly pledge ourselves to be faithful to each other and to be married to one another on the return of Henry Morton Stanley from Africa. We call God to witness this our pledge in writing.'

Alice Pike was only 17, and Stanley was in his thirties, but they seemed nonetheless well matched. She had a cool self-assurance that came from being the beautiful and talented daughter of a millionaire; the Pike residence was in that part of Fifth Avenue, between 42nd and 72nd Street, which tycoons such as William K. Vanderbilt and John Jacob Astor had lined with imitation châteaux and palazzi. Although Stanley could not compete in wealth, he was forceful and flamboyant in a way that suited the surging optimism of America in the years following the Civil War. He smoked Havana cigars at breakfast, handed out signed photographs to the merest acquaintances, walked with his head thrown back and chin defiantly forward, and liked to brag. He was only 5 feet 5 inches tall, but powerfully built. His years in Missouri, Kansas, Colorado, and Nebraska had made him expert with a six-shooter and a rifle; he had prospected for gold, ridden the Plains in the Indian wars and could bring out a string of anecdotes about such figures as Colonel Custer and Wild Bill Hickok. It was small wonder that Stanley had carried the Stars and Stripes into the middle of Africa, and meant to do so again.

Yet there was another side to him. Amid the pellmell gusto of *How I Found Livingstone* – which had sold 70,000 copies and been castigated by Florence Nightingale as 'the very worst book on the very best subject' – were passages of real sensitivity. Stanley wrote with feeling about the beauties of forests and mountains. Often his handling of Africans seemed to derive from the treatment he had seen imposed on Red Indians, but such toughness was oddly mixed with tenderness. He enjoyed talking to children about his adventures and had a knack of capturing their interest. On the search for Livingstone he had been presented with a slave boy named Kalulu by an Arab trader. Stanley brought the boy back with him from Africa and treated him almost as an adopted son; his recently published adventure book for children was called *My Kalulu*. Above all, Livingstone had become far more for him than a journalistic prize – he wrote and talked about the famous missionary with an awe that was near to mysticism.

Alice Pike was not in the least afraid of the glitter in Stanley's grey eyes when he was enraged by petty upsets. He would do anything for her: she told him that Henry was not nearly so melodious as his second name, so he at once began signing himself, in his fondly phrased letters, 'Your loving Morton'. Alice felt proud that the portable boat with which Stanley planned to explore the lakes and rivers of Africa would be called after her. Only a few chosen friends knew this secret – how the *Lady Alice* would be a constant reminder of the girl he had vowed to return to and claim as his bride. He told Alice he must be away for two years, which to someone of 17 seemed like eternity. But she would occupy herself with the delights of New York society and her lessons in singing and playing the harp.

Stanley and Alice had met in London. This gave him an initial advantage, for whereas she was on a first visit to Europe that Spring, with her mother and elder sister, he knew his way around in the British capital. He had been based on London, Paris or Madrid since 1867, when he joined the staff of the *New York Herald*, and although feeling more at ease in the United States he did not care to argue about his postings with the capricious and autocratic owner of the paper, James Gordon Bennett. By now, Stanley had built up a wide circle of contacts in London – which was not to say that he got on well with many British people. They seemed aloof and super-cilious; he had quarrelled wildly in 1872 with the Royal Geographical Society, which had at first seemed sceptical about his claims to have found Livingstone, then rather jealous. The RGS members were a cross-section of the British Establishment, and to them his lack of decorum and his new-style journalism seemed to epitomise all that was worst in America. As Queen Victoria wrote, after he had been brought to meet her in a Scottish ducal home: '. . . a determined, ugly, little man – with a strong American twang.' Stanley had clearly fought his way to success from nowhere. Questions about his origins only stirred up his notorious temper, or reduced him to sullen silence.

These shortcomings in British eyes did not worry Alice. Her own father, who had recently died, came from poor Jewish stock in the small German town of Schwetzingen, near Heidelberg, and at twenty-six had founded his fortune by distilling a whisky he called 'Magnolia' in Cincinnati. Alice had grown up in a world where what mattered was how much people could make of themselves; you did not ask about their pedigrees. After all, her industrialist father had written poetry, played the flute and devoted half a million dollars to building an opera house in Cincinnati.

The verve Stanley showed was exciting. His third book, telling of his experiences as a correspondent with two British military campaigns in Africa, had just appeared, and *The Times* said in its review (April 25, 1874): 'As might be expected from his energy and enterprise, Mr Stanley is first in the field.' The reviewer thought the book showed signs of the race 'which the author has been running against brother correspondents', but praised its typically forthright manner.

The vividness he brought to his writing also made Stanley a brilliant conversationalist. But he was best in the company of only two or three people; then his voice lost its aggressive harshness and became softly melodious. His smile was caressing. Unlike Victoria, Alice did not find him ugly: he had wavy black hair, flecked with grey, highly arched brows over those remarkable eyes, and a firm mouth lurking behind his flowing moustache.

She studied him over dinner at the Langham Hotel, near Regent's Park. The recently-built Langham was almost an American enclave in London – Stanley lived there and his friend Mark Twain used it as a base when he was in Britain on his lecture tours. It was far bigger than the traditional British hotel and among its numerous attractions had 300 WCs, a lift, and its own well as a protection against cholera. The size and modernity of the Langham made the Americans who poured into London after the Civil War feel more at home.

A young man named Armour, from a prosperous meat-packing family, was staying at the Langham and had offered to introduce Stanley to the Pikes. At the start, Stanley was his usual wary – even cynical – self. He had already met Alice's brother, and dismissed him as 'one of those useless young men fashionable New York produces every year, who become nothing, whom nobody ever hears of.' However, it cost little effort to go along to the dinner party, where he was greeted by Mrs Pike – who was 'good-looking, stout, and exceedingly good-tempered'.

The first of the Pike girls to appear at the dinner was Nettie. Stanley decided that she was healthy and handsome, but seemed 'rather fast' and spoke 'disagreeably loud'. Her coiffure was done up in the popular frizzles, which he called 'a lot of untidy hair hanging over the forehead'. When Alice came into the room she showed none of the exuberance of her elder sister, and for a while he saw only her 'soft, girlish, profile'. Then he drew her into conversation, and she slowly turned towards him in a self-contained way that contrasted with the style of the 'more volatile Nettie'. Alice was pale, had a broad forehead, and big blue-grey eyes. He later wrote in his diary: 'Her mouth was large but well-formed, her nose had a certain Jewish fullness at the point with the slightest possible rise halfway down.' She wore too many diamonds for Stanley's taste, but he had to concede that she was attractive; when she rose from the table in her black silk dress, he noticed that her figure was 'very elegant . . .'

After dinner, the girls began to question Stanley about Africa. The awe-inspiring funeral of Dr Livingstone had taken place in Westminster Abbey a few weeks earlier and Stanley had been one of the pall-bearers. He was the last white man to have seen the old explorer alive; although failing to persuade Livingstone to come out of the African wilds to safety, Stanley had given him enough supplies to fend off the inevitable end of his obsessive wanderings for another eighteen months. Alice in particular seemed genuinely interested in hearing about these experiences. But his afterthought on the Misses Pike was disapproving, or perhaps defensive: 'They are both very ignorant of African geography, and I fear of everything else.'

He also soon discovered that Alice already had a number of suitors. One was an elderly judge in St Louis called Mumford. Another was a young French count, whose latest letter – a 'very lover-like effusion' – Alice unashamedly read out, between bursts of laughter. Stanley was shocked by this behaviour. But a few days after the meeting at dinner, he wrote: 'I fear that if Miss Alice gives me as much encouragement long as she has been giving me lately, I shall fall in love with her.' One May afternoon they went out together in a carriage in Hyde Park. Later they made a trip to Windsor, where in a carefree manner he weighed himself at a chemist's shop: he was 178 lb. That was far too much, but he knew from his Livingstone expedition that a few months of travel in Africa, with all its fevers and anxieties, would soon reduce him to gauntness.

Stanley saw Alice almost every day in London, but he could not allow his romantic feelings to deflect him entirely from his plans. He had bought a large library of books on Africa, and studied them until the early hours of the morning. He made careful notes about climate and geography in his tidy, tightly-controlled handwriting.

An Irish journalist gave an account of how the famous Stanley worked: 'The chairs, tables, sofas and settees, nay even the very floor itself – are laden with books, newspapers, manuscripts and maps. Nobody has ever ventured to dust a single article in Mr Stanley's room ever since he first took possession. He sits all day long on a wicker stool about eight inches high . . . and writes on a little table

Alice Pike at seventeen, in the Spring of 1874. This photograph was taken in Paris, and she gave it to Stanley to carry with him across Africa. Alice was born in Cincinnati, but when she was ten her industrialist father moved the family to New York

of perhaps treble that height just large enough to hold an inkpot, a quire of foolscap, and the meerschaum, his faithful companion through all his African travels . . . he can lay his hand on any book or paper he may want without losing a moment in the search, so well does he remember the place where he has stowed it away.' Stanley sketched routes across the continent, sometimes just above the equator, and sometimes just below. He drew up precise lists of the equipment he would need, with a skill remembered from his time as a clerk in a country store in Arkansas.

On June 12, Alice had to sail home to New York, and Stanley accompanied her to Liverpool, to see her off. As soon as he arrived back in London he called at the *Daily Telegraph* office in Fleet Street

Henry Stanley, journalist turned explorer, was in his early thirties at the time of his pledge to Alice: on his return from the 'Dark Continent', they would be married. He confided the details of their romance to his diaries

and asked for financial backing. It was a somewhat unorthodox move, seeing he was still employed by the *New York Herald*. But it was also astute, because his relations with James Gordon Bennett were fragile. The *Herald* had backed the search for Livingstone, and although Bennett had given the orders, Stanley gained the kudos. 'Who paid the bills?' Bennett would demand. He was sure to reject the proposal for a new African expedition if Stanley made a direct approach, but would not dare to if another journal was already declaring its support. The *Daily Telegraph* had recently come to the front among British newspapers, and had an adventurous, popular touch that made it close in outlook to the leading American dailies. The deputy editor of the paper, Edwin Arnold, was a tireless traveller and versifier; he was also one of the few Fellows of the Royal Geographical Society with whom Stanley was on friendly terms.

Arnold helped Stanley to persuade the owner-editor, Edward Levy – Lawson (later Lord Burnham), to put up £6,000 if the *Herald* would match the figure. In return, Stanley would send back from Africa exclusive despatches about his discoveries. A message was sent to Bennett by Transatlantic telegraph, asking whether he would come in on the venture. After twenty hours he gave a terse, one-word answer: 'Yes.'

The preparations now began in earnest – and with much urgency, for Stanley meant to leave for Africa within two months. First of all he must select several white assistants, because he had decided that the expedition would need at least three hundred black porters, guides and mercenary soldiers, whom he could not hope to control on his own. There was a young and energetic clerk at the Langham Hotel named Frederick Barker; he had heard about the expedition and begged to be taken along, so Stanley signed him up. Then Edwin Arnold mentioned the Pocock brothers, two sons of a fisherman who looked after his yacht on the Medway in Kent. They were scantily educated, but strong and resourceful. When Stanley met the Pococks he was taken with their cheerful enthusiasm, and promised them a chance of fame. After that, he sought no more recruits, and brushed aside suggestions that he might take along botanists, geologists, or army officers with proven powers of command – he wanted nobody who might contest his leadership.

At the end of June he interrupted his planning to make a quick journey to New York. He had been given a free passage on a White Star steamer in return for an assurance (which was carefully kept) of some publicity for the company in his writings. Ostensibly, he made the crossing to see Bennett. But for several days Bennett refused to fix an appointment, and when Stanley did see him it was only to learn that he would not sign a contract drawn up by the *Telegraph*. Bennett would merely lodge his share of the outlay for the expedition in a bank, to be drawn on as needed. The conversation was at an end.

Stanley noted: 'This is rather an unkind way to receive one he is about to send to complete the discoveries of so many great travellers in Central Africa.'

At 613 Fifth Avenue, a short walk from the *Herald*'s offices on Broadway, there was a more heartening welcome. Alice and Stanley spent as much time as possible together during his busy week in New York. They talked about the expedition, and the life they would share when he was home again. Stanley was only too well aware of the dangers and trials he must endure before their reunion. He wrote in his diary: 'But two years is such a long time to wait, and I have so much to do, such a weary, weary journey to make before I can ever return. No man had ever to work harder than I have for a wife.' Perhaps they could be married right away? Alice was willing, but her mother would not hear of it. Nettie was to be married in the autumn, and there was already so much to think about for the wedding and the reception for a thousand guests. In any case, Alice was still too young.

On July 17, Alice and Stanley spent their last evening together. After dinner, they walked near Central Park in the dusk. That morning, the *Herald* had come out with a long announcement about the expedition, saying that Stanley would set out from Zanzibar as 'the ambassador of two great powers'. It praised his many qualities, which could 'overcome the hundred perils of an explorer', and forecast that the expedition would bring great benefits by wiping out the slave trade and uncovering the last secrets of African geography. Yet there were rancorous overtones to the announcement, which showed signs of Bennett's own hand. It stressed how much money the *Herald* had spent to find Livingstone, and how much it was putting at risk a second time. It ended by pointing out that the expedition was an alliance of resources and purpose between 'the proprietors of the two journals'.

This was not the moment, however, to brood on Bennett's jealousy. Stanley was buoyed up by his love. After the walk in the dusk, he sat with Alice in the parlour of her home. They were alone together: 'She raised her lips in tempting proximity to mine and I kissed her on her lips, on her eyes, on her cheeks and her neck, and she kissed me in return.'

The next morning Stanley left New York. His mind was racing. He would have little more than a fortnight in Britain to complete his preparations before he must sail for Africa. Alice came to see him off at Pier 42 on the North River; with her were Nettie and the man she was engaged to, David Goin. As they stood on the quayside, Alice promised that she would write regularly, although they both knew it was possible to go for months, or even years, in the depths of Africa, without seeing any mail. She gave him two photographs, to carry on his journey: one was just of her face, passionately intelligent; the other showed her standing in a tightly-waisted silk dress with a full embroidered skirt.

Alice and Stanley exchanged a last few words: 'She repeated her vows to me as we stood together, and as I clasped her hands to bid her goodbye, she gave me such a look – a long, earnest, wide-eyed look – during which I thought she was striving to pierce the dark, gloomy picture, but I turned away – and the spell broke.'

He hurried up the gangway and found a place on the deck from where he could see the quay. Alice and her companions were still there. 'I could not bear that the scene should be protracted, or that she should be pained with standing, and I motioned with my arm for them to be gone . . .

'Alice kissed her hand to me, and resolutely turned away . . .'

2. To the Great Lakes

Stanley stepped ashore at Zanzibar on September 21, 1874, a little more than two years since he had last seen the island. It greeted him with a hubbub of voices and familiar tropical smells. Off the water-front, the tall stone houses, with their carved and brass-studded doors, maintained a secretive yet watchful air. This was the Arab town; beyond a maze of alleyways it merged into a sprawl of mud huts where the bulk of the island's 200,000 people lived in traditional African fashion. The dusty suburbs swarmed with goats, chickens and naked children. Farther in the distance were vast plantations of coconut trees, and gardens producing the cloves for which Zanzibar was renowned.

The place seemed to live according to an old and immutable pattern, but Stanley knew well that it was in the midst of far-reaching changes. The seventy white residents no more felt themselves to be exiles, languishing in a remote and humid corner of the Indian Ocean. The outside world had a growing interest in Zanzibar: a mail steamer had begun to call every month, and Europe was now only four weeks away through the Red Sea and the Suez Canal. There was increasing activity in the harbour, and from a vantage point on the flat roof of an American merchant's house, Stanley was able one morning to count 135 vessels.

The trade of Zanzibar was no longer based upon the export of human beings. The island's slave market had been shut down the year before, the Arabs yielding at last to a British threat of a naval blockade. As though to underline this victory over Islam, the market site had been bought by Anglican missionaries, and on it they were building a massive, red-brick church. The Sultan, Barghash-bin-Said, was praised on every hand as tractable and good-natured – a startling change, for in his rebellious youth he had been deported for nearly two years to Bombay; now he was preparing to visit London and meet Queen Victoria. There could be no doubt about the supremacy of the British in Zanzibar. Their warships were constantly in the harbour, and their consul-general had recently moved to a huge house on a headland well away from the rest of the foreign community.

Stanley noted these developments with his sharp reporter's eye. He took no pleasure in the dominance of the British in Zanzibar. It was his success in bringing back the letters and diaries of Livingstone, with their revelations about the horrors of the slave trade, that had stirred Gladstone's Government to mount the decisive campaign against the Zanzibar market. Yet he knew how his British critics said he had merely done good by accident, that all he had been after was a sensational story; this rankled because to an extent it was true – he had only learned to care about Africa and its problems after meeting Livingstone at Ujiji.

One development in Zanzibar which he had least expected made him even more critical of the British. The wages demanded by the *askari*, the armed escorts needed to protect any expedition in Africa, had soared in the past two years; the rates for guides and porters were correspondingly higher. All Stanley's meticulous calculations were now in disarray. For such inflation, which meant he must hand out advance payments of more than £1,000 before he could even start his travels, he blamed a young Royal Navy officer, Lieutenant Verney Lovett Cameron. It served to reinforce Stanley's dislike of Cameron, who had rebuffed his offer to mount a combined expedition in Africa, and furthermore was a protégé of the Royal Geographical Society.

Cameron had been sent out by the RGS six months after Stanley had returned in 1872, with a brief to give Livingstone any further help he needed. This was largely based on the sense of pique and humiliation that a 'Yankee journalist' had saved a British national hero from starvation. In his anxiety to set off from Zanzibar Cameron had offered more than three times the usual rates for men to serve in his expedition. It was common knowledge that the RGS had been so astounded by the bills sent back by Cameron that it had at first refused to honour them. Stanley was quick to hit this sensitive point. One of his first despatches to the *Daily Telegraph* (November 12, 1874) said that the 'somewhat inordinate liberality' of the Cameron expedition 'only shows too plainly how the money has been expended.'

Although he did not admit it openly, Stanley was worried that Cameron might forestall him in the race to uncover the remaining secrets of Central Africa. After learning that Livingstone was already dead – having met the bearers of his body marching down to the coast – Cameron then pushed on westwards, towards Lake Tanganyika and the mysterious Lualaba River, which so far no other white traveller but Livingstone had seen. It was known that Cameron had suffered a series of disasters and was moving slowly – but he did have eighteen months' start. Might he not snatch the honours? It was an unbearable thought to Stanley, who had come to see himself as 'Livingstone's heir'.

Soon after his arrival in Zanzibar, Stanley wrote (September 24, 1874) to Livingstone's daughter, Agnes. He gave her news of his activities, then turned to explaining how the doctor's remaining possessions had been auctioned in Zanzibar for £3 after being brought down to the island by porters. This had happened well before Stanley had arrived. He protested hotly: 'If Dr Livingstone had been a common soldier, and his family so devoid of feeling as to appreciate such a sum, above the possession of the valuable souvenirs of a great man, I could have understood the feeling that could have prompted the sale, but knowing that you would have valued such things a thousand times more than their pecuniary value – I must say I was shocked, and indignant that men could be found to be so stupid and so asinine.' It was a barbed comment on the way the British consulate was run, and reflected a hostility derived from Stanley's previous visit to Zanzibar.

Although the new 'Anglo-American expedition' had no official status, the fact that Stanley was representing a paper in London as well as one in New York gave the British – and the Arabs – a far greater interest in his intentions. He said openly in a long interview with the Sultan that he intended to 'complete the work of Livingstone' – a programme that could hardly fail to threaten Arab power on the mainland. For his part, the Sultan told Stanley that the disclosures in Livingstone's letters had brought an end to the slave trade in Zanzibar. Even so, explained the Sultan, Arabs did not regard slavery as wrong: 'Our Koran does not say it is a sin, our priests say nothing against it, the wise men of Mecca say nothing against it . . .'

Despite the further trouble which Stanley was likely to cause him, the Sultan was friendly. He really had no alternative: it was a popular saying that when you played the flute in Zanzibar, all Africa as far as the lakes would dance – but white men were more and more deciding the tune. To anybody with political foresight, where it would end was absolutely plain.

If Stanley had any intuition about how his new travels might speed up the colonial process in Africa, it concerned him far less than personal ambition. He was fired by his sense of grievance, which he made no effort to hide when writing from Zanzibar: 'Though I had many reasons for not undertaking a second journey to Africa, I was conscious that by the acceptance of this command I would compel those who doubted I had discovered Livingstone at Ujiji to confess themselves in error . . .' He felt elated that he had been recognised as having enough 'integrity and honesty' for the task; if he lived, his 'unjust enemies would be silenced forever'.

Stanley hurried forward with his arrangements for the departure to the mainland. He prided himself on being equipped for anything: when he went in search of Livingstone he even remembered to pack a bottle of champagne, with which they were able to toast their meeting. It had given a capital touch to the story.

Now there was the time-consuming labour of bargaining with local traders for the expedition's long list of basic needs – beads, wire, cloth, bedding, ropes, tents, medicines, ammunition, and countless other odds and ends, all done up into bundles weighing 60 lb each; the total weight was more than eight tons. Stanley's own impedimenta was formidable, including two crates of photographic equipment, sextants, chronometers, compasses, binoculars, water-bottles, whistles, knives, guns, chisels, unspillable inkwells . . . Then there were his more personal items: five cut-throat razors in a case, shaving mirrors, ivory-backed hairbrushes, eau de cologne, and several meerschaum pipes – including one with a monogram 'HMS' on the bowl. Once away from the coast, on a journey that was going to take far longer than the Livingstone expedition, it would be useless to bemoan any oversights.

Before leaving London, Stanley had spent some time designing equipment for crossing rivers and lakes, and giving orders for it to be made in such a manner that it could be carried over hundreds of miles of bush tracks on the heads of porters. One of his inventions was an inflatable pontoon named the *Livingstone*, which proved of little use. The other was his portable boat, the *Lady Alice*, in five sections; when assembled she would be 40 feet long, 6 feet in the beam and equipped with sails and oars. He had given this order to a boat-building yard at Teddington, on the Thames. By the time he departed for Zanzibar, the work on the boat was not complete, and he arranged for her to be sent after him by the next mail

On a roof in Zanzibar: Stanley's companions for the great journey. On the left is Frank Pocock, and beside him Frederick Barker, the clerk from a London hotel. In the centre sits a Zanzibari boy, with Edward Pocock and Kalulu on the right. This engraving was made from a photograph by the explorer

steamer. When the *Lady Alice* arrived, he was well advanced with his preparations.

After the boat was brought ashore and examined, Stanley was dismayed to realise she was too heavy and bulky to transport along the narrow jungle paths. One section, weighing 310 lb, he decided to abandon completely. The rest must be sub-divided, and he persuaded a carpenter who was aboard the mail steamer to spend a month in Zanzibar cutting the boat into smaller pieces. The success of the expedition might well depend on the outcome of this labour so Stanley gave the carpenter two helpers. These were the Pocock brothers, the Englishmen whom Stanley had chosen in the face of 1,200 applicants ranging from generals to circus performers. They were already proving themselves efficient and cheerful.

The senior and more forceful of the Pococks was Frank, aged 24; he was fair, blue-eyed and wore a small beard. Edward Pocock – nicknamed 'Slipper' – was two years younger, possessed a large drooping moustache, and displayed a rather sentimental nature. Both boys had fine tenor voices and at their home village of Upnor in Kent were leading members of the church choir. Frank played the concertina, whereas Edward was an expert bugler, having been trained at Chatham and Aldershot; at Stanley's suggestion he gave a much-admired demonstration for the Sultan. The Pococks also knew all the latest London music-hall hits, and put on a concert for the Zanzibar merchants.

While the alterations were being made to the *Lady Alice*, Stanley was helped by his young clerk, Frederick Barker, in assembling and listing the stores. He also pushed on with the seemingly endless work of hiring men. Each Zanzibar recruit had to be assessed for experience and character, for such expeditions attracted not only the adventurous, but also the criminals of Zanzibar – men who might desert at the first chance with all they could steal. Losses from starvation and war were always high; Stanley had to find men who would be both reliable and brave, rather than a horde of reckless desperadoes forever likely to abscond. This was made harder by the disclosure that he did not mean to go simply to the trading towns of Tabora and Ujiji, but to remote lands far beyond the lakes.

Stanley had the advantage of being known to the expedition veterans of Zanzibar, and he was able to recruit as his 'captains' some of the men who were with him in search of Livingstone or had acquitted themselves well as followers of Livingstone during his final wanderings. This nucleus of twenty-three included the wily Manwa Sera, who was appointed chief captain, the head guide Kachéché, the dogged Chowpereh, Mabruki Speke (named after the explorer with whom he had travelled) and Edward Gardner – a Livingstone 'faithful' who had been educated at a mission in India. All of these were given presents by Stanley as a show of his good intentions, and invited to help in weeding out all the 'roughs, rowdies and ruffians' from the multitude of would-be recruits; but this did not save him from hiring a man who had committed seven murders, and many others who only wanted to draw some advance pay.

By the middle of November the remodelled boat had been tested by the Pococks, declared seaworthy, and taken to pieces again for carrying. Five *dhows* were hired, and the men and materials transported across the narrow stretch of water to the mainland harbour of Bagamoyo. Stanley had wanted to stay there until he had recruited more than 100 porters, but before he could do so there was so much trouble between his *askari* and the local Arab garrison that he decided to hurry inland. The expedition's recruits were accused of theft, rape and other offences, and so many were thrown into the Bagamoyo jail – as well as Stanley's own improvised prison – that it looked as though his forces might disintegrate before a day's march had been achieved. On the evening of November 16, 1874, Stanley composed a letter about his will and personal affairs to his London publisher, Edward Marston.

The next morning, Edward Pocock sounded his bugle at dawn and the great caravan took its leave – 356 strong, and stretching out for nearly half a mile. At the head were twelve guides in crimson robes, followed by the porters with their head bundles, the bearers of the *Lady Alice*, several dozen wives of the captains and their children, then the Europeans riding their donkeys; at the front and rear armed *askari* watched for marauders and runaways. Alongside the caravan trotted Stanley's five dogs – three of which he had chosen from the Battersea Dogs' Home in London.

There was an excitement soon after the start when a contingent of Baluchi soldiers overtook the caravan to reclaim fifteen women who had fled with it from Bagamoyo to accompany new-found lovers. After much screaming from the women and protests from their men, the soldiers marched back to the coast with their captives.

There is no doubt, from the way Stanley writes, that he was deeply stirred by being back on the African mainland, despite all the anxieties caused by his vast and unruly force. But the Pococks and Barker must have been hard pressed to hide their apprehensions. Life had been agreeable in Zanzibar, as Edward Pocock noted in his diary. He and his brother, coming from the Medway, had felt very much at home with the sailors on the British warships in Zanzibar harbour. One of Edward's entries reads: 'Evening, visited HMS *Thetis* to a theatrical performance, play 'Merchant of Venice'.' In a letter (September 24, 1874) to his parents, he remarked: 'It is beautiful weather, something like summer in England, if you wasn't to see the blacks.'

But the relative calm of Zanzibar was now yielding to something far more ominous, and the violence in Bagamoyo had been a hint of what lay ahead. Also, away from the breezes and cool, high-ceilinged houses of Zanzibar, Stanley's young assistants found the heat of tropical Africa overpowering; as the sun climbed higher behind them, they sweated in the heavy woollen clothing that was the fashion of the time. The parasols held up by their servants seemed to give little relief.

The three newcomers to African travel waited for symptoms of malaria, and remembered that Shaw and Farquhar, their leader's companions on the search for Livingstone, had both died. The Europeans with Cameron had fared just as badly: John Moffat, a nephew of Livingstone, succumbed within a few weeks of leaving Bagamoyo, and Dr William Dillon blew out his brains in a moment of delirium, pointing a rifle to his head and firing it with his toes.

The first casualty of the *Telegraph-Herald* expedition was one of Stanley's dogs, a huge mastiff given him by an English friend, Baroness Burdett-Coutts; only a few hours from Bagamoyo, it collapsed from heat-stroke. Frank Pocock noted that gloomy fact in his diary, and the next entry reads: 'Locked three men up in chains, very wild country.' Although the expedition was still on a well-trodden route, it again and again saw human skulls lying in the coarse grass beside the path. Stanley does not even mention putting the men in chains – it seemed a matter of course to him that in lawless regions you made your own rules and chose the most direct methods to impose your will on malcontents.

Although the Pococks and Barker may have sensed they had entered a fatally hostile environment, the progress the caravan made to Mpwapwa village gave Stanley a glow of confidence. It was reached in twenty-five days, whereas his rival Cameron had taken four months. In a despatch to his papers on December 13, Stanley boasted: 'We have suffered less sickness, less trouble, and, altogether have had more good fortune than any expedition which ever came into Africa.' Yet within days he was to rue such hyperbole, for his troubles began as soon as he turned northwards towards Lake Victoria, and began marching by the compass across barren country. He was no longer on the route taken by Cameron, who had gone due west. Intense heat alternated with torrential rain, food was scarce, and the thorny forests made progress slow and painful. Two more dogs died.

To add to these woes, both Stanley and Frank Pocock were now struck by severe bouts of malaria – far more acute than what Stanley blithely called their 'seasoning fevers'. With less supervision, porters began to look for the chance to desert. The outlook was bad – a big expedition could only carry enough food for a week or two, and was soon starving if it could not barter along the way.

Just before Christmas, the weather worsened and one night the camp was flooded. Stanley wrote the first of his letters to Alice Pike from the interior of Africa and it offered a miserable picture: 'How your kind woman's heart would pity me and mine . . . I am in a centre pole tent, seven by eight. As it rained all day yesterday the tent was set over wet ground, which by the constant passing in and out of the servants has been trampled into a thick pasty mud . . . Outside my tent things are worse. The camp is in the extreme of misery and the people appear as if they were trying to make up their minds either to commit suicide or to sit still inert until death relieves them . . . there is a famine in the country . . . I myself have not eaten a piece of meat for ten days, I have lived on boiled rice and tea and coffee . . . I have but three days ago recovered from a severe attack of fever . . . Three of my dogs are dead . . . One of my donkeys was killed last night by a hyena . . .'

When Alice eventually read this, it must have seemed impossibly remote from her own world. A few weeks earlier she had written to Stanley, enclosing a cutting from the *Cincinnati Enquirer* about Nettie's wedding. Reporting from New York, it said: 'Miss Alice Pike, another sister, appeared in a Paris dress, composed of alternate widths of white silk and black velvet, heavily embroidered in massive wreaths of flowers. She is well known here as a reigning belle and looked lovelier than a fairy princess.' Alice lived in a social whirl, but found time to write several letters a week to the man she hoped to wed: 'I do love dancing so much. Honest, I would rather go to the opera though than a party . . . Almost every evening some fellows come in – I get awfully tired of them . . . All the papers say Mr Stanley had arrived at Zanzibar and was well and making active preparations to go into the interior . . .' Her letters raced on inconsequentially about everything: 'I hope you are a Democrat. Are you? I am. Nettie and Mr Goin are enjoying themselves. He says it is awfully jolly to be married . . .' But many of Alice's carefree descriptions of driving in Central Park and strolling in Fifth Avenue would not be seen by Stanley until long after. By the time these letters reached Zanzibar, the expedition had lost contact with the outside world. It was absorbed in its own affairs.

Frank Pocock's diary entry on December 25 was terse: 'Christmas Day spent drying clothes. No difference made in the day (worse luck).'

Just before the New Year, Stanley met the first serious challenge from the less faithful of his Zanzibaris. He heard that a group of fifty men had arranged to abscond *en masse*, and had to capture the ringleaders and disarm their followers. From then onwards, troubles proliferated: hunger, desertions and deaths from dysentery harried the expedition every mile of the journey towards Lake Victoria. As Stanley was to admit very frankly, in a despatch (March 1, 1875) sent after they had reached the lake: '. . . I imperilled the expedition and almost brought it to an untimely end, but which, happily for me, for you and for geographers, a kindly Providence averted.'

There was no kindly providence for Edward Pocock. On January 12 he complained of feeling ill, and rapidly worsened as the expedition staggered upwards to a village called Chiwyu, more than 5,000 feet above sea level. Stanley arranged to have him carried in a hammock, roofed with canvas against the sun, but as delirium set in and Edward's body became covered with red pimples, it was clear that this was something less normal than malaria. Stanley diagnosed typhus. The end came on January 17, as the camp was being organised in Chiwyu. Frank Pocock wrote: 'He was buried at night under a mambo tree with a deep cross cut in the tree. The burial service was performed by Mr Stanley . . . His head lays east, his feet west, God rest his soul.' In a letter delivered long afterwards to Henry Pocock, who had been so proud to see his sons go out to Africa, Stanley wrote a long message of consolation, praising Edward's cheerfulness, his energy, and his patience; every morning the camp had woken to the sound of his bugle, and in the evenings his singing had charmed all who heard him. But the family should take courage, for it looked certain that Frank would come home to Kent 'with honour and glory'. Such reassurances could not disguise the truth: it had taken precisely two months for the first death to occur among Stanley's white assistants.

Yet far more critical for the outcome of the expedition was the loss of twenty-one men in a battle with tribesmen at Vinyata, immediately after Edward Pocock's death. The hostility of the neighbourhood had been clear for several days, and when a straggler was hacked into pieces and left on the road, Stanley knew he was faced with war. The Nyaturu warriors were allowed to attack first, and after Stanley's men had fought their way out of several ambushes the advantage of modern rifles was at last demonstrated. Orders were given to burn and plunder every village in the district, and this at least gave the expedition enough grain to last for six days. After the battle, Stanley took a roll-call: out of the original 356 there were only 173 people left – seventy-seven had died in the fighting or by disease, and the other losses had been through desertion. Several dozen men had been abandoned at villages along the route because they were too ill to march. Three months of travelling had created havoc. He wrote in his diary: 'This is terrible, but God's will be done. My men are still failing me; I have a great number on the sick list.' The hope lay in reaching Lake Victoria, but that was at least a month's journey away.

The expedition was rescued from despair when it reached a district with abundant game, and Stanley went out with his rifle to shoot everything eatable within range. His eyes stared down the sights; his face was haggard, for he had now lost more than fifty pounds in weight. In two days Stanley shot a giraffe, six zebra, a buffalo, several antelopes, and a variety of ducks and other birds. The camp gorged itself upon meat, and what the men could not eat they dried and took with them: some of the porters carried more than 30 lb of meat as well as their 60 lb loads. Spirits also surged when new porters were hired from tribesmen *en route*, bringing the expedition up to 280 strong, excluding women and children. The new men would travel as far as the lake and then be paid off.

On the morning of February 27 the caravan came over the summit of a ridge and saw the blue water before it. Frank Pocock cheered at the sight and ran back to tell Stanley and Frederick Barker, who was ill and riding on a donkey. Barker managed a smile. As the porters marched down into the village of Kagei, on the lakeshore, they burst into an extempore song of celebration, enlivened by the firing of muskets. The first objective of the journey had been reached in 103 days, although the cost in lives had been high: the permanent members of the expedition now numbered only 166.

As Stanley stared out at the lake, dotted with islands – some half lost in mist – he knew he was on the verge of his first great geographical achievement. Before his arrival now with Frank Pocock and Barker, only three white men had ever seen Lake Victoria, and there was much argument about its extent. Sir Richard Burton and Livingstone had both suggested that it was really a group of lakes, whereas Speke believed it was one huge expanse of water. But nobody had been able to chart it accurately; Stanley gave himself a week to recuperate before setting out to sail around its shoreline.

The *Lady Alice*, which had been a burden on the 720-mile march, was now assembled and tested. Her hull, masts, sails and oars were all in perfect condition, and while she was being loaded with flour, dried fish, trade goods and scientific equipment, Stanley sat down to compose a long letter (March 4, 1875) to his fiancée. 'My darling

Alice,' it began – and launched into a businesslike 1,000 word account of his tribulations on the way from the coast. This part, he explained, could be offered to the *Herald* for publication. (It never appeared; either Alice did not hand it on, or else the *Herald* had already received a longer, parallel account that Stanley also wrote just before his lake journey.) The last third of Stanley's letter is personal and passionate: 'In one of your very last letters which I received before starting from the sea, you asked me if you could not get married at once on my return, to which I answer that it shall be as you desire. The very hour I land in England I should like to marry you, but such a long time must elapse before I see you, that even to see your dear face again appears to me as a most improbable thing . . . I have often wondered how you pass your time. I suppose it is in one constant round of gaieties? What a contrast to yours are my surroundings . . . My present abode is a dark hut; through the chinks of the mud I can but faintly see these lines as I write. Outside naked men and women create a furious jangle and noise, bartering with my people for beads.' After commending himself with all his heart to her love and prayers, he obediently signed his letter 'Morton'.

As Stanley prepared to explore Lake Victoria, he realised that its reputation had scared all his men. There were tales that around it were evil giants and dwarfs, and monstrous dogs. When he asked for ten volunteers to man the *Lady Alice*, the Zanzibaris offered one excuse after another, so that in the end he had to choose the ten strongest and most intelligent he could see and order them to get ready. The journey began on March 8, the crew rowing reluctantly as the boat headed for open water beyond the bay upon which the expedition was encamped. As Pocock and Barker waved to Stanley, seated in the stern, they were doubtless concealing some qualms. Pocock noted in his diary that he had been 'left in charge of men and property'. He was just approaching his twenty-fifth birthday, and in the two months that were to pass before Stanley's return he was to find himself hard put to it in combating the wiles and truculence of some of the more experienced Zanzibari 'captains'.

Shortly after Stanley began his journey, sailing up the eastern shore of the lake in an anti-clockwise direction, he was able to recruit a local African as a guide. Named Saramba, the man looked loutish and slow, but he did know the lake and showed himself to have courage. The manner in which the *Lady Alice* was swept along as the wind stiffened so impressed him that he declared they would soon 'finish the world'. There were a few bloody skirmishes with lakeshore people who came racing out aggressively in their canoes, but in general the progress was good.

Stanley's optimism grew as he reached the northern end of the lake and turned westwards, for he now knew he was nearing the domain of Mtesa, king of Buganda; there was intense interest in Mtesa, for even if he did not qualify as civilised by Victorian terms, at least he ruled a country that was well organised and boasted a permanent capital. Three white men had already visited the king: Speke and Grant more than ten years earlier and an American officer employed by the Egyptians, Charles Chaillé-Long, a year before Stanley's arrival. There was a feeling that whoever controlled Buganda held the key to Central Africa.

General Gordon, governing Equatoria province in the Sudan, wanted to set up links from the north for the Khedive of Egypt. From the south the Arabs of Zanzibar had their eyes on the commercial possibilities, and a subject of the Sultan had reputedly converted Mtesa to Islam. The Ugandans were showing themselves to be very curious about the outside world, and in 1872 had sent emissaries bearing ivory and other gifts to Zanzibar, for which King Mtesa

Arrival in Buganda. As the *Lady Alice* sailed into a bay on Lake Victoria, muskets were fired and drums thundered a welcome. Stanley was 'very much amazed at all this ceremonious and pompous greeting'

vainly requested in return a Goan cook and a white woman. The latter fancy was doubtless inspired by the visit of Florence Baker with her explorer husband to Central Africa; even though she never went as far as Buganda, her long fair hair and other feminine charms had become a legend far and wide.

When Stanley arrived there was some disappointment among Mtesa's 200 wives that he lacked a spouse against whom they could measure themselves. But this in no way lessened the warmth of the reception. The explorer sent messengers on ahead, and Mtesa moved his court to a lakeside camp to welcome him. An escort of six canoes was sent to guide the *Lady Alice* through the islands. The impression on Stanley was immense: 'On the fourth of April I landed amid a concourse of two thousand people, who saluted me with a deafening volley of musketry and waving of flags.'

The Ganda were immaculately dressed in red, white and black robes, and Stanley feared his rather tousled boat's crew in no way matched the splendour of the hosts; his own face was red and peeling from the sun on the lake. But the visitors made themselves as presentable as they could, and even Saramba was smartened up after some small pages of Mtesa's court loudly derided him as a pagan slave 'worth about a goat'.

Stanley was allocated quarters, and loaded with gifts of food – including fourteen oxen, sixteen goats and sheep and one hundred bunches of bananas. At this stage, he had not met Mtesa, who through an official invited him to present himself later in the day.

The two men sought very different benefits from their encounter. Stanley needed to write about Mtesa for the outside world, because that was his job. Secondly, he was keen to solicit Mtesa's aid in future explorations. Finally, he had a clear idea that here lay a good chance of following Livingstone in 'opening up Africa to the shining light of Christianity'. For his part, Mtesa was frightened of Egyptian penetration from the Sudan, and saw Stanley as representing a counter-balancing force. Furthermore, he might be the source of arms and expertise that would allow Buganda to spread its borders and gain mastery over neighbouring tribes.

So as they met, they both regarded one another carefully. Stanley saw a 'generous prince and a frank and intelligent man', who was tall and somewhat nervous, dressed in a black robe with a gold belt. A wide variety of gifts were accepted by Mtesa with cool dignity. Stanley much regretted not being able to present an accordion he started out with. He could also have given a demonstration, for he had often played it in the evenings for his Zanzibaris to dance to. But the instrument was ruined by the floods on the journey.

Stanley was closely questioned by Mtesa and by the courtiers on a wide variety of topics. He was also asked to demonstrate the power of his rifle, and managed to kill a small crocodile at a range of 100 yards with a three-ounce bullet – 'an act which was accepted as conclusive proof that all white men are dead shots'. Then the Ganda put on an elaborate show of naval power with forty big canoes, which contained a total of 1,200 men.

Stanley very quickly turned the conversation to religion, and set about persuading Mtesa that Christianity was much superior to Islam. It seemed he had a receptive listener, and soon the idea grew in his mind that a stirring call for missionaries in Buganda might have dramatic consequences. The influence of Islam had clearly wrought great improvements since the time when Speke visited Mtesa – so Christianity could surely do much more. Stanley's sincerity is beyond question: he was no theologian, but had a positive Victorian faith in the deity. The sincerity of Mtesa is another matter. Stanley always reacted angrily to subsequent arguments that he had simply been 'duped' and used by the king for political ends.

While the campaign to convert Mtesa was in progress, there was startling news – of another white man approaching, with an escort of forty soldiers. It turned out to be Colonel Ernest Linant de Bellefonds, an emissary from Gordon. To maintain dignity, neither white man spoke as Linant was led into Mtesa's court, where Stanley was sitting.

When a chance to offer one another greetings occured, Linant said, 'Have I the honour of speaking to Mr Cameron?' Stanley quickly disabused him of that idea; the two fell silent once more until they were able to talk in the privacy of the hut allocated to Linant. Then they exchanged news throughout the day and half the night, Stanley explaining what he had discovered of Lake Victoria and showing Linant the sketches he had made. They drank many mugs of tea, smoked cigars and enjoyed the Frenchman's supply of *pâté de foie gras*, sardines, Marseilles biscuits and coffee. Linant wrote in his journal for the Ministry of War in Cairo on April 12: 'Stanley is a first-rate traveller – a brave, light-hearted gentleman, a good comrade, a patient explorer, taking everything as it comes . . . He has travelled far and wide and seen a great deal. He knows the whole world. It was four months since I had heard a single French word pronounced. It was a great pleasure, therefore, to hear Stanley speaking for, without expressing himself with perfect accuracy, he yet talked French sufficiently well to enable us readily to converse.' This regard was reciprocated by Stanley, although he disapproved of the way Linant posted armed soldiers at the corners of his compound and kept everybody out. His own compound was full of people awaiting their chance to interrogate him on every imaginable topic.

Stanley found to his satisfaction that Linant was a Protestant, and so well able to back up his own religious arguments. Mtesa was impressed that when he talked to them separately they both gave identical answers to questions about Christianity. As Linant departed, Stanley gave him a letter (April 14, 1875) to the *Telegraph* and the *Herald* – a stirring call for missionaries to be sent out to Uganda. Linant handed over the letter in Khartoum to be forwarded to London, by the time it appeared he had been killed fighting hostile tribesmen.

Stanley's call for missionaries was one of the most significant messages to come out of Central Africa in the second half of the nineteenth century. More than £25,000 was quickly raised in Britain to speed the Gospel to Mtesa's subjects. Missionaries were to be murdered and converts put to death, but the political effect was the further involvement of Britain in East Africa. It also advanced Mtesa's aim of keeping the Egyptians at their distance. The letter is a revealing insight into Stanley's view of what Africa needed to 'bring it into the light'. After describing how Mtesa had earlier been converted to Islam, Stanley claimed that he had defeated the Arab influence by a single interview with the king: '. . . I flatter myself that I have tumbled the newly-raised religious fabric to the ground, and, if it were only followed by the arrival of a Christian mission here, the conversion of Mtesa and his court to Christianity would be complete.' The Ten Commandments had been written on a board at Mtesa's request so that he could study them daily, together with the Lord's Prayer and Christ's injunction – 'Thou shalt love thy neighbour as thyself'. A few years later Mtesa was to show where his real faith lay by having hundreds of people sacrificed in the belief that this would save him from a serious illness.

Rather more realistic was the advice Stanley gave about who should be sent to help the heathens: action, not talk, was needed by the Ganda (people of Buganda). The ideal missionary must be a practical man, able to build houses, teach farming, cure disease, and turn his hand to everything 'like a sailor'. Having made the point, Stanley took an almost mystical flight: 'Such a one if he can be found would become the saviour of Africa. He must be tied to no Church or sect, but profess God and His Son and the moral law, and live a blameless Christian life, inspired by liberal principles, charity to all men and devout faith in heaven. He must belong to no nation in particular, but the entire white race.' Stanley listed the equipment this paragon would need to advance Uganda – every kind of carpenter's tool, nails and tacks, anvils, a plough, garden seed, shovels, pick-axes, linseed oil, some illustrated journals, plus some gaudy prints, a magic lantern, rockets and a photographic apparatus. There might be other things that common sense would suggest, and the mission should also take care to bring along the right kind of gifts for Mtesa, including several military uniforms liberally sprinkled with gold braid, a 'cheap dinner service of Britannia ware', a bed-stead and counterpanes. Any guns should be of good quality – 'for the king is not a barbarian'. The leaders of the missionary groups should take heed of the message, for this was their finest chance yet of winning more converts than had ever been thought possible: 'Here gentlemen, is your opportunity – embrace it!' He then offered another bait as exciting as souls, by promising that the mission to Uganda would repay its outlay ten times over in ivory, coffee and otter skins 'of a very fine quality'.

However quaintly it reads today, the letter electrified the buyers of the *Daily Telegraph*, and to a lesser extent those of the *New York Herald*. More significantly, it gave Stanley himself another dimension, for no longer was he the minion of James Gordon Bennett, finding Livingstone for a scoop, or even the hired explorer seeking a fame that would outshine Burton, Baker, Speke and Cameron. Now he put himself forward as the heir of Livingstone in a very particular way: Stanley the evangelist.

This role was set aside, however, a few days after he departed from Mtesa to collect the rest of his expedition and guide it to Buganda. Sailing down the western side of Lake Victoria, he reached a lofty island which he named after Alice Pike (the honour did not last – it has reverted to Bukerebe), then raced with a north-east wind behind him to Bumbiri, a bigger island close to the coast. Here he met trouble, for when the boat went inshore to barter for food a crowd of apparently friendly inhabitants seized the gunwales and dragged the *Lady Alice* and her crew out of the water and surrounded them with spears poised. 'Twice I raised my revolvers to kill and be killed, but the crew restrained me . . .'

For three hours, the Zanzibari interpreters tried with skill and patience to talk their way out of the threatening impasse, while Stanley sat silently in the stern of the boat. All at once, after having been paid a tribute of cloth and beads, the local chief ordered his warriors to seize the boat's oars. It was done before Stanley and his men knew what was happening. Then 500 warriors gathered on a hill overlooking the beach, and a war drum started beating. Still the Zanzibaris tried to negotiate, but when fifty warriors rushed to the boat and announced that they were about to cut the throats of the white man and his crew, it was plain that some desperate stratagem was needed.

Stanley told Safeni, his coxswain, to walk towards the enemy with two expensive pieces of red cloth, as though to barter. At a signal the rest of the crew must push the *Lady Alice* into the water, with Stanley seated in her, and Safeni must turn and run for his life after them.

The manoeuvre had hardly begun when the islanders saw through it, and raced down the hill yelling and waving their spears: Safeni stood for an instant on the water's edge, with the cloths in his hand. The foremost of natives was about 20 yards from him. He raised his spear and balanced himself. Stanley relates what took place next:

'Spring into the water, man, head first,' I cried. The balanced spear was about to fly, and another man was preparing his weapon for a deadly cast, when I raised my gun and the bullet ploughed through him and through the second. The bowmen halted and drew their bows. I sent two charges of buckshot into their midst with terrible effect . . .

Safeni swam out to safety.

While this was happening, the crew were hanging on to the boat and pushing it farther from the shore. Stanley hauled aboard one man, who helped in another. In place of oars, the men tore up the bottom boards of the boat and used these as paddles, for there was now no wind to fill the sails. The warriors shouted in rage from the shore, and as though there was not trouble enough, the boat was attacked by two hippopotami; Stanley shot one between the eyes and wounded the other. Next the crew of the *Lady Alice* saw the Bumbiri warriors preparing to launch canoes, and although Stanley kept hitting men who exposed themselves to his rifle, four boats put out to engage the *Lady Alice*. The Zanzibaris stopped paddling, and he filled his elephant rifle with explosive balls. When the canoes came close he took careful aim, sinking two of the canoes and killing five men. The other canoes retreated.

Stanley made a vow. When he came back with the main body of his expedition, he would teach the Bumbiri people a lesson so harsh that they would never forget it.

After the fight, night fell and the *Lady Alice* drifted on the vast expanse of the lake. With the improvised paddles the crew could only make three-quarters of a mile an hour, and they did not know where to go for rest and sustenance; the only food in the boat was four bananas, which the men shared between them.

The efforts to reach a place of refuge took 76 hours, during which the boat was buffeted by squalls and the Zanzibaris became weak and dispirited. Stanley made a fire in the stern with a chopped-up thwart and boiled some coffee given him by Linant de Bellefonds; each man drank a cupful but the need for food was desperate. At last the *Lady Alice* reached an uninhabited island, and the men tottered ashore. Stanley picked up his shotgun from the bottom of the boat and went in search of birds, while the crew looked for fruit. By nightfall, they were able to feast off two ducks, four bunches of green bananas and some wild cherries. 'And what glad souls were we that evening around our camp fire with this gracious abundance to which a benignant Providence had led us, storm-tossed, bruised and hungry creatures that we were but a few hours before! Bananas, ducks, berries and coffee! The tobacco gourd and pipe closed one of the most delicious evenings I ever remember to have passed.'

A week later, Stanley was at Kagei, where two months before he had left Frank Pocock, Frederick Barker and 166 men. He had no knowledge at all of what had been happening there while the *Lady Alice* was making the first 1,000-mile circumnavigation of Lake Victoria, and it was a relief to see men dancing with delight on the shore as the boat approached. Frank Pockock was waiting, as he jumped ashore. But where was Barker? Pocock turned and pointed to a cairn of stones: 'He died twelve days ago, Sir.' Once again, Stanley had the task of writing to a bereaved parent in England. In his letter to Mrs Charlotte Barker he warmly praised her son's energy and cheerfulness, and promised to bring home his Bible.

Pocock had written in his diary about the way Barker had died:

'He was as usual in the morning until about nine o'clock when he complained of being cold. I gave him brandy and put a hot stone to his feet, he seemed to revive a little . . . He was very bad, foaming at the mouth and breathing very hard. At half past ten there was a change took place, I thought for the better. He breathed so much freer. He did not for long, he fixed his eyes and lay motionless . . . And I was alone, the only white man with one hundred and sixty-six men under my charge. I had the pants taken off him and drawers put on him in a shroud . . . I performed the burial service myself . . .'

Stanley had grown fond of Barker. But sorrow was not the only reaction, for within six months of leaving Zanzibar he had lost two out of three white assistants – and the expedition was not a quarter completed. Six more leading Zanzibaris had also died during his absence on the lake, the most discouraging loss being that of Mabruki Speke, who had travelled loyally with Stanley on his first expedition, and saved him from being killed in a mutiny. The forebodings Stanley felt were in no way lessened when he was gripped by three bad attacks of malaria, which reduced his weight to below 110 lb. 'But I quininized myself thoroughly from dawn of day to set of sun, and on the fifth day stepped out, sallow, pale, weak and trembling, it is true, with jaundiced eyes, palpitating heart and ringing ears – but the fever had been conquered.'

Stanley fretted to be gone from Kagei for good. Mtesa had promised to send down a big fleet of canoes to escort the expedition, but as the weeks passed there was no sign on the horizon. It seemed impossible to muster enough canoes locally, and to march around the lake to Uganda would mean fighting a way through hostile tribes.

This was a situation in which Stanley showed all his tenacity. In a letter to Felix Lafontaine, a friend in New York, he sent greetings to colleagues on the *Herald*, then plunged into a recital of his experiences. The catastrophic losses from disease had to be taken philosophically; he had done his best, even to the extent of personally vaccinating 300 men against smallpox. 'The evil humours of men's bodies will out somehow, and if men must die, one mode of death is as good as another.' At the present rate, the expedition would be wiped out before his programme of exploration was half completed. But he was going on.

It cost a month of tedious negotiation to acquire enough canoes to start the journey to Buganda. In the end, Stanley had to take boats from a local tribe, after bribing the chief. It would need several journeys to and fro to move everybody up the lake – the flotilla had to carry nearly 200 people, several tons of equipment, and eighty-eight sacks of grain to provide food on the way. The first journey was begun on June 20, with Stanley leading the way in the *Lady Alice*, and was not without its drama. In the darkness several of the canoes began to leak and sink, and frantic cries for help rang across the water. To see what was happening, Stanley set fire to a book he had been reading earlier in the day. The *Lady Alice* sped through the night on rescue missions, and although nobody drowned the loss of supplies was severe.

Stanley chose an island well out in the lake as a halfway station to Buganda. Leaving Pocock and Manwa Sera in charge he went back again to Kagei to collect the remainder of the expedition. Life had not been quiet there in his absence, for the Zanzibaris had been fighting; a man Stanley greatly valued was found with his throat cut. A court was set up, consisting of the local chief, an Arab trader and several of the leading Zanzibaris. It sentenced the murderer to death, but Stanley would not accept that and ordered instead that the man be given 200 lashes. On July 6, the rearguard of the expedition said farewell to Kagei, which had been its headquarters for nearly five months. Stanley took a long look at the graves of Frederick Barker and Mabruki Speke: 'There was not one feeling of regret in my breast at leaving this place . . .'

At last, the next stage of his explorations could begin; but before that, he would visit Bumbiri again to settle accounts.

By the time the expedition was reunited Stanley had been joined by several groups of Ganda in war canoes. They had been sent out by Mtesa to look for the *Lady Alice* following rumours of trouble on the lake. Stanley effectively brought these reinforcements under his command, and on July 30 sent an ultimatum to the paramount chief of Bumbiri, saying he would attack unless amends were made. This was ignored, and on August 4 a force of 250 men set out in six large canoes led by the *Lady Alice*. They flew the Stars and Stripes, the Union Jack and the red flag of Zanzibar. Stanley had been working out his tactics for some days, and sailed around to the western side of the island so that his adversaries would have the afternoon sun in their eyes. At the entrance to a large bay the boats were drawn up in line of battle, waiting until the local warriors made their inevitable appearance on the shore with spears, bows and rocks. As the moment arrived, Stanley gave the order to come within 50 yards and then open fire. The marksmen in the boats poured volley after volley into the warriors, who fell in heaps.

Stanley wrote in his diary: 'The Savages were not a whit disheartened. Relief after relief came gallantly down, and with a frenzied courage stood the brunt. Several of the boldest even advanced into the water and seemed to shoot their arrows in scorn, but these were soon seen gasping in the water, and a few gurgles only marked where they stood.' The firing went on for an hour and a half, until Stanley decided he had inflicted enough harm. An interpreter shouted to the remnant on the shore that 'the white man had punished them in a manner they would remember, and warned them in future to leave strangers alone . . .' The bugle was sounded by Frank Pocock and the expedition sailed away, having suffered not a single casualty itself.

The exact deathroll on Bumbiri could never be known exactly. In his diary Stanley estimated thirty-three killed and one hundred wounded. In his despatches to the *Telegraph* and the *Herald* he raised this to forty-two. Frank Pocock wrote in his diary: 'They were very thick on the shore, but in ten minutes they were thinned from the fire of our rifles. After about two hours firing we left the bay with from thirty to forty killed . . . Arrived in camp about seven o'clock with songs and shouts of joy. We counted what we knew to be dead – thirty-three. Master shot fifteen himself.'

Stanley felt he had done well, and as his expedition sailed northwards towards Buganda the lakeside people pressed gifts of cattle and fruit on him: 'Thus was our victory at Bumbiri productive of great good and plenty to us. The fame of it was already spread widely along the shores of the mainland, for though these natives do not possess the means of Europe and America to communicate news, yet rumour is swift and industrious.'

The tidings took longer to reach the outside world. Stanley's despatches did not arrive in London and New York until a year later, but when they did the effect was immediate. Liberal groups expressed shock and indignation that such deeds could be committed in the name of civilisation. Protest meetings were called at the Royal Geographical Society, and journals of opinion thundered their disapproval. Viewed from the calm of offices and clubs in Central London, Stanley's behaviour on Lake Victoria – as told in his own words – lacked any mitigating factors. The *Saturday Review* said: 'Here is an expedition got up for commercial purposes by a pair of

48

notorious newspapers, and it takes the form of what is practically filibustering; and this outrage on a peaceful and comparatively unarmed people is held forth to the world as countenanced by the English and American flags. This is surely a question worth the attention of the two foreign ministers.' The *Saturday Review* warned Stanley that he had carried the 'American method of treating savages' too far. It was not merely the bloodshed, but the graphic manner in which it was described, with such seeming relish.

Lord Derby, the British Foreign Secretary, was drawn into the Bumbiri controversy when a protest was delivered to him by the Aborigines Protection Society and the Anti-Slavery Society. He expressed the hope that Stanley might later be able to 'afford some explanation or justification of his proceedings'; in the meantime, it was plain that Stanley had no right to hoist the British flag, and Her Majesty's consuls on the East Coast of Africa would be 'instructed to intimate this to him, if any opportunity of communicating with him should arise.' As everybody knew, there was scant hope of doing so.

Perhaps the most balanced comment came from another explorer of Central Africa, Colonel James Grant. In a letter to the Royal Geographical Society he refused to support a motion of censure on the Bumbiri incident, but added in sad bewilderment: 'Even Stanley's best friends cannot but regret his pugnacity and want of discretion.'

One point was missed by everyone: Stanley was obeying his journalistic calling, in the style he had been taught. He always gave his imagination full play when writing about his African battles, in the confidence that the readers enjoyed violence. In chasing popular success, he shaped his buccaneering image.

3. The Cauldron of Slavery

After the punitive visit to Bumbiri, it seemed to Stanley that he could now take leave of Mtesa and hurry off to new fields of discovery. In ten months he had marched more than 700 miles, settled the shape and extent of the world's second biggest lake, established relations with a powerful African kingdom, and planted in it the seeds of Christianity. By comparison with other explorers, he was making swift progress; but even so, the great bulk of his task lay ahead. The expedition must first go westward to Lake Albert, which had been sighted by Sir Samuel and Lady Baker in 1864, but never properly explored; it was thought that the Nile, coming from Lake Victoria, flowed into it and out again at the northeast corner.

Once Stanley had reached Lake Albert, it should be possible for him to assemble the *Lady Alice* and make a second voyage of discovery. It might take a month to march to the lake, and as long to sail around it. After that, he would head south overland for 400 miles, to Ujiji on Lake Tanganyika. Once more the boat would be launched, for yet another circumnavigation – and that would be three of Africa's great lakes vanquished.

Finally, he would lead the expedition westward again, towards the vast, mysterious Lualaba River, which Livingstone had been the first white man to see. Stanley must follow the river wherever it led; some geographers thought it joined the Niger, others believed it swung westwards to form the Congo, whereas Livingstone had died convinced that it fed the Nile. Laying bare the secrets of the Lualaba would be the climax and Stanley felt encouraged by his accomplishments so far, despite the losses in men and equipment. He was sure that Mtesa would give him guides, and a strong military escort, to take the expedition safely to Lake Albert.

While he set off to negotiate with the king, he left the main body of his followers in camp at Domu, two-thirds of the way up the western shore of Lake Victoria. From there the expedition would be able to strike off directly towards its next objective. The camp was put in charge of Frank Pocock – in whom Stanley noticed a growing air of assurance – and Manwa Sera, who had become known as the 'father of the expedition'.

As he neared the Bugandan capital, Stanley received tidings that filled him with dismay. Mtesa proposed to make war against his main enemies at the northern end of the lake, a tribe called the Vuma. 'When I heard this, I felt more than half inclined to turn back, for, I knew by experience that African wars are tedious things.' But Stanley had to rely upon Mtesa for the military escort to Lake Albert, so there seemed no alternative to going on and exerting his skill to give Mtesa a quick victory.

In the midst of this dilemma, Stanley was confronted with trouble from his own followers. Two of the senior Zanzibaris had been caught selling their guns and pistols to the local Africans. There was a scent of mutiny in the air. The two were sent under guard to Pocock, with a letter of instructions, dated August 18, 1875:

(1) I send Chowpereh and Muccadum to you to camp. You will put Muccadum in chains until I return. Keep him close prisoner.

(2) You will put Islam in chains also until I return to camp. You will thus have Fundi Rehani, Alsassi, Wadi Baraka, Muccadum and Islam in chains. Five smart men. The rings which slip over the collar must be watched . . . The ring must be beaten almost flat so that it cannot be slipped over the chain.

(3) Muster all the Wangwana, and take their guns away and put them in your house, except a few of the most faithful . . .

(4) Let no fire be kindled near your house anywhere. Be careful of these instructions as you value our success. Our common safety depends upon your sleepless vigilance . . .

This note of anxiety was reiterated in a postscript; but it is a sign of how often such emergencies afflicted the expedition that Stanley says nothing about it elsewhere.

Pocock makes a passing mention in his diary, but he had other troubles to cope with. He had been punched in the face by a Zanzibari whom he had told, in what he felt was a friendly way, how to plait rope: 'I struck him again, as it was not in my nature to stand that. He was arrested and put in chains.' For good measure the prisoner was given a lashing. Pockock was also having difficulties with the wife of one of the men who were away with Stanley. When Pocock asked her to grind some flour, she refused. When he told her not to light a fire inside her house, she ignored him – and the house burnt

51

down. She was given another house, and again Pocock found her with a fire inside it:

'I put water on it but she made fun of me. She had the fire close to her bed and thought it right – to keep herself warm.'

It was just over a year since Pocock had signed on with Stanley at the Langham Hotel in London, with his father and his brother Edward as witnesses to the contract. It would be harvest-time now in Kent, but England seemed very far away. Writing to his parents (August 14, 1875), Frank said: 'Don't forget to make some wine, if possible. We expect to be home about Christmas, 1876. My thoughts are ever on you all.'

The day after he finished the letter, he was dressing a wound in a man's throat when he heard that one of the Zanzibaris had drowned after falling out of a canoe. He recovered the body before it was eaten by crocodiles, and to avoid offending the superstitions of local Africans by burying it on land, tied a large stone to the feet and threw it overboard well out in the lake. 'All's well,' he wrote phleg-matically in his diary.

By this time, Stanley was deciding how he could best help Mtesa in his war. The king was encamped at the point where the Nile flowed from Lake Victoria, and the Vuma enemy were within sight on an island. It would be a naval conflict, for each side had several hundred canoes. Stanley was not at all optimistic about the outcome, for the Vuma were expert sailors and used a daring tactic of diving under enemy canoes and cutting the cords which held them together. Before the serious fighting began, he looked across at the enemy through his binoculars: 'They are very boastful and exhibit mad antics to us.' As the days drifted by he decided to return to his work of religious conversion, and noted on September 6: 'I have begun to translate the Scriptures for Mtesa in the intervals of war business. A cannon I aimed at the island has caused five deaths. Today I dropped two with a Snyder rifle.'

Throughout September the war continued with sporadic canoe fights on the lake. Gradually the Ganda gained the upper hand – partly, in Stanley's view, because Mtesa had threatened to burn alive any of his warriors who showed cowardice. Between his labours on the Scriptures, Stanley designed a two-storey floating fort which he thought might strike terror into the enemy. It so pleased him that he put in his diary a quotation from Milton's *Paradise Lost*, beginning 'The invention all admired . . .' Admired though it may have been, he could find no volunteers to sail in this outlandish vessel; the Ganda regarded it as a death-trap from which they could never escape if surrounded. No mercy might be expected from the enemy, as had been demonstrated when Mtesa sent across the bay a peace party led by one of his favourite young warriors. 'We watched the canoe until it touched the shore, and then it became engulfed in a mad crowd of black demons who slaughtered them to a man before our eyes and laughed the King to scorn.'

Peace was agreed on October 14, the Vuma sending two young girls as symbolic tribute. Stanley moved off with Mtesa to the capital and felt gratified when the king declared once and for all his adherence to Christianity. He sent a letter to Pocock (October 22, 1875): 'Now the king wants the prayer book in order to conform with the Christian religion. You will therefore look in my leather portmanteau and find a little prayer book which formerly belonged to Fred. Wrap it up in paper carefully and give it to bearer who will return in haste . . .'

His attitude towards Mtesa varied from day to day. He confided his feelings to his diary – that the king was the most intelligent African he had ever met, but 'too fond of women', and a victim of flattery . . . Perhaps the greatest vexation was Mtesa's indifference to European concepts of time, for although it was agreed that Stanley could have an army to escort him through the warlike regions to the west, it seemed impossible to pin the King down to a starting date. In a note to Pocock on November 2, Stanley asked for details of conditions in the main camp, and ended: 'I am thirsty for news, and tired – God knows how much – of this country.'

As a gesture to Mtesa, Stanley promised him a young mission-trained Zanzibari called Dallington, who could read and write. He would help the king with his study of the Bible and act as his scribe. Dallington was keen to stay in Buganda, and took with a will to despatching royal messages far and wide. (General Gordon in Khartoum was later to receive several rather imperious letters, couched in Dallington's odd style.) At last, Stanley extracted the promise he needed and left the king to return to his own camp; he had been away from his people for three months – time frittered away, in which no exploring had been possible. The delay had lowered morale at the main camp, where the Zanzibaris were fractious and relations uneasy between Frank Pocock and Manwa Sera. Villages round about had been raided for food and Pocock

53

The woes of travelling in Central Africa: swamps concealed leeches, crocodiles, snakes – and malaria

suspected that some covert encouragement to the raids had come from Manwa Sera himself.

But the reappearance of the 'Great Master' soon lifted the expedition from its gloom. Now there would be action. Stanley let the various miscreants out of their chains, and roared with delight at a joke by one of the local Africans: 'Why is it that you Whites have all long noses and your dogs have short noses, while we have short noses and our dogs have long noses?' Orders were given for the breaking up of the camp, and on November 26 – less than a week after his return – Stanley led the march away from the lush, soporific environs of Lake Victoria. The expedition soon found itself plunging through waist-deep swamps. The nine months spent on and around the lake had dimmed memories of what it meant to struggle through the wilderness. Malaria soon began to wreak havoc and both Stanley and Pocock fell sick. But nothing could dim Stanley's joy at being on the move again, and the men responded to his mood.

On December 4, a baby was born to the wife of Robert Feruzi, one of the mission-educated leaders of the expedition. It was christened 'Alice'.

Two days before Christmas, Stanley made his rendezvous with the spearmen he had been promised. He drew up a table of the various contingents, and added to his own 180 followers, found that he was commanding a force of 2,270 people. But it might not be enough for the opposition they must expect to meet – he had originally asked Mtesa for 50,000 men. On Christmas Day a spear hurled out of the forest buried itself in a Baganda warrior's hip; it was the first show of force from the resentful people whose land they were invading. The march halted and a Christmas dinner was set out: tea, boiled bananas and cold beef. 'I am content and thank the Almighty I have got so good food to eat,' wrote Frank Pocock. He had now been away from home for nearly eighteen months.

By early in January the expedition was passing through wild country which no white man had ever entered before. The exact route is hard to trace from Stanley's account, but he was near the 'Mountains of the Moon' – the Ruwenzori range, which rises to 17,000 feet. Although lost in cloud, the peaks were said to be capped with snow, and streams of icy water had to be forded. All the time, the caravan was being harassed by hostile bands, who hid in the grass to loose off showers of arrows. Deep pits had been dug along the path and several of the expedition's men fell into them.

Despite all these obstacles, the expedition pressed on towards the expanse of water that was its objective; Stanley looked forward to the moment when the *Lady Alice* could start her new voyage of discovery.

But with every mile of the advance, the leader of the Ganda soldiers, General Sambuzi, became more and more nervous. He warned that the expedition was creating a trap for itself in which everyone might die. Reinforcements were at least 100 miles away. Stanley recognised this as true: if they were overrun by the Nyoro warriors and their allies, there would be no survivors, for the Ganda themselves had set a merciless pattern in war. He had heard at Mtesa's capital of how the king's father had lured 30,000 enemy warriors into a stockade to arrange peace terms, overcome them with 100,000 of his own men, and given orders that they should all be hacked into small pieces. The massacre took five days to complete. The tribes around Buganda were always watching for a chance to take revenge for deeds like that.

In a mood of growing tension, the army stuck to its westward course. It was against Stanley's nature to admit defeat, and Sambuzi knew that his certain fate would be execution if the white man accused him before Mtesa of being a coward. So on January 11, 1876, Stanley came within sight of his prize: he stood on a plateau and looked down to the blue expanse of a lake, 1,500 feet below. It seemed to him that he had reached the southern extremity of Lake Albert, although from the longitude and latitude he wrote in his diary it must have been a smaller, and completely unknown, stretch of water which later was named Lake George. He was eager to be on the shore, and a powerful reconnaissance party was sent out to find the best route for carrying down the sections of the *Lady Alice*.

Stanley was closing his eyes to reality. As his forces halted on the plateau, thousands of warriors moved in from the surrounding villages. It seemed as though danger waited behind every rock around the camp. Sambuzi sent out emissaries for peace, with no avail. A mocking reply was brought back: 'It is true you have come, but tell us how you will get away from here. Can you fly in the air?' If Stanley did reach the lake, he and his crew would have no hope of assembling the boat and launching her before being slaughtered. In the meanwhile, what would be the fate of the rest of his followers?

All lingering hopes were quelled when the courage of the Ganda failed. Stanley learnt that Sambuzi's warriors planned to steal away in the night. The white man and his people would be left to their fate. The panic quickly spread to the Zanzibaris; they also wanted to flee, as far and as fast as they could, away from this menacing land. Stanley faced the prospect of being, by dawn, left alone with Frank Pocock and a handful of the most loyal followers.

He made one final bid to salvage a little from the disaster, by calling a conference of his captains. Perhaps they could put forward a plan which would be less shameful than joining the general retreat. When they were seated around him, he asked the men to speak their minds freely about the situation; he did not need to tell them that it could hardly be more desperate. The captains chose as their first spokesman the chief guide and 'detective', Kachéché. Speaking in Swahili, he said, 'Master, I don't know what my brothers here think of the pit in which I see we are fallen, but I would tell you truly what I think. I will do exactly as you say. Either live, or die, all is one to me. If you say go on, I am ready; if you say return, I am with you; but I want you to tell me, if we go on to the lake, have we any chance at all to be able to start on our journey?'

After that, there was nothing more to say or to discuss, except the

56

preparations for retreat. Stanley had no wish to lead men like Kachéché to certain doom.

The flight from Lake George was ignominious, but when the local people saw the invaders scurrying back the way they had come they did nothing more than harry the rearguard. In one skirmish five men were killed, but after a week the expedition reached a village called Kawanga, on the edge of Mtesa's domain. Everyone was exhausted, hungry and frightened. Stanley sat down and wrote a rather breathless, and very revealing, despatch for the *Telegraph* and the *Herald*. He admitted that his latest journey had been 'great folly', only slightly redeemed by penetrating an unknown region.

His journalistic acumen never deserted him, and he used this mistake to draw his readers closer: 'Honestly I do not suppose I have been guilty of such a hare-brained attempt as this before.' (When the despatch arrived, in a quite speedy eight months, both papers printed this 'confession' with apparent complacency.) To support his claim that the journey had not been utterly in vain, Stanley devoted several racy paragraphs to telling how he had met amazingly pale-skinned Africans in the Ruwenzori region. They might almost be taken for Greeks or Syrians, he declared, and the women were 'singularly beautiful'.

He ended by promising to look for another route to Lake Albert – but he never did so, even though Mtesa sent a message promising to supply an army of 25,000 men this time. As Pocock drily noted in his dairy: 'If an attempt had been made to return, a great many of the Wangwana (Zanzibaris) would have deserted, others would have gone sick and died on the road, as they dreaded the thought of returning to Unyoro.'

Stanley rejected an appeal from Mtesa to come back and visit him yet again. A letter from the king's new amanuensis concluded: 'I Dallington, the servant of white men, I won't tell you a lie, but I will tell you the truth. The Sultan (Mtesa) is not bad.' Stanley was in two minds about that. As a parting gift he sent Mtesa the Bible that had belonged to Edward Pocock, then turned south towards Lake Tanganyika. Time was slipping away.

With visits to several important chiefs along the way, the march to Ujiji occupied a tiring four months; but as Stanley drew near once again to the main Arab trade route he was able to make contact with a pioneering ivory hunter, Philippe Broyon. He had first encountered Broyon, a Swiss, not long after leaving the coast in 1874, and now sent messengers across country with a letter describing the best places around Lake Victoria for buying ivory. In return, Broyon sent two bars of Castile soap, a bottle of castor oil and some old copies of *Le Figaro*. The castor oil was especially welcome, as Stanley often suffered badly from constipation through the effects of malaria and the medicines he took to suppress it. Although he noted the exchange with Broyon in his diary, he made no mention of it in his newspaper despatches – probably to avoid giving the impression that there were too many rival adventurers in the wilds; but in fact, the Swiss was the only other white man in the Central African interior.

As Lake Tanganyika came into view on May 27, 1876, Stanley remembered nostalgically how he had sailed on it with the 'grand old hero', David Livingstone. For all its beauty, the lake seemed uninteresting and forlorn without him. Stanley stared at the mountains beyond the western shore, knowing that there he must eventually go, in the missionary's footsteps, to the land of the Manyema cannibals. It was a place, according to Livingstone, where men were afflicted by a strange sickness: broken-heartedness. There the Arabs hunted for slaves, and the supply seemed limitless. Although the trade in humans could no longer take place in Zanzibar, the slave-market of Ujiji still flourished as ever. A girl could be bought for fifty lengths of cloth; a bullock cost ten.

Yet if Ujiji was a magnet for slavers, it also offered tired travellers the prospect of rest. By Central African standards, the town was a haven of peace. Seven hundred miles from the sea, the authority of Sultan Barghash still had some force. Stanley's expedition had been travelling for seventeen months and had covered, by land and water, nearly 3,500 miles. There would now be a chance to recover and reorganise.

The satisfaction of walking down into the town, and being greeted by Arabs who had been in Ujiji during the time of Livingstone, was soon replaced by disappointment. Stanley and Pocock were expecting that here they would find a vast accumulation of mail, sent up from Zanzibar. There was nothing. Stanley could not even feel confident any more that the despatches he had sent from points along the route had safely arrived with his editors in New York and London. He expressed his dismay in a letter (June 2, 1876) to Alice Pike: 'As I thought of Ujiji I flattered myself daily that I should receive letters and newspapers. I daily fed and lived on that hope ... You may imagine how I felt when after enquiry about letters, I was met with "There are none" . . . what would you have done, oh my Alice? Tear your hair, clothes, and shriek distractedly, run about and curse the Fates? I did not do anything so undignified, but I soberly grieved and felt discouraged . . .'

He went on to tell his fiancée how he now looked. For the moment he was well, but 'awfully thin'. He was down to 118 lb, and recalled being 178 lb when he had weighed himself at Windsor two years earlier. 'My cheeks are sunk, my eyes large and sickly, my bones feel sore even lying on two blankets.' He wondered what Alice's mother would think of him. Would she not ask how her daughter could have seen anything in Henry Morton Stanley? 'Yet the same heart still throbs with deepest love, as it did long ago, there is sincere friendship for Mrs Pike, and admiration for your sisters.'

He was well aware that it was within a few weeks of two years since he had parted from Alice in New York. She was now 19. He knew that with her beauty and talent, she would have no lack of suitors. But he buoyed up his confidence by looking at the two photographs of her, wrapped in oiled silk, which he kept in his breast pocket. In his diary was written the promise Alice had made: '. . . when the two years are gone, if you come back to claim me I will marry you, so help me God . . .' He could not be back within two years, that was sure, but there was still some time to go to the date she had fixed for their wedding: January 14, 1877. He must hurry on with his exploring.

Shortly before the middle of June, the *Lady Alice* was assembled and launched on Lake Tanganyika. As an escort she had a massive teak canoe, loaned to Stanley by Ujiji's Arab governor. Both boats were equipped with sails and Stanley worked out that his journey would take two months at the most. As was now his custom, he put Frank Pocock in charge of the main camp; after much hand-shaking, the *Lady Alice* put off from the beach and headed south. Stanley knew he was far behind Cameron, his rival from the Royal Geographical Society. Cameron had crossed Lake Tanganyika and had reached the Lualaba River; but the Arabs reported that from there he had turned south and headed towards Angola. When the moment came for Stanley to explore the Lualaba, he would go north, into the region shunned by even the most daring slave-traders.

The journey around Lake Tanganyika was as uneventful as he could have wished. He noted that the Arabs had established a new trading centre called Karema and that a few lakeside villages had been ravaged by bandits. On the western shore the effects of the slave trade were woefully plain, and in his diary he recorded the sight of a caravan with more than 1,000 people chained or roped together. They were in the last stages of hunger, and the children in particular had suffered from the march: 'The chests jutted out with the protuberence of a skeleton frame, while the poor bellies were in such a fearfully attenuated state like an empty bladder . . . legs were mere sticks of bone, trembling weak supports to the large head and large chest.' As he looked at them the men prisoners held down their heads in shame at their condition.

Later he was to compose a bitter despatch (October 28, 1876) about the slave trade in the heart of Africa, and tell how it had depopulated vast areas in a few years. In his view, Sultan Barghash was ultimately to blame, for the Arab slavers were his subjects; indeed, Stanley had seen a large consignment of slaves going to Said bin Salim, governor of the important trading centre of Tabora – and Salim was directly responsible to the Sultan.

After a voyage of 800 miles, the *Lady Alice* arrived back at Ujiji on the last day of July, to find that a smallpox epidemic had broken out. The precaution Stanley had taken to vaccinate his recruits now proved its worth, and only those who had deliberately evaded this treatment fell victims to the disease. But the effect upon the Arabs and their slaves in Ujiji had been severe. As many as seventy-five people were dying every day, and when Stanley brought out his reserve of vaccine he found that it had all dried up; there was nothing he could do to help. The best course was to leave Ujiji as soon as possible. It was a painful choice, because men he had sent east to the Arab town of Tabora to search for mail had not yet returned.

Stanley sat down to write a series of long despatches on geographical topics. One of 5,000 words was entirely devoted to the Lukuga River, a potential outlet for Lake Tanganyika. In it he was bent on showing that whereas he made a proper scientific study, Cameron had been content to take the opinions of local African chiefs. In what he wrote for publication, Stanley was ostentatiously polite to his rival, the 'gallant young naval officer,' but a personal letter to Edward Levy of the *Daily Telegraph* (August 13, 1876), had a far less charitable postscript: 'We have obtained a signal triumph over Cameron . . . Possibly he would have been more careful had he suspected a "damned penny a liner" for a successor in that locality.

By crossing the Lualaba and striking off in a wrong direction he has left the question of the Lualaba where Livingstone left it.'

Ujiji was the last place from which it was possible, with any confidence, to send mail down to the coast; even then, it might be almost a year on the way. So both Stanley and Pocock were busying themselves with letters to relatives and friends. Frank wrote (July 20) to one of his brothers in Rochester, and recalled the death of Edward more than eighteen months before: 'In the time of "Mabruki" – such was my brother's African name – his morning bugle call was always loud and clear . . . Even now I hear the people of an evening, sitting around the camp fire, talk of "Bwana Mabruki", what a merry fellow he was.' In Ujiji, said Frank Pocock, the sound he most often heard was the screaming of a slave being beaten, or the roaring of the waves on the lake shore. But he hoped to be home 'one fine day in May, 1877.' The date was still slipping back.

Stanley spent the morning of August 14, 1876, using his photographic equipment, which was still in working order after nearly two years of being carried through Africa. He took several views of Ujiji, and arranged a picture – by delaying the shutter action – in which both he and Pocock appeared. It shows them 'conferring' in the courtyard of their mud house at Ujiji: Stanley is posing with his right hand on his hip and the other holding one of the long oars of the *Lady Alice*. The oars and the rudder of the boat are stacked against the side of the house. Stanley is clad in a belted, thigh-length jacket, knee-boots, and what looks like a Moslem *tarboosh* on his head. Frank Pocock is sitting on the ground, with several Africans lounging around him in a semi-circle; he is wearing a cap and sports a luxuriant beard.

Later in the day, Stanley sat down to compose a letter to Alice. Spontaneous and direct, it is among the most moving things he ever wrote. Although he only once speaks of death, he knew well that the chances of surviving the last stage of his journey were anything but good. His strength, and that of his followers, had been eroded by two years of wandering – and now they must face the unknown perils of the Lualaba. At the start of the letter Stanley gives a brief account of his journey around Lake Tanganyika, and praises the performance of the *Lady Alice*. He then remarks that he was at the southern end of the lake on July 4, the anniversary of the first hundred years of American independence. Doubtless she had gone to Philadelphia, where a vast exhibition was being held to mark the occasion: 'How the city of Philadelphia must have groaned under the millions which thronged the streets, how the air must have been disturbed throughout Pensylvania with shouts and cannon, nay indeed, the United States from New York to California . . . Then all taking place under a terrible, broiling, suffocating heat. Yet where is the patriotism that would not stand it, because such a day only takes place once in a hundred years. Think how forgotten you and I and most now living will be before another such day comes over America . . .'

He goes on to say how he has been waiting in vain for the men he had sent to Tabora to come back with mail. So still without news, he must leave this letter in Ujiji, to be sent down to Zanzibar as soon as possible. He spells out what he hopes to achieve after leaving Ujiji; these paragraphs reveal – more plainly than any of his published writings – how he was already in little doubt about where the Lualaba would take him.

It is now within a few days of twenty-five months since I parted from you, and nearly twenty months since leaving Zanzibar. I am in the centre of Africa, and want to strike from here to the western ocean, the Atlantic, to come to *you*. The eastern half is done, the western half must be traversed now and it is an entirely new country. With good fortune I could reach the ocean in nine months from the day I leave Ujiji, but I doubt whether it is to be done under the circumstances in that time. I permit myself to hope I can do it in a year. I am not sure whether I shall attempt to reach the western ocean, or to reach some known point on the Congo, and return to Zanzibar . . . if I went on westward and so to England, I might reach England in August or September 1877, if I returned to Zanzibar, by November or December 1877. If I adopted the first road I should have traversed 5,400 miles of Africa, and across by the latter I should have done 6,000 miles. The time engaged in doing it would be three years, just a year longer than I estimated. But the estimates are invariably wrong, and it is not fair to tie a man down to mere estimates. We have all done our best, no expedition has done so much, nor nearly so well as we have . . .

Then, my own Darling, if by that name I may call you, let us hope cheerfully that a happy termination to this long period of trial of your constancy and my health and courage await us both, that the time may come when we can both laugh at these silent, gloomy days to be, both be amused at our experiences, various and different as they are ... Give my most cheerful salutes to your mother. For you, my own Alice, what treasures of love would I pour out before you if I could see you ... What means have I to convey my heart's load of love to you, but this letter which must go through a thousand miles of savages, exposed to all dangers of flood and fire and battle until it reaches the sea? And to go well it must be light, not heavy. I thus am prevented from enlarging upon my love, and perhaps properly, lest too much would render its declaration insipid. Time is also precious with me, for I have but little to write letters. Grant then that my love towards you is unchanged, that you are my dream, my stay and my hope, and my beacon, and believe that I shall still cherish you in this light until I meet you, or death meets me. This is the last you will get, I fear, for a long time. Then, my darling, accept this letter with one last and loving farewell.

MORTON.

In an earlier part of this long letter Stanley talked about Kalulu, the slave boy he had brought back from the Livingstone expedition. Alice knew Kalulu, whom Stanley had taken through France, Britain and America, then sent to a private school in Wandsworth, South London. At the funeral of Livingstone, Kalulu had walked behind the coffin in Westminster Abbey. With some reluctance Stanley took him out of the school, where he was just learning to read and write English, to return to Africa with the *Telegraph-Herald* expedition. Kalulu settled easily back into African life and acted as a general factotum to his master, who now told Alice: 'You would wonder to see how tall he is grown, he has shot up like a palm tree.'

The pride Stanley took in this young attendant was shattered a few weeks after the letter was written, because Kalulu deserted. In a terse diary entry, Stanley said Kalulu had run away 'for no known reason'. Perhaps it was because of some premonition about what lay ahead.

The 'detective', Kachéché, was sent out to hunt for Kalulu, and caught him on the island in the lake. The runaway was paraded before Stanley, and sentenced to the customary punishment – he was put in slave chains, and would have to march in them for a week or more, until he had purged his crime. Even Kalulu's special status could not save him from this humiliation – which was then the standard treatment for deserters.

Kalulu was by no means the only deserter before the expedition

63

could shake itself free from the allures of Ujiji. Nearly forty men out of the remaining 170 made their escape, during the journey to the western side of the lake. It was a depressing setback – Stanley knew he was going to need every able-bodied man he could muster in the months ahead.

He was ill with malaria, and his spirits were low. In one of the brief entries in his diary he confesses to being 'terribly weak'. Frank Pocock, who was worried about him, asked if he could go back to Ujiji in search of the deserters. That, at least, was the reason put forward: 'But my idea was to get news from the coast and things for Mr Stanley, as he was sick so often.' At first he met with refusal, then Stanley called him and said: 'I give you seven days to go and return and you can take three men.'

By this time, Pocock was himself fighting off a bout of malaria. He had also dismantled the *Lady Alice* for porterage. But he went down to the shore to look for any canoes setting out for the eastern side of the lake. He found one, packed with more than sixty slaves: 'I saw the canoe coming crowded and a drover standing aft like the captain of a man-of-war. When he came to the shore I asked, "Is this the way you treat human beings?" He said, "They are my money and I take them to Ujiji for sale". But I said, "I want room in this canoe". He said, "Sit there". But I am not a slave, therefore I want room . . . I took my stick and drove from thirty to forty half-starved slaves on the shore, much to his astonishment. He said, "I thought this would come when I saw an Englishman standing on the shore." My men pushed the canoe in the lake and with many rough words we sailed away, leaving his money on the shore to desert if they wished. We made good way, by my giving the rowers a present and we reached an island at 9 p.m. Here we moored for the night, myself still suffering from the effects of fever.'

Pocock only managed to capture four deserters, the rest being hidden in and around Ujiji by friends. He was also dismayed that still nothing was known about the men who had been sent to Tabora for mail; any hope of seeing them must be abandoned. He loaded a canoe with the deserters, and all the provisions he could buy, and sailed back to the west. He was given a warm greeting by Stanley, who had recovered his health and seemed cheerful again.

The month-long march to the Lualaba was uneventful, although the area was ravaged by smallpox. On October 17, 1876, the expedition climbed over a low ridge at the side of a mountain and saw ahead the confluence of the Lualaba with another, smaller river. Stanley was filled with excitement and awe. His men threw down their loads and sat to enjoy the view. In the distance they could see a mountain, beyond a wide expanse of grassland. The Lualaba was nearly a mile wide, pale grey in colour and winding slowly from the south: 'In the bed of the river are two or three small islands, green with the verdure of trees and sedge. I likened it even here to the Mississippi, as it appears before the impetuous, full-volumed Missouri pours its rusty brown water into it. A secret rapture filled my soul as I gazed upon the majestic stream. The great mystery that for all these centuries Nature had kept hidden from the world of science was waiting to be solved.'

The Zanzibaris wondered if their earlier fears had been exaggerated, for the Manyema country did not seem so dangerous as it was reputed after all. Food was cheap: the daily ration money for each man on the expedition was six cowrie shells, which served as currency, and the local villagers would sell a chicken for three cowries and ten cobs of sweet corn for two shells. All the deserters had been let out of their chains, and for the moment nobody had any thought of running off. A short way ahead, along the banks of the Lualaba, lay a town called Kasongo, where there were known to be several Arab traders. So the next morning the expedition set off early and covered eighteen miles in nine hours, until it marched into Kasongo with drums beating and trumpets blaring.

It was here that Stanley first came face to face with Tippu-Tib, the most powerful Arab leader in the whole of Central Africa. He was really called Hamed bin Muhammed, but he was always known by his nickname; that, said the Africans, was the sound of his guns as he came to attack you. Tippu-Tib was in his late thirties, but had been trading in Africa since he was twelve. He gave allegiance to the Sultan of Zanzibar, but had not been back to the island for more than five years. Over a vast area, south and west of Lake Tanganyika, he had usurped the powers of the African chiefs; his lieutenants raided far and wide for slaves and ivory. Tippu-Tib and Stanley were quick to size one another up. Stanley gave his impressions of a tall, black-bearded man in the prime of life, quick in his movements and courtier-like in his manners. Tippu-Tib was half-caste and had negroid features; he also had a nervous twitching of the eyelids. But there was no mistaking his calibre: 'After regarding him for a few minutes I came to the conclusion that this Arab was a remarkable

65

Tippu-Tib was the greatest Arab freebooter in Africa. His followers ravaged vast areas of the interior for slaves and ivory. Yet his courtesy impressed many Europeans. This photograph was taken some years after Stanley first saw him on the Lualaba in 1876

man . . .' Tippu-Tib travelled through the interior of Africa in style, with his harem and a retinue of young Arabs who served him devotedly.

Tippu-Tib's version of the meeting is to be found in his memoirs. Writing in Swahili, he tells how he had recently come to Kasongo: 'A month passed there until one afternoon Stanley appeared. We greeted him, welcomed him and gave him a house. The following morning we went to see him and he showed us a gun, telling us, "From this gun fifteen bullets come out!" Now we knew of no such gun firing fifteen rounds, neither knew of one or had seen such. I asked him, "From a single barrel?" He said they came from a single barrel, so I asked him to fire it so that we could see . . . At that he went outside and fired twelve rounds. Then he took a pistol and fired six rounds. He came back and sat down on the verandah. We were amazed . . .'

Having given Tippu-Tib this cause for thought, Stanley quickly made him a proposition. If the Arab would accompany him for sixty days' marching, with a force of 200 armed men, Stanley would pay him 5,000 dollars. After several sessions of haggling detailed terms were agreed, the main ones being that Stanley would choose the direction the joint force would take, that one day in three would be a halt, and that each day's march would be for four hours. The marches would start just north of Kasongo at Nyangwe, the last Arab trading centre on the river. Stanley promised to give Tippu-Tib a draft for the money, which could be collected in Zanzibar.

The size of the offer was governed by one fact: Stanley now realised that without some bold strategem, his explorations must end at Nyangwe. The courage of his followers had risen on reaching the Lualaba, but was now ebbing away at terrifying speed. If he tried to lead them farther north, they would desert almost *en masse*. Then he would have to admit defeat, or plunge on with Pocock and a loyal remnant to what could only be certain death. Nyangwe had been the farthest point reached by Cameron, who had turned back there sixteen months earlier. Tippu-Tib said Cameron had been baulked because he could not get canoes. Also, the tribes to the north were so savage and cannibalistic that his men would not go with him; so finally, Tippu-Tib had escorted Cameron over a well-defined trade route to the south, where he met a party of Portuguese half-castes and went off to Angola.

By hiring Tippu-Tib, with a force much larger than his own,

Stanley was making his men virtual prisoners. They dare not desert, and sixty marches would take them so far into hostile country that they could not run away with any chance of survival. They could only stay with Stanley, wherever he went.

The expedition force of 150, which included about a score of women and children, was now combined with Tippu-Tib's caravan – which had 200 men armed with muskets, plus a horde of porters, concubines and camp-followers. Some of Tippu-Tib's men were 'Ruga Ruga' mercenaries renowned for their ferocity; they wore blood-red cotton cloaks and headdresses of feathers and skins. The march from Nyangwe began on November 5, 1876, the plan being to journey for several days through the rain forest, rather than to follow the winding Lualaba from the outset.

Before they started, Stanley confronted Pocock with the hazards they were about to face. If the Lualaba did become the Congo, its course might run for nearly 2,000 miles before it reached the Atlantic. There was still time to turn back, rather than risk the unknown. Frank Pocock was in no doubts about going on. He said he had been told by his father to 'stick by Stanley to the end,' and he would do so. Pocock's own diary entry was typically matter-of-fact: 'We held a consultation this evening concerning our journey from Nyangwe. The decision is we go north to settle the question concerning the Lualaba and the Nile.' But in retrospect for his readers, Stanley describes the moment with a great flourish – how he and Frank sat talking it over in the candlelight; they tossed a coin, and it told them to go south; they drew straws and got the same result; but in the end they agreed they must head north, for that was their destiny, and they shook hands solemnly.

It was an historic decision for Africa. But Stanley's determination to go on, whatever the cost, was much more concerned with proving that he kept his word: the vow to perform the greatest exploring journey of the age came before everything. He put it clearly in a letter to Edward King, a Boston journalist with whom he had once shared a flat in Paris: 'I can die, but I will not go back. I anticipate trouble and many disagreeable things – possibly the digestion of myself in some cannibal's stomach – but I cannot picture to myself the idea of me standing, hat in hand, explaining personally to the proprietor of the *New York Herald* why I came back without fulfilling my promise.'

The trouble the explorer anticipated was not long delayed. The journey through the dense and humid forest exhausted the porters and lowered the spirits of everyone. Stanley one evening tried to compose a poem, which quickly degenerated into clumsy doggerel. He left it unfinished, the last line reading, significantly, 'Our people lamented aloud . . .'

By the end of November the travelling conditions were somewhat better, but the people were more threatening. There were signs of depravity everywhere; in the villages, rows of skulls were stuck on posts. Pocock recorded: 'These people are real cannibals. They cut the ears off slaves and captives and eat all flesh. Human flesh they are fond of.'

Showers of arrows fell into the camp at night, and Stanley had to send out armed groups to clear the surrounding areas. Progress was erratic, for while part of the combined force was travelling down the Lualaba in the *Lady Alice* and a fleet of captured canoes, the rest was marching along the riverbank and had to be waited for. Tippu-Tib progressed in a maddeningly slow fashion, starting at dawn and stopping by mid-morning. He was also trying to alter the contract for the march to his own advantage, and circumstances made it hard to resist him. Stanley's earlier admiration for Tippu-Tip had begun to wane. Pocock only referred to him contemptuously as 'this Arab.'

By the middle of December the waterborne force, led by Stanley, was fighting off bands of warriors as much as 500 strong. The land force, still lagging behind, was also meeting opposition – and was infected with smallpox. One of the victims was Tippu-Tib's favourite concubine, and it was becoming clear that the Arab leader had had enough of marching. When they reached a district called Vinya-Njara, less than 180 miles north of Nyangwe, the contract was abandoned. Tippu-Tib was given a draft for 2,600 dollars and Stanley promised, rather incongruously, to send a photograph of himself from London. The combined force now began to divide up.

It was Christmas Day, the expedition's third Christmas in Africa. The main meal was rice and jam – one pot to every ten men. 'Thank God we got that,' wrote Pocock. In an effort to lend a festive air to the occasion, Stanley organised races among the women and children, and contests between teams in the captured canoes. The Ruga Ruga mercenaries put on an impressive war dance, but the highlight of the day was a race, from one end of the camp to the other, between Tippu-Tib and Frank Pocock. The Arab won by fifteen yards, which must have irritated the younger white man considerably. He does not mention the defeat in his diary, only saying cryptically: 'We spent the evening walking to and fro the camp.'

The moment that filled Stanley with most dread – and most elation – had now been reached. He dreaded it because he could not know what his followers might do. He was elated because before him lay the great prize, which he had feared for so long would be snatched from him by Cameron.

For three days the final preparations were made. The *Lady Alice* and twenty-two canoes were loaded with the expedition's remaining trade goods and equipment. Enough food for fifteen days was packed. There was a mood of deep foreboding among Stanley's captains, and a rumour that part of the expedition might try to return to Nyangwe with Tippu-Tib. But the Arab did not want the blame for a mutiny among the caravan of followers of a white man, who might later denounce him to the Sultan of Zanzibar. Tippu-Tib gave a warning: 'If any man follows me back to Nyangwe, I shall kill him.'

On the morning of December 28, 1876, there was a cold grey mist over the Lualaba. Stanley waited for it to clear, then embarked his expedition. He had 143 men, women and children, two donkeys, two goats and one sheep. With the *Lady Alice* at the head, the flotilla made its way into the current, along the western bank. Somebody tried to raise a song, but there was scant response. From beneath the trees, Tippu-Tib and his people watched them go.

4. Down the Congo to the Sea

From the forest came the sound of drums and war-horns, proclaiming the advance of strangers along the waters of the Lualaba. Groups of men could be seen crouching among the trees, with drawn bows in their hands. If any canoe was heedless enough to come within range, they would let fly a volley of poisoned arrows. Yet neither was it safe to stay in midstream, because sudden storms whipped the mile-wide river into a frenzy. That lesson was quickly and bitterly learnt: two canoes were sunk, two men drowned, and four guns lost.

Stanley stood up in the bows of the *Lady Alice* and stared back at the 140 survivors of the Anglo-American Expedition, paddling rhythmically in his wake. 'How few they appeared to dare the region of fable and darkness!' He had led them such a long way since the palms of Zanzibar had faded from sight in November 1874 – to Lake Victoria, to Buganda, to the foothills of the Ruwenzori, to Lake Tanganyika . . . Now it was almost 1877, and he was about to take a gamble with their lives, and his own, in which he had no means of calculating the odds. They were 250 miles south of the Equator and travelling inexorably northwards. The remaining beads, cloth and shells on which they relied to barter for food might last six months, but there was no certainty of meeting people with whom to trade. The expedition was left with only fifty guns out of the hundred it had possessed at the start, and Stanley knew there were about thirty men with him who could be relied upon in battle. The rest of his followers were 'mere dummies', a show of heads to impress the ignorant, and their loyalty always in doubt.

He had been badly afraid of a mutiny when the two men had been drowned soon after the parting with Tippu-Tib, for then it was still just possible to turn back and struggle upriver to Nyangwe. But the response to the incident was curiously apathetic: it had been Fate, the will of Allah. 'They are terribly dull people to lead across Africa,' he wrote in his diary on New Year's Eve. At night they smoked cannabis until they fell down half smothered, and by day showed a lack of confidence on the water that was astounding. He had

71

ordered that the canoes be lashed in pairs for greater security; it also halved the number of units he had to worry about. Even so, he shouted himself hoarse in his efforts to keep the flotilla safely together.

He was endlessly busy. Through his binoculars he scoured the riverbanks and islands ahead for any signs of war-canoes that might be skulking for a chance to dash out and attack. Notes must be kept about tributaries, islands, distant mountain ranges; soundings of the river bed had to be taken with lead and line; at noon, if the sun was visible, he must bring out his instruments to record the geographical position; then he must start looking for a safe place to camp for the night. Once ashore, he had to supervise the building of a stockade, send out foraging parties, give medicine to the sick, bandage wounds and ulcers, and write up his diary. At last, before he closed the flaps of his tent, there might be a little while to read a book by candlelight, or to think his private thoughts. Alice had said in one of her treasured letters: 'So you dream about me, do you – and such dreams! I guess you dream with your eyes open. Still, if you like it, I am glad.'

Every morning, when he awoke to the sound of Frank Pocock blowing his dead brother's bugle, to the shouting, to the cries of children and the harsh chorus of jungle birds, there was the river. It awaited him with another day of untold hazards. The river and its power obsessed him. In a direct line, he was about 1,000 miles from the Atlantic – but how far would the river go before it arrived there? He wrote: 'I pen these lines with half a feeling that they will never be read by any other white person; still as I persist in continuing the journey, I persist in writing, leaving events and their disposal to an All-Wise Providence.'

Shortly after New Year, Stanley received the news he had been awaiting with apprehension. A few days journey farther on lay a series of cataracts and rapids. He discovered this by interrogating three prisoners taken as retaliation for a dusk attack on the expedition's camp. The prisoners were questioned through an interpreter named Katembo and said that the falls were too high to be sailed down by any boat. Moreover, the approaches were controlled by a people called the Mwana Ntaba, and beyond them were even fiercer tribes. He knew that the cataracts would be the absolute point of no return, for if his men managed to fend off the Mwana Ntaba, and then dragged the canoes and the *Lady Alice* to the river below, the last possibility of retreat would be gone.

As he came within sound of the falls, Stanley worked out that the expedition was less than 30 miles from the Equator, and still travelling almost due north. The people along the river were so uniformly warlike that he devised a regular procedure for dealing with them: he rarely attacked first, however threatening their manner, but as soon as the spears and arrows began to fly, the sharpshooters of the expedition would open up. Then raiding parties would go ashore to seize all the food they could find. It was one way of husbanding his resources, and possessed an element of rough justice.

Stanley describes a typical encounter: 'Today has been a lively day with us. At Lombo-a-Kirio, we made friends, and permitted four large canoes, one about ninety feet long manned with thirty-five paddlers, to pass by with a peaceful salutation. After giving the word "Peace" and going down a little, we saw we were followed by them and others coming from Kibombo Island and Amu Nyam. It seemed to me we were about to have a busy time. I did not wait to be surrounded, but at once dropped anchor and opened fire, while the canoes were sent ashore to do damage. The people seeing we were not to be victims as they had intended, ran away, and we seized eatables and canoes and captured two women. One we have released to carry a message of peace to her friends, with a promise that if they make peace we shall release the other, as we are not come for war but to see the river. At Katumbi about dusk a native was seen thrusting a spear into the camp. About six natives fell today in the passage down the river.' Ten years before, he had reported a campaign against the Red Indians in Kansas by General Winfield Hancock, who followed a simple precept: 'If they want to talk, I will talk, and if they want to fight, I shall fight them here and now.' Stanley also believed that once you started fighting, there were no half-measures.

At the first cataract the opposition was desperate, and the expedition was hard pressed to get ashore and encamp before being swept to doom by the whirlwind force of the water. Stanley wondered at the reasons for so much fury being hurled against him. Was it merely cannibal lust, or had rumours from the south about Tippu-Tib's slave raiders turned every outsider into a foe? But his mind was soon occupied with the more basic problems of moving the canoes and the *Lady Alice* downstream. Rough roadways had to be cut through humid jungle, and working parties under Pocock were set up to push the task forward by night and day. Downpours of rain slowed progress, and dragging the canoes overland with lianas tired the strongest of his men. It seemed that six more cataracts lay ahead scattered over a distance of forty miles.

In stretches of clear water it was possible to refloat the boats, and when the villagers showed signs of belligerency it was provocation enough to go ashore and plunder for goats, chickens and bananas. The people knew nothing of firearms and a few shots served to send them scurrying into the undergrowth. On one island an old woman was caught; a large ulcer on her foot had stopped her from getting away. Stanley treated the ulcer and through his interpreter Katembo tried to find out something of the country ahead. But only a few words of what she said were intelligible – which proved that very soon the expedition would be among people whose language related to no known dialect. Yet the local skills in ironwork, weaving and leatherwork were remarkable, and for all his preoccupations with finding a way past the cataracts, Stanley made many sketches of captured spears, knives, baskets and drums.

By mid-January, four cataracts had been circumvented with a road hacked out by fifty axemen working night after night. The worst labours seemed over when Stanley was faced with a drama that drew out all his powers of leadership. The canoes were being floated through turbid waters to a new camp when one went out of control, overturned and was smashed to pieces. Two of the three men in it swam to safety, but a third clung to the wreckage and was swept at ever-increasing speed towards a waterfall. At the very moment when he was about to be flung over, the remains of the canoe struck a pointed rock standing little more than a foot above the water. In desperation the man grasped it and climbed up, with his legs dangling in the torrent; a wide expanse of river plunged down into angry whirlpools on either side of him. The trapped man was Zaidi, one of the expedition captains, a veteran who had served with Livingstone. His friends on the bank stared in horror, for it seemed only a matter of time before Zaidi must be carried to his death.

Stanley was called to the scene. Zaidi sat motionless on his tiny splinter of rock. He gave no sign in reply to shouts – because he heard nothing above the roaring water. Stanley looked for a means of rescue, and first lashed several length of creeper to a canoe, which was then manoeuvred into midstream. But as soon as the canoe approached the rock, the creeper snapped and the boat hurtled over the waterfall. Near Zaidi was a larger outcrop, but he had no hopes of reaching it. Everything thrown in his direction was at once swept

'The desperate situation of Zaidi, and his rescue by Uledi, the coxswain of the boat.' This reconstruction was one of the most celebrated illustrations in Stanley's book about the long struggle with the Congo

away. Stanley pondered what might be done, then sent for all the rope the expedition possessed, and for a second canoe. The rope was woven with creeper, and tied to the bow, centre and stern of the canoe. Stanley next asked for two volunteers.

Nobody moved. He asked again, demanding how they would like to be in such a position as Zaidi, with no friend willing to help him. Uledi, the coxswain of the *Lady Alice*, then stepped forward and said: 'My fate is in the hands of God.' He was followed by a boat-boy called Marzouk, and the two of them stepped into the canoe 'with the air of gladiators'. Slowly the canoe was let down the river towards Zaidi on his rock, and when it was only a few yards from him, Uledi threw him a rope. As he seized it, Zaidi toppled back off his perch and fell into the flying water. It seemed he was lost – until his head appeared half a minute later. He was still holding on to the rope. 'Haul away!' shouted Stanley to his team on the bank, but at the first pull the woven cables began to snap. It now looked as though all three men were beyond hope. Then the watchers on the bank realised that Zaidi, with his length of rope braced against his former perch, had acted as an anchor for the canoe, which was being swept

75

by the current against the larger of the two outcrops on the edge of the waterfall. Uledi and Marzouk jumped on to the rock, and desperately pulled Zaidi up and across to join them.

'But although we hurrahed and were exceedingly rejoiced, their position was still but a short reprieve from death. There were 50 yards of wild waves, and a resistless rush of water, between them and safety, and to the right of them was a fall 300 yards in width, and below was a mile of falls and rapids, and great whirlpools, and waves rising like little hills in the middle of the terrible stream, and below these were the fell cannibals of Wane-Mukwa and Asama.' A stone was tied to a long piece of whipcord, and after twenty attempts, it was caught by the stranded men. They attached their remaining tent-rope to the cord and this was hauled across to the shore. But by now it was dusk, so there was no alternative to leaving Uledi, Zaidi and Marzouk on their rock for the night. As Stanley went back to the camp, he grimly heard that another canoe had been overturned and a man lost.

Early next morning Stanley sent thirty men to cut rattans in the forest, with an equal number to guard them against attack, and soon strong lengths of woven cables linked the outcrop with the bank. The three men carefully secured these lines to their rock and prepared to swing themselves across, hand over hand. Uledi went first, often floundering beneath the water, then he was followed by Zaidi. Both survived the 50 yards safely, and after them came the young Marzouk; by the time he was near the bank his strength was failing and his hands were slipping on the ropes. 'Pull away, you fool! Be a man!' shouted Stanley. With the last of his strength Marzouk reached the bank. He was embraced and applauded. The cheers were so loud, noted Stanley, that the tribes all around 'must have known, despite the roar of the waters, that we had passed through a great and thrilling scene.'

By the last week of January the expedition had struggled to the lower end of the cataracts (which were to become known as the Stanley Falls). The river crossed the Equator, but was at last turning steadily towards the west. It was smooth and sluggish, broadening at times to more than ten miles wide, as it wound across a vast plateau. Since the height above sea level was now less than 1,500 feet, there might be many hundreds of miles of unbroken water ahead. Near the Congo's mouth Stanley knew there was another series of steep and tumultuous rapids – the unscaled obstacle which had defied all efforts at exploration of the river from the Atlantic since the arrival of the Portuguese in 1484.

The satisfaction Stanley felt at putting one series of cataracts behind him was soon wiped out. This feat only served to plunge the expedition into worse dangers than it had ever faced. Unknown tribes came racing out from the banks in gigantic canoes, some carrying more than a hundred armed men. There was no respite from war, until the very will to go on seemed to drain away. Every day, attack after attack had to be beaten off, and ammunition was running low. The odds against survival were longer than Stanley had ever thought.

Livingstone once said it was 'foolhardy' to tackle the Lualaba. If Stanley had known what he was in for, he bitterly decided, he would never have started with a force of less than 200 armed men. Day and night the drums sounded, warning of his approach, and he now had no interpreter who could plead on his behalf for a peaceful passage. 'Either bank is equally powerful, to go from one side to the other is like jumping from the frying pan into the fire. It may truly be said that we are now "running the gauntlet".' Stanley added up the number of fights the expedition had been in on the river: the total was twenty-six. Often the wide surface of the river was dotted with islands, and it was sometimes possible to use these as cover, to avoid being spotted from the banks. This tactic saved ammunition, but left unanswered the problem of finding food. Since it was rarely possible to meet people who seemed friendly enough to barter, he had no compunction about sending raiding parties ashore to plunder.

The most spectacular battle of the journey took place at the junction of the Congo with a tributary named the Aruwimi. Fifty-four canoes holding almost 2,000 men suddenly bore down on the expedition, at the end of two days of ceaseless fighting. The sight of this armada was so appalling that two expedition canoes turned to flee. They were driven back into line. Stanley arranged his force in a tight formation, with the *Lady Alice* in the forefront. The men without guns, and the women and children, held up shields. Stanley shouted in Swahili, giving the marksmen his last instructions: 'Wait until you see the first spear, then take good aim. Don't fire all at once. Keep aiming until you are sure of your man. Don't think of running away, for only your guns can save you.' His calm befitted a man who had been on both sides in the American Civil War.

The leading war-canoe had eighty oarsmen, ten warriors at the prow and ten more racing up and down; eight men at the stern guided the vessel with long paddles. Stanley waited, his Winchester to his shoulder, and when the first canoe was 50 yards from the *Lady Alice* its spears began to fly. The order to fire was given, and for five minutes the slaughter was relentless. Spears were no match for the rifles of the Zanzibaris; the attackers turned and fled, despite their ten-to-one superiority. The expedition became possessed by a kind of frenzy: 'Our blood is up now. It is a murderous world, and we feel for the first time that we hate the filthy, vulturous ghouls who inhabit it. We therefore lift our anchors, and pursue them upstream along the right bank, until rounding a point we see their villages. We make straight for the banks, and continue the fight in the village streets with those who have landed . . .'

Huge stores of ivory were found, and these the exultant Zanzibaris carried off to their canoes. Only one man had been lost in the Aruwimi River battle, although several were gashed by spears. Stanley justifies having met force with greater force by the evidence in the villages that cannibalism was an accepted part of life; he makes a grim little joke about his enemies having 'enjoyed a cold collation on an ancient matron's arm'. The account of the Aruwimi fight became one of the great setpieces in his writing.

On February 8, 1877, there was a sudden change of fortune. By this time, the river was flowing almost due west, although it was still on a parallel at least 500 miles north of the Congo estuary. The riverside was lined with closely-packed villages, the homes of unknown people, and Stanley feared more trouble. But if there was any chance at all, he would avoid fighting and come to peaceful terms. His followers were once again starving, and the expedition captains had come to him late at night to demand that he get food somewhere the next day. To fight for it would mean further losses, and there were now only thirty of his men who had not been wounded.

He halted the flotilla in midstream and went cautiously in the *Lady Alice* towards a village. Near the shore he dropped the anchor and began an elaborate pantomime to show that he was stricken with hunger. He rubbed his stomach with one hand, and raised one of the expedition's few remaining bananas to his mouth with the other. Again and again he repeated the performance, while the villagers watched him silently. He pushed his battered sun helmet well back on his head, so that they could see his face. Then he waved beads, copper bangles and bracelets in front of him. There was a long pause, while the villagers lined the bank, the *Lady Alice* swung at its anchor, and the rest of the expedition watched from a quarter of a mile away.

At last an old chief appeared and walked down to the water's edge. Around him were several headmen, with whom the chief began a long consultation. At last came an invitation to land. Stanley raised anchor, and his boat swept to the shore. He climbed out, and shook the chief eagerly by the hand. At last he had found friends on the river.

Several members of the crew hurriedly went through blood brotherhood ceremonies with the chief's entourage, to endorse the new relationship: incisions were cut in their arms, and each 'brother' sucked blood from the other. Frank Pocock was called ashore by the chief to go through the ritual with him. Presents were handed out, and the expedition was supplied with enough bananas and fish to fend off its hunger. That night Stanley set up his camp on an island facing the village, which was named Rubanga, and went to sleep in a mood more confident than he had known for months.

The chief had confirmed, although talking with him was difficult, that the river was called the Congo. The Zanzibaris were amazed, then delighted, to be shown four ancient Portuguese muskets. These could only have come from the Atlantic coast. The expedition had crossed a watershed – for the slow, tenuous trade routes of the African interior now led to the west. In his diary, Pocock is more explicit than Stanley: 'They tell us there are white men below us and it is evident they know something of people from the coast because they understand trade . . .' Food was cheap and so were slaves – a man could be bought for twenty cowrie shells. The women of the district were expert canoeists and went completely naked; their top teeth were filed to points. 'A fine race of people,' decided Pocock, although he had to admit they were expert at stealing when they came into the expedition's camp to barter.

With guides provided by the chief of Rubanga, good progress was made downstream. There was still at least 700 miles to go to the nearest white settlement, but a sense of euphoria ran through the flotilla. The river was at last turning south. Pocock stopped singing hymns, a habit which had begun to get on Stanley's nerves. The Zanzibaris thought fondly of how much money they would get for all the ivory taken as booty in recent fights. Stanley found himself inventing problems and working out how to solve them, from having become so used to ceaseless trouble.

The relief was short-lived, for early one morning the expedition was attacked – in what it had imagined to be friendly waters – by eighty canoes. Two spears were thrown at Pocock, who managed to catch one; Stanley immediately brought out his elephant gun, and blasted holes in the bows of four canoes bearing down on him. Water rushed in, and scores of spearmen were soon struggling in the current. Pocock summed up the skirmish: 'We told them to go away but they wanted to fight. We gave it to them in good style.'

After this came another interlude of peace, and Stanley sat under an awning in the stern of the *Lady Alice* to write up notes on the flora and fauna. He was in poetic mood: 'We glide down narrow streams, between palmy and spicy islands, whose sweet fragrance and vernal colour cause us to forget for a moment our dangerous life.' There was a richness about the foliage which made life an eternal Spring. Hippopotami snorted and sported in the water, elephant and buffalo browsed on the islands, and birds were everywhere in great variety. Stanley saw storks, cranes, flamingoes, geese, ducks, king-fishers and ibis. He was eager to go shooting, because the expedition was short of meat, but knew that the sound of gunfire would alarm the local Africans and perhaps rouse them for war. It was better to paddle quietly between the islands, and be seen as little as possible, although this made it hard to get supplies.

There were sixteen women with the expedition. Most of these were the wives of the captains, and had travelled all the way from Zanzibar. A few others were acquired en route, either as offerings from chiefs or as captives in battle. One of these was Amina, wife of the captain Kachéché: she was expecting a baby, but the strains of the journey had proved too much. One afternoon Kachéché called to Stanley, to say that Amina was dying, and the *Lady Alice* pulled over to the canoe where she lay stretched out. She was conscious, but very weak. Stanley talked to her, and she answered; 'Ah, bwana, I shall never see the sea again. I have so wished to see the coconuts and the mangoes; but no – Amina is dying; dying in a pagan land. She will never see Zanzibar.' That evening they wrapped her body in a shroud, weighted it with stones, and flung it into the middle of the Congo.

Going ashore or stopping to barter were still hazardous. The villagers were often drunk on palm wine or beer, and demanded intolerable payments in shells and beads for food. Stanley saw his stocks diminishing too fast and made anxious calculations about how many mouths he had to feed, and for how many more months. He had also noted with alarm that it was harder to counter the skill and courage being shown by the Africans who came to attack them. The four guns which were hailed as proof of some faint contact with civilisation had not been, after all, such a happy omen. Although muskets packed with nails and pieces of old iron were no match for repeating rifles, the expedition might easily be overwhelmed by a big and concerted attack. One running fight lasted for five hours. Stanley wrote: 'The hostility which these people bear for us is most strange, for as soon as they see us, without a word being spoken on either side, they man their canoes and fire away at us as if we were lawful game.'

The last fight, the thirty-second, took place when the expedition had gone ashore to prepare a meal and cut grass for its three donkeys, which had survived the journey from Nyangwe. As Stanley and Pocock sat waiting for a dish of manioc porridge, shots rang out from the trees and three men fell wounded. Everyone rushed for their guns and began blazing away at the unseen assailants. There was a

Execution of slaves by the Kuti tribe near the Upper Congo. As the head was severed it was whipped up into the air by the spring of the sapling, and flung to the far side of the clearing. This ritual was carried out upon the death of a chief

confused encounter, after which both sides separated with 'a little more respect for each other'. In one account, Stanley says the expedition had fourteen men wounded, but two other versions record four and six casualties; the page in Pocock's diary is missing.

Throughout the second half of February the expedition followed the Congo as it flowed south-west, and sometimes almost due south. Stanley took his positions regularly at noon and found he was well south of the Equator again. The river had clearly completed its great arc to the north and was heading steadily for the sea at 6°S. Every day there was increasing evidence of trade with the coast. Canoe caravans were paddling upstream, and in the village markets there was a display of cheap cups, plates, printed calico and looking glasses. Yet such symbols of outside influence were deceptive, and they watched a man condemned for witchcraft being tossed into the river with his hands bound and a wooden gag in his mouth. As the executioner pushed the man out of the canoe he shouted: 'If you are a magician, cause this river to dry up and save yourself.' The victim was carried downstream by the current, until a crocodile slipped out from the bank and dragged him under the surface.

By the start of March the expedition had reached Bolobo, midway between the northernmost point of the river and the sea. The ruler of the area was Chumbiri, whom Stanley dignifies with the title of 'king'. Without much trouble friendship was established: Chumbiri was anxious to trade, the expedition was short of food, and the cultivated hillsides near the river showed that the people were expert farmers. Blood brotherhood was exchanged and the king promised guides to help the expedition on its way to the coast. Stanley gives a colourful description of Chumbiri, with his handsome wives in heavy brass necklaces. He tells how the king had a passion for snuff, wore a tall hat like an Armenian priest's, and brushed off flies with an elephant tail. Pocock's attitude was more sceptical – he called Chumbiri a 'complete beggar'. He went to have a meal with the chief in his palace ('if we may so call it') and met twelve of the wives and their children. He put a string of beads on each child, which then ran off delighted to its playmates. The meal was fish, palm oil and bananas, flavoured with salt, and everyone had a spoon to eat with; it was the first time, Pocock realised, that he had seen Africans eating with metal spoons since he had left the East Coast, two years and four months before.

Chumbiri managed to cajole his visitors into paying more than

1,000 cowrie shells and several lengths of cloth – which the expedition could ill afford to part with – in return for the promised guides. Success seemed so near at hand, and Stanley was reaching out for any way to hasten the expedition's arrival at the Atlantic. But the guides, led by Chumbiri's eldest son, were untrustworthy; they abandoned Stanley long before their job was done. 'A prodigious liar' was his bitter verdict on the king.

This annoyance was softened by a geographical discovery. On the morning of March 12, 1877, the expedition emerged from between high cliffs, where monkeys played in the trees, into a circular lake. A thousand miles below the Stanley Falls, the Congo had spread itself so wide that from one bank the other was almost out of sight. In the centre of the lake were sandy islands where fishermen worked at their nets. Frank Pocock took Stanley's field-glass and climbed to the top of a mound to make a survey. The lake was surrounded by hills, whose outlines became indistinct in the distance. To the south-east was a jagged peak, jutting above the long sweep of forest and savannah. At noon, Stanley took the latitude and found they were slightly more than 4° off the Equator. The lake was 1,100 feet above sea level.

The expedition was tired and close as ever to starvation. But the sight of this wide, smooth inland sea lifted morale. Stanley knew that on the same latitude the Atlantic was only 300 miles away to the west. Pocock saw that much of the northern bank of the lake was flanked by rugged, white sandstone cliffs, topped by grassland. He pointed them out to Stanley, and suggested a name: Dover Cliffs. 'I feel we are nearing home,' he said.

Frank could not hide his severe nostalgia for his Kentish birth-place, which was only 30 miles from Dover. In one of his last letters to his family, sent from Ujiji nine months earlier, he had said they should expect him 'some fine day in May 1877'; that might now be almost possible. He had told his brothers to look out for a wife for him, and said that the local girls should not be downhearted at his absence: '. . . if the cottage is still in the wood, we will give it a good African warming.' Pocock missed his friends and relations – 'kiss all the children for me', he had written – and his dog Sailor. Yet the worst of the dangers now seemed passed. He had noted in his diary a few days earlier that the villagers seemed 'very civil', quite different from those higher up the river who wanted to fight 'without knowing us to be friends or foes'.

Stanley accepted the idea of inserting the Dover Cliffs on his chart of the Congo. He also decided to honour himself a second time as an explorer; having called the cataracts a thousand miles upriver the Stanley Falls, he entitled this new-found lake the Stanley Pool. In his later writings he asserted the name had been pressed on him by his white companion, although there is no hint of that in Pocock's diary.

Sparing little time to savour this new prize, Stanley hurried on to investigate the cataracts lying just ahead – the roar of the first could be heard from the southern end of the Pool. A local chief declared there were only three falls to be passed; they were known as the 'Mother', the 'Father', and the 'Child'. The maps Stanley had brought with him were based upon the discoveries of Captain James Tuckey of the Royal Navy, who tried to go up the Congo in 1816 but died in the attempt. It seemed that the chief was too encouraging, because Tuckey had charted some high cascades farther down the river. They would certainly need to exist, to explain the drop in altitude between the first cataract and the sea.

But a 'bunch' of falls, spread over a few miles, could soon be defeated by making detours – as had been so triumphantly demonstrated in January. A month or less might see the expedition safely at Boma, a trading post which Stanley knew had a small European community and was visited by ocean-going ships. The 'weary, weary journey' was almost done. With his spirits high, despite the shortages of food, he prepared on March 16 for the lowering of the *Lady Alice* and the canoes through the cataracts.

It was the start of a nightmare, an unparalleled disaster that almost destroyed the expedition in the last stage of its 7,000-mile crossing of Africa. Yet a quick reconnaissance, a round trip of 50 miles, would have proved to Stanley that his scheme must tax his men beyond endurance. Perhaps he was illogically reluctant to leave the river after staying with it so long, through such a variety of hazards. It may be that his judgement was faltering towards the end, and only his relentless will drove him on to attempt the unfeasible. His sense of theatre should also be taken into account – he must have been looking forward eagerly to leading his flotilla jubilantly into Boma, to leaping ashore from the *Lady Alice* and proclaiming his historic exploit.

The possibility of leaving the boats and marching the last 150 miles alongside the river is never even mentioned in his diary. But

Stanley admitted in retrospect: 'There is no fear that any other explorer will attempt what we have done in the cataract region. It will be insanity in a successor. He may travel overland. Nor would we have ventured on this terrible task, had we the slightest idea that such fearful impediments were before us.' He blamed the inaccuracy of his maps, and the ignorance of the chiefs, for his calamitous decision.

The struggle with the cataracts was to last five months, and in that time the expedition covered 180 miles. Sometimes the boats were raced through torrents, at others they were dragged over steep hills to by-pass rapids in which no boat could hope to survive. The perpetual clamour of the water was nerve-wracking: Stanley likened it to the sound of two express trains passing in a tunnel. Famine constantly gripped the expedition, for although the local villagers were placid enough, they asked exorbitant rates for food; sometimes a gun was the price of a single chicken.

Pocock once noted an ominous silence in the camp, for most of the people had not eaten for three days – and all the time they were called on to drag the canoes over rough paths and slippery rocks. They were a ragged band, looked on with a mixture of sympathy and contempt by the Africans of the Lower Congo. Now and then the villagers helped, without any prior offer of gifts, to clear the pathways and drag the canoes. It was out of pity for the famished and impoverished strangers, condemned to such mad labour.

The first week gave an indication of what had been embarked upon. The canoes were moved less than ten miles, sometimes by taking them through the calmer stretches of river with ropes held by teams on the bank, and at other times by manhandling them across the rocks. Stanley's diary shows his anxiety: 'The people fainted for lack of food ... Accidents were numerous ... One dislocated his shoulder ... We lost our best canoe, seventy-five feet long, three feet wide, by twenty-one inches deep, the rapids were too strong for us ... Horrible and slow work...' On March 26, at the end of the day, Stanley fell backwards into a pit between two rocks, and dropped twenty-five feet. He stunned himself, but his only injuries were several bruised ribs.

As the work became more desperate, the emergence of Pocock as the expedition's deputy commander – in fact if not in name – probably saved Stanley from collapse. The two of them discussed the possibility of death, and Stanley admitted he felt physically spent; he put his private papers in order, and advised Frank what he must do if he found himself left alone. In the thirty months they had been together, the younger man had moved from the status of a servant to being a close and loyal friend.

Pockock had just passed his twenty-seventh birthday, the third spent in Africa. He found the work with the canoes very 'tedious' (he has some difficulty spelling the word in his diary) but every scrap of news about Boma and the ocean he could extract from the local Africans kept him up to the task. His only real worry was about the ulcers on his feet, for his last pair of shoes had fallen apart. He tried to make sandals out of pieces cut from a portmanteau, but they did not last long on the rocks. Stanley could not help him, because he only possessed one pair of boots, which were held together with brass wire. In the end, Pocock was reduced to going barefoot. He was treating the ulcers with native herbs, which seemed to have some effect.

By March 29, the expedition had survived, with several injuries, a frenzied stretch of water that Stanley named the Cauldron, and was engaged in setting up a camp overlooking a waterfall. The current in the centre of the river was overwhelming, and he ordered that all the canoes must follow the *Lady Alice* and stay very close to the right bank until they had rounded a bend and reached the camp. As he was about to set out, he noticed Kalulu sitting in one of the biggest canoes with five other men. He was surprised, having expected Kalulu to be with the party bringing supplies overland. 'I can pull, sir!' answered Kalulu. Stanley shrugged and smiled at him – since his one lapse at Ujiji, in trying to desert, Kalulu had behaved well and was back in his guardian's fond esteem.

Stanley had just arrived at the camp when he saw the large canoe hurtling by in midstream. Kalulu and the other paddlers could do nothing, as they sped faster and faster towards the waterfall. As it toppled over the edge, the canoe buried its head in the waves and vanished. Then it whirled around below the falls and floated away with its stern pointing upwards. All the watchers knew that the six were lost – the first victims of the expedition's assault on the lower cataracts.

For several days the drowning of Kalulu and his colleagues threw Stanley into utter despondency. Frank Pocock dreamt three nights later that he saw Kalulu in the camp, that he had not been lost in the river after all. But it was fantasy – there was no hope for Kalulu.

Kalulu and Frank Pocock – drawings made in Britain shortly before they set out for Zanzibar

Both Pocock and Stanley knew he would never return to the school in Wandsworth.

But the struggle with the cataracts must go on. Stanley had the canoes hauled over the top of a mountain 1,200 feet high. There was no other way to pass a series of whirlpools. It seemed like witchcraft; the local people locked their doors and moved their valuables away from the area, out of certainty that no good could come of such deeds. Indeed, so many canoes had been smashed or lost that Stanley resolved that he must have new ones made, although days and nights of labour would be needed. Two large trees were selected, and to speed the job a team of axemen was put to work at night under the direction of Pocock. The days went by relentlessly. It was the middle of May: in two months, they had advanced less than ninety miles towards Boma.

A mood of sullen resentment was now overtaking the Zanzibaris, and in his heart Stanley knew they were hardly to be blamed. Yet he acted with his usual toughness when he found that some of the senior men, including several of his trusted captains, were stealing beads to buy food. The scanty resources of the expedition must be protected. A sudden search of everyone's private possessions was made. Five men with beads found upon them were flogged.

On June 3, the expedition was laboriously making its way through a series of rapids to a spot named Zinga. Still no more than 100 miles had been covered, but there was hope of making faster progress through calmer waters within a week. Stanley hurried ahead to Zinga, to meet the local chiefs. The bulk of the expedition was to follow him overland, and he had arranged to send back a hammock to collect Frank Pocock, who was suffering badly with his ulcerated feet. The canoes might be able to travel part of the way down the river, although in several places the rapids were far too wild for any craft to shoot through them. Stanley had narrowly escaped drowning in a futile bid to reach Zinga in the *Lady Alice*.

Early in the afternoon, he settled himself on a high point over-looking the rapids and waited for Pocock to join him. Using a field-glass, he gazed towards the rapids – and suddenly saw a capsized canoe whirling in the centre of an expanse of water called Bolo-bolo. Several men were clinging to the canoe, which was upside down. They next managed to climb on to it, still holding their paddles, and work their way towards the shore. When they were near enough they abandoned the canoe and swam to safety, leaving the boat to hurtle down to the Zinga cataract.

Stanley sent messengers to find out what had happened, and whether any men were lost. Within minutes the news had been passed down the river: three men were drowned, and one of them was Pocock.

The story was simple, and tragic. Frank Pocock had grown tired of waiting, and demanded to be taken straight down to Zinga in a big canoe known as the *Jason*. Several of the Zanzibaris resisted the idea, saying it was impossible to survive in the torrent, but Pocock laughed and accused them of cowardice. This had stung Uledi, coxswain of the *Lady Alice*; he was renowned for his bravery, and had taken the lead in rescuing the man stranded on a rock in the Stanley Falls several months before. He climbed into the canoe; so did nine other men. Because of his feet, Frank Pocock was carried.

Soon they reached a spot where Uledi intended to leave the canoe, and have it guided down to Zinga on ropes. After climbing on a rock and looking ahead, he insisted that it was impossible to go farther – but Pocock again accused him of cowardice. In the end, Uledi made an appeal to Allah, and set off towards the waves of the Bolo-bolo. Almost at once the boat went out of control, was swept over a rapid and drawn down into a vortex of water. When canoe and occupants came to the surface, Frank Pocock and two others were not to be seen. Then the white man floated up, moaning as he did so.

Uledi tried to reach him but could not, and the survivors made a desperate journey to the water's edge.

That night, Stanley wrote in his diary a long, rambling and almost incoherent description of Pocock's death. It is headlined 'A BLACK WOEFUL DAY!' He praises Frank's good spirits, his courage, his honesty. Then he laments his rashness on water and contempt of danger. 'As I look at his empty tent and dejected servants, and recall to mind his many inestimable qualities, his extraordinary gentleness, his patient temper, his industry, his cheerfulness and tender love of me, the pleasantness of his society, and his general usefulness, I feel myself utterly unable to express my feelings or describe the vastness of my loss.'

He collected together Frank's possessions, and looked at his diary. The last entry was very brief, the work of a sick man: 'June 2nd. Halt. Repairing tent.' Stanley drew a line under it and wrote out an account of the disaster. Less than three years before, in Zanzibar, he had taken a group photograph of Edward Pocock, Frederick Barker, Kalulu, and Frank Pocock. Not one of them was still alive.

The expedition still tried to struggle forward, but all resolve and confidence had ebbed away. It took nearly three weeks to muster the strength to leave Zinga. The men threatened to mutiny, and Stanley told them openly that he wanted to die. They could go, and leave him to his fate with the *Lady Alice*. He would drown in the river. Then he had another thought: he could take a few picked men, and march to Boma; but that would be leaving the rest, perhaps 110 people, to almost certain death. So he did nothing, except directing the interminable labour of dragging the canoes. He was rash enough to ask one man why he was not working, what was the matter with him. The man turned on him: 'We are tired, that is the matter.'

Thirty men did desert, but Stanley sent out orders to the local chiefs to arrest them, and the men finally came back of their own accord. They were not punished or even reproved. There were more casualties in the river, and one man died from ulcers on his legs and feet – 'literally eaten up with them', noted Stanley in his diary. Several men were arrested by the local chiefs for thieving from the villages, and taken into slavery. Huge ransoms were demanded, and since Stanley could not offer enough, the men had to be left to their fate, so far from their homes. On July 26, Stanley was suddenly embraced by one of his senior captains, Safeni, and realised the man was mad. Safeni danced and sang, crying that he was happy to have

89

reached the sea at last. Then he fled from the camp, holding his pet parrot on a stick. Men were sent in pursuit, but Safeni was never found.

On July 31, the decision was made, at a place called Isangila Cataract: 'We have decided to abandon the River, as it is not in our power to continue the warfare longer.' As a last gesture, the *Lady Alice* was dragged to the top of some rocks overlooking the cataract, to bleach and rot in the sun. Then the march across 50 miles of rough terrain towards Boma was begun. 'Tough work over mountains. Terribly hungry, I fear for my people,' said Stanley's diary entry for August 2. Two days later at the village of Nsanda, he prepared a letter and gave it to three of his strongest and most reliable men – Kachéché, Uledi and Muini Pembe. To them he added Robert Feruzi, who had been educated at a mission and spoke good English. He told them to hurry as best they could to Boma, for the lives of all the survivors would depend on their success. The letter said:

To any Gentleman who speaks English at Embomma.

Dear Sir,

I have arrived at this place from Zanzibar with 115 souls, men, women and children. We are now in a state of imminent starvation. We can buy nothing from the natives, for they laugh at our kinds of cloth, beads and wire. There are no provisions in the country that may be purchased, except on market days, and a starving people cannot afford to wait for these markets. I, therefore, have made bold to despatch three of my young men, natives of Zanzibar, with this letter, craving relief from you. I do not know you; but I am told there is an Englishman at Embomma, and as you are a Christian and a gentleman, I beg you not to disregard my request. The boy Robert will be better able to describe our lone condition than I can tell you in this letter. We are in a state of the greatest distress; but if your supplies arrive in time, I may be able to reach Embomma within four days. I want three hundred cloths, each four yards long, of such quality as you trade with, which is very different from that we have; but better than all would be ten or fifteen man-loads of rice or grain to fill their pinched bellies immediately, as even with the cloths it would require time to purchase food, and starving people cannot wait. The supplies must arrive within two days, or I may have a fearful time of it among the dying. Of course I hold myself responsible for any expense you may incur in this business. What is wanted is immediate relief; and I pray you to use your utmost energies to forward it at once. For myself, if you have such little luxuries as tea, coffee, sugar and biscuits by you, such as one man can easily carry, I beg you on my own behalf that you will send a small supply, and add to the great debt of gratitude due to you upon the timely arrival of the supplies for my people. Until that time I beg you to believe me,

Yours sincerely,

Henry M. Stanley

Commanding Anglo-American Expedition

for Exploration of Africa.

P.S. You may not know me by name; therefore I add, I am the person that discovered Livingstone in 1871. – H.M.S.

Stanley wrote out versions of the letter in two other languages he knew – French and Spanish – and told his four picked men to go. They left him at noon, as gaunt and silent groups were setting out from the camp to scavenge through the countryside for food.

The next day the survivors began to march again, and managed twelve miles. It was now only 20 miles to Boma. On the evening of August 7, as a camp was being prepared, Stanley heard excited shouts: Uledi and Kachéché were approaching with a long string of porters behind them carrying sacks of food. The expedition was saved. The survivors took up the remainder of the day in filling themselves with rice, potatoes and fish. Some were so desperately hungry that they ate the food raw in handfuls. For Stanley there were all the 'little luxuries' he had asked for, as well as bread and butter, gooseberry jam, tinned fruit, and three bottles of pale ale. One of the crew of the *Lady Alice*, a boy named Murabo, led an extempore song, telling in Swahili of the dangers they had been through, the battles they had fought, and how at last they had come to the sea. Stanley ran into his tent to hide his tears.

In two days, the expedition was in Boma, and on August 10 he found the strength to write out a cable of 500 words, summarising what he had done. It began: 'On the 8th, inst. I arrived at this place from Zanzibar, with 115 souls, in a fearful condition.' He was still much confused, for he had actually reached Boma on the 9th. The expedition was quickly taken down the estuary of the wide brown river which had cost so much anguish and death, to the bigger trading centre of Kabinda. Stanley was now well enough to prepare a longer despatch, which he gave to an English trader who was just about to take ship to Liverpool. But he pleaded for an understanding of his condition: 'While I would gladly avail myself of this opportunity, still I am so prostrated just now, and I may say, so excited at the sight of white faces, and the scores of "Welcomes" I hear, and so confused with the good things of life they press on me, that, with the keenest desire to do my duty to you, I yet am constrained to ask you not to exact too much from your very willing servant, but to give him a week's breath.'

Towards the end of August, the expedition was moved in a Portuguese gunboat to Luanda, the capital of Angola. There Stanley was the guest of honour at a banquet given by the Governor-General; the care and housing of the Zanzibaris was taken over as a government expense. More than a month was spent in Angola, and Stanley compiled a series of long accounts of his journey, which he sent off on the mailships to Europe. He knew that many people must have given him up for dead, and the sceptics would have derided his efforts to be a great explorer, the true 'heir of Livingstone'. But who could gainsay him now? He had kept his word, and he was coming home to claim the rewards of all his suffering.

There is an exuberance about those first despatches from Luanda, a denial of the utter exhaustion to be seen in the photographs taken of Stanley at the time. He had made the acquaintance in Kabinda of Major Serpa Pinto, a Portuguese traveller who was preparing to walk across southern Africa. Before he wrote any of his long despatches, Stanley gave Pinto a letter to Alice Pike, and asked him to send it to New York as quickly as possible. Pinto wrote to a friend in Lisbon, remarking that the 'Yankee Stanley' was very worried that his 'pequeña' (girlfriend) might have forgotten him.

In late September, the Zanzibaris were sufficiently recovered to start their journey home, although several had died in a mood of strange listlessness since reaching the coast. The Royal Navy had two ships in Angola waters, and offered Stanley free passages to Cape Town, and on to East Africa. He was relieved that he would not have to find the money to transport more than a hundred people around the continent.

The first full news of how his discovery was being hailed in Europe and America was given to Stanley when he reached Cape Town in October. The cable he had sent from Boma had never been handed to a telegraph office, and finally reached the *Daily Telegraph* in London on September 17 – through the post from Holland. The 'filling in of Africa's blank space' was at once everywhere acclaimed as the greatest work of exploration of the century. The praise was unstinting from such veterans of African travel as Burton, Baker and Grant. The Royal Geographical Society said that Stanley was 'unsurpassed', and Agnes Livingstone, eldest daughter of the great missionary traveller, declared that her heart was filled with gratitude and delight. Even Cameron (now promoted to the rank of commander) sent an elegant compliment. Learned societies were competing to shower honours upon Stanley; newspapers and publishers were waiting for his every word.

Only one thing was needed to seal his triumph. Stanley was eager to reach Zanzibar, for he knew that bundles of mail would be awaiting him there. The Royal Navy warship finally arrived at the island on November 26. After seeing his followers – eighty-eight men, thirteen women and six children – safely ashore, he hurried to the house of his American merchant friend, Augustus Sparhawk. There he found the packet of letters he sought, with their familiar, dashing handwriting. As he read them, he learned that his deepest fear, the thought so long suppressed, was indeed a reality. Alice had jilted him. Even if he had managed to complete his journey in two years, as he at first hoped to do, he would still have been too late.

Alice was married on January 11, 1876, and now she even had a daughter, born the following October. The wedding took place at the Pike home in Fifth Avenue, where Alice and Stanley had kissed in the parlour that night in July 1874. She had once written to him: 'I should hate to be poor, how envious I would be of rich people. Just think if I had to give up my beautiful laces, silks and diamonds, my home and piano, horses and carriage . . .' There would be no risk of that. Alice had become the wife of Albert Clifford Barney of Dayton, Ohio. Barney was the heir to a huge fortune his family had amassed by making railway carriages.

In his diary, Stanley makes no mention of the crushing disappointment he must have felt. He went stoically about the time-consuming work of paying off the Zanzibari survivors and compensating the widows of the many men who had died. Then he caught the steamer back to Europe, travelling by way of Marseilles and Paris. In the French capital he was met by his friend and publisher, Edward Marston, and together they faced the array of dinners and receptions hurriedly arranged in the explorer's honour. Stanley seemed 'very lonely and depressed' when they went to a banquet at the Hotel du Louvre: 'He was evidently suffering acutely from a bitter disappointment; what that was I could well guess, but need not disclose. "What is the good of all this pomp and show?" were his words. "It only makes me the more miserable and unhappy." It was not easy to arouse him out of this unhappy mood.'

From Paris, Stanley caught the boat train back to London. Among all the mountain of congratulations was one further letter from Alice. It had been written on November 17, three days after the *New York Herald* had published his two best despatches from Luanda:

Dear Morton,

Among the many congratulations and praises showered on you, receive my humble rejoicings also, of all you have accomplished. I am proud to know how bravely you have borne your many hard trials.

Poor Stanley! How much you have lost, but your gain has been great indeed. I shed tears when I read of the fate of Kalulu and the 'Lady Alice'. I had hoped she would have proven a truer friend than the Alice she was named after, for you must know, by this time, I have done what millions of women have done before me, not been true to my promise. But you are so great, so honoured and so sought after, that you will scarcely miss your once true friend and always devoted admirer of your heroism. For indeed you are the hero of the day. That alone should console you for my loss. No doubt before long you will think it a gain, for Stanley can easily find a wife all his heart could desire to grace his high position and deservedly great name . . .

If you can forgive me, tell me so; if not, do please remain silent. Destroy my letters, as I have burnt all of yours. Adieu, Morton, I will not say farewell, for I hope in some future time we may meet – shall it be as friends?

Alice Barney

Only a tiny handful of his close associates knew why Stanley, in his moment of fulfilment, suffered long spells of melancholy. When his two-volume bestseller, *Through the Dark Continent*, appeared in mid-1878, he gave no explanation for the name of the boat in which he had achieved so much. Nothing appeared in the newspapers, except for two rather cryptic references in American dailies. In the middle of a complex account of Stanley's discoveries, a writer in the *New York Times* (November 4, 1877) remarked: 'He would have returned to New York first, but that the lady to whom he was betrothed, tired of waiting for him, has lately married. I hope in reporting this I am not casting a reflection upon the constancy of a New York lady who is said to be as charming as she is good.' The other report was less discreet. It was headlined 'Betrothed to a Jewess and Jilted while in Africa'. With several inaccuracies it proclaimed the secret behind Stanley's 'sullen, morose, discontented and savage' behaviour, why he seemed to enjoy nothing but making himself disagreeable at public dinners where everyone was anxious to lionise him. Alice's identity was hinted at, but she was not named.

This report suggested that there had been other romantic misfortunes in the explorer's life. But it did not explain why Stanley was so much less able than any ordinary man to bear the rejection of his love and the wounding of his emotions.

The explorer at the end of his journey from the Indian Ocean to the Atlantic. This photograph was taken in Cape Town

PART TWO

A Quest for Identity

5. The Workhouse Rebel

Stanley never celebrated his birthday. Perhaps he chose not to know exactly when it was. He liked to suggest he had been born in 1843, and everything he wrote about his age was carefully misleading. The confusion was never cleared up until long after his death. When a memorial service for him was held in Westminster Abbey in 1904, a plaque on his coffin gave June 10th, 1840 as the date of birth. A massive obituary in *The Times* would only venture to say he had been born 'about the year 1840'. The Encyclopaedia Britannica, Eleventh Edition (1911) settled for 1842. The Dictionary of National Biography has June 10th, 1841; at least the year is right.

He pretended in his first years of fame to come either from St Louis or New York. After the finding of Dr Livingstone, a letter of congratulation arrived from Mark Twain, applauding Stanley on his courage as a 'fellow Missourian'; Twain was to learn he had been deluded, but the two became the best of friends. Sometimes, there were newspaper stories that Stanley was really a Scot named Garret Baldwin, or even Stanislaus, a Polish aristocrat. As late as 1895, a book appeared in London to 'disclose a mystery hitherto unexplained, but much discussed': sustained by an abundance of detail, it asserted that the great explorer had been born in Carmarthenshire, South Wales, in November, 1840.

In fact, Stanley came from Denbigh, a small county town in north-east Wales; he was born on Thursday, January 28th, 1841. Most biographies say he was christened in the sixteenth-century church at Tremeirchion, a village a few miles from Denbigh, but while he certainly had relatives there, a search of the Tremeirchion baptismal records reveals no trace of him. It is now possible to say he was christened at a Denbigh church called St Hilary's, of which only the tower still exists. The register shows that John Rowlands, a farmer aged 26, was willing to admit paternity, and the mother was Elizabeth Parry, a butcher's daughter of nineteen. The baby was christened John, and while the listing of both parental surnames was evidence enough, the word 'Bastard' was inserted on the entry, according to the custom of the times.

Elizabeth Parry was to have three more illegitimate children during the next 15 years. This behaviour must have won her a certain notoriety in a town such as Denbigh, with its 5,000 inhabitants. Although one child in ten was born out of wedlock in North Wales at this time, most girls overcame the stigma by quickly slipping into marriage; but Elizabeth Parry's career verged on the eccentric. Two of her children were put in a workhouse, including John – the future Stanley – and at one time she was in such straits that she had to take refuge there herself. At last, when almost forty, she was married to a man named Jones, the father of her two youngest children. Yet, despite her feckless way of life, Elizabeth Parry was able to command a certain respect, long before she became renowned in Denbigh as the mother of a man whose feats amazed the world.

She was the youngest daughter of a family once well-to-do, and her father Moses was only late in life reduced to living humbly beside the ruined walls of Denbigh Castle. There was a time when he had presided at dinner over a household of forty people, including servants and labourers; at the end, he was sharing a cottage with the eldest of his sons, who poleaxed calves in a shed at the bottom of the garden.

A picture of Elizabeth Parry can be gleaned from contemporary sources, and it is common ground that for all her frailties, she had presence and style. In his unfinished autobiography, Stanley gives a childhood memory of seeing his mother come into the workhouse: 'A tall woman with an oval face, and a great coil of dark hair behind her head . . . she was regarding me with a look of cool, critical scrutiny.' No photograph of her survives, only an amateurish drawing done in 1872, when she was fifty – showing an ample, bespectacled woman beside a garden gate with some knitting in her hand. Ten years later, she was interviewed for *Drych*, a Welsh-language paper put out in the United States; the report contains a sentence which, for all its pomposity, conveys something about her: 'Mrs Jones is taller than the generality of women, and certainly of a more ladylike and handsome appearance than the ordinary Welsh-women of her age.'

One of the most valuable witnesses is Dr Evan Pierce, who not only delivered Elizabeth of the future Stanley in 1841, but attended her during her final illness in 1886. Pierce was a man of some distinction, a product of the local grammar school who had gone on to be educated in Edinburgh, London and Paris; he was five times mayor of Denbigh. In his fiery Welshness, Pierce was proud that Denbigh Castle, standing grey and massive on a steep hill above the town, was the last fortress in the land to surrender to Cromwell. Writing what he knew of Stanley's origins, in a letter to the *Denbigh Free Press* in 1889, Pierce twice broke into verse, and was well nigh beside himself with eloquence: 'It would almost seem that the spirit of those chivalrous defenders – General Salusbury and his faithful band – and, perhaps of Prince Llewelyn himself, had descended upon the infant born so close to those renowned precincts, and endowed him with their fearlessness, courage, determination and indomitable pluck.'

In his letter, Pierce relates how on her deathbed Elizabeth Parry asked him to quote again the lines he had told her the day Stanley was born. He did so, in Welsh and English, rendering the latter thus:

> There, on the nurse's lap, a new-born child,
> We saw thee weep while all around thee smiled;
> So live, that sinking in thy last long sleep,
> Thou still may'st smile, while all around thee weep.

Hearing it, she looked happy and said. 'Ah, Doctor, the Welsh is by far the best.' It was a sentiment he approved.

At the time he was writing these reminiscences, Pierce was in his old age, but still alert enough to hold the office of coroner for the western division of Denbighshire. He pointed out that he had been 'intimately and professionally acquainted' with the explorer's parentage on both sides for more than half a century.

Yet research now shows that in one recollection, Pierce was startlingly wrong. This concerns the self-confessed father of Stanley, the very shadowy John Rowlands. He is said by Pierce to have died when the baby was only a few months old. This also fits with Stanley's own statement: 'My father I never knew. I was in my "teens" before I learned that he had died within a few weeks after my birth.' In fact, John Rowlands died as late as May 24th, 1854, when the future Henry Stanley was thirteen. The cause of death was delirium tremens.

This presents a conundrum. Since John Rowlands was willing, at a public christening, to have himself put forward as the father of Elizabeth Parry's first child (even if he did not care to take her as his wife), it is odd that he was so uninterested thereafter. Although the Rowlands were a solid farming family, he provided nothing for the child's upkeep and was seemingly indifferent to its fate. For his part, Stanley never showed the slightest curiosity about the man whose name he had borne until adolescence; there is no hint in his diaries that he ever tried in later life to make contact with the Rowlands family – although he does mention one brief, chilly meeting as a youth with his paternal grandfather.

It may be because Rowlands was reputed to be a drunkard, and an unlikely father for such a man as Henry Stanley, that the 'Vaughan Horne legend' has persisted in North Wales. James Vaughan Horne was a solicitor, and when he was only thirty-two he was Denbigh's town clerk and deputy recorder. Almost forty years after his death the *Denbigh Free Press* recalled that he had been 'very widely known and esteemed'. But Vaughan Horne was not a happy man: his marriage was childless and he died at forty-six of chronic liver disease and dropsy, which suggest alcoholism.

The legend says that Elizabeth Parry worked in a bakery behind the offices Vaughan Horne shared with another solicitor in Denbigh's main thoroughfare, Vale Street. It is claimed that Vaughan Horne took a fancy to Elizabeth, made her pregnant, then bribed John Rowlands to say he was the father.

There is no documentation and there are no portraits of Vaughan Horne to set alongside Stanley's photograph. But a search of the records yields a piece of circumstantial evidence: Vaughan Horne had property at Llanrhaeadr, a village in the hills just south of Denbigh, and is buried in Llanrhaeadr Church; John Rowlands had also lived at Llanrhaeadr, and rests in the churchyard there. Moreover, when Elizabeth's second illegitimate child, Emma, was born in 1843 the father was listed as 'John Evans, of Liverpool, farmer (late of Ty'n Pwll, Llanrhaeadr).' And once again, the putative father proved utterly indifferent to his offspring.

Soon after Elizabeth Parry's first child was born early in 1841 she went off to London and became a domestic servant; she was back in Wales by the summer of 1842, when her daughter Emma was conceived. If Vaughan Horne was the true father of the future Stanley, was Emma also his child? It is a maze of speculation, and only hearsay that Vaughan Horne's aged widow always stayed indoors when the famous explorer visited the district, because his features looked too familiar. Nobody can now say why, or when, the legend began about James Vaughan Horne, so the paternity of Stanley remains something of an enigma.

Until he started work on an autobiography, Stanley could never bring himself to write about his Denbigh childhood, and when questioned on it would be uncommunicative, answering with that stare of cold hostility few men could equal. When he wrote a summary of his boyhood experiences in a private journal, he felt driven to use Swahili, the language he had used with his Zanzibar porters. It was one thing to go home and visit old friends and relatives, or even address a jubilant audience of fellow Welshmen about his African adventures, but relating the details of his origins produced an intense surge of emotion.

Once having made himself put pen to paper, Stanley writes with brimming sentiment about the miseries of poverty. In the first paragraph of the autobiography he derides the attention paid by aristocrats to their family pedigree and talks defiantly about 'all of us plebians' and 'we baser creatures'. On the other hand, he never manages to admit that he was illegitimate. As he advances into his story, he is often moving and sometimes maudlin. It is also plain that this is an exercise in self-justification and excuse, to explain away the brusque exterior his critics never tired of attacking. In his most flowery manner, he paints a Wordsworthian picture of how he was in childlike fancy: 'See what a change forty years have wrought in me. When a child, I loved him who so much as smiled at me; the partner of my little bed, my play-fellow, the stranger boy who visited me; nay, as a flower attracts the bee, it only needed the glance of a human face, to begin regarding it with love. Mere increase of years has changed all that. Never can I recall that state of innocence . . .'

Some of Stanley's earliest memories are of living in the primitive cottage on Denbigh Castle green – also called the 'Digs' – and sharing the upstairs part with his grandfather, Moses Parry, the one who had known better days. 'My grandfather appears to me as a stout old gentleman, clad in corduroy breeches, dark stockings, and long Melton coat . . .' Downstairs lived two of Moses Parry's sons, one of whom took a wife called Kitty, to the general decline in the happiness of the household. When he was four, Stanley began attending the 'free grammar school' in the dank crypt of St Hilary's church, where he had been christened. The school was in a wretched state, although it dated back to 1726; the teaching was in Welsh.

One summer day in 1846, Grandfather Parry dropped dead while working in the fields; he was in his eighties. Almost immediately, his small grandson John was moved out of the cottage and boarded with neighbours, who were paid 2s. 6d. a week for having him. The money apparently came from the boy's two uncles.

The arrangement only lasted a few months, and one Saturday afternoon, in late February 1847, the six-year-old John Rowlands found himself in the St Asaph Union Workhouse. The admission book gives the 'cause of relief' as desertion, and once more John Rowlands has the label 'bastard' written beside his name. Before he was taken in among the orphans, the local idiots, and the poor, decrepit old people for whom the workhouse was a last resort, the Board of Guardians must have been convinced that the child was rejected by the families of both his parents.

St Asaph lies five miles north of Denbigh, and is in the main notable for possessing the smallest cathedral in Britain. It is an out-of-the-way, drowsy place, surrounded by meadows, and has a long history: the Romans made a fort here called Varae, the Saxons built a church, and a Dominican friar named Ainan was appointed the local bishop in 1268 and laid the plans for a cathedral. Two centuries later, the town was razed by the Welsh nationalist Owen Glendower, and in 1645 was ravaged by the Roundheads, who used the cathedral as a stable. Since that time, there have been few events in St Asaph to stir the blood.

Here Henry Stanley received all his formal education, while wearing the drab grey uniform of the workhouse. There was in Victorian times a tendency to refer very euphemistically to the place as the 'St Asaph public school' and when Stanley became famous, some of the orphans and destitute boys who had been there with him wrote to reminisce about their childhood. Perhaps time lent enchantment to their memories, but they seemed less embittered about the workhouse school than Stanley always declared himself to be. One of his correspondents, who became a tailor in Chester, recalled that Stanley made a good impression on everyone as a boy. Another former pupil with memories to offer was Tom Mumford; he asserted that the erstwhile John Rowlands had been the 'most noble boy in the school', who was made a prefect and put in charge whenever the headmaster, James Francis, went away. 'He would then assume the cane and would not hesitate to use it . . .'

Allowance must be made for a gap of forty years, and the desire to shower compliments on a famous compatriot. But there is supporting evidence to be found in a long-forgotten book on Stanley written when he first achieved fame in Africa – only sixteen years after leaving the workhouse. This says he was a bright pupil, good at geography and drawing; he was so strong at arithmetic that he was put in charge of the school accounts, and at the age of nearly fourteen was presented with a Bible signed by the Bishop of St Asaph for 'diligent application to his studies, and general good conduct'. Often on Sundays the forty boys and thirty girls were marched half a mile from the workhouse to the Cathedral for morning service, and the Bishop, Dr Vowler Short, took a general concern in their wellbeing. At Christmas he had them to his house, and in summer played games with them in the gardens. Dr Short was known as a reformer, with a keen belief in raising educational standards. Sometimes, the chairman of the Board of Governors would take a group of boys to the sandy beach at Rhyl, six miles away, for an afternoon's swimming.

The importance of such treats may be exaggerated, for life in the St Asaph workhouse was decidedly no idyll. (The two-storey building still exists, converted into the 'H.M. Stanley Hospital'; despite architectural merit it must have had a forbidding air for the first inmates.) The food was mainly bread and porridge, with meat once a week. Even so, it is hard to reconcile all the other accounts with Stanley's own descriptions. 'Tyranny of the grossest kind lashed and scowled at us every waking hour', he says. 'Day after day little wretches would be flung down on the stone floor in writhing heaps, or stood, with blinking eyes and humped backs, to receive the shock of the ebony ruler, or were sent pirouetting across the school from a ruffianly kick, while the rest suffered from a sympathetic terror during such exhibitions, for none knew what moment he might be called to endure the like.'

Again and again, Stanley returns to gruesome memories of what he and his classmates went through. He brands as the villain, the instigator of all the horror, the workhouse teacher James Francis. Since by any interpretation Francis must have had a vital influence on Stanley's character, it is worth recording such details as survive about him.

The one easily verifiable fact about Francis is that he died in the North Wales Hospital for Nervous Diseases, generally known as the Denbigh Lunatic Asylum, on January 13th, 1866. He had been committed to the place in 1863, seven years after Stanley had left the workhouse. For most of his life, Francis had only one hand, having been maimed in the left arm during a colliery accident at Mold, a small town near Chester; after this injury he had been forced to give up his job as a miner to take the lowly-paid but onerous post as the instructor at St Asaph. Francis possessed rare attainments for a miner in the middle of the nineteenth century; at the workhouse he had to teach every subject in the curriculum – and in English, although most of the children, Stanley included, had been brought up talking Welsh.

When Stanley arrived at the workhouse, Francis had been teaching for seven years, and was thirty-two. His pupils were social outcasts, but their scholastic level was considered good enough for them to be entered for the traditional Welsh cultural festivals, the eisteddfods; in 1851, when he was ten, Stanley was the school candidate for the Rhuddlan Eisteddfod, but could not take part because he caught measles.

At the moment when Stanley was adjusting to workhouse life, an official commission of inquiry was studying education in Wales. The commission's report, published in 1848, was an unusually detailed and methodical work for its time. Descriptions of every school in the principality, backed up by statistical tables, were heightened by impassioned protests about the state of things. Nothing was missed by the commissioners; producing the fact that 71·5 per cent of schools in North Wales were without lavatories, they said: 'The germs of the barbarous and immoral habits which disfigure Welsh civilisation are thus implanted in the minds of the children . . .' The standard of teaching came in for severe attack: 'Any person who is supposed to understand the English language better than his neighbours is encouraged to undertake the office of schoolmaster.' The level of instruction in arithmetic was deplorable, and Welsh teachers spent far too much time upon handwriting lessons.

The eight workhouse schools in North Wales were among those investigated. The commissioners found the workhouses 'filled with the mothers of illegitimate children, and the children themselves.' The children were exposed to immoral acts of every kind; the small girls were made to work in the wards, among the newly-born and the dying. The boys spent a large part of their time gardening. St Asaph Workhouse School was no exception to the pattern, and the master had been unable to obtain materials for teaching arithmetic, as the majority of the Guardians thought the subject superfluous.

The survey at St Asaph was made on March 10, 1847; this was only eighteen days after Stanley was admitted. The commissioners were always sparing with praise, so what they had to say of Francis is significant: 'He speaks very broken-English . . . but by catechising carefully, and requiring his pupils to converse always in English, he has brought them to understand more of what they hear and read than would be expected in so elementary a school . . .' Five months after Stanley finally left his hands, Francis was selected by a schools inspector for an efficiency award. He was sent a certificate from London and his wages were increased.

One account written a few years after Francis had died in the Denbigh asylum said 'he was an excellent teacher and a worthy man'; his kindness and attention to the children in his charge were said to be beyond praise. This account also asserts that when Stanley left the workhouse school in May 1856, Francis came to see him off. He borrowed sixpence from a barber whose shop was near St Asaph Cathedral, and handed it over as a parting gift.

This fulsome picture of life in the workhouse bears no resemblance to Stanley's own. He relates how the behaviour of Francis grew more and more violent until a fateful day when the whole senior class was to be birched because a table had been damaged and nobody would own up to having done it. As his turn drew near, Stanley 'felt himself hardening for resistance'. He gives an account of what happened when Francis saw he was in a mood of defiance:

'How is this?' he cried savagely. 'Not ready yet? Strip, sir, this minute; I mean to stop this abominable and bare-faced lying.'

'I did not lie, sir. I know nothing of it.'

'Silence, sir. Down with your clothes.'

'Never again,' I shouted, marvelling at my own audacity. The words had scarcely escaped me ere I found myself swung upwards into the air by the collar of my jacket, and flung into a nerveless heap on the bench. Then the passionate brute pummelled me in the stomach until I fell backwards, gasping for breath. Again I was lifted and dashed on the bench with a shock that almost broke my spine. What little sense was left in me after these repeated shocks made me aware that I was smitten on the cheeks, right and left, and that soon nothing would be left of me but a mass of shattered nerves and bruised muscles.

Recovering my breath, finally, from the pounding in the stomach, I aimed a vigorous kick at the cruel Master as he stooped to me, and, by chance, the booted foot smashed his glasses, and almost blinded him with their splinters. Starting backward with the excruciating pain, he contrived to stumble over a bench and the back of his head struck the stone floor; but, as he was in the act of falling, I had bounded to my feet, and possessed myself of his blackthorn. Armed with this, I rushed at the prostrate form and struck him at random over his body, until I was called to a sense of what I was doing by the stirless way he received the thrashing.

I was exceedingly puzzled what to do now. My rage had vanished, and, instead of triumph, there was a feeling that, perhaps, I ought to have endured, instead of resisting. Someone suggested that he had better be carried to his study, and we accordingly dragged him along the floor to the Master's private room, and I remember well how some of the infants in the fourth room began to howl with unreasonable terror.

After the door had been closed on him, a dead silence, comparatively, followed. My wits were engaged in unravelling a way out of the curious dilemma in which I found myself. The overthrow of the Master before the school appeared to indicate a new state of things. Having successfully resisted once, it involved a continued resistance, for one would die before submitting again . . .

After learning that the master was not dead, Stanley decided to resolve his difficulties by running away for ever. He climbed over a wall and fled in the direction of Denbigh. He was free after nine years in the workhouse, and was now 15 years old.

His own version of the last moments at St Asaph rings true in many details – such as the infants howling as Francis is dragged by their door. Yet it is hard to accept unreservedly. There are too many echoes of Chapter 13 of Dickens' *Nicholas Nickleby*, where the heroic young Nicholas rebels against the sadism of Squeers. The episode in Dickens starts with an exchange of orders and refusals, then goes on to the moment where Nicholas strikes back. '. . . Nicholas sprang upon him, wrested the weapon from his hand, and pinning him by the throat, beat the ruffian till he roared for mercy.' It ends when Squeers is thrown to the floor, where he lies 'stunned and motionless'.

Nicholas leaves Squeers to be restored to consciousness, and retires to 'consider what course he had better adopt'. He decides to flee from the school – as Stanley did.

One curious aspect of Stanley's case is that he was never caught and punished, as might be expected. A few weeks later, he was working openly as a pupil teacher in a school less than 10 miles from St Asaph. So some mystery surrounds Stanley's departure from the workhouse. The entry in the register for May 13, 1856 confirms that he left on that day, and has the comment: 'Gone to his uncle at the National School, Holywell.' But there is a blank in the column for character. The evidence builds up an impression that Stanley was an oustandingly clever boy, but emotionally unbalanced. It is known that he had several times tried to run away from the workhouse before his final departure.

The first photograph of him dates from 1856. He sits awkwardly on a straight backed chair, his jacket unbuttoned to display a crumpled woollen waistcoat. His chin rests on an ill-fitting wing collar. The expression is remarkable, his mouth curves down and is slightly compressed at the corners. The eyes are very penetrating.

There is also a word-portrait of him as a youth, given by a teacher called Hughes of Llandudno: 'I knew every ingredient in his nature, I thought, and used to sum him up as a full faced, stubborn, self-willed, round-headed, uncompromising, deep fellow. In conversation with you, his large black eyes would roll away from you as if he was really in deep meditation about half-a-dozen things besides the subject of conversation. He was particularly strong in the trunk, but not very smart or elegant about the legs which were slightly disproportionately short. His temperament was unusually sensitive; he could stand no chaff, nor the least bit of humour.'

It is small wonder that the workhouse could not hold Stanley, and he was lucky when after wandering about the countryside for some days he found a welcome from his cousin, Moses Owen. Although only four years older than Stanley, this hospitable relative was already running a small National School – a Church of England establishment for poor children – at a hamlet called Brynford. Moses was clever, and had attended Caernarvon College, but not strong (he was to die before thirty). Already he was employing a younger brother to help him run the school; so, when a cousin appeared, equipped with nine years' education from the workhouse, family duty went in step with convenience. Stanley was enlisted as a pupil

teacher in return for bed and board and a promise of help to further his education.

This proposal did not find much encouragement, however, from Moses's mother, a widow named Mary Owen. She made it plain that the family had enough to surmount already, without taking in the illegitimate son of her youngest sister. Mrs Owen felt little sympathy for the loose-living Elizabeth; when Elizabeth was 'punished for her sins' a few years earlier by having to go into the St Asaph workhouse, Mary had only looked on grimly from her home at Tremeirchion, three miles away. Elizabeth had just given birth to a fourth child out of wedlock – in fact, only two days after her

Left, John Rowlands (the future Henry Stanley), a few months after he left the workhouse in St Asaph. Above, the end of his letter to an uncle in Liverpool pleading for help in finding a job. There were few prospects in North Wales in the 1850s

firstborn fled the workhouse. In contrast, Mary devotedly sustained her family by running a shop on the outskirts of Tremeirchion. The shop occupied the downstairs part of her square solid house, which stands in a hollow beside a clear spring from which it takes its name: Ffynnon Beuno – St Beuno's Well. Mary also made beer and kept a few cows, sheep and hens.

Stanley graphically conveys the mood when he brought the news to his aunt that Moses had decided to take him on as a helper at Brynford school. 'She stood in the centre of her kitchen floor, as I handed her her son's letter to her. The contents surprised and annoyed her.' Moses had asked his mother to equip Stanley – then in his workhouse garb – with a suit of clothes (the outfit in which he was to be photographed), and send him back from Tremeirchion to Brynford in a few weeks. Mrs Owen made the encouraging first gesture of giving her nephew a meal, but he could not mistake the overtones in her behaviour: 'Each time she came in to add some dish to the fare she was spreading for me, I felt her searching eyes on me. This was an ominous beginning, and made me feel subdued as I sat in the shadow of the ingle-nook.' Later he was to hear her complaining about his arrival to customers who came in to buy beer.

Yet life at Tremeirchion, after the miseries of the workhouse, was not entirely bleak. Behind the Owens' house was a huge rocky hill, called Craig Fawr, which was exciting to climb on a May afternoon; there is a local tradition that Stanley asserted in later years how he acquired an early taste for adventure by scrambling up to its peak. Tremeirchion was also a village of unusual beauty and distinction. Beside the church stood a handsome inn named the Salusbury Arms, after the local squirearchy. Mrs Thrale, the life-long friend of Dr Samuel Johnson, was a Miss Salusbury before marriage, and Johnson had stayed at Bryn Bella Hall, which she built; the gates leading to Bryn Bella face the house where Aunt Mary Owen ran her shop-cum-tavern.

When Stanley began his teaching work with Cousin Moses, he found life far less agreeable than he had hoped. For a start, the pupils were rough and loutish: 'They were vilely irreligious, and to my astonishment acted as though they believed manliness to consist of barefaced profanity. Most of them snuffled abominably . . .' They were not easy to control, especially as the new pupil-teacher was small for his age. Stanley admits that an old blacksmith in Denbigh had, on seeing him, declared that 'I could not belong to one of the big-boned Parry breed'. To make his anguish greater, all the boys at Brynford knew of his origins and mocked him in Welsh. But there was one compensation: Moses Owen was a tireless instructor and for several months pushed him forward academically, far beyond the limited curriculum of the workhouse.

Stanley might have stayed indefinitely at Brynford, but for the influence of Aunt Mary. With every week-end visit, to bring food she had lovingly cooked for her son, she undermined their relationship: 'I suspected that her wishes were gradually perverting his original intentions towards me.' Soon there were bitter scenes between the two boys, the younger one weeping as Moses grew more and more hostile and sarcastic. After nine months, Stanley was sent back to Tremeirchion, and earned his keep by helping his aunt in the bar and looking after her sheep.

She now had plans for getting rid of him, and these plans centred upon Liverpool. The city was only a short ferry trip from Wales across the estuary of the River Dee. It was one of the great ports of Europe, sending out to the Empire and the Americas all the products of Lancashire, the gritty core of England's industrial might. The cotton exporters of the Southern States of America maintained a ceaseless traffic with Liverpool, their ships returning with British emigrants and manufactured goods. Mary Owen had relatives in Liverpool, including a sister. Surely, the family could find some job – as a clerk perhaps – for Elizabeth's child; she wrote off to them to ask.

While they waited for an answer, Stanley was anxious, but happy. It was the summer of 1857, he was sixteen and full of energy. With memories of those months in Tremeirchion he was often to while away 'many a lonely hour in African solitudes'. His favourite spot was the summit of the Craig, which gives a wide view over the lush Vale of Clwyd, from the seashore at Rhyl to the ruined castle at Denbigh. 'There I was happiest, withdrawn from contact with the cold-hearted, selfish world, with only the sheep and my own thoughts for company.'

On Saturday nights at Tremeirchion he was fascinated to watch the local yeomen downing quarts of Aunt Mary's ale, until they sang and shouted and threatened to fight one another. When the customers grew too wild, the dark-eyed termagant would emerge and silence them with her glance. The young Stanley was developing views about his compatriots. He was later to measure their nature by what he saw in other races: 'The North-Welsh are a compound of opposites – exclusive as Spaniards, vindictive as Corsicans, conservative as Osmanlis; sensible in business, but not enterprising; quarrelsome, but law-abiding; devout but litigious; industrious and thrifty, but not rich; loyal, but discontented.' Some of those traits were deep in himself.

As the months went by, there was scope enough for discontent. An uncle in Liverpool had said confidently that he could arrange a clerk's job in an insurance office, but nothing seemed settled. Although the dates are somewhat uncertain, and Stanley does nothing in his published and unpublished writings to clear them up, it would seem that he lingered at Tremeirchion as a shepherd and beer-server for more than a year. So at the start of June, 1858, he wrote a fairly desperate letter to his uncle in Liverpool. It shows the level of literacy he had achieved by the time he was seventeen, and is also the only surviving letter he signed with his baptismal name;

Dear Uncle,

My Aunt and I have waited with much anxiety expecting every day to receive an answer from you, is there a chance for me or no to have that place, now having past the month of May.

Dear Uncle, I sincerely hope I have not displeased you in anything, as my Aunt thinks I have done. Dear Uncle, also I hope you have not taken it unkind of me in plaguing. It's a hard case on me and would be harder still if I could not procure a situation. Dearest Uncle, I sue to you for kindness. I have nowhere to go unless I procure a place. I am quite well, thank Providence for it, so also my Aunt's health is better, and we hope that you are all the same. Our sincerest love to you all, and also the blessing of God be with you. We have no particular news to inform you at the present time.

They have not succeeded in finding me a situation at Mold Railway Station as the master was a very bad scholar and his health was very imperfect, and he was very unlikely to stay there long. Hoping sincerely you will return me an answer by return of post. I shall feel extremely obliged to you, so I remain,

Your very Humble nephew,
John Rowlands

My character if wanted may be procured of the Curate, Mr W. Williams.

The job he had wanted at Mold, which boasted a station, was presumably in the National School there; one of the Owen boys was already teaching at Mold.

A few weeks after the letter had been sent, the move to Liverpool was made. Mary Owen took her nephew across by steamer, gave him a sovereign, wished him luck, and left without delay. Stanley records that he wept on leaving Tremeirchion, for although there had been scant love between him and his aunt, she was the nearest thing to a mother he had known. They never met again, because before he returned to Wales, she had died, drifting into a long decline from exhaustion: 'Her face was thin and sharp, and showed traces of bad health, as well as of anxiety. The querulous voice and frequent sighing proved that she suffered in body and thought.'

Liverpool was not a success for Stanley. There was no job as a clerk, his relations were down on their luck and the optimistic Uncle Tom hid his worries behind extravagant bonhomie. It was a wretched transition from the peace of Tremeirchion to the noise, smoke and squalor of Lancashire. The ill-born nephew wandered helplessly around the slums, taking temporary jobs as an errand-boy. His sovereign was expropriated to keep the house from starvation, then his precious suit and overcoat were carried off to the pawnshop. Was there any way out – a possibility, however slight, of making a real start in life? Liverpool was the very place for making such a start: the wave of emigration was at its peak, and every week nearly a thousand families passed through the port on their way to the New World.

More and more often, Stanley lingered in the docks, looking at the sailing ships preparing for their voyages, away from the advancing winter on the Mersey. One day, he had to take a load of provisions to a packet boat called the *Windermere*. At the suggestion of her Master, Captain David Hardinge, he signed on as a cabin-boy. It was December 1858, and the *Windermere* would be bound for New Orleans. It is a sign of his loneliness, and of how little there was to keep him in Liverpool, that Stanley parted from his relatives five days before Christmas. Four months after being so nervous about leaving Tremeirchion, he revealed that capacity for sudden, determined action which would become his hallmark.

6. New Life in the Deep South

Stanley was to receive hard lessons in self-preservation during the seven-week voyage to New Orleans. But for the first few days he had no heart for studying his new environment or thinking about what lay ahead. He was below decks, being seasick. The memory was vivid: 'I became troubled with a strange lightness in the head, and presently I seemed to stand in the centre of a great circle around which sea, and sky, and ship revolved at great speed. Then for three days I lay oblivious, helpless and grieving...' But he was not allowed to grieve too long, for with a tornado of oaths he was driven to work by the second mate. Stanley had any romantic notions of ocean life knocked out of him by a succession of back-handers. The language was equally stunning – the account he has left of his first voyage is strewn, in the Victorian manner, with dashes.

The home port of the *Windermere* was Boston, and at that time American merchant ships were renowned for their hard discipline. Even so, living conditions and food were better than could be found in the despised British 'lime-juicers' – so-called because of the daily ration of juice given out to counteract scurvy. The life was brutal, but after Stanley had found his sea-legs and thrown off the sea-sickness, he took to it. Much of his next five years was to be spent afloat, and his spirit exulted in the drama and danger. He describes the first storm encountered by the *Windermere* as she sailed beyond the Bay of Biscay: 'Then it was that the mates bawled out aloud, and sailors clambered up the shrouds in a frenzy of briskness, and the deckhands bawled and sang after a fashion I had not heard before, while blocks tam-tammed regularly, great sail-sheets danced wildly in the air, and every now and then a thunder sound, from bursting canvas, added to the general excitement... A gale at sea is as stimulating as a battle.'

He was soon disabused of any idea that he would work in comfort as a cabin-boy. He was ordered 'before the mast' to be a deckhand. A young English sailor named Harry had already made the crossing to New Orleans and explained what to expect. The captain wanted

Stanley to jump ship in America, and by making conditions rough for him would try to force him to desert. Then the captain would pocket the wages due to him. It was an old trick, often practised on wide-eyed youths who wandered around the docks of Europe. Stanley was alarmed by the news; when he had signed on for the *Windermere*, he had imagined the captain would be only too happy to give him the choice of sailing back to Liverpool, or staying in New Orleans. Now he faced being penniless again, in a city where he knew nobody.

Harry's forecast was true. On the voyage, Stanley was scarcely better off than three stowaways who appeared when the ship was well out to sea. The stowaways were a man and two ragged boys even younger than himself. His sole advantage over them was in being beaten a little less often; even so, as he listened to the yarns of Long Hart, the cook, he realised himself lucky not to have been at sea twenty years earlier. Hart had spent his life under sail, and knew the world from California to Callao and tropical Africa; he wore a blue Phrygian cap and gold earrings, which Stanley suspected must have belonged to his dead wives. When Hart was young, sailors were keel-hauled and tied naked to the windlass, or hoisted up the yardarm at midday. As Stanley listened in awed silence, the names of distant places he had learnt about in the schoolrooms of St Asaph and Brynford became real. His mind struggled to adjust, to absorb so much that was strange. Recreating his first experiences on the lower deck, he hits off the vivid language of the first mate, who has caught him loafing: 'Now, my young pudding-faced joker, why are you standing there with your mouth wide open? Get a swab, you monkey, and swab up this poop, or I'll jump down your – – – – – – throat. Look alive now, you sweet-scented son of a sea-cook.'

By the start of February, the *Windermere* was in the Gulf of Mexico. Stanley had just passed his eighteenth birthday – although he did not know it and looked far younger. The ship prepared to enter the Mississippi, by furling sails and dropping anchor, to await a tug to pull her a hundred miles up-stream to New Orleans. This was Stanley's first sight of a great river, and of a land where the sun held stronger sway.

When they had docked in New Orleans, he gazed at the mile-wide, brown Mississippi, and the flat country of Louisiana. From the crowded wharves came the smells of molasses, tar, brine and coffee. At that time, the Crescent City – so called through being built on a crescent-shaped bend in the river – stood at the apogee of its power. It was the gateway to the cotton-growing lands of America, and to its port came ships from all the world; they brought manufactured goods, and immigrants. From New Orleans there was a river-steamer network covering many hundreds of miles of the Mississippi and its tributaries, then continuing up the Missouri and the Ohio, to such burgeoning centres as Louisville, St Louis and Cincinnati. The strength and confidence of the Deep South and its premier city had been boosted a few years earlier by the Mexican War and the allegiance of Texas, the vast 'lone star' state.

There was an elegance and grandeur about New Orleans which caught the imagination of new arrivals from Europe. It had been founded early in the eighteenth century by the French, then fallen for a time under the sway of Spain; finally the United States had bought Louisiana in 1804. The Spaniards had left their mark with such dignified buildings as the neo-classic Cabildo, the palace of justice; the influence of France showed itself in the fine ironwork on the buildings, the graceful colonnades and the many Catholic churches.

Stanley's first sortie ashore did not show him that side of New Orleans. Under the tutelage of the young sailor Harry he visited a brothel – places with which the port was well supplied. All innocence, he was led in by Harry and sat down in a parlour – when there 'bounced in four gay young ladies, in such scant clothing that I was speechless with amazement'. He must have seemed to the girls an unlikely customer, looking little more than fifteen. As he puts it, the girls 'proceeded to take liberties with my person', whereupon he fled into the street and could not be persuaded by Harry to return. Next they called at a bar, where Harry invited him to have a drink, but once more he defied temptation: 'I belong to the Band of Hope and have signed the pledge, so I must not.' However, he did try a cigar and was sick, which brought the evening to a close.

The next day, back aboard the *Windermere* Stanley was subjected to calculated harassment by the second mate. He firmly made up his mind to jump ship, rather than cling on and be carried, by a reluctant Captain Hardinge, back to the dank futility of Liverpool. He liked the ebullient style of the white men he saw in the streets: 'They had a swing of the body wholly un-English, and their facial expressions differed from those I had been accustomed to.' So after dark he emptied out his sea-bag, chose his best clothing and personal treasures – which included the Bible from the Bishop of St Asaph – and crept ashore to hide for the night amid some bales of cotton. He was in the act of becoming an illegal immigrant, although it was an age when such niceties did not matter much.

With daylight, fortune proved generous. Almost at once, he found a temporary job as a junior clerk with a firm of merchants in Tchoupitoulas Street, one of the city's main thoroughfares. Stanley distinguished himself there by his energy. The owner, James Speake, soon took him on permanently at twenty-five dollars a month, and showed a warm interest in his welfare. The white employees were also friendly and one of them gave him an old brass-bound trunk in which to keep his few possessions. Stanley writes affectionately about the trunk, how he locked and unlocked it to gaze at the partitions for all the shirts and collars he did not yet have, and the picture of a girl stuck inside the lid.

He had found himself cheap lodgings in a boarding house run by a Negro woman. Her place in St Thomas Street had been recommended to him by two slaves who worked for Speake. The pair were called Dan and Samuel, and as the most junior white employee in the firm he was often thrown into their company during the day. This was to be his first encounter with black people, but it did not end very happily – because it was Stanley who revealed that the slaves were stealing provisions from the store, by taking them home after work in their tin lunch-boxes. There had been shortages noticed in wines, spirits, biscuits and other food, and the new clerk looked into a lunch-basket in the backyard and found it three-quarters full of golden syrup. He reported this discovery to Speake. The slaves were sent for, quickly confessed, and pleaded in vain for mercy. Stanley records the upshot quite phlegmatically: 'A constable was called in, and Dan and Samuel were marched off to the watch-house, to receive on the next day such a flogging as only practised State-officials know how to administer. Dan, a few days later, was reinstated in the store; but Samuel was disposed of to a planter, for field-work.' It is a glimpse of the old South with its four million slaves, the America Stanley first knew.

At this time, he was still, reluctantly, calling himself John Rowlands; very shortly that would change. He was also starting to hide his uncertainties behind a façade of boldness: '. . . within a few weeks of arriving in America, I had become different in temper and spirit.' He felt that mood of reckless excitement gripping the South just before the Civil War.

Some idea of how Stanley was changing can be gained from several letters, among his private papers, written to him in sentimental vein after he had become famous. One is from a Swiss army officer, A. Schumacher, living in Berne: '. . . I can see you yet before my eyes in Delord Street, your tawny face, your rich light brown hair, your clear eyes with a little melancholy look; you wore a straw hat and generally a blue checkered jacket, and you were always remarkably clean and tidy.' Writing after a gap of more than thirty years, Schumacher can be forgiven for not recalling the colour of Stanley's hair.

Perhaps the most convincing description of Stanley in New Orleans comes from an 1891 newspaper interview with an anonymous 'lady of undoubted veracity.' She recalled several meetings with a John Rollins when she was living near Annunciation Street and he was visiting a house nearby. At the time, she said, he stayed in a 'sailor's lodging-house' and worked as a clerk for a commission agent's office in Tchoupitoulas Street. He said he came from Wales and that a mystery surrounded his birth. Her reminiscences ended: 'When I knew him, he was always a boy of good habits, smart as a whip, and much given to bragging, big talk and telling stories . . .' But such glimpses of Stanley in his New Orleans period are rare. They are overlaid by his own, carefully contrived account.

How Stanley found a second father and assumed his name is one of the best-known stories about these formative years. The phrase by which he introduced himself to a friendly stranger – 'Do you want a boy, sir?' – is given almost as much importance in his autobiographical writing as the famous greeting to Dr Livingstone twelve years later. He declares that the man who befriended him was a prosperous cotton broker, dealing between planters along the Mississippi and the merchants in New Orleans. The elder Stanley, who had no children of his own, helped the runaway to find his first job, encouraged him to read more widely, and taught him the elements of polite behaviour. There was also a Mrs Stanley – frail, gentle and pious – who entertained the shy Welsh lad to breakfast on Sunday mornings and filled him with wonder by her ladylike qualities; we are told she died suddenly in November 1859.

A few weeks after this bereavement Stanley senior took John

Rowlands of Denbigh to be his adopted son, telling him that in future their names would be identical. The kindly cotton broker had in his youth been ordained, so he felt qualified to conduct a baptismal ceremony: '. . . he rose, and, dipping his hands in a basin of water, he made the sign of the cross on my forehead . . .' This ritual, and the relationship that followed, are created for the reader in the explorer's memoirs at great length, with solemnity and emotion.

After his adoption, Stanley was equipped with entirely new clothes, and even more books to supplement the volumes of Shakespeare, Jonson and Cowper he had already been given. His mentor was intent on turning him into a 'complete gentleman', able to make a distinguished career. Together they travelled up the Mississippi, as the elder man followed his business affairs. They lived well and were treated with respect, according to the fulsome picture we are given.

For all this new-found affection, the younger Stanley was made to study for several hours a day, and ordered to read aloud to improve his intonation. He was also warned by his adopted father to be more precise and honest: '. . . I was led through gushes of healthy rapture into excesses of speech; but he would turn on me, and gravely say that he was not accustomed to carry magnifiers with him . . . Sometimes he would assume a comical look of incredulity, which brought me to my senses very quickly, and made me retract what I had said, and repeat the statement with a more sacred regard for accuracy.' Occasionally there were quarrels, with the adopted son breaking into fits of temper: 'I was one who could not always do the right and proper thing, for I was often erring and perverse, and at various times must have tried him sorely.'

In the autumn of 1860 they parted, never to meet again. 'Many years later' the explorer (by his own account) learnt that the man who meant so much to him had died in 1861 in Havana; he had gone there to see a brother. Several letters came from Cuba, then there was silence. Stanley says he was left only with a photograph of his 'father', a lock of his hair, some books and clothes, and the precious memory of their happiness together.

But these memoirs are a tangle of truth and fantasy. The relationship ended in a quarrel, although only a most veiled hint of this is given; it was too painful to admit that after giving all his loyalty and love, which nobody had wanted in the bleak years of childhood, he was eventually to part on bad terms from his mentor.

Nothing is said about the origins of the elder Henry Stanley (his middle name is never mentioned) except that he turned to commerce from the ministry through 'becoming lukewarm' about religion. He had preached in Tennessee before moving down to New Orleans, and an impression is conveyed that he was born and bred in the South. The memoirs assert that the pair were together for two years, whereas an examination of the dates shows that the time was no more than nine months.

At last, it is possible to draw back the curtain that has lain for more than a century across this crucial episode in the explorer's formative years, and to reveal the carefully concealed identity of the 'father'. Henry Hope Stanley was born in 1815 in Cheshire, England, and emigrated to America when he was twenty-four. He was never ordained, although his mother had, after the death of her first husband, been re-married to a Presbyterian clergyman. Henry Hope Stanley stayed in regular touch with his well-to-do family in England, and kept up his British citizenship. His mother – widowed for a second time – was living in Cheadle, south of Manchester. With her were two bachelor sons: John Stanley was, like his elder brother, in the cotton business; the other son was a solicitor.

Henry Hope Stanley was twice married, first to a Texan girl whom he met shortly after arriving in America. She was to die of yellow fever while he was on a business trip, and although the tragedy occurred years before the adopted Henry Stanley appeared on the scene, he seems to have appropriated the story for his own interpretation of events. The senior Stanley briefly returned to England after the loss of his first wife, and there took a second bride, a Miss Miller whom he had known in his childhood. This was the Mrs Stanley who befriended the future explorer and so impressed him by her elegance. His account of her death in 1859 is entirely fictitious.

It is true, however, that the Stanleys were childless. They adopted several children, including a girl called Anna who disappointed them by running away with the coachman. Henry Hope Stanley was known for his benevolence. After his death, one of his employees said: 'Often when we had to work unusually hard and long, he waited until our tasks were completed, then took us to the theatre and after the performance to supper. Everybody liked him.' The wealthy merchant was distinctively British in his dress and manners; he had a rubicund face and luxuriant black beard.

The death of his first wife made Stanley resolve to keep away from New Orleans in the hot weather, because of the epidemics that so often swept the city then. He built a mansion at Arcola, to the north of the capital, in Tangipahoa parish. The countryside at Arcola was handsome and well-wooded. Stanley spared no expense on his house, which had wide verandahs and tall columns at the entrance; the marble fireplaces were imported from Italy. But there was little chance to enjoy this retreat, because of the mounting hatred between South and North. Henry Hope Stanley was determined that if civil war broke out, he would have no part of it, and would return to England with his wife until the fighting ended.

The knowledge that Henry Hope Stanley came from Cheshire explains why his interest was aroused by the boy who asked him for a job in New Orleans: the county of Cheshire borders Wales, and he would at once have recognised the sing-song accents of the runaway.

He soon came to regret this latest adoption, as his 'son' proved hard to control and several times ran away; when he returned, the youth's explanations of what he had been doing were unconvincing. It is likely that he wandered along the Mississippi, taking any odd jobs he could find. In the *Autobiography* there is a graphic account of a journey on an old-fashioned flatboat, carrying timber down-river from St Louis. He also spent some time tending an elderly sea-captain, who had fallen ill aboard ship in New Orleans harbour.

In Arcola a bitter and decisive dispute took place. It made the cotton broker decide to send his unruly protégé away to work on a friend's plantation in Arkansas, several days' journey to the north. In later years he always refused to discuss the details, but they were said to involve a local girl with whom the younger Stanley had been too familiar. There is no question of H. H. Stanley's having died in Cuba in 1861; he lived for another seventeen years, returning to New Orleans from England in 1865 at the end of the Civil War.

None of this is touched upon in the explorer's memoirs, and there is no shred of evidence about what really happened to cause the separation. He only says that he did not get on with the plantation owner in Arkansas to whom he had been sent when 'his father went to Cuba'. There was a quarrel, so he decided to leave. He had a letter of introduction to a German-Jewish trader named Altschul at Cypress Bend. That was forty miles away, and he decided to go there at once on foot. When he reached his destination, he would send for his trunk to be collected. 'In another quarter of an hour I had left the plantation with a small bundle of letters and papers, and was trudging through the woods . . .' Ever since his flight from the Welsh workhouse four years earlier, Stanley had shown this trait – an urge for sudden and dramatic departures.

He was in some fear of the journey, along a lonely dirt road. On every side were tall pines and oaks, and he wondered what he would do if he met a bear or other wild animal; but this was only his imagination running free, and he arrived at Cypress Bend without incident. Altschul gave him a friendly welcome, and set him to work as a clerk and junior salesman.

Cypress Bend was in the swamp-lands of Arkansas, which were notorious for both malaria and the quick-tempered nature of the white settlers. In Stanley's view, one may have followed from the other. He himself soon experienced exhausting bouts of fever, and one day when he stood on the scales found his weight down to 95 lb. But life was full of diversity, and the whole neighbourhood seemed to revolve around Altschul's well-stocked shelves – not to mention the liquor room at the rear.

A character who provoked Stanley to wonder was the head salesman, a New Yorker of Irish origins called Cronin. He drank heavily, but his talents outweighed his weaknesses: 'He was assiduous, obliging, and artful beyond anything with the ladies. He won their confidences, divined their preferences, and, with the most provoking assurance, laid the identical piece of goods they wanted before them . . . Cronin was a born salesman, and I have never met his equal since.' With the men customers, the tight-lipped planters, Stanley's idol had other tactics. First he would take them out to sample the liquor, before pressing upon them shotguns, revolvers and saddles; in everything he was an expert. Unfortunately, Cronin fell into disrepute for 'gross familiarities with female slaves' – this was the unpardonable sin, so he had to leave.

Stanley soon began to take the measure of his customers, and gives a telling portrait of life in the South on the eve of the Civil War. The planters ruled over their own domains 'like princelings' owning hundreds of slaves, and had developed such egotism that any slight was enough to make them flare with rage. 'Though genially sociable to each other, to landless people like myself they conducted themselves as though they were under no obligations.' In this environment, it was natural that the young counter-clerk was resolved to prove himself a man. Everybody carried a gun, and Stanley soon possessed a Smith and Wesson with which he practised for hours on end. After a while, he declares, he could sever a pack-thread at twenty paces; later in life, his experience as a marksman in Arkansas would prove its worth.

He might have stayed in that remote corner of Arkansas, working his way up from 200 dollars a year under the tutelage of Altschul. But in March 1861, he overheard a discussion between two customers which made him aware of formidable events on the horizon. One of the men was a local politician, Dr Goree. His son was the same age as Stanley and came home on vacations from a college in Nashville, Tennessee. Through the son, Stanley soon gained a heady view of the struggle to come. In May, 1861, Arkansas joined the Confederacy.

As the talk of war grew, plans were made for volunteer companies to fight under the Confederate flag. At first, Stanley saw himself as an outsider, and had no thought of enlisting. He was Welsh, and this was not his conflict: 'I had a secret scorn for people who could kill each other for the sake of African slaves.' But as he stayed behind the shop counter, customers began to gaze at him with a query in their eyes. What did it matter if he was not an American citizen? He was in the South – didn't he believe in its cause?

Still Stanley did nothing. Then one morning he was sent a petticoat, wrapped in a parcel. He recognised the handwriting – it had come from a quiet girl called Margaret, a cousin of the Gorees. He had always been fond of her.

That afternoon, Stanley went out and signed on for the Dixie Greys.

7. From Dixie to the Federal Fleet

When Stanley put on his Confederate uniform, to play a part in the greatest conflict of the nineteenth century, Southern morale was at its peak. The first shots of the Civil War had been fired only three months before, and from Virginia to Texas there was a confidence that the Federals would never find enough spirit to make a fight of it. The North, with its 20 million population, might be four times stronger on paper than the Southern whites, and had industrial power to sustain the war effort – but courage surely meant more than numbers. The Confederacy even had the best tunes: as Stanley marched out of Little Rock in August 1861, with the Sixth Arkansas Regiment of Volunteers, the streets echoed to the singing of 'Dixie'. The girls wept and waved their handkerchiefs, the bands played and sun glinted off a thousand bayonets. 'We strode to the "levee" with eyes front, in the manner of Romans when reviewed by their tribunes,' says Stanley.

Such excitements helped to overcome his reservations about going to war. A fine silk banner had been stitched for Company E by the womenfolk of Cypress Bend, and beneath it Stanley pledged loyalty to the South alongside the sons of wealthy planters. His friend Dan Goree had even brought along a personal slave. The officers included a first lieutenant named Penny Mason, from an old Virginian family, and a second lieutenant whose uncle was none other than the heroic Confederate general, Robert E. Lee. 'As compared with many others, the company was a choice one, the leaven of gentlehood was strong, and served to make it rather more select than the average.'

Stanley became popular with the Company's 'ballast' – uneducated veterans of the Mexican War of 1847 – as a letter-writing scribe. It was a task that sustained his pride, gave some scope to his embryonic literary skills, and showed off the graceful penmanship he had learnt in the workhouse. Proof of his talents in this direction is shown by an inquiry he received almost thirty years later from a survivor of Company E named James M. Slate. It recalled old times and ended: 'This is enough for you to say, in reply, you are the identical Boyish Soldier. You have wrote many letters for me. Please answer by return mail.' Stanley sent a warmly sentimental reply to Slate, who was by then living in Blue Ridge, Georgia.

On March 25, 1862, the 6th Arkansas Regiment began assembling in Corinth, Mississippi, with various other Confederate brigades and regiments; there were 40,000 men under the commands of Generals Pierre Beauregard and Albert Sidney Johnston. Coming against them was General Grant with nearly 50,000 Federal soldiers, and on both sides the preparations started for one of the crucial battles of the Civil War. Stanley and his comrades spent several days bracing themselves, but on April 2 they were finally given orders to make three days' cooked rations; two days later they set out for Shiloh near the Tennessee River, leaving their knapsacks and tents behind them. For two nights the army bivouacked miserably in the damp countryside, and before dawn on Sunday, April 6, rose to catch the enemy by surprise. Forty-eight hours later in the wooded countryside around Shiloh, there would be more than 4,000 dead and 17,000 wounded – a casualty rate of almost one in five.

Shiloh was the first of many times when Stanley would see men fight and die. The account he has left about this desperate initiation is sometimes marred by heavy moralising. At its best, however, it has passages which stand comparison with Stephen Crane's descriptions in *The Red Badge of Courage*.

The battle started slowly, and for the Confederates well, as they overran the front lines of the Federal blue-coats in the pale flush of dawn. They were to have the advantage of surprise, despite the inferiority in their equipment and numbers. 'As we tramped solemnly and silently through the thin forest, and over its grass, still in its withered and wintry hue, I noticed that the sun was not far from appearing, that our regiment was keeping its formation admirably, and that the woods would have been a grand place for a picnic; and I thought it strange that a Sunday should have been chosen to disturb the holy calm of those woods.'

At first the firing was desultory. 'Stand by, gentlemen,' said Captain Smith to Company E, as they neared the Federal positions and regiments around them began to blaze away through the trees. Stanley and his colleagues were equipped with the antiquated flint-lock muskets which were dangerously slow to load. The ammunition was rolled in cartridge paper, which held powder, a round ball and three buckshot; the men had to tear the paper with their teeth, empty some powder into the pan, lock it, empty the rest of the powder in the barrel, press the paper and ball down the muzzle, and ram both home. To perform this operation in the extremities of combat, against an enemy armed with Enfield rifles, was discouraging enough – and the similar activities of men around added to the hazard. Stanley recalls being angry with the man in the rank behind him, for making his eyes sting with the powder from his musket and his ears deaf with noise. Soon the whole battlefield was roaring with sound, which seemed to him like rocks tumbling and thundering down a mountain-side.

Yelling and cat-calling, the Confederates fixed bayonets and broke into a run, until they had captured an enemy encampment. The surprise element in their advance was proved by the way many of the dead and wounded were still half-dressed. Abandoned equipment was strewn amid the tents. Stanley and his colleagues were elated, fancying the battle was almost won. But much more lay ahead. Once again they advanced towards the Tennessee, to be met by a furious storm of bullets and shells as they came near the next line of tents. A dozen members of the company sheltered behind a fallen tree.

'How the cannon bellowed, and their shells plunged and bounded, and flew with screeching hisses over us! Their sharp rending explosions and hurtling fragments made us shrink and cower, despite our utmost efforts to be cool and collected . . . One man raised his chest, as if to yawn, and jostled me. I turned to him and saw that a bullet had gored his whole face, and penetrated into his chest.'

As the Confederates drove a path through the second line of tents, Stanley was flung to the ground by a missile that struck him on the clasp of his belt. He was stunned and exhausted, and crawled to the shelter of a tree where he lay for a while, until he was able to grope in his haversack for something to eat. After half an hour he walked on again through the battlefield, to search for his regiment. Among the dead he saw another Briton from the Dixie Greys, a heavily-built sergeant who had been nicknamed 'John Bull', and close to him was a young lieutenant with a bullet-hole through the centre of his forehead. 'I can never forget the impression those wide-open dead eyes made on me.' Stanley wrote from the viewpoint of a private soldier; a somewhat more detached appraisal was later offered by one of the senior officers involved, General D. C. Buell: 'The battle of Shiloh was the most famous, and, to both sides, the most interesting of the war.'

The Confederates had the advantage of being able to plunder the rations in the camps they had occupied, before lapsing into uneasy sleep. At daylight they were hurried into line by their officers for further action; yesterday they had failed to reach the Tennessee, and now they must do it. But fortunes were to change, for the Federal troops had been reinforced by 20,000 fresh men who had crossed the river at night under the leadership of Buell. After hours of desperate battle, the Confederates were forced from all the ground they had taken and Beauregard saw there was no hope left of pushing the Federals into the water. He withdrew to Corinth in good order – General Grant deciding that his own men were too worn out to mount a pursuit. So despite its welter of casualties, the Battle of Shiloh (also known as Pittsburg Landing) ended inconclusively.

But Stanley was not there at the finish. Early on the Monday morning he had found himself, mentally stunned but unhurt, a captive of the Federals. His account of how it happened gives a glimpse of his character and courage under fire:

'With my musket on the trail I found myself in active motion, more active than I would otherwise have been, perhaps, because Captain Smith had said, "Now, Mr Stanley, if you please, step briskly forward!" This singling-out of me wounded my *amour-propre*, and sent me forward like a rocket. In a short time, we met our opponents in the same formation as ourselves, and advancing most resolutely. We threw ourselves behind such trees as were near us, fired, loaded, and darted forward to another shelter. Presently I found myself in an open, grassy space, with no convenient tree or stump near; but, seeing a shallow hollow some twenty paces ahead, I made a dash for it and plied my musket with haste . . .'

Suddenly, Stanley realises his position is curiously changed. No longer can he see any grey uniforms about him, and all are blue. He has run too far ahead of his company, which has retreated from this hopeless encounter and left him stranded. He is surrounded by Federals: 'Half a dozen of the enemy were covering me at the same instant, and I dropped my weapon, incontinently. Two men sprang at my collar, and marched me, unresisting, into the ranks of the terrible Yankees. *I was a prisoner!*'

With several hundred other Confederates taken at Shiloh, he was put on a steamer for St Louis. Once again he was travelling along the great American waterway – but now he could not tell where his journey would end. In St Louis there was a brief lift to the spirits of the prisoners, for many citizens there did not hide their sympathy for the Southern cause; Missouri had almost joined the Confederacy. In a diary, made up later from notes put together soon afterwards, he writes: 'April 13, 1862. Arrived in St Louis, put in college. People St Louis very generous. Ladies sent presents of food and flowers.' But quickly the captives were transported far from the fringes of Confederate support, to a prisoner-of-war centre near Chicago, named Camp Douglas. Stanley now found himself, willy-nilly, much farther north than he had ever been before in America, and almost a thousand miles from where he had stepped ashore in 1859. He was soon brought to his lowest ebb.

The camp was riddled with dysentery, typhus and vermin. The prisoners were housed in vast huts, each one holding more than 200 men, with continuous wooden bunks giving thirty inches a man. There was nothing to read, nothing to do except brood; disease spread relentlessly. Stanley writes an anguished account of his time in Camp Douglas, and the journeys to the open ditches behind the barracks: '. . . we saw crowds of sick men, who had fallen prostrate from weakness, and given themselves wholly to despair; and, while they crawled or wallowed in their filth, they cursed and blasphemed as often as they groaned.' Every day men were carried in their blankets to the crude camp hospital, and none returned. He watched the bodies piled up in the early mornings on the death-wagons 'as the New Zealand frozen-mutton carcases are carted from the docks.'

He had been put in charge of one of the platforms in a hut, which meant he was responsible for collecting rations and keeping a record of the men. But there was little honour or satisfaction in that, and only one escape from the nightmare of Camp Douglas presented itself: to desert the Confederates and sign on with the North. At first Stanley rejected this suggestion from the camp authorities; it cost six weeks of misery, after the arrival from St Louis, to make him change sides. On June 4, 1862, he took the oath of allegiance to the Union and was sworn in with the First Regiment of the Illinois Light Artillery. It was less than a year since he had pledged loyalty in the Dixie Greys – but he was, after all, only a Southerner by chance. He felt a romantic attachment to the Confederacy, but the political arguments of the Civil War meant little to him.

Almost as soon as Stanley had been given his blue Federal uniform and drafted south from Chicago, the dysentery he had picked up in Camp Douglas took him totally in its grip. He collapsed at a camp near Harper's Ferry and was sent into hospital. On June 22 his condition was so bad that he was discharged – penniless, weak and with nowhere to go. He was again near the battle areas, but too weak to care.

It took him a week to struggle more than halfway from Harper's Ferry to Hagerstown, 24 miles away. Then he staggered into the farmhouse of a man called Baker, who let him sleep in a barn. After several days of unconsciousness he awoke to find he had been put on a mattress and dressed in a clean shirt. He was lucky – the family he chanced upon decided to befriend him. They made him sit quietly in their orchard; it was a hot, Maryland summer, the war had begun to recede from the neighbourhood, and gradually Stanley recovered enough to join in the placid rural life by helping with the harvest. By mid-August he was clear about what he wanted to do: his thoughts were concentrated upon Wales, which he had last seen four years before. The nearest port to the Bakers' farm was Baltimore, and there he might find a place on a ship going to Liverpool. The Bakers were sympathetic: they took him in a pony and trap to Hagerstown, and bought him a railway ticket to Baltimore.

A diary entry shows that soon after reaching Baltimore, Stanley went to call on the girlfriend of a Confederate soldier named W. H. Wilkes, who had been with him at Fort Douglas. (This fellow-prisoner was the nephew of a famous Federal naval captain – a good example of how the war divided families.) It may be that Stanley was hoping the girl would be rich enough to give him financial help in return for news of her beau; but she is not mentioned again. He found a job aboard an oyster schooner in Chesapeake Bay – an experience not without drama, since the captain fell over the side and was drowned. A few weeks later he signed on with a sailing ship, the *E. Sherman*, for a month-long voyage to Liverpool.

At this point Stanley's own chronicle of his life peters out. When starting to write of events from 1861 onwards he had noted: 'I am now about to begin a period lasting about six years, which, were it possible, I should gladly like to re-live, not with a view to repeating its woes and errors, pains and inconsistencies, but of rectifying the mistakes I made . . .' Soon afterwards he found that various actions in which he could take no pride were too clear-cut for literary art to camouflage. He may also have shied away from telling the full story of his humiliating return to Britain.

For all his adventures during four years in America, Stanley looked far from successful. He walked the forty miles from Liverpool to North Wales: 'I was very poor, in bad health, and my clothes were shabby. I made my way to Denbigh, to my mother's house. With what pride I knocked at the door, buoyed up by a hope of being able to show what manliness I had acquired, not unwilling, perhaps, to magnify what I meant to become . . .'

This first meeting was not a good augury, for after giving him a bed, a meal and a shilling, his mother told him to clear off.

Elizabeth Parry was now married and middle-aged. Two years before, in the chapel at St Asaph, she had become the wife of Robert Jones, father of two of her children. Together they were running the Cross Foxes, a small inn with mullioned windows in the village of Glascoed. They had just suffered a misfortune, however, with the death of their youngest child, James, from meningitis at the age of six. It is easy to see how the unheralded appearance of the erstwhile John Rowlands, the illegitimate child of her teens, would be shaming to Mrs Jones. In a tiny place like Glascoed this dishevelled stranger would be a talking-point for weeks among the customers of the Cross Foxes.

The bleak welcome has been made much of to explain away Stanley's austere behaviour in later years – not least by Stanley himself: '. . . I found no affection, and never again sought for, or expected, what I discovered had never existed.' This would be very well, if, in fact, he had been permanently alienated. It is far from the case. But he did realise that he must cut more of a dash next time he came home. He may also have been paying the penalty for some rather extravagant letters he had written to Denbigh from New Orleans. One was sent in 1860, when he changed his name; bearing the unfamiliar signature 'Henry Stanley', it told his half-sister Emma that John Rowlands was 'dead'.

After the rebuff he received in Wales, the impoverished vagrant made his way to Manchester; there he threw himself upon the good-will of relations of the man who had adopted and rejected him in Louisiana. Although there is no evidence of a reunion with Henry Hope Stanley, by then living in England, he was given clothes and some money, and put on the road to Liverpool.

At the start of 1863 he was having his first look at New York, after sailing there from Liverpool in a ship named the *Ernestine*. He was still without money or friends, and the only solution to his predicament was to sign on again as a deckhand. For the next nine months he was in a succession of merchant ships, generally sailing between Boston and the Mediterranean.

One entry in his sparse diary of this period stands out: 'May 1863. Barcelona, Barque *Jehu*, naked night. Barracks of carabiniers.' Lloyds of London record that the *Jehu* arrived at Barcelona on June 25 from Boston, and sailed a fortnight later for Girgenti in Italy. She was a 250-ton wooden ship, built at Newburyport, Massachusetts in 1859 and commanded by a Captain Smith. Stanley's diary note was written up long after the event, so that the difference of a month can be attributed to a lapse in his normally faultless memory. It is a cryptic entry, but more light is shed in yet another retrospective diary. This says: 'Wrecked off Barcelona, crew lost, in the night. Stripped naked, and swam to shore. Barrack of carabiniers... demanded my papers!' But the *Jehu* was not wrecked off Barcelona in 1863; she was in service until 1890.

There are two other versions of the incident, based on separate interviews with Stanley in 1872. Examined together they reveal how he wove fancy with fact to contrive a life-story in which his earlier years seemed consistent with his eventual fame. One is a magazine biography (*The Graphic*, August 17, 1872) much of which is accurate. It begins: 'Of a roving disposition, he commenced his travels early. While yet a boy he ran away from school, went to sea, and deserted his ship in the harbour of Barcelona. In swimming to land he lost his bundle of clothes, and was thus obliged to make his way ashore naked. In this condition he was found by a sentry and taken to the castle, where he was allowed to sleep the night on some straw. In the morning a captain took pity on him, gave him some clothes, and bade him *adios*, after conducting him through the suburb of Barcelonetta. He started to Marseilles without a copper in his pocket, and though several times in danger of being imprisoned as a vagabond, continued his journey on foot through Southern Catalonia, and finally arrived at the frontier, sustaining himself by asking alms. In France his forlorn appearance attracted the attention of the police, and at the little town of Narbonne, in the department of the Aude, he was apprehended, but after a short detention released. Having received means from his friends upon arriving in Marseilles, he began his travels in a more respectable fashion, visited almost all the ports of Europe . . .'

The second interview has this anecdote: 'When he was sixteen he

133

ran away to sea (much against the wishes of his father) from a country hamlet. He experienced a severe shipwreck in the Atlantic Ocean. The waves swept away most of his clothes, and he landed on the coast of Spain and walked as far as Narbonne. When I asked him how he got on at Narbonne, he said, "Oh, it was all right there: my father sent me money, and I travelled to Athens like a prince".'

That Stanley was the source of both these fanciful versions is proved by his unpublished diary, which says: 'July: Back in America via Narbonne.'

In October 1863, Stanley abandoned life at sea and took a job with Judge Thomas Irwin Hughes of Brooklyn. He later told friends that he had once thought of being a lawyer, but found the work too dull, and it is likely that Hughes hired him to copy out documents. Hughes was not a judge in the strict sense, but the status of notary public and 'attorney for prosecuting government claims' would make it natural enough for him to assume the title. Stanley tells nothing about his work for Hughes, but he appears to have lodged with him in Brooklyn – the directory for the period shows that Hughes lived at 313 Ryerson Street. There is a melodramatic diary entry for the end of 1863: 'Judge drunk; tried to kill wife with hatchet; attempted three times. I held him down all night. Next morning, exhausted; lighted cigar in parlour; wife came down – insulted and raved at me for smoking in her house!'

Despite the hazards of life with the Hughes family, he appears to have stayed with them, and to have gone on working until mid-1864 at the legal office in Cedar Street, lower Manhattan. It was here that he became friendly with a young captain in the Federal army, Louis R. Stegman, who was home on leave in New York early in 1864. Before joining the army, Stegman had probably also worked for Judge Hughes. The two were of the same age, and both had romantic notions of prospecting for gold in Australia or South America; this emerges from a nostalgic letter Stegman wrote to Stanley many years afterwards. It is likely that they also talked about entering journalism when the war was over, because Stegman set himself up as a photographer in Brooklyn in 1866. The stimulus of war had led to many changes in the newspapers of the North, and dailies such as the *New York Herald* were building up a corps of correspondents to report from the battlefronts.

Stegman went back to his regiment, to be wounded almost at once by a Confederate bullet in Georgia. Stanley took a sudden, inexplicable step at about the same time: he signed up for three years in the Federal Navy. The files show that he joined on July 19, 1864 as a 'landsman' (non-sailor) giving his age as twenty, although he was twenty-three. He described himself as a clerk, born in England and living in King's County, New York. The navy noted that he was 5 feet 5 inches tall, with dark hair and complexion, and hazel eyes.

This was Stanley's third entry into the Civil War: he had barely escaped with his life from the ranks of the Confederates, and his time with the Federal Army had been brief and miserable. Now the conflict was nearly over and there was little chance of promotion. It has been asserted that Stanley joined up again to report on action at sea, for the advancement of his career as a newspaperman; there is no basis for this. It is more likely that he joined on a whim, from boredom with his life behind a desk, and perhaps from envy of Stegman in his officer's uniform. It would seem that he did not disclose his seaman's experience while signing on, so that he could take the slightly more genteel role of ship's clerk.

Stanley went to the receiving ship *North Carolina*, and from there to the frigate *Minnesota*, lying at Hampton Roads, Virginia. But he managed to be in New York in November, as shown by an entry in his diary: 'Maggie Mitchell, testimonial, Niblo's, Shadow Dance.' Unravelled, this refers to a performance on November 18 at Niblo's Garden, a Broadway theatre, with a popular actress of the time in the leading role. Maggie Mitchell was playing in *Fanchon*, a romantic drama adapted from a work by George Sand; Act 1, scene 2 was always known as the 'Shadow Dance'. The *New York Times* advertised 'A farewell benefit to Miss Maggie Mitchell, whose perfect portraitures of her original character, the Little Cricket ... have been universally praised by all.' Stanley was evidently among the admirers of Maggie Mitchell.

Before leaving New York, he briefly visited what Stegman called 'the old den in Cedar Street'. Stegman was back on leave, after recovering from his wounds, but was applying to be re-mustered for service. In a sentence Stanley might well have composed for him, he told his commanding general: 'The old feeling of soldierly ardour is rampant'. But Stanley was the first to see action. On December 20, 1864 he was off Fort Fisher, North Carolina, for the bombardment of one of the last Confederate strongholds on the Atlantic. The fort guarded the port of Wilmington, from which the embattled Southerners maintained tenuous links with the outside world. The

Federals exploded a vessel filled with gunpowder near the walls of the fort. But the defenders proved dogged, and a bloody onslaught on Christmas Day was abortive. The fleet retired to Beaufort, to prepare for a decisive attack.

By an odd coincidence, a fortnight before Stanley arrived off Fort Fisher, another young Briton with whose surname his own would forever be linked died inland in North Carolina, a prisoner of the Confederates. Like Stanley, he had assumed a new name in America, and was known as Rupert Vincent. Shortly before he died he wrote home to his father: '. . . I am convinced that to bear your name here would lead to further dishonours to it.' His father, Dr Livingstone, was at that moment preparing for his last great expedition to the interior of Africa.

Stanley at 23, when he was serving as a clerk in the frigate *Minnesota*.

8. The Vagabond Freelance

Day-dreams helped Stanley to escape from his routine as a clerk in the warship *Minnesota*. His mind ranged over the adventures he had had since first crossing the Atlantic six years earlier; they did not satisfy his imagination. Fanciful ideas of how he might have joined the navy came to his mind . . . He had persuaded the captain of a Confederate cruiser to take him to New Orleans, after giving a precise description of the city to prove he had been brought up there. He told the captain he would spy for him, to pay for his passage. But when the cruiser was anchored off a port in Virginia, and he was stationed on guard, he stole a rowing boat and daringly made his way to a Federal ship not far away . . . Then he saw himself as a hero in the attack on Fort Fisher. He swam 500 yards under fire and tied a rope to a Confederate ship, so that the admiral's flag-ship could secure her as a prize. He had been the admiral's secretary, but for such bravery was promoted to the rank of ensign on the spot . . . Stanley kept these inventions in the back of his mind, while he laboured over his paperwork.

A picture of him is given by a shipmate, Lewis H. Noe: 'Stanley hardly spoke to anybody. He would be sitting by himself reading whenever he had the chance.' But when he did emerge from his books he displayed a 'pleasing address' and an air of confidence. He talked well, and although he was just a ship's clerk he adopted the manners of an officer. Stanley revealed his thoughts to Noe: 'He was full of aspirations for adventure; told marvellous tales of foreign countries, and urged that when we should leave the service I should accompany him on a proposed tour in Southern Europe. Being of a romantic turn of mind, I was pleased at the suggestion.'

The two became close companions. They had joined up on the same day and Noe was overwhelmed by Stanley's flair as a story-teller and his 'marked ability, intelligence, and skill as a penman'. There was a big difference in their ages, for while Stanley was well into his twenties, Noe was only fifteen. Their relationship exposes a trait that was to appear throughout the explorer's life: the desire for

Stanley arrived in America the second time. Enlisted in the United States navy as an ordinary seaman. The first month he was promoted to be the clerk of the ship - "Ship's Writer". The fourth month he was appointed a secretary of an Admiral, and for swimming 500 yards, and tying a rope to a captured steamer, while exposed, to the shot and shell of a battery of ten guns was promoted to an Ensigncy with a salary of £350 per annum. By working hard he managed to make the sum of £450 per annum. He was in several battles on land, as well as on the water, and was engaged in the last great battle on sea between the rebel and the Union fleet Fort-Fisher. which took place Jany 16th 1865 Two months afterwards, the ship in which he was was sent to cruise. It made a voyage nearly round the

Stanley's account of his naval career was highly fanciful. He wrote this for a girl in his native Wales

a younger man at his side to give unquestioning loyalty and be a confidant on whom he could, without constraint, try out new ideas. But if Noe met a psychological need in Stanley, there were practical advantages in return: the older friend composed letters for Noe to his family back in Long Island. A Christmas letter to Noe's father was written while the *Minnesota* was off Fort Fisher.

After the fleet had returned in mid-January to attack the Confederate stronghold – successfully this time – Stanley's private musings had come up with a bold scheme. He put it to Noe: they should abscond together when they reached harbour. The frigate went to Portsmouth, New Hampshire, for repairs soon after the battle; the two became deserters on February 10, 1865.

According to Noe, Stanley forged a pass out of the dockyard and put the commodore's name on it. As soon as they were clear of the gates they stripped off their uniforms, under which they wore civilian clothes bought from the naval carpenters who had been overhauling the *Minnesota*.

But Noe came in for a storm of family condemnation when he had made his way back to the sleepy village of Sayville. His parents and an older sister, who was a school-mistress, told him to hurry back to New Hampshire and rejoin his ship. He agreed, but in New York visited Stanley who warned him that it would only mean 'disgrace and punishment'. So Noe decided the next best thing would be to join the army and signed on for the Eighth New York Mounted Volunteers. He did so with an assumed surname, which Stanley had suggested: Morton.

As for Stanley, he boldly stayed in New York and looked for a job. There is evidence that he first worked in the office of a lawyer named Lyons, but by April 14 he was seeking a foothold in journalism. An entry in his diary for that day says: 'New York. Assassination of Lincoln. Great Excitement. Office of Evening Post.' Then he saw brighter hopes elsewhere of putting together the funds he needed to begin his travels in Europe. By the end of May he was out of New York, heading west by train and stagecoach. Stanley had urged Noe to desert once more and come along, but he refused.

The mid-sixties of the last century were a time when the young and daring of America were following the advice of Horace Greeley: 'Go West, young man, go West!' Gold had been discovered in Colorado in 1858, and a rush of prospectors flocked to the mining settlements in the Rockies above Denver. These outposts had extravagant names, and one of the best-known was Central City. It was called the 'richest square mile on earth', and Stanley pinned his hopes upon it. He was ready for the West, and his hours of practice with a six-shooter in Arkansas had not been in vain. By June 1865 he was in St Louis – which he had last seen as a bedraggled prisoner – and there he persuaded the owners of the *Missouri Democrat* to accept him as an 'attaché'. This meant he was a recognised freelance contributor, paid by results. It was to be a fruitful alliance.

He did not linger in St Louis, but hurried on towards his goal. By late June he was in St Joseph (where Jesse James later met his end), and there took the 'Pony Express', which crossed the plains to the Rocky Mountains and California. By July he was in Salt Lake City, and he reached San Francisco during August. Then he quickly turned back from the Pacific to Colorado, where he was to spend the rest of 1865 and part of 1866. Denver was his base, but most of the time was spent in Central City and other mining centres such as Black Hawk. He could not live by writing alone, and the reminiscences of people who knew him show that he took a variety of jobs.

Two men called Mullen and Webster recalled that Stanley worked as a bookkeeper in Central City. 'He was a bright fellow and took well with everybody, and especially the business community,' said Mullen. According to Webster, Stanley tried to organise a group to go to Alaska, where gold had been reported: 'He often talked about prospecting expeditions to distant points.'

Two other accounts confirm that Stanley worked for the Central City newspaper, the *Miner's Daily Register*. But he was hired as an apprentice printer, not a journalist. An early report says: 'He directed his time between the press room and the prospect hole; he picked type and picked rocks with equal facility . . . He had not the Midas touch, however, in those days, and finally left Central never to return.' As a prospector, Stanley worked with five friends to discover the Huff Lode in Central City. While in a mountain camp he scarred his arm in the flames as he prepared a meal over the open fire; sometimes he said the scar was caused by an Indian arrow.

The West was a disappointment to Stanley in one sense. He did not make his fortune by striking gold. But in the year after leaving New York he made another discovery: his skill as a word-spinner could bring the success he craved. He had found a *métier*. One of his articles took the attention of another young freelance writer, William Harlow Cook. The piece so impressed Cook that he sought out

Stanley, and a friendship developed. Cook gives the impression of being somewhat docile, and he was soon hypnotised by Stanley's enthusiasms. They talked about making some bold adventures together – and agreed to go around the world. Stanley had managed to save up some money, and his new companion was even better off. They would start at once.

As a prelude, to test their fitness, they decided to travel more than 600 miles down the Platte River from Denver to Omaha. The Platte is a shallow, fast-flowing torrent with many obstacles, and had been swollen by snow water when Stanley and Cook launched themselves upon it. But not only the perils of the river must be watched, for Redskins roamed the banks.

There is a brief account of the trip by Stanley, telling how they bought planking and tools, built a raft in a few hours, stacked it with arms and provisions, and set off at dusk. 'After twice upsetting, and many adventures and narrow escapes, we reached the Missouri River.' There are also a few lines about the exploit in one of Stanley's notebooks. The journey began on May 6, and ended on May 27. In the notebook, there has been a deliberate mutilation to hide some event between May 17 and 18.

The pair reached Omaha, took a steamer to St Louis, then a train to New York. There they collected Lewis Noe, who Stanley said was his half-brother. Stanley had never stopped writing to Noe while he was in the West. As a result of these letters Lewis's family had forgiven Stanley for the desertion episode and accepted the proposal that their son – now honourably discharged from the army – should go on the world trip. Several of Stanley's letters had been addressed to Noe's sister, for whom he may have felt some attraction – she was 'full in person, with voluptuous lips, dark glittering eyes and very black hair, falling loosely to her waist.'

Stanley and Cook explained the itinerary they had in mind. The party would go first to Turkey, and then travel by way of Armenia and Georgia to Kashmir; after that, through China and back across the Pacific to America. Ultimately they would publish a book describing their discoveries and experiences. It was risky, but Noe was dazzled by the prospect Stanley held up before him: 'He told my parents that he desired to educate me and give me the polish that could best be obtained by intercourse with the world. He told me of diamonds, and rubies, and precious stones, and rich India shawls and other fabrics in Central Asia, the real value of which the natives knew scarcely anything, which could be procured by us for insignificant sums of money, and could be sold at an enormous profit.'

Preparations complete, the party left New York for Boston and set off in a barque, the *E.H. Yarrington*, on July 10, 1866. To cut down costs, they helped to work their passages – which was no new experience for Stanley, although his 'half-brother' later complained of it. After fifty-one days they reached Smyrna (now Izmir), the main port of western Turkey. The entry in Stanley's notebook reads: 'September 3: left Smyrna for interior intending to cross Asia by Tartary and China.' It was not long, however, before these hopes were brought to the ground.

The party set out from Smyrna with two horses; Noe was on foot. The idea of taking a guide was abandoned when a man Stanley had been negotiating with asked too much money. There was a fracas soon after the start when Noe set fire to a hedge for amusement. This annoyed people in a nearby village, and Stanley punished Noe by thrashing him. According to Stanley, he administered a 'few strokes of a switch'. Noe later asserted that Stanley tied him to a tree and lashed him on his bare back for hours, declaring that 'whipping does boys good, whether they have done anything or not'; afterwards Stanley said that Noe had proved that he would be a good companion, by the way he had accepted the beating.

However, the pair seem to have been soon reconciled, and the party plodded on through the mountains in the September heat. Disaster occurred near a village called Chi-Hissar, when Stanley – by his own account – struck the leader of a gang of brigands with a sword for insulting Noe. A dozen Turks then surrounded the adventurers and led them off into captivity. All three were bound up and beaten. To make the position even more desperate, their captors spread the story that the Americans were thieves. Villagers crowded around to spit on Stanley and his colleagues, and throw stones at them.

According to Noe, Stanley had tried to murder an old Turk they met on the highway to steal his two horses; he failed to kill the intended victim – although getting the horses. The Turk then collected a party of friends, who chased the Americans into the mountains and dragged them back to captivity. Noe tells what followed: 'Each day we were drawn up over the limbs of trees by ropes and lariats around our necks to compel us to give them money. At other times they laid our heads on blocks and sharpened knives before us, and by signs made us understand that we must give them money or they would cut our throats.' Eventually the travellers were freed and their tormentors arrested.

Stanley wrote his own version as soon as possible (October 17, 1866) for the English-language paper at Constantinople, the *Levant Herald*. It was done in graphic style, saying unequivocally that he and his colleagues had been attacked and robbed of 'all our money, valuables and clothing', to the tune of about 80,000 piastres (equal to about 3,700 dollars). He goes on to describe the rough treatment when they reached the village of Chi-Hissar, and adds: 'We had instantly acquiesced in all their demands, and were as docile as lambs in their hands, and though when attacked we were armed with the best Sharp's fliers and Colt's revolvers, we had offered no resistance.' The letter goes on to tell how the three were freed with the help of a Mr Peloso, agent of the Ottoman Bank in the area. 'We arrived at Constantinople via Broussa yesterday, to lay our case before the American Minister, through whose influence I hope justice will be meted out to the unbaptized rogues. Hoping you will give this letter a small space in your valuable paper, I remain one of the victimised, HENRY STANLEY.'

In a notebook written by Stanley shortly after the event, the entry for September 18 reads: 'Mr Cook and myself were beaten. Louis a boy of 17 was – – – ' (The final word has been scratched out later.) An unpublished manuscript by Stanley says specifically that Noe was raped, and comments blandly that he 'looked somewhat effeminate'. Later two of the Turks were convicted of sodomy.

At first, however, the sexual affront was of far less significance than the loss of the expedition's goods and property. The American minister to Turkey, Edward Joy Morris, keenly felt his duty to rescue his compatriots from their dilemma: 'If ever the condition of men presented the traces of cruel treatment, theirs did. Mr Stanley's own plight fully corroborated his story.' Morris describes how Stanley reached Constantinople with neither shirt nor socks and was put up for the night at the embassy residence. The next morning, the minister gave him a cheque for £150, without security and any conditions, as a loan. 'I regarded him as a young man of great courage and determination; his countenance showed this, being stern, almost to serenity, but with nothing sinister about it.'

Without being asked to do so, Stanley gave in return a draft for £150 drawn on a completely fictitious 'father' at 20, Liberty Street,

New York. Morris sent the draft to his agent in Philadelphia, who inevitably found out that there was no such person in Liberty Street. The minister is also on record as saying he was told by Stanley that the brigands had stolen a draft for several thousand dollars payable by a merchant in Tiflis – the city for which the expedition had been heading – but he doubted this from the outset.

These facts were given by Morris, with reluctance, several years later, after disclosures by the resentful Noe. According to Noe, he had been sharing a hotel room with Stanley on the night after the valueless draft for £150 had been presented to Morris; Stanley could not sleep. Noe was awoken by his companion, who threatened to kill him unless he signed a statement that he had received one third of the money. Noe claimed he did so, since there was a revolver on the bedroom table beside the document.

The American minister next saw Stanley looking distinguished in 'a kind of semi-navy officer's coat and vest, with gold lace on the sleeve and Turkish buttons . . .' The outfit was made up in Constantinople and Stanley posed for several portraits in it at the studios of Abdullah Brothers, Photographers to His Imperial Majesty the Sultan. The naval uniform may have been suggested to Stanley by the arrival at the Turkish capital of the USS *Ticonderoga*, a steam-powered warship on a world cruise to show the American flag. The *Ticonderoga* had reached Turkey on September 3. (His subsequent claim to have been a member of the crew is disproved by US naval archives.)

Stanley and Noe left Constantinople suddenly, without calling to say farewell to Morris. This puzzled him, and he heard later that they had gone to Broussa, where Cook was awaiting the trial of the robbers.

The Turkish episode is given cursory treatment in all Stanley's writings. His surviving notebooks are evasive. An entry for October 16 simply mentions the return to Constantinople. There is a gap until October 25, when an entry has been made and erased. The last entry says that he and Noe finally left Cook 'at the base of Mount Olympus' and caught a ship to Marseilles.

Weeks later, the case at Broussa was heard. The brigands and rapists were convicted and sentenced. Morris put in a claim for compensation on behalf of the travellers, who had sworn affidavits that their losses totalled 2,000 dollars – a little more than half the figure given by Stanley in the *Levant Herald*. A settlement for 1,200 dollars was agreed. Out of it Morris took his £150, at the suggestion of Cook, then sent the remainder to Cook's address in Illinois. But while the patient diplomat was unravelling these financial tangles, Stanley was showing off his uniform to the citizens of Denbigh.

9. *Wronged Children of the Soil*

On December 14, 1866, a singular entry appeared in the visitor's book at Denbigh Castle, Wales. It read: 'John Rowlands, formerly of this castle, now ensign in the United States Navy in North America, belonging to the U.S. Ship *Ticonderoga* now at Constantinople, Turkey, absent on furlough.'

Henry Stanley had come home in style, to sign his baptismal name for the last time. He was wearing the naval uniform made up in Constantinople and had reached Denbigh in a carriage and pair hired from the Black Lion Hotel, Mold. He was resolved that he would not be greeted with contempt, as had been the case four years earlier. After their arrival in Britain at Newhaven, he and Noe had gone by train to Liverpool. There Noe was left with Thomas and Maria Morris, the relatives Stanley had stayed with while still a youth. Stanley did not want to take his companion to Wales with him: in the first place, he would confuse matters, and in the second they were somewhat estranged. Money was tight, the £150 supplied by the minister in Constantinople having been stretched to its limit, and on November 28 a document was exchanged between the two in which Noe acknowledged having received 'the amount of £27 (Turkish money) and 93 piastres'. According to Noe, a tirade in Welsh was launched against him by Stanley to his relatives – who remonstrated that the young American, not knowing the language, did not have a chance to put his own case. 'Mr Morris is a good kind-hearted man,' decided Noe, who was left kicking his heels throughout Christmas and New Year in Liverpool.

There is little in Stanley's own papers about his activities in Wales. One notebook has the entry: 'November 27, left London for Liverpool.' Following that about half a page is torn out and the next surviving entry is for January 7, 1867. Another version, made up later, has a cryptic note for December 1866: 'Hope Vicarage. George Williams receives Turkish silver filigree cigarette holder. He advises me, "It won't do, you know."' In the posthumous *Autobiography*, Stanley's widow avoids any mention at all of the period between October 1866 and Spring of the following year.

Never commissioned, Stanley had an officer's uniform made and claimed to be a Civil War hero. He gave this photograph to a young friend, Edwin Balch, who wrote the inscription many years later, upon the explorer's death

Dec 14 2/ 1866.

– – – – John Rowlands formerly of this castle, now Ensign in the United States Navy in North America belonging to the US Ship "Ticonderoga" now at Constantinople, Turkey, absent on furlough

In his imposing uniform, Stanley made a dramatic re-appearance in Denbigh in 1866, and signed the castle register with the name by which local people still knew him

After going to see his mother, Stanley visited St Asaph in his uniform. The workhouse children were treated to tea and cakes to celebrate his success in life. Afterwards, he gave a short talk to his young audience, saying he was proud of all he had learnt at the school; they should be equally thankful, and strive to show what they could achieve. The visit was a triumph. One of the workhouse Governors said the ex-pupil came back 'gratefully, and, I may say, gracefully' to return thanks for the kindness he had received. It would appear that Stanley was slightly disappointed, however: he had asked the Governors if he could take a boy back with him to America, but they regretted that there was no suitable lad in the workhouse.

Immediately after the New Year, 1867, Stanley made a journey down to London to see the *New York Herald* representative, Colonel Finlay Anderson. A letter from Anderson dated January 3, 1866 (presumably an error for 1867) shows this meeting was inconclusive; later the two were to have a close friendship. Stanley found it amusing, and perhaps cheering, that Anderson was smaller than himself: 'He is almost a dwarf in stature – and quite two inches shorter than I am and also exceedingly slight in figure.'

On January 8, Stanley was back in Liverpool and re-united with Noe. They had somewhat resolved their differences, for the diary entry for that day records: 'Met Louis and went with him to the museum and library.' At last the two of them sailed for America, but in different ships. A declaration made by the younger man at

Early in 1867, Stanley parted company with Lewis Noe. But he always kept this photograph of Noe at the age of 15

this time says: 'I hereby renounce all claims on Henry Stanley, having made up my mind to work my passage home to New York, receiving clothes in exchange for the passage money.' On January 12, Stanley gave Noe a long letter for his mother, explaining in detail what had happened since the departure from Boston in the previous July. For another two years, he went on sending jovial greetings and photographs of himself to Noe, although they never met again; Noe refused to be mollified, and the repercussions of the ill-starred Turkish expedition were to last for another forty years.

But Stanley could not foresee this. Apart from wondering if he could launch himself on a lecture tour in his Constantinople uniform (which he now announced as being 'the costume of a Turkish naval officer') he was ready to cut his losses and return to where he felt most at home – the territories beyond St Louis. Almost as soon as he had stepped ashore in New York, he bought a train ticket, and by mid-February 1867 was back in Missouri. This moment, when he was just twenty-six, was a watershed in his life.

He was about to obtain his first staff position in journalism, and with it his behaviour was transformed – no longer would he be so feckless, or need to sail quite so close to the wind. Perhaps the colourful, if hazardous, return to Denbigh and the fleeting re-appearance of John Rowlands – a name he had not used for nearly seven years – closed some wound deep in his personality. The cycle of 'mistakes' was over, although into these years had been packed a profusion of experience on land and sea, from Arkansas to Asia Minor. Late in life, Stanley ruminated: 'Looking backward upon the various incidents of these six years, though they appear disjointed enough, I can dimly see a connection, and how one incident led to the other, until the curious and somewhat involved design of my life, and its purpose, was consummated.'

The first job offered to him by the *Democrat* was on a freelance basis, to report the meeting of the Missouri legislature in Jefferson City, to the west of St Louis. Covering the assembly for the rival *Missouri Republican* was a veteran civil war reporter, William Fayel. They quickly became friends and some years later Fayel was to write Stanley to reminisce about the disaster of Stanley's attempt to lecture in Jefferson City. He wrote: (August 19, 1872) 'You recollect that cold, bleak February night, when you made your advent to the Tennessee House – full of your lecture on Turkey, and about twenty dollars worth of printed tickets of admission – most of which in a fit of disgust you consigned to the stove . . .' The exuberant notices put out by Stanley describe him as 'The American Traveller' and said that he had taken a grand tour through Asia Minor, where he had been cruelly robbed and stripped of all his possessions, letters of credit and more than 4,000 dollars in cash. During the lecture he would wear a Turkish naval officer's uniform, display a Saracenic coat of mail, needlework by a Turkish maiden, a whetstone from Mount Olympus, and much else besides. Moreover, he promised to repeat the Moslem call to prayer, in Arabic, and to close the 'exercise of the evening' by singing a Turkish song. The lecture-goers of Jefferson City were not impressed – when the great American traveller mounted the platform, he faced an audience of 'four deadheads and four who had paid.'

Soon he was far removed from the scene of this humiliation. He had been given an assignment at fifteen dollars a week and expenses to report the campaign by General Winfield Scott Hancock, with 1,500 men – the biggest army seen in the West for twenty years – against the Indians in Kansas and Nebraska. This was Stanley's true début as a correspondent. At last his writing becomes identifiable – his *Democrat* despatches are signed off 'Stanley' or with an 'S' – and it is possible to trace the workings of his mind as he is confronted with the complex Indian problem. It was basically a racial issue, and Stanley's experiences in April–November 1867 were to have a bearing on many of his attitudes in later life.

America was in an imperialistic, expansionist phase in the 1860's. The Indians stood in the way of the railroad (destined to span the continent by 1869), of the Civil War veterans taking up their rights to land in the West, and all the concepts of material civilisation. General Phil Sheridan, a commander in the Indian wars, put it succinctly: 'We took away their country and their means of support, broke up their mode of living, their habits of life, introduced disease and decay among them, and it was for this and against this that they made war. Could anyone expect less?' But much more common was the sentiment expressed by the Topeka *Weekly Leader* (June 27, 1867): '. . . a set of miserable, dirty, lousy, blanketed, thieving, lying, sneaking, murdering, graceless, faithless, gut-eating skunks as the Lord ever permitted to infect the earth, and whose immediate and final extermination all men, except Indian agents and traders, should pray for . . .'

Stanley found Hancock after going first to Solomon City, Kansas, and then to the general's headquarters on the Saline River, where he was given a friendly welcome. He had the advantage of being the only newspaper correspondent with the expedition in its early stages, but there was one journalistic companion – the artist Theodore R. Davis, of *Harper's Weekly*. Both of them caught up with the expedition at the same time, and had to struggle through a blizzard to reach

Fort Zarah. They joined forces, working in the evenings over their despatches and sketches by the light of a candle or the camp fire. In his unpublished memoirs, Davis, recollected how the *Democrat* correspondent was equipped: 'Stanley's outfit, a thoroughly sensible one, made him a sufficiently characteristic figure to attract attention, but not to occasion remark – from the loose-fitting blue felt cap, with its reversible band for ear protection – to the stout rawhide boots such as lumbermen wear . . . and the ample blue-black overcoat with a cloak for a cape, completed what was usually visible of Stanley's costume.' Davis recalled that he rode a big 'sorrel nag' and used a simple snaffle bit with a short rein.

The two newspapermen had several private adventures during the expedition. One arose from the flight of some deserters who stole, among other things, Stanley's saddle blanket. The idea of chasing the deserters with the help of 'Wild Bill' Hickok was suggested by the irate reporter. 'Wild Bill' was a dandified freebooter who travelled the plains in a scarlet jacket and black velvet trousers. The pursuers set out at midnight with a party of army scouts and after riding 12 miles found the deserters lying drunk in an abandoned adobe house. At Stanley's suggestion the captives were brought back in single file at the end of lariats. The incident raised the young reporter in the eyes of Hancock and the other senior officers. Later, Davis went hunting for rattlesnakes, which he and his colleague ostentatiously fried and ate.

Davis studied Stanley's characteristics. One he noticed was an ability to copy any style of handwriting after seeing it for only a few moments. Another was his ability to ride all night without tiring. He summed him up as 'methodical and indefatigable'.

Stanley's earliest despatches display his jocularity at its worst. The first, on April 2 from Fort Harker, Kansas, ends with a laboured compliment to the wisdom of readers of the *Missouri Democrat*, and says: 'In the meantime, assure them of the deep respect we entertain for them as a body, and should anything else turn up in these hyperborean regions, they shall hear it.' In another message he offers a joke about scalping: 'It is a horrible sight and the operation is one, we earnestly hope, will never be performed on our worthy self. While writing, we assure you our scalp is intact, but how long it will remain so we cannot as yet inform you . . .'

He dilated on the 'savagery' of the Indians, and asked emotive rhetorical questions: 'Are delicate women to be carried by the remorseless savage to his wigwam to be sold to vile bondage and for other purposes for which we have no name?' Step by step, however, his despatches began to show understanding and sympathy – which he had never felt for the Negro slaves in New Orleans. Early in the campaign, Colonel Custer (later to gain immortality for his Last Stand) chased a party of Cheyenne Indians, failed to catch them, and burnt down a nearby village. Stanley saw no sense in it. Gradually his sympathies turned, until he captured a memorable phrase to epitomise his view of the Indians: 'These wronged children of the soil.'

The massive expedition led by Hancock completely failed to solve the Indian problem in Kansas and Colorado. No effective treaties were concluded, and only four Redskins were killed – two of them being 'friendlies' shot by accident. Stanley made the most of it by colourful reporting and liberal theorising. It seems that the nearest he came to action was meeting a delegation of Cheyennes, including Chief Big Mouth, who had helped to massacre eighty-one soldiers in the previous December. After his account of the pow-wow at Fort Laramie with Big Mouth, he tacks on a ponderous comment to gratify the many Irish immigrant readers of the *Democrat*: 'Were these people on English territory, every reader could foresee their fate; but, forsooth, the leading civilised nation of the world must treat them with forbearance. So be it.'

As the expedition ground to a halt, Stanley was in Omaha, which he had last visited after his journey down the Platte River with Cook in early 1866. This time he had the opportunity to pause for a few days, whereupon he fell in with a theatrical group and became enamoured of a comedienne named Annie Ward. Together with two other suitors, Esterbrook and Bird, he arranged a benefit performance for Annie at Corri's music hall in Omaha. According to his notebook, the plans were made on July 1, but the performance did not happen until the 26th. Between those dates, Stanley went down the Missouri to St Louis to be given further orders by the *Democrat*. He had done well with the rather aimless Hancock campaign, his despatches appearing nearly every day and sometimes filling almost two columns; some were passed on to East Coast papers, since the great migration of settlers across the plains and the resistance of the Indians was a major domestic topic. Stanley's energy and journalistic fluency is reflected in the way he was independently filing stories to papers in Chicago and Cincinnati.

His success was in harmony with the optimism of St Louis at that moment. The city's confidence was limitless. Nobody asked too many questions about the next man's past, in case he might be asked about his own. Among Stanley's journalistic contemporaries was Joseph Pulitzer, of subsequent 'Pulitzer Prize' fame. One incident in which he was involved exactly captures the mood of Missouri at the end of the 1860's – the atmosphere which gave free rein to Stanley's impetuosity and shaped his style of journalism. Pulitzer fell out with a Captain Augustine in Jefferson City in January 1870, and below the headline 'Pulitzer as Shootist' a report in the *St Louis Despatch* by one Wallace Gruelle reads:

'Tonight, at about half past seven o'clock, Mr Pulitzer shot at and wounded Mr Augustine in the office of the Schmidt Hotel. It appears that Mr Pulitzer – and by the way, I am on Pulitzer's side, not because he is a newspaper man, but because he is a clever, affable gentleman, whose portrait I intend to paint some day, and he voted right on the Richland county bill – had sent an article to the *Westliche Post*, at which Mr Augustine took offense and mildly told Mr Pulitzer he was a liar. Mr Pulitzer cautioned Mr Augustine against using such strong language. Mr Pulitzer left the hotel and got a pistol and returned and went for Mr Augustine. Had not his pistol been knocked down, Missouri would have been in mourning this day for a loyal slaughtered son. As it was, only two shots were fired, one of which took effect in Mr Augustine's leg. Augustine struck Pulitzer on the head with a Derringer, or some other kind of pistol, cutting his scalp and ending the battle. Mr Pulitzer was arrested and given bond for his appearance before the City Magistrate in Jefferson City.' The penalty was a hundred-dollar fine.

Back in Omaha, Stanley did his share of fighting. The benefit of Annie Ward duly took place, and the lovestruck reporter hid a bouquet under his coat and threw it on to the stage, only to have Annie kick it back into the stalls. The incident amused the Irish editor of the *Nebraska Watchman*, F. W. MacDonough, who wrote a satirical piece on it. Stanley went to 'Little Mac's' office and started a fight. He gave his version of the dispute some years later: 'This local editor had me brought up before the mayor, Charles Brown, for assault and battery. The jury returned a verdict of "Not Guilty" and "Little Mac", besides suffering the indignity of a vigorous kicking in his rearward parts, was compelled to pay costs.'

MacDonough had his own interpretation. He regarded Stanley

as an 'illiterate and cheeky Bohemian fraud' and a 'romantic deadbeat' who had lain in wait for him in a store and assaulted him in a 'cowardly manner'. He claimed that his foe was always afraid to meet him face to face, and was far too busy chasing women to do his job properly as a correspondent.

The romance with Annie Ward did not go well. Among Stanley's papers is a letter from her (August 14, 1867) notable for its simple honesty. She declines to go out on a picnic party to the 'Bluffs' with him, saying that she cannot accept any invitations from gentlemen. Annie thanks him for the poetry he had written about her, and cannot resist asking if he will publish it anywhere. The verses to Annie do not survive, but judging by his later poetic efforts there is little to lament.

The wooing of Annie Ward and the brush with 'Little Mac' were only diversions from the business of reporting the Indian troubles. Stanley was being sent back West by the *Democrat* to follow a Peace Commission headed by Nathaniel G. Taylor, a Methodist minister, and having among its six members General William Sherman. Stanley watched the performance of Sherman on the Peace Commission with some distaste, recording how he mixed paternal advice to the chiefs with cajolery and threats: 'When they submitted to Sherman they were compelled to do so, for the naked law of force was apparent in his every gesture and articulation.'

The man who made the deepest impression upon Stanley was Governor Andrew Jackson Faulk of Dakota, a lawyer who for his day had progressive views on how Indians should be treated. Faulk thought that many of the conflicts on the plains sprang from white intolerance. Stanley quoted him at length in despatches to the *Democrat* and a variety of other papers. Echoing Faulk, he advocated the bringing together of the Indians in one vast reservation, where they could be taught the skills of stable agriculture, be educated and christianised. He even suggested that the Indians should be granted US citizenship and the right to vote; it would mean they must pay taxes, but these might be taken off the annuities they were entitled to for surrendering their lands to settlers.

It is a sign of Stanley's widening horizons that he was able to deploy such arguments, and to draw comparisons with other racial dilemmas: 'We know that if the red man could have been enslaved, he would have been before this; but there was a free spirit in his nature which made it impossible; he could die, but he could not be enslaved . . . Every man on the frontier goes armed because the Indian is a wild beast and must be shot. So every man went armed down South because they had slaves, and the slaves might rise.'

The first stage in the Peace Commission's work was sailing up and down the Missouri in a steamer, looking for suitable reservation sites. It would seem that Stanley left the party for a while at Omaha, with one of his old colleagues from the *Missouri Republican*, William Fayel. Years later, Fayel recalled that Stanley had there given him a book called *The Footprints of Travellers;* it was a popular, two-volume account of exploration in all parts of the world. No time was wasted in Omaha, however, for Stanley had an appointment in the small settlement of Julesburg, Colorado, to give a lecture. According to his private notebook, he talked on 'The Irish in the United States' – a topic which would have gone down well with many of the labourers on the Union Pacific Railway; at the time when he spoke, the rail-head was between Julesburg and Cheyenne, 150 miles farther west.

The Peace Commissioners travelled up the Union Pacific to the Platte River, and Stanley watched them negotiate in October with 4,000 Comanches, Arapahoes, Apaches and Kiowas at Medicine Lodge Creek, Kansas. He was critical of the behaviour of the army, and remarked that soldiers tended to talk to the Indians in 'a tone which is extremely galling'. He spoke with pity about the dignified but hopeless pleas of the chiefs and grew indignant about the partiality of justice in the West: 'If a white man shot an Indian, what law touched him – what power tried him for the offence and made him pay the penalty for his murderous deeds? It was as if he had shot a buffalo. Nothing was done, nothing was thought of it. And the red man, to make matters straight killed the first white man he came across, took interest in the shape of stock and called the account settled. Immediately a cry went up to heaven . . .'

The peak of Stanley's performance was his coverage of the Medicine Lodge peace councils, which was being reported by ten other journalists, including a group from New York, Cincinnati and Chicago. He turned this rivalry to advantage by giving character sketches of the men in the Press tent, and engaged in light-hearted mockery of the debates among them: 'The romantic members giving full rein to their vivid imagination, soar away on eagle's pinions beyond the ethereal dome above, and come down again gently gliding, sailing over regions unknown to the dull few until they alight on mother earth, and find themselves only in the Press tent, but still admired by the wondering crowd around.' He attempts everything in his despatches, sometimes being ungrammatical and using adjectives with a wrong meaning, but always sweeping his sentences fluently on. His readers are offered a phonetic rendering of Indian speech, taken down in shorthand, and even fragments of private dialogue between the commissioners – as when two generals have been shaking hands with chiefs, and Stanley overhears them afterwards:

'Well, by God, I am glad that this wearisome task is over.'

'So am I.'

'Let's go and wash our hands.'

'I wonder if these fellows have got the itch.'

'Gad, shouldn't wonder.'

Stanley gives his despatches variety with word-pictures of the women who appear at Medicine Lodge. One is an Indian interpreter, who wears a crimson petticoat, black cloak, and 'a small coquettish velvet hat, decorated with a white ostrich feather'. A colonel's daughter named Julia Bent catches his interest: 'She is of medium height, and rather coarse features, but has a charming, ringing laugh . . . her feet are of the most diminutive size, and a peep at her trim ankles might drive an anchorite insane . . . She is about fifteen years old.'

Yet, however much he might be interested in everyone else, Stanley never forgot to keep himself in the reader's eye. When he had a cup of coffee he praised it as 'even excelling in my opinion the best Mocha I ever drank in an Egyptian khan.' He recalled how 'graphically and distinctly' the Hancock expedition had been reported by the 'special correspondent Stanley'. He was never afraid of the first person singular, or of airing his opinions.

He expressed outrage that the Sioux had been persuaded to sell their land in Minnesota and then never been paid for it. Such double-dealing by the government led only to bloodshed and continuing distrust. Stanley ended his last despatch to the *Democrat* on November 21, 1867, with a prophetic paragraph: 'Now, what have the Commission accomplished? There were only two nations at war, the Cheyennes and Sioux. With the Cheyennes, a much inferior nation to the Sioux, we have made peace – or truce rather – but the Sioux, the most formidable and numerous, still remain defiant.' More than twenty years later, this failure to reach any accord with the Sioux was to have its last and most bitter sequel, just north of where Stanley was writing, at a place called Wounded Knee.

For all his theorising, Stanley was adroit enough to maintain a proper leaven of 'colour' and racy dialogue. Once the *Democrat* carried three of his despatches on the same day. He worked in the beat of tom-toms, the war dances, a train ambush, and the fierce behaviour of small Indian boys. He was fast learning the professionalism with which to exploit his innate flair for writing.

Such exuberant material did not pass unnoticed in the offices of the leading American dailies. Stanley had already been mailing overtures in several directions. Early in 1867 he wrote to Horace Greeley of the *New York Tribune*, asking for a job – after all, he had certainly obeyed Greeley's advice to 'Go West'; but there was a rather stiff rejection from the managing editor. So Stanley turned his attention to the all-conquering *New York Herald*, to which he was already contributing as a freelance. He felt confident enough in early December to resign from the *Democrat* and take a train East. He had a bold proposition for the *Herald*.

10. A Coup in Abyssinia

While Stanley was travelling the plains of America, he managed to keep track of affairs in the Near East. He wanted to go back there, despite his ignominious retreat from Turkey in the autumn of 1866. Putting aside the thought of a journey to China in the footsteps of Marco Polo, he looked for some exciting event to report. At first, his attention was taken with a threat of war in Crete between the Turks and the Greeks. Then came news of British preparations to invade Abyssinia; Stanley felt sure this would take the fancy of the *New York Herald*. He asked them to send him to cover the campaign.

Abyssinia was the legendary domain of Prester John, a brave Christian defying his Muslim enemies from a mountain fastness near the Nile. The country did indeed have a Christian ruler, the Emperor Theodore, and it was against him that the British were going to war. By the time Stanley made his proposal to the *Herald* in the middle of December, a military advance party had already landed on the western shore of the Red Sea.

The problem which Victorian England was about to settle, with the most majestic invading army that Africa had known since the days of Imperial Rome, was essentially ludicrous. Yet in it lay the seeds of tragedy; for Theodore, who now must be made to kneel, had in him a half-demented greatness. Twelve years earlier, when Theodore had fought his way to the mastery of most of Ethiopia, he had been regarded by the European powers – in as far as they regarded him at all – as quite enlightened. Missionaries went in, and Britain even opened up diplomatic relations; Queen Victoria presented Theodore with a pair of engraved pistols.

It was in 1862 that the skies of amity clouded over, and although the Emperor was by this time growing slightly erratic through an excess of drink and women, the British were really more at fault. Theodore sent a letter, awash with Christian piety to Victoria, ending with a request that she might receive his envoys in London. In the course of his message Theodore explained that by the power of God he had killed all his enemies, even if they were members of his own family, and was now preparing to wrestle with the Turks, who refused to leave the land of his ancestors. Perhaps Theodore's sentiments and phraseology were thought in Whitehall to be somewhat droll. The overture was ignored.

As Stanley puts it: 'The letter arrived in England safely in February, 1863; was received by Earl Russell, opened, read, thrown upon the table, docketed, and in the pigeon-hole it rested.' Six months later there was no reply, and the emperor displayed his ire by throwing the British consul, Captain Charles Cameron in jail. Three months later, the British letter came but said nothing about envoys. So Cameron stayed in jail, where he was joined by the French consul and more than twenty white missionaries, male and female, with several children. At times they were put in chains, and listened to Ethiopian prisoners being tortured to death in neighbouring cells.

Efforts at diplomacy were slow and unrewarding: Theodore grew ever more suspicious, his reasoning became chaotic, and by now he ruled Ethiopia through fiendish atrocities. He refused to free Consul Cameron or any of the missionaries. So in the middle of 1867, Britain declared war.

The interest of the *New York Herald* in all this was slight. There was no denying that Abyssinia was remote and little-known; in fact, so remote and little-known that the American reader cared nothing for it. Stanley's proposal was discouragingly received by a sardonic young man, about his own age, who was just taking over control of the paper from his father. The son, James Gordon Bennett Jr, was already renowned as a debauchee; he belonged to the New York 'fast set' which produced Jennie Jerome, who was to be the mother of Winston Churchill.

If Stanley wanted to go to Abyssinia, said Bennett, then he must cover his own expenses and write exclusively for the *Herald*. He would be paid by results, and if he did well there was every prospect of a staff job. Stanley accepted the offer: his writing in the West had been so successful that he had managed to save up 3,000 dollars, and 1,000 would see him through the Abyssinian venture. He knew that he and the *Herald* were made for one another – the paper attracted him to the extent that he often falsely claimed to have represented it while in Turkey.

There was no time to lose. On December 22, he was aboard a fast steamer bound for Liverpool. Stanley spent Christmas at sea, as he had ten years earlier in the sailing ship *Windermere* on the way to New Orleans.

After landing in Britain, he caught a train to London and called on Colonel Anderson, the *Herald* representative. He used the paper's office in St Martin's le Grand as his base as he hurried around buying equipment for Abyssinia. He was not much impressed with London in the January weather, but wrote in his diary: 'Nevertheless, I cannot forget that I am also one of the breed, and despite the bad impressions which a cold day begets, I feel it would take little to renew my affection for them.' On January 3 he went to the East End to look for his half-sister Emma, who had been working in the Mile End Road, 'but I find she has returned to Wales'.

Travelling by way of Paris and Marseilles, he reached Suez – at the northern end of the Red Sea – towards the end of January. Hotels were crowded with officers and civilians eager to catch up with the main force advancing on Theodore. The campaign was proving a magnet for archaeologists, botanists and geographers; they had pioneering work to do in the Abyssinian mountains. Stanley hired a servant and bought a horse, then applied for a passage in the next ship to the landing-place at Annesley Bay. To his alarm, he was told that he could not travel there without proper accreditation. The War Office would have no truck with unknown Yankee journalists. He suffered further because while he might be unknown, his paper was not – the *Herald* had an international notoriety; as the novelist Anthony Trollope observed: 'It has an enormous sale, but so far is it from having achieved popularity that no man on any side ever speaks a good word for it.'

Stanley sent a telegram to Finlay Anderson in London, and sat down in his hotel to wait. Anderson proved to have good contacts in Whitehall, and approval for Stanley to join the Press corps in Abyssinia came back by wire. While he was calling at the Suez telegraph office, he worked out a discreet arrangement which was to put the British correspondents at some disadvantage. He gave a large bribe to the head telegraphist, to ensure that his despatches would go first. In America, after all, you would have been thought half-witted to leave such matters to bureaucratic chance.

His dispositions complete, Stanley made his way to Annesley Bay, intent on overtaking the army led by Sir Robert Napier. He was to witness a masterpiece of military logistics.

General Napier was not a man to tackle Theodore with inadequate forces. Britain had found few chances for fighting since the Crimea and the Indian Mutiny, so there was a glut of well-born officers anxious to show their valour in the Ethiopian wilds. Napier had spent most of his army life in India and China, which had given him a chance for action, so he was as indulgent as possible. If Stanley thought he had seen something when Hancock went after Indians with 1,500 men, he was to be stunned by war in the British manner. The force deployed in Abyssinia had 520 officers, 13,600 soldiers, 26,000 'followers', 44 elephants, 16,000 mules, 4,700 camels, 2,500 horses, and 20,000 sheep and bullocks for food. This horde of men and beasts had been put ashore on a sun-parched beach by an armada of ships.

For his part Stanley travelled light, the way he had been taught in the West. This did not satisfy the commissariat officers who received him. They said he needed six horses and four servants, otherwise 'people would only look down on him'. Stanley relates this first encounter with a skilful irony. But it may be that people did look down on him somewhat, sleeping in the open with his Colorado buffalo robe around him and wandering off on sorties of his own. One of the officers branded Stanley a 'howling cad'. He was given the rather apt nickname 'Jefferson Brick', after a character in Charles Dickens's *Martin Chuzzlewit*. In the novel, Brick was a war correspondent for an American paper called the *Rowdy Journal*, and was described as a 'small young gentleman of very juvenile appearance' who was intent upon achieving worldwide fame.

In return, Stanley mocked the foibles of the British officers, their elaborate modes of speech and flamboyant uniforms. He describes a parade: 'The officers wore silver helmets on their heads. Behind the cavalry regiment came Sir Robert Napier and Sir Charles Staveley, attended by their respective staffs, well dressed and well mounted. A good deal of effeminacy was visible here which detracted much from their otherwise martial bearing. One young lordling wore kid gloves and a green veil.' He had some decidedly bleak exchanges before he was able to meet Napier – who thereupon treated him in a quizzical but amiable way and invited him to dinner with a distinguished gathering of officers.

Sir Robert (later Lord Napier) had a slyly humorous face, in the craggy Scottish style, and was nearly sixty; he had recently lost his first wife and married again to a girl in her teens. Stanley liked him: 'What a charming old gentleman!' he jotted in his diary. Yet it must have been a somewhat unnerving experience for Stanley, with his Welsh background, to pass himself off in such company as an American born and bred.

He also had an awkward time with the Press corps; 'I was made to feel that, though a journalist like themselves, an American journalist was not of such fine clay as a Briton of the same profession . . . There was no great harm that a number of English Pressmen should make merry at my expense, but had an English correspondent visited an American Press tent, the American who should have ventured to ridicule England and her institutions, would have been shamed to silence.' In his published writings, however, he muffles this anger: 'The English Press was very ably represented in Abyssinia . . . I give them the credit of being the most sociable mess in the army, as well as the most loveable and good-tempered.'

He takes his readers through the campaign with expertise, stage by stage. The army comes to Magdala at last and the fighting is brief – for the soldiers whose loyalty was still with Theodore were no match for the weapons and tactics of the invaders. The fortress is taken, Theodore commits suicide and Consul Cameron, with all the other prisoners, is freed. The British losses have totalled less than forty, mostly from dysentery; of the eleven officers who died, two were accidentally drowned, one committed suicide and one had apoplexy.

Stanley's moment to show what a Yankee journalist could do had now arrived. After hurriedly buying some souvenirs – including a strip of Theodore's bloodstained shirt – he made a dash for the coast; his British rivals followed at a more gentlemanly pace. To catch the first ship up the Red Sea from Annesley Bay he had to risk going through a torrent – an incident brilliantly realised in the book he was to write about the campaign.

Bodies of men, oxen, mules and horses are swept by in the raging storm-waters which have suddenly filled a ravine. There seems no chance to cross and live – then the rain slows and Stanley and his servant Ali decide to make a dash for the opposite bank. A mule is drowned, Ali gets through, then Stanley prepares to spur his Arab horse, Sayed, into the torrent: 'Now, I am a capital rider on a smooth, level prairie, or even on an Abyssinian road; but it is quite a different thing to leap a horse into a deep pool of water from a height, and it was with considerable misgiving that I mounted him . . .'

But he survived (and later sent Sayed to the Gordon Bennett stables in America). He caught his ship, and reached Suez in company with Colonel Millward, who had the official despatches – and the reports of the British journalists – in his bag. But at Suez, because of a cholera outbreak, the ship was put in quarantine for five days; Stanley smuggled ashore a long report of the capture of Magdala and the death of Theodore – and addressed a covering note to his friend, the head of the telegraph office. 'I do not think Colonel Millward sent anything on shore', he wrote in his notebook, 'and if so I shall be ahead yet'. He was very well ahead, and when his report was received in London, passed on to the *Herald* in New York and then relayed back, there was general confusion and doubt. The British Government had not had a single word from Napier about the outcome of the expedition.

More astonishments were to follow. When the quarantine was over, Stanley hurried ashore with further despatches. They were again, for the obvious reason, given precedence over Millward's official messages and the reports of the British correspondents. If that were not enough, the cable line suddenly broke down between Alexandria and Malta, so that just after the last 'take' of Stanley's deliberately spun-out copy had gone, silence fell again. All the other despatches had to travel on from Alexandria to Malta by ship and could only then be telegraphed. By this time, Stanley had gone off to Cairo – knowing he had done well, but never guessing at first just how well. The *Herald* was being accused of the blatant invention of news when the official messages from Napier were released by Whitehall, confirming all the details the paper had long since published.

Stanley had made very sure of his staff position, and waited in Egypt for further orders. In his private journal he wrote: 'Alexandria, June 28, 1868. I am now a permanent employee of the *Herald*, and must keep a sharp look-out that my second coup shall be as much of a success as the first.'

11. *Two Loves Lost*

Stanley was made to earn his £400 a year as a staff correspondent for the *Herald*. From the middle of 1868 to the autumn of 1869 he was kept constantly on the move. Paris, Madrid, London, Athens, Cairo, Aden . . . He led what he called 'a life of railway celerity', and declared that pleasure could never deflect from his aims. Some of the traits which manifested themselves in his earlier, desperate years were to serve him well in journalism. He was quick to see an opening, ruthlessly competitive, and eager to make an impression.

While passing through Egypt in the New Year of 1869 he met a wealthy Philadelphian named Balch, whose home was in Paris at 48 Avenue Gabriel, near the Concorde. Balch was taken with Stanley's verve and gave him a letter of introduction to his family. When Stanley called at the Avenue Gabriel at the end of February he found there was a son, Edwin, aged thirteen, who spoke good French and was only too willing to show him the sights of the capital. Edwin was much impressed by the romantic tales this new friend of the family poured out. The admiring letters he wrote show Stanley led him to believe he had 'run away from college' before plunging into a life of adventure, and that his dream was to spend two years exploring Central Asia.

Every morning in the last days of February 1869, Stanley would wait in the foyer of the Hôtel du Louvre, where he was staying, to be collected by Edwin for visits to such places as Vincennes, Versailles and St Cloud. They also went to the Louvre and Notre Dame; Balch later recalled Stanley's intense interest in 'Le Stryge' – a gruesome portrayal of a vampire. At the end of a week, Stanley had to go on to London. As a parting gift he gave his youthful guide two books, and the inscription in one is significant. It reads: 'To my dear young friend Edwin, from Henry Morelake Stanley, February 27, 1869.' Stanley was just beginning to assume a second Christian name and was experimenting with Morelake, Moreland and Morley, before settling on Morton. Six months earlier he was simply calling himself 'Henry Stanley'. There was a further sign of self-assurance

As he achieved success as a journalist, Stanley became more sure of himself. But he had a fondness for adopting disguises

in the inscription: he now underlined his name with an exuberant flourish. Another memento he gave Edwin was a photograph showing him in the uniform made in Constantinople in 1866; he told Edwin he had worn it during the naval attack on Fort Fisher in 1865.

Edwin replaced Lewis Noe in his regard at about this time. For the past two years, Stanley had made a point of posting Noe a New Year greeting. In 1868 he had sent one saying effusively: 'To brother Louis, primer of boys and best of companions – a Happy

166

> *To my dear Young friend*
> *Edwin*
> *from*
> *Henry Morelake Stanley*
> *Feb₇ 2ᵈ 1869*

For several years he tried out various middle names, before settling upon 'Morton'

New Year to you, Louis and a hundred more of the same sort. In your rejoicings, forget not the exiled friend and brother, Henry.' At the start of 1869 he had sent a letter and photograph from Somaliland, inscribed: 'Still your friend – Khan Bahadoor, alias Stanley.' In the photograph, he was wearing a turban and Turkish costume, and in front of him was a small Negro boy and behind him an old man; but Noe did not respond – he still bore a grudge for having received no financial compensation for his tribulations in Asia Minor. Stanley never wrote to him again, and instead began a correspondence with Balch.

After the farewell in Paris, Stanley hurried over to London for a briefing. There was every likelihood of prolonged civil war in Spain, and he must go to Madrid, as chief of the bureau, by the end of March. But before he set off there were family duties to observe, and he at last felt able to take his mother and half-sister Emma on holiday. His success in life had now made him the family hero, and he was proud to have their admiration. What could be better than to display his newly acquired familiarity with Paris?

It must have been with no small amount of trepidation that his mother got herself ready in Denbigh, and then caught the train to

London with Emma. They were met at Paddington station by Henry (as they must now call him) and went with him to his hotel near the Strand. Then all three crossed over to France from Dover.

Spring was just bringing the trees of Paris into leaf and every vista was a subject for delight. These were the dying months of the Third Empire, with its brittle gaiety, and Stanley wrote in his journal: 'Mother is in raptures with Paris – the life on the boulevards, the Bois and the Imperial Palaces.' He noted the insistent maternal advice he received about care in choosing a wife – French women might be pretty enough and some might even be wealthy, but he should not let them steal his affections. 'She does not scruple to exaggerate the virtue of British girls . . .' It is likely that he had told his mother of his involvement in the previous year with Virginia Ambella, a Greek girl to whom he had been introduced on the island of Syra. Marriage had been seriously discussed, and Stanley was for a while eager at the prospect; in the end the Ambella family postponed the wedding plans because they knew too little about their daughter's suitor, and Stanley slipped away from Greece, never to return.

His mother was keen that Stanley should take a bride who would restore his links with Wales. She may have had a share in presenting him with a possibility in this direction shortly after the holiday. He was called upon at his London hotel by Thomas Gough-Roberts, a retired Denbigh solicitor whose daughter Katie had made some impression on Stanley during a visit home in the previous autumn. She was buxom and fair-haired; Gough-Roberts declared that if there was a mutual attraction, he would have no objection to the marriage. Indeed, Katie was an heiress and would bring to the union a considerable fortune. In his journal, Stanley mentions £1,000, and admits that he was strangely flattered to find a professional man who knew all about him yet regarded him as a suitable son-in-law. '. . . When a well-to-do solicitor of one's native town is so frank and so good-natured as to be oblivious of St Asaph, it must be that he thinks more highly of me than I can persuade myself to do.' Thomas Gough-Roberts knew about Stanley's background for the very good reason that Emma was a maid in his house. But he must also have known, as one of Denbigh's small circle of lawyers, the gossip about barrister James Vaughan Horne and his possible role in Stanley's parentage. After Katie's father had left, Stanley wondered if this was not the hand of Fate, trying to overwhelm his reserve and awkwardness with women. But as he made notes of the interview in his journal he kept his journalistic sharpness: Gough-Roberts looked as though he drank far too heavily.

On the morning of Easter Sunday, March 22, 1869, Stanley sat down and wrote to Katie a letter nearly 2,000 words long. It is gauche in places, boastful and untruthful in others; but it gives a window into his innermost thoughts, showing how deeply scarred he was by his origins. He begins by telling her that he is glad 'arrangements have been made' – presumably referring to his interview with her father – so they could carry on a correspondence that would be neither 'illicit nor secret'. There was no need for them to be hasty, but he had to confess that when he first saw her he was struck with admiration 'and this admiration begot something warmer, and this something warmer begot another deeper and more lasting feeling'.

He then starts to flounder about woefully, as he braces himself to tell Katie his life story. He plunges in:

'I am the illegitimate child of Elizabeth Parry and John Rowland of the Digs. I was a waif cast into the world, treated as circumstances developed themselves. Neither of my parents ever deigned to take the slightest notice of me . . .' He then goes on to give a fairly accurate account of his early years, until the point where he is put into the workhouse. 'This waif now became a burden, an annual expense (the amount of which is just one-tenth the sum I yearly expend on choice Havannahs); the waif must be got rid of, but how? What a pity he did not die . . .'

He then relates his experiences in the workhouse, the years at Tremeirchion, the pawning of all his possessions in Liverpool, and the trip to New Orleans in the *Windermere*. He recounts his adoption by Henry Stanley senior, his work as a clerk in Arkansas, and his enlistment with the Confederates. At this point he cannot resist claiming he had been promoted to orderly sergeant by the Confederate Army, and that he escaped from a Federal jail by swimming a river under fire 'on an awful night'. He lays the bravado on even heavier when he comes to relate his service in the Federal Navy, saying that he had been promoted to an ensign at Fort Fisher by swimming under fire to put a rope on a rebel ship. Then comes an account of his first successful return home in 1866. 'He had £5,000 in the bank and a farm of 140 acres in Omaha. Stanley's mother was very happy to see him now. Everybody else was; they were proud to see him because he was well dressed and a gentleman and an officer of the United States Navy.' Next he gives a broadly accurate account of his progress as a journalist, although rather ambitiously claiming that he is known 'all over America' as a traveller, gentleman and author.

He rounds off his autobiography by declaring: 'This waif – this boy Rowlands – this Stanley, is he who addresses you now. I assure you that he is very ambitious, and means, God willing, to rise to some notoriety before he dies. He could do better if he had a wife, not a pretty, doll-faced wife, but a woman educated, possessed of energy; there is no more wanted with her but herself; along with her aid and encouraging presence of a woman of such attainments I would defy the world . . .' He adds a postscript: 'Tell me how I must address you, Miss Roberts is so formal, almost unkind. Address me by my name, Henry.'

Having despatched this letter, he packed his possessions and started off once more for Spain. Notwithstanding all his other preoccupations, he was to send Katie letters and signed photographs with great frequency – sometimes as often as twice a week.

His reporting of the civil war in Spain was of the highest calibre. Sometimes finding little time for sleep, he raced about the country from one trouble-spot to another. His despatches captured not just the action – they also showed insight and compassion, especially when he described a desperate battle at Saragossa of which he was the only independent eye-witness. He was moved by the heroism of the anti-Government fighters, going down to inevitable defeat: '. . . they appeared like characters suddenly called out to perform in some awful tragedy; and, so fascinated was I by the strange and dreadful spectacle, I could not look away.'

His virtuosity was not being missed by Douglas A. Levien, the *Herald's* new bureau chief in London (Finlay Anderson had returned to the United States). On July 12, 1869 he wrote a significant letter to Stanley: 'Mr Bennett Jr arrived at Queenstown in his yacht the *Dauntless* on Sunday afternoon after an unexampled run of 12 days 17 hours across the Atlantic. He will be in town I hope in a few days and I have then a proposition to make to him which I think you may like. I will not mention it, however, until I have learnt his views, in case it should end in a disappointment.' About this time Stanley had a letter from Edwin Balch, mentioning the conflicting newspaper reports about the fate of David Livingstone. One of these said he was

James Gordon Bennett inherited one of America's biggest newspapers. He sent Stanley to find Livingstone

at Zanzibar; another quoted Sir Roderick Murchison, president of the Royal Geographical Society, as forecasting that the long-lost explorer was intending to cross Africa along the line of the Equator. Nine months before, Stanley had spent several weeks waiting in vain at Aden, when it was rumoured that Livingstone was 'returning to civilisation'.

It is not clear whether he had troubled to keep abreast of the Livingstone saga during his busy months in Spain. The correspondence with Edwin Balch suggests that his long-term ambitions were still centred on Asia, and when an urgent summons reached him from Bennett on October 16, he could only have known that he was to be sent on some wide-ranging assignment.

The highly-dramatised version of their late night meeting in Bennett's bedroom in the Grand Hotel, Paris on October 17, was later published by Stanley and became so much a part of newspaper mythology that he could never alter it. Yet it must be viewed with reserve, for when Stanley wrote it he was still in the employ of Bennett, a temperamental man who inspired fear in all his subordinates. According to Stanley, the interview began with Bennett's order to 'find Livingstone', cost what it may, and to give him any help he might need. The dialogue is put down verbatim, including Stanley's initial incredulity and his demand to Bennett about what he imagined such a 'little journey' (Stanley's thudding irony) was going to cost. Bennett's response was cool: 'Well, I will tell you what you will do. Draw a thousand pounds now; and when you have gone through that, draw another thousand, and when that is spent, draw another thousand, and when you have finished that, draw another thousand, and so on; but FIND LIVINGSTONE.' Bennett could afford to be expansive, for at that time his family had the biggest assured income in the United States after the Vanderbilts and the Astors; however, he was for a time to refuse to pay Stanley's bills when the expedition into Africa had been launched, and only relented when he realised the historic nature of his coup.

Stanley's account of the bedroom interview goes on to explain that Bennett did not want him to go straight to Africa. Far from it. Stanley must first attend the opening of the Suez Canal, travel up the Nile and write a tourist guide, visit Jerusalem, Constantinople, the Crimea, the Caspian Sea, the ruins of Persepolis, the Euphrates, and India; all of this must take something like a year. From Bombay, he was finally to make his way across the Indian Ocean to Zanzibar – and then start looking for Livingstone. There is a submerged hint that Stanley was given orders to go on to China from India if the Livingstone story was no longer worth pursuing.

In journalistic terms, all this is odd. By October 1869, Livingstone had not been seen by any white man for three years and eight months. He was in his late fifties, was known to be in poor health, and had several times been reported dead. The longer he remained missing, the less would be the public awareness of him. The latest of many unconfirmed reports had appeared in *The Times* on October 14, 1869 – three days before the Bennett-Stanley meeting: it said

Arab traders had reached Zanzibar from Ujiji, on Lake Tanganyika, and had seen Livingstone there some months earlier. If Bennett's real motive in calling for Stanley was to send him searching after Livingstone, expense no object, he would scarcely have ordered him to make a rambling journey through Asia to do mainly 'timeless' stories about ruins and former battlefields.

However, even if there was time to leave Livingstone in his African limbo, the Suez Canal could not wait. The official opening, which promised to be a ceremony of dazzling splendour, was due to be held in only a month, on November 17. Stanley must not dally long in Paris or London.

He hurried at once to London and asked Katie and her father to come and see him. A whole page in Stanley's journal has been cut out and lost, covering the period October 17–23, but there is firm evidence that Stanley made a dashing proposal: he and Katie should be married at once, and spend their honeymoon in Egypt at the opening of the Canal. Then they would travel across Asia. It may well be that Stanley's idea was prompted by the recent, and much-publicised, explorations by Sir Samuel Baker in the company of his Hungarian mistress – later his wife. But this was all too much for the Gough-Roberts, accustomed only to the placid tenor of life in Denbighshire. It was decided that the wedding must wait until Stanley was home again. He was sad that his inspiration had fallen on stony ground, but the parting was warm; he promised to write often, and kept his word.

Dashing once again through Paris, he called at the Balch home in the Avenue Gabriel and offered to take Edwin up on his suggestion, in a letter, of coming along as a companion on the journey through Asia. Not surprisingly, since Edwin had only just turned fourteen, his parents declined. Stanley caught an express from the Gare de Lyon for Marseilles, and then a steamer for Alexandria. On the way, he wrote Edwin a letter from Malta, telling him how to improve his English.

At the opening of the Canal, Stanley did all that might be expected of him. He described the elaborate palaces built by the Khedive Ismail, with their huge chandeliers and works of art assembled from all over Europe, the banquets attended by the Empress Eugenie and a plethora of other heads of Europe's royal families – the voluptuous grandeur of it all, which so soon was to drown Ismail's vision in a torrent of debt. Then he sailed up the Nile as far as the first cataract, dutifully wrote his guide for tourists, and by his own account prevented a duel between a Mr Higginbotham and a Frenchman. Next he went to Jerusalem, where he hired as his personal servant a young Christianised Arab, and made a tour of the archaeological excavations in progress.

The next stop on his itinerary was Constantinople, a place with disturbing memories of a little more than three years before. Stanley reached Turkey in early February, 1870, and discovered that the American Ambassador was still Edward J. Morris, who had been given the valueless draft for £150 on Stanley's non-existent father in Liberty Street, New York. It seems that at first Stanley was afraid to approach Morris, although he must have known that the £150 had been retrieved long ago from the compensation paid by the Turks.

He asked an American clergyman with whom he had made friends on the sea trip from Palestine to act as an intermediary. This man, Dr Henry Harman of Dickinson College, Pennsylvania, told Morris that Stanley wanted to make an apology; the reporter was immediately invited to dinner. The ambassador found the draft in a drawer, tore it up in front of his guest and gave him a letter (February 8, 1870) declaring that no debts existed between them and that the ambassador 'had no cause for any complaint'.

Morris gives an account of the change in Stanley in the three years since he had last seen him: 'The uncouth young man whom I first knew had grown into a perfect man of the world, possessing the appearance, the manners and the attributes of a perfect gentleman . . . He was changed in his manner and was riper in his mind and character, and I became very favourably impressed with him. He was at my home frequently . . .' So warm did the relationship grow that Morris presented him with a repeating rifle as a parting gift, and handed him letters of introduction to the various authorities he might meet along his somewhat perilous route to India.

The long trek to the Persian Gulf offered Stanley much opportunity for colourful writing. At Persepolis he slept out amid the ruins, and left his mark on one of the temple pillars. Inside a diamond-shaped border he carved his name deeply: 'Stanley, New York Herald, 1870'. (It is still very visible today, and has done little to enhance his reputation with history-conscious visitors to Persepolis.)

At last, by way of Karachi, he reached Bombay, at the start of August 1870; if Livingstone were still missing, he must now follow Bennett's instructions – take a passage to Zanzibar, and begin his search. But the news was still as confusing as it had been when he left Paris. It was merely known that Livingstone was still alive in the middle of the previous year.

More recently there had been vague statements from Portuguese sources that Livingstone had been killed and burnt for witchcraft. This might be possible, because in a letter he had written in the previous May, the doctor said he proposed to head for the Lualaba river: 'The people west of this, called Manyema, are cannibals if Arabs speak truly. I may have to go there first, and down the Tanganyika, if I come out uneaten, and find my new squad from Zanzibar.'

After waiting two months for a boat, Stanley was able to set off in a barque named the *Polly*; but instead of sailing direct for Zanzibar he was obliged to go southwards to Mauritius. The journey took six weeks, and was uneventful except for a violent quarrel between the drunken captain, Jabez Petherick, and his consort, a Mrs Wilson. In his private journal, Stanley records how Petherick had tried to smash down Mrs Wilson's cabin door with a hatchet, and that he had kept the captain at bay. At this intervention, Mrs Wilson had shrieked out: 'Oh, thank you! Oh, the murdering villain! May your soul rot in hell, Petherick!' Stanley says there was much else of 'vile, un-adulterated language', but leaves it to the imagination. His defence of a woman in peril strongly recalls the affray with Judge Hughes in Brooklyn in 1863.

From Mauritius, Stanley went northwards to the Seychelles in a brigantine, which took up another sixteen days. Then at last he caught a whaling ship heading for Zanzibar. Efforts to chase whales were generally unsuccessful, and he complained mournfully in his diary: 'Still at sea, light breezes every day. Oh! how I suffer from ennui! Oh, the torments of an impatient soul! What is the use of a sailing boat in the tropics? My back aches with pain, my mind becomes old, and all because of this dispiriting calm.'

He also made a far more practical entry, being a most assiduous recorder of monetary details: 'My entire fortune in this world amounts to £553 11s. 3d. after 13 years hard work, that is from 1857. At a rate of £42 11s. 8d. per annum.' The last days of 1870 were ebbing away, and it was now well over two years since his first coup for the *Herald*, following the capture of Magdala. The moment had now come to do something much more sensational.

12. *Friends and Foes in Zanzibar*

As he prepared to search for Livingstone, it was not only the state of his personal finances that worried Stanley. In Zanzibar, nobody knew anything about the guarantees James Gordon Bennett had promised would be awaiting him. Stanley had with him eighty dollars in gold, the sum of his immediate resources. 'No letters and no money from Bennett . . .' he wrote gloomily in his notebook. In this awkward moment, he was rescued by the American consul, Captain Francis Webb.

The consul told the island's business community that the *New York Herald* man was creditworthy. Stanley was able to sign a series of large drafts on Bennett, one of them for 3,750 dollars. As he explained later: 'The expense you were incurring frightened me considerably; but then "obey orders if you break owners" is a proverb among sailors, and one which I adopted. Besides, I was too far from the telegraph to notify you of such expense or to receive further orders from you; the preparations for the expedition therefore went on. Eight thousand dollars were expended in purchasing the cloth, beads and wire necessary for my dealings with the savages . . .'

East Africa had never seen anything to compare with the massive expedition he mounted in the *Herald*'s name. On arrival in Zanzibar on January 6, Stanley had with him only two companions: Selim Heshmy, a servant he had hired in Jerusalem, and William Lawrence Farquhar, a sailor from Leith in Scotland. Although Selim had been with his master all the way across Asia, Farquhar was employed specifically for the journey in Africa. The tall and brawny Scot had been the first mate of the *Polly*, the barque in which Stanley had sailed to Mauritius. (His own time at sea had made Stanley an enthusiast for the all-round skills of sailors; he may also have thought it advisable to take along a man who could speak to Livingstone in his own accents.)

Within weeks, Stanley was to increase his following from two to nearly 200. The need for so many men was dictated by the piles of supplies he assembled. They weighed six tons, and even he was alarmed at what had to be transported nearly 1,000 miles through the unmapped tropics: 'I confess I was rather abashed at my own temerity.' He had been reading the books of earlier explorers, and recalled that Burton and Speke had taken only 132 men on their historic trip to Lake Tanganyika in 1856. Since that date there had been several other white-led – and abortive – attempts to penetrate the so-called Dark Continent from Zanzibar, but never on so lavish a scale. Stanley even bought two rowing boats, one capable of holding twenty men, so that if need be he could hunt for Livingstone all around Lake Tanganyika. To reduce the weight of the boats, he stripped them himself of their outer boards, which he replaced with tarred canvas, and divided them up into sections.

By his own account, the only person to whom Stanley revealed what his intentions would be after crossing the 30 miles of sea between Zanzibar and Bagamoyo on the African mainland was Captain Webb. He could hardly have done less, for Webb and his wife invited him to stay in their house and allowed him to pile it up with his supplies. To everyone else he was carefully vague, just saying that he was off on an exploring trip: David Livingstone's name was not mentioned. The captain of the *Falcon*, in which Stanley had come from the Seychelles, merely recorded: 'I have taken a man as passenger to Zanzibar that is travlin to central Africa for the New York Herald . . .'

It must have given Webb no small pleasure to learn Stanley's secret, for the Americans were feeling embattled in Zanzibar at that time. For a Yankee to brave the interior and bring back the truth about Livingstone would be a lesson for the British – and in particular for Webb's opposite number, Dr John Kirk. There was only a thin veneer of goodwill between the consulates, as Webb's private correspondence makes plain; by the time Stanley and the *Herald* had played their part, not even the veneer would be left.

The reasons for Anglo-American hostility on Zanzibar in 1871 were both commercial and political. Until a few years earlier, the Americans had dominated the foreign trade of the island, their sailing ships bringing in huge quantities of 'Merikani' cloth, which the Arab slave caravans on the mainland used as a basic trade good: 'Merikani' was unequalled for its hard-wearing qualities. The United States' ships, based mainly at Salem and Boston, took back hides, ivory and gum copal. It was a long-established connection, and Webb represented a Salem merchant, who had been trading with Zanzibar since the 1830's. For many years the American dollar had exact parity with the 'Maria Theresa' dollar, specially minted in Austria as the common currency of East Africa.

But the Civil War gave the Americans a severe setback, regular sailings being threatened by the Confederate warships. Just as the conflict ended, the era of steamships fully arrived and the opening of the Suez Canal gave British and German ships a great advantage. The extent of the transformation was shown by the Zanzibar shipping figures: in 1859, out of sixty-five ships putting in at the island, thirty-five were American, but by 1869, only eight out of fifty-three. For a naval man such as Captain Webb, this must have been painful.

Interwoven with commercial antagonism was the political suspicion rife between the consulates on the island – British, French, American and German. Of the four, only the Americans had no wish to influence the course of events in Zanzibar. They had no active or latent imperialistic ambitions there, and sought only a *status quo* in which trade could thrive. Men like Captain Webb were happy to see life drift along placidly, beneath the sway of the Sultan.

On the other hand, the British had the self-appointed task of making the Arabs mend their ways. British warships sailed up and down the East African coast to enforce the 1845 treaty with the Sultan which forbade the export of slaves from Zanzibar to foreign countries such as Arabia. Imperceptibly the British applied more and more pressure, reinforced by the almost continual presence of British gunboats in Zanzibar harbour. The Americans felt convinced, despite British assurances to the contrary, that the time was coming when the island would be taken over as part of Queen Victoria's empire.

Since the British and Americans shared almost the same language, they might have been expected, in such a faraway spot, to be personally friendly, however their respective governments chose to differ. It was not so, for the Americans were conscious of being looked down upon. The British Consuls were full-time professionals. They were never in trade. All the American consuls were, and when they bought a consignment of hides would dry them on the flat roof of the residence. As one remarked: '. . . then Kirk can't bear the "American stinking hides". His aristocratic nose we often see go in the air as he goes under our windows, making some such remark to whoever may be with him.'

So Stanley, who identified totally with America and carried a

John Kirk, Britain's man in Zanzibar, seemed supercilious to his 'Yankee' guest

United States passport, would have felt predisposed against Kirk from the outset. Yet Kirk was of vital importance to him in his mission, for this thirty-nine-year-old Scottish surgeon was one of Livingstone's closest friends. He had been with the great explorer during his 1858–63 Zambesi Expedition, and had shown his tenacity by staying on for six years; most of the other members of the expedition had resigned after quarrels with their leader, or had been dismissed. Livingstone had rewarded Kirk by using influence to have him appointed as official surgeon in Zanzibar in 1866. As his superior, Henry Churchill, gave way to ill-health after 1867, Kirk advanced towards the consulship he dearly desired. A few weeks before Stanley reached the island, illness had finally driven Churchill to give up his post, leaving Kirk in complete charge.

The crucial meeting between Stanley and Kirk took place on January 17, and at the time the journalist only noted in his diary: 'Had a talk with Dr John Kirk this morning. He gave me a very bad account of Livingstone.' There is a conflict between this entry and the version in the book *How I Found Livingstone* of when the interview with Kirk took place. The book says it was during an evening reception at the British Consulate where the refreshment was 'a kind of mild wine', and the conversation petty scandal.

Kirk drew his guest aside and showed him a rifle: 'Then I heard anecdotes of jungle life, adventures experienced while hunting, and incidents of his travels with Livingstone.' Taking this cue, Stanley asked Kirk for the latest news of the explorer, and was told that he might well be dead, but was probably alive. Kirk thought that Livingstone should give up: 'He is growing old, you know, and if he died, the world would lose the benefit of his discoveries. He keeps neither notes nor journals; it is very seldom he takes observations.' Then, according to Stanley, Kirk said the old doctor was 'a very difficult man to deal with generally', and most unwilling to have white company on his travels.

The 'Yankee reporter's' subsequent readiness to publish this informal conversation was regarded as ungentlemanly, but his version is almost certainly accurate. In private, Kirk often made bitter criticisms of Livingstone – who was, indeed, a cantankerous man. Once he had noted: 'Dr L. is a most unsafe leader . . . it is useless making any remark to him.'

Stanley was careful to hide his objectives from Kirk, and told him he was planning to explore the Rufiji river. Kirk must have had his suspicions, for the Rufiji was of small importance. He would have been anxious to deflect a journalist – and an American one, to boot – from getting precise news of Livingstone. He was under pressure from London to do that, and as the 'man on the spot' he would not have his standing improved by being pre-empted by a stranger.

The feeling between the two is well reflected in Stanley's description of Kirk at their first introduction: 'I fancied at the moment that he lifted his eyelids perceptibly, disclosing the full circle of the eyes. If I were to define such a look, I would call it a broad stare.'

However, Stanley had no time for exchanging stares and sophistry with Kirk. Although still a novice at organising African expeditions, he was determined to be on the mainland within a month, and needed to hire at once the nucleus of his armed escort. He sought out veterans who had been employed by Speke and Grant. The most renowned of these was a small grizzled man known as 'Bombay', whose appearance was rather marred by a large gap in his teeth where Speke had hit him during a quarrel. Stanley appointed Bombay as his captain, with a wage of eighty dollars a year, half in advance, and a uniform. Five other men who had been with Speke were taken on at forty dollars a year, and eighteen more employed at slightly less.

Stanley decided that Farquhar and Bombay would not be enough to help him control his caravan, and he looked around for another white assistant. In one of the bars of Zanzibar he found a Cockney, John William Shaw, formerly third mate in an American ship, who for some undisclosed reason had been paid off in East Africa. Shaw declared his readiness to travel on the mainland, and straightway proved his practical worth by sewing the canvas saddles for the donkeys. He was taken on at 300 dollars a year.

By the end of January, Stanley was ready. He records: 'My answer to all questions, pertinent and impertinent, was, I am going to Africa. Though my cards bore the words "Henry M. Stanley, New York Herald", very few, I believe, coupled the words "*New York Herald*" with a search after "Doctor Livingstone". It was not my fault, was it?' He retained this artfulness when taken by Captain Webb to meet Sultan Barghash. Most of the interview at the Sultan's palace was concerned with Stanley's account of the Moslem countries through which he had passed during his recent tour of Asia; at the end, the Sultan gave him letters of introduction to his officials at Bagamoyo, and a *firman* (effectively, a passport) to be shown to Arab merchants he might come across in the interior.

Stanley felt no need to master the intricacies of Zanzibar's power structure. Quite clear, however, was the volatile nature of the Sultan's position. Barghash had only succeeded to the throne in the previous October, after the death of his brother, Majid, and was generally regarded as being of a tiresomely independent disposition.

181

After Barghash had come to power, Kirk at first accepted suggestions that his forcible overthrow should be arranged. In a letter to Livingstone, Kirk put it bluntly: 'He (Majid) has been succeeded by Barghash, who throwing off the mask turns out a fanatic who would if he could turn out all Europeans. I much fear we shall have to turn him out ...' But instead he used diplomacy on the new Sultan. Kirk recorded his success in an official despatch: 'So far from keeping me at a distance, nothing is done by him without informing me or asking my advice, and justice is obtained for all British claims with a rapidity unknown in the latter days of Seyyid Majid ... With the French, American and German consulates I find that His Highness has greatly lost favour since he has treated this agency with proper respect and as taking precedence in everything without question.' Kirk was justifiably pleased, and such confident messages were calculated to evoke pleasure in Whitehall.

It was only in the matter of his old leader, Dr Livingstone, that Kirk did seem slack to some of those in London. It was true that he had much to occupy him in Zanzibar itself, and was fortunate that his young wife, Helen, could help him with the secretarial side of his office work, for the large Indian community was remarkably litigious. Yet the problem of Livingstone's welfare nagged away in the background; after all, the explorer had been appointed a sort of 'roving consul' for inner Africa in 1866, and still held that status. Kirk had shown himself somewhat hasty in 1867, in accepting a report that Livingstone was dead.

After that was disproved he seemed to veer towards a casual optimism. Supplies were despatched intermittently to Ujiji, the trading centre on Lake Tanganyika where Livingstone was believed to be. But small concern was shown about whether he ever received them. The latest consignment had been sent off from Zanzibar by Kirk and Churchill jointly at the start of November, 1870, with a seven-man armed escort – four of whom were slaves. The cost of this caravan came from £1,000 supplied by the British Government in response to growing public disquiet about the fate of Livingstone. Neither Kirk nor Churchill (who was chronically ill with malaria) went over to Bagamoyo to supervise the recruitment of the thirty-five porters needed to carry the supplies; in a letter to the Royal Geographical Society, Churchill expressed a hope that the caravan would reach Ujiji in February 1871, then added warily 'but nothing certain can be said about it'.

Kirk made his first visit to Bagamoyo for some months early in February. He was taken across in HMS *Columbine*, a ship from the anti-slave patrol, to go on a hunting trip near the coast with several Royal Navy officers. The first news as he stepped ashore on the glittering sand was that the relief caravan was still loitering on the coast. It had not even started the 700-mile march to Ujiji.

Stanley had arrived on the mainland shortly before in one of a fleet of five Arab sailing *dhows* he had hired to bring over his soldiers and supplies. According to him, the official caravan for Livingstone fled inland hurriedly upon learning that Kirk was about to arrive. In a despatch to Whitehall (February 18, 1871), Kirk gave a different version, saying that he had been told 'through a native' that the 'men sent off by Mr Churchill' were still in Bagamoyo, and therefore arranged to cross over from Zanzibar in the *Columbine* to hurry them up: 'However, by using my influence with the Arabs I succeeded at once in sending off all but four loads, and followed inland one day's journey myself. The remaining four loads I arranged on my return were to be taken as far as Unyanyembe by an Arab caravan, and thence sent to Ujiji by Said bin Salim, the governor . . . had I not gone in person they might have loitered yet several months.'

Stanley met the party from the *Columbine* at the French missionary centre, just north of Bagamoyo's straggling outskirts. The mission was attractively laid out amid tall palm trees beside the Indian Ocean, and the hospitality of the nuns and priests was notable – when he went to dinner with them a few nights earlier, a bottle of Veuve Cliquot had been brought out. Kirk and Stanley exchanged greetings over a glass of wine with every appearance of amity, and the next morning the consul called at the journalist's tent for a cup of tea. But the matter of the caravan that had been motionless for a hundred days would not be forgotten. As Stanley was to point out, at least fifteen Arab caravans had left Bagamoyo for various points inland since mid-December.

After Kirk was gone, Stanley pressed ahead with the recruitment of porters. He needed 150 men who would contract to come with him as far as Tabora, about two-thirds of the way to Ujiji; but before he was able to acquire his full quota there were all manner of exasperating problems. A downpour of rain drenched some of the supplies, stacked in a leaky tent, so that the carefully-packed bundles had to be opened out and dried, then lashed up again. The men brought across from Zanzibar filled in the time by pursuing local women, which caused arguments with the Arab governor of Baga-moyo. Also, Stanley had anxieties about John Shaw, his new white recruit. William Farquhar had been sent off with an early section of the caravan, and he felt more confident about him, but Shaw seemed to be losing his nerve and regretted ever coming to Africa.

In the calm and relative cool of the evenings, Stanley composed letters to friends in America and Europe; if the fortunes of most white travellers in East Africa were any guide, his prospects for returning alive were not good. One of the letters was to Katie Gough-Roberts, his fiancée in Denbigh; it was the last he ever wrote her. If he already knew through letters from Wales that she had been married four months earlier to a young architect, Urban Bradshaw, he gives no hint of it.

Although it contained no momentous tidings, he did get one last-minute letter, and this he carefully preserved. Brought across by *dhow*, it was from Mary Webb, one of the American consul's two small children. In a laborious copperplate, Mary wrote: 'Did you see us hoist Charlie's flag when you started that morning? Do the men like their tent? How do you like your tent? Does Selim sleep in your tent?'

After six weeks the last of the five sections of the expedition was assembled. As it set out westwards, to the noise of muskets fired in celebration, Stanley rode at its head with John Shaw. The American flag was raised, and the *Herald*'s man had some difficulty in suppressing any show of emotion.

13. Blazing a Trail to Ujiji

The principal discouragements to exploration in Africa during the last century were illness, the terrain and the people. Stanley was soon tested for the first time in his life by all three. He had an attack of malaria only a few weeks after reaching the mainland, and was 'made aware that my acclimatisation in the ague-breeding swamps of Arkansas was powerless against the mukunguru (fever) of East Africa.' He dosed himself heavily with purgatives and quinine, which was the accepted treatment, but soon suffered new attacks, followed by dysentery. He said in a despatch to the *New York Herald* (July 4, 1871): 'From a stout and fleshy person, weighing 170 pounds, I was reduced to a skeleton, a mere frame of bone and skin, weighing 130 pounds.'

Not until the 1890's was a connection established between fever and insect bites – so that there is a macabre aspect to reading the accounts by Stanley and his contemporaries of wading through swamps, and then a few pages later the inevitable descriptions of fighting for life against bouts of malaria. A wide range of optimistic treatments were put forward. Stanley relied upon a concoction not far removed from the formula drawn up ten years earlier by Livingstone, of a pill having equal parts of resin of jalap (a strong purgative) and calomel, rhubarb and quinine. For a powerful man, said Livingstone, the pills should have an extra element of jalap, and when properly administered rendered African fever 'not a whit more dangerous than the common cold'. This formidable cure was to be known as 'Livingstone Rousers' and although missionaries swallowed the pills with Christian fortitude for almost a century, the truth is that Livingstone watched his wife die of malaria several years after he had devised this 'perfect' remedy.

The problem of finding a *modus vivendi* with the African people was also tackled in various ways. A few white travellers relied mainly on persuasion – Livingstone being the prime example (although the extent to which even he used beating and shooting in extreme moments has been overlooked). Others demanded absolute obedience.

Stanley is generally regarded as the epitome of the second, more draconian, type of European explorer.

There can be no doubt that he was impatient by nature, and saw Africa as a place where violence was a *lingua franca*. Sir Samuel Baker once said of him: 'All must be struck with Mr Stanley's candour ... It was not at all necessary for him to write about the fights and the bloodshed that had occurred between him and the natives.' Yet Stanley's almost naïve approach to Africans had its merits. He was able to command great loyalty from his 'dark companions', as he called them. Unlike men such as Baker, he did not regard Africans as *essentially* inferior – if they could measure up to his standards, in energy and determination, they were his equals.

The route of the expedition was well defined as far as Tabora. This was the relatively easy part of Stanley's journey, following the paths from one African village to the next. As long as the peoples were at peace, the main hazards were from the weather. Heavy rains flooded the rivers which had to be crossed and turned plains into swamps.

Stanley soon saw he would be hard put to it to reach Tabora in three months, as planned. He caught up with the fourth section of his expedition, which complained of sickness and fatigue, and angrily drove it on ahead. Then his own porters began to flag. His two horses died and the donkeys began to follow suit. He was having a taste of the trials and frustrations of travel in Central Africa.

When one of the porters deserted with two goats, a tent and another man's personal belongings, Stanley sent out a search party. The deserter was found just as local tribesmen were about to kill him; he was brought back and by general agreement given a flogging with a donkey whip. This was the first of numerous occasions when Stanley had men beaten; as he grew more anxious he took to putting deserters in slave chains – a method of exacting obedience which white travellers had learnt from the Arabs.

The caravan battled on, leaving dead donkeys in its wake. Shaw, whose behaviour and attitudes were already irritating to Stanley, threatened to desert. The next setback was discovering the condition of Farquhar, whose section of the expedition had been overtaken in a hot and dirty village. Farquhar was suffering from elephantiasis, with his face and legs horribly swollen, and had not moved from his tent for two weeks.

Everyone sensed Farquhar was doomed, only three months after leaving the coast. In hope that he would recover with rest, Stanley left him at a place called Mpwapwa, with a servant. When the expedition later met a powerful trader, Sheikh bin Muhammad, on his way to the coast, Stanley asked the sheikh to collect Farquhar and take him to Zanzibar. But it was too late. Farquhar was dead.

As Stanley neared Tabora the march grew easier and he joined up with Arabs heading in the same direction. The enthusiasm of the porters who had been hired at Bagamoyo soared as they looked forward to being paid off. The final 180 miles were covered in 16 days and at the end of June the caravan entered the town with guns firing and horns blaring. Tabora proved to be an oasis of comparative order, with many strongly-built houses occupied by the richer traders, and a market where fruit, chickens and goats could be bought. Stanley set himself up in a place just to the south called Kwihara.

He was now only 200 miles from Ujiji by the most direct route. But would Livingstone be there? If he were, would he run away to the other side of Lake Tanganyika at the approach of another white man rather than consent to be rescued? Obsessed by such speculations, Stanley was eager to hurry on. Burton and Speke had found it hard enough just to reach Ujiji, without trying to meet somebody on arrival.

From Tabora Stanley sent a long despatch to the *New York Herald* about Livingstone. It ended in his best rhetorical manner: 'Until I hear more of him or see the long absent old man face to face I bid you a farewell; but wherever he is be sure I shall not give up the chase. If alive you shall hear what he has to say; if dead I will find and bring his bones to you.' The despatch was sent to the coast in the care of an Arab trader, for Francis Webb to forward by the first ship sailing out of Zanzibar. Stanley also received a letter from Webb (June 11, 1870), which declared confidently: 'You will doubtless see Dr Livingstone at Ujiji and we hope to see you back here in October.'

But the expedition was to be stranded for three months in Tabora, trapped by a war between the Arabs and a powerful African freebooter called Mirambo. The route to Ujiji was effectively shut, despite a series of battles in which Stanley and his men took part. Mirambo delivered a telling counterblow by ambushing his enemies at night, and several of Stanley's men were killed.

It looked for a while as though the search for Livingstone might end in Tabora, for Mirambo was boasting that he would sack the town and 'drive the white men back to the sea'. But Stanley had to go on. He did not know, but might have guessed, that Webb had received the alarming news from America that James Gordon Bennett was refusing to honour Stanley's massive drafts. He could be quite certain that if he turned back now, he was finished as a *Herald* man. It was by no means enough that he and Shaw were the first Europeans to reach Tabora since the visit of Speke and Grant ten years earlier.

With desertions and the losses in fighting Mirambo, Stanley was now reduced to a permanent force of little over a dozen men. Mirambo had been driven off at a cost of 200 warriors when he tried to overrun Tabora, but all hopes of coinciding with Livingstone in his expected arrival at Ujiji seemed to fade as the days went on. Stanley stared fretfully at the sunburnt plains and distant mountains.

He was also suffering further heavy attacks of malaria. In one bout he was unconscious for a week, but was told by Shaw – himself half comatose – that it lasted a fortnight. In his delirium he saw his past floating before him and imagined he was with the cotton broker in New Orleans who had adopted him and given him a name.

At last the expedition began to recover some strength and confidence. Only Shaw showed no spirit, even when Stanley tried personally cooking delicacies for him and promised big rewards after the task was done. When Stanley announced that he planned to strike out for Ujiji by making a long detour through little-known regions to the south, Shaw grew even more alarmed. They by now knew that Farquhar had died at Mpwapwa.

'There is one of us gone, Shaw, my boy! Who will be the next?' Stanley had said with more heartiness than tact on hearing the news. Shaw had a fairly clear idea that it would be he. All he now wanted was to get out of Africa alive and never return.

Stanley would not be deflected from his new route, even though the Arabs warned that it lacked water and was ravaged by blood-thirsty bandits. By patient effort the caravan was built up again; to supplement his own stores and give himself more men, Stanley also took under his control the supply party Kirk had seen off from Bagamoyo in February, since it was also loitering at Tabora.

On September 20, Stanley shook off a fresh attack of malaria and prepared to march out of Tabora to the south. He had hired guides who professed to know the desolate country the expedition must traverse. As he began, several of the Zanzibari 'faithfuls' such as

Bombay pleaded with him to leave Shaw behind – which was exactly what Shaw wanted. But he was determined to avoid any show of weakness by his surviving white companion: 'Now, Mr Shaw, I am waiting, sir. Mount your donkey, if you cannot walk.'

At last the caravan was on its way. Apart from a few hardy women followers, whom Stanley did not count, it numbered 55. This included the guides, the remnants of the official supply party, and a small slave boy who had been presented to Stanley by an Arab. At the suggestion of Bombay, the boy was given the name Kalulu, and Stanley made him his personal servant.

After a few days, Stanley knew he had made a mistake in ignoring the advice about leaving Shaw behind. He himself was so weakened by fever that he could hardly keep moving, and Shaw was only a hindrance. The two men spent a last evening together. 'Shaw played some tunes on an accordion I had bought for him in Zanzibar; but, although it was only a miserable ten-dollar affair I thought the homely tunes evoked from that instrument that night were divine melodies. The last tune played before retiring was 'Home, Sweet Home'; and I fancy that before it ended we had mutually softened towards one another.'

Next morning, Shaw was sent back to Tabora on a litter, and there he died. There is a rumour that he shot himself in despair. It might have been an accident, for Stanley recorded vaguely that Shaw wounded himself in a paroxysm. But Shaw was certainly unpredictable with guns: on the journey to Tabora he had, in a spasm of anger, fired a bullet through the tent in which Stanley was sleeping.

It was already October, and Stanley drove himself forward with fanatical haste. It was as though he possessed some sixth sense – for by an amazing coincidence, Livingstone had just arrived at Ujiji after a year of wandering along the far side of Lake Tanganyika. The old missionary was on the edge of death; in a shaky hand he wrote on the back of a tattered envelope a fragmentary diary: 'Rest, dispirited and sore . . . very hot, feverish – rain soon.'

There is a nightmare quality about Stanley's account of his final weeks on the way to Ujiji. Once several of his men combined in a conspiracy to kill him; there was a climax when he faced the guide Asmani, who stood more than six feet tall and towered far over him – and ordered him to drop his gun. Stanley began to squeeze the trigger of his own double-barrelled weapon: 'Never was a man

On the last stage of the journey to find Livingstone, Stanley was faced with a mutiny, led by the giant Asmani

nearer his death than was Asmani during those few moments . . . but if I did not succeed in cowing this ruffian, authority was at an end. The truth was, they feared to proceed farther on the road, and the only possible way of inducing them to move was by an overpowering force, and exercise of my power and will in this instant, even though he might pay the penalty of his disobedience with death.' As the two faced one another. The veteran Mabruki Speke knocked Asmani's gun aside. Stanley had survived the crisis, and to make his control beyond dispute gave a flogging to Bombay for having encouraged the mutineers. But within a few days the incident had been forgotten. Such was the peril which they all shared that no deserter could hope to make his way safely back to Tabora; they must live or die together.

Food was scarce, and as the caravan passed through each new locality, the chief would demand huge amounts of *hongo* (tribute). In one place, Stanley was forced to hand over nearly 500 yards of cloth; it looked as though the expedition might be beggared long before it reached Ujiji. Every river was infested with crocodiles. Stanley narrowly avoided being seized in a pair of snapping jaws, and had to watch as one of the remaining donkeys was dragged under to its death. As they crossed a marsh the travellers sank up to their necks in slimy mud filling the holes where elephants had walked. Stanley remarks: 'Decency forbade that I should strip, and wade through the sedgy marsh naked . . . it would have been cruel to compel the men to bear me across. Nothing remained, therefore, but to march on, all encumbered as I was with my clothing and accoutrements . . . it was very uncomfortable, to say the least of it.'

On November 3, about a week's march from Ujiji, the expedition had its first definite news that Livingstone was in the vicinity. A group of Africans said they had seen a very old white man, who had come from Manyema. He was sick, they declared. Stanley was elated by the news, but realised he must hurry.

The last week of Stanley's dash to Ujiji was almost the worst, despite the prospect of success. More and more *hongo* was demanded, until Stanley resorted to creeping furtively past villages in the night. One morning there was an incident which Stanley related with gusto in his *Herald* despatches and in *How I Found Livingstone* (but cut from later editions). As they ended a night march, and were crossing a shallow river, a wife of one of the soldiers began to shriek loudly for no clear reason. Alarmed at the certainty of being given away by the noise, and surrounded by the villages of hostile warriors, Stanley began to beat her with his whip: 'I was compelled to stop her cries with three or four smart cuts across her shoulders, although I felt rather ashamed of myself.' Another version said nothing of being ashamed, and told how the beating went on until the woman was subdued into silence. She was then gagged and bound, and put on the end of a rope which was held by her husband – 'who threatened to cut her head off if she made another cry.'

At last, more than eight months after leaving Bagamoyo, Stanley paused on the hills overlooking Lake Tanganyika. A few miles below was Ujiji. Here Burton and Speke had stood, thirteen years before. But Speke had been almost blind through the rigours of the journey, and Burton had an ulcerated jaw and could not eat. Stanley was emaciated and tired, but he felt he could put on a braver show than they had as he marched into the town. It was, after all, going to be a moment of history – and he would not only make it, but record it, too. Everyone in the expedition brought out their best remaining clothes. Stanley put a new band around his topee, donned some clean white flannels, and had his boots well oiled: '. . . I might well have paraded the streets of Bombay without attracting any very great attention.'

When the caravan was a mile outside Ujiji, Stanley gave the order 'Commence firing!' and volley after volley roared into the air from the muskets. The flags of America and Zanzibar were unfurled – 'Never were the Stars and Stripes so beautiful to my mind.'

As the expedition nears the glittering lake, Arabs rush up to shake the white man by the hand – 'but I have no patience with them'. Stanley is consumed with anxiety. Has Livingstone fled? Where is he? Why hasn't he appeared?

'Suddenly a man – a black man – at my elbow shouts in English, "How do you do, sir?"

"Hello, who the deuce are you?"

"I am the servant of Dr Livingstone," he says; but before I can ask any more questions he is running like a madman towards the town.'

14. 'Doctor Livingstone, I Presume?'

When Stanley uttered his renowned greeting at Ujiji on November 10, 1871, his aim was still just as it had been when he arrived in Zanzibar almost a year earlier: to waste no time in squeezing as much information out of Livingstone as he could, then leave him. He would offer him some supplies in return for the interview, and hurry away to telegraph the story. He might do this by returning to the East Coast and catching a steamer to Aden, but also fancied going northwards to the Nile and Egypt – which should be quicker and would allow him to renew his contacts in Cairo. He envisaged staying with Livingstone for a week or two; the warnings by Kirk that the doctor was misanthropic offered little hope of a friendly reception, and the fact that Stanley did not like Kirk gave no grounds for thinking that he would like Livingstone any better. Neither was it an advantage to be representing the most scandalous newspaper in the English-speaking world when meeting an elderly, dedicated missionary whose name was almost a synonym for self-sacrificing idealism. Indeed, Stanley dared not say much about himself until the morning after his arrival at Ujiji, and in polite Victorian fashion Livingstone expressed no curiosity. But when Stanley asked if he knew the *New York Herald* the response was harsh; despite having been almost *incommunicado* for five years, Livingstone at once said: 'Oh, who has not heard of that despicable newspaper!' In his published accounts Stanley merely removed the adjective.

Yet it was not only doubts about Livingstone which made Stanley resolved to get away quickly, but the thought of James Gordon Bennett and his unpredictable rages. A man who could tear off all the tablecloths in a fashionable Paris restaurant, scattering glasses, plates and crockery on the floor, could not be forgotten across thousands of miles of desert and jungle. In his diary, Stanley wrote: '... I serve a hard taskmaster. I should say Bennett would never forgive me for running away from my duty to him. From what I know of him he would even begrudge the few days I must naturally stay here ...' This motivation sets Stanley apart from other African travellers – the pressure to supply the words to earn his salary. He had a scoop on his hands now, but in journalistic terms it was valueless until in print.

That was why he refused Livingstone's almost immediate proposal, that they should join forces to explore beyond the far side of Lake Tanganyika, towards the Lualaba River. The doctor was at once captivated by the wealth and range of his equipment: the caravan which had made the laborious trek from Tabora was regarded as a 'flying column' by its leader, but the impedimenta it brought even included an enamel bath, a variety of silverware and a Persian carpet, as well as basic trade goods. It seemed to Livingstone that the supplies Stanley unpacked were enough for pursuing what really mattered – a solution to the geographical problem of the Nile-Congo watershed. But Stanley could not be tempted. Reporting was his business, he kept telling himself, not exploration.

Yet Stanley ended up by staying with Livingstone for more than four months, and happily went with him by canoe to the northern end of Lake Tanganyika, in a bid to settle the watershed difficulty. When they finally had to part, Stanley was in tears: 'I was so affected that I sobbed, as one only can in uncommon grief.'

The critics of Stanley (generally the more slavish admirers of Livingstone) scorned the idea that there could have been any true, mutual attraction. From the outset, however, their relationship had a special strength, despite the differences in age, personality and outlook: they shared a fundamentalist faith in divine purpose, and felt their remarkable meeting must have been ordained by God. Shortly before, both were oppressed by visions of death. Stanley had seen a grim portent in Farquhar's end, and knew when he left Shaw he was moribund. As his own strength waned he realised that any severe attack of malaria, such as the one he had barely survived in Tabora, must prove fatal. Yet he could only go on. He had written in his diary: 'I feel I must die, sooner than return.'

For Livingstone, who had not encountered another white man since March 1866, the meeting must have seemed even more providential. When he arrived at Ujiji, 16 days before Stanley reached the town, he had made a note about his condition on the last stage of the march from the Manyema country: 'I felt as if dying on my feet.' He had dysentery and internal bleeding, but lacked the goods to barter for the delicate food he might be able to digest, and had to subsist on little else than tea and African porridge. Almost all his followers had deserted him and the Arabs were passively hostile; they would not let his letters reach the coast, in case these revealed the atrocities he had seen committed by slave-traders in Manyema. He lacked either the means or the strength to go to Tabora, the only place in the interior where he might find help – and in any case the war with Mirambo had cut the route. His last reserve of trade goods would be exhausted in a fortnight. Death could only be a matter of time – and a brief time, at that.

In this extremity, Stanley's arrival with so many luxuries must have appeared miraculous. Soon after the two sat down to talk, Stanley cried out: 'Oh, by George! I have forgotten something.' He sent his servant Selim hurrying for a bottle of champagne which had somehow survived the hazards of the journey. He raised one of the two silver goblets he had also packed in the hope of this moment: 'Dr Livingstone, to your very good health, sir.' At banquets in England, Livingstone had learnt to appreciate wine, but he never expected to be offered champagne at Ujiji.

The two ate an enormous meal together, seated side by side with their backs against the mud wall of Livingstone's house. 'You have brought me new life,' Livingstone said, again and again. The local Arabs were impressed by Stanley's verve, and by the manner in which he had circumvented Mirambo. All but one or two had been content to let Livingstone die, but they sensed the young newcomer

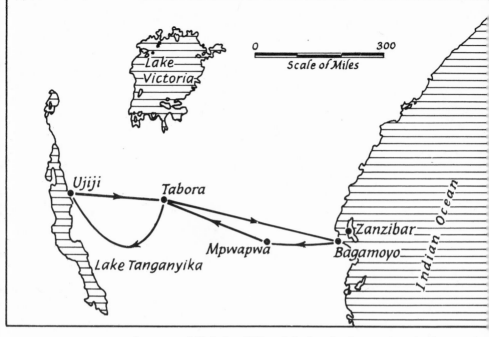

Stanley's search for Livingstone 1871-72

was not to be treated lightly. Gifts of choice food were hurriedly sent in to the white men.

As Stanley was to write in his account for the *Herald*, it seemed as though he and Livingstone had been marching together to an appointed rendezvous. Yet for some days afterwards he could not help wondering if it was all a dream – that here he was alone in the middle of Africa with the man whose fate was such a mystery to the world. Stanley writes with great frankness on his own reactions, and in particular about his astonishment that Livingstone was friendly and forthcoming. The explorer was entirely ready to co-operate with the *Herald* when Bennett's orders had been explained: he would write a personal letter to the paper expressing his gratitude, and felt in no way put out that his rescuer was an American (Stanley never revealed his Welsh background to him).

In fact, Livingstone's lifelong concern with slavery made him especially eager to have a first hand report of what had been happening in the United States since the end of the Civil War. He had earlier named after the assassinated President Lincoln a lake about which he had heard reports – but not yet seen. Stanley dutifully wrote: 'To the memory of the man whose labours on behalf of the Negro race deserves the commendation of all good men, Livingstone has contributed a monument more durable than brass or stone.' Sadly, some years later the lake proved to be fictitious. However, the choice of Lincoln's name was a reflection of Livingstone's pre-occupation. In a letter to his son Tom (September 22, 1869), he wrote: 'War brought freedom to 4,000,000 of the most helpless and hopeless slaves . . . War has elevated and purified the Yankees and now they have the gigantic task laid at their doors to elevate and purify 4,000,000 slaves . . . The day for Africa is yet to come.' So it seemed quite significant that an American newspaper should have sent an expedition to look for him. As Livingstone said in a letter to James Gordon Bennett: 'Now that you have done with domestic slavery forever, lend us your powerful aid towards this great object.'

There was also a more personal reason why Livingstone should feel an involvement with America: his eldest son had died in uniform there. Stanley mentions hearing about Robert Livingstone (who had called himself Rupert Vincent) from the old missionary, and doubt-less revealed something of his own experience in the war. Livingstone neglected his four children deplorably, and although his letters to Robert had been harsh and minatory, the matter lay on his con-science. Stanley was only a few years older than Robert Livingstone, and made the gap seem even less by saying that he was twenty-eight – whereas he was almost thirty-one when he arrived in Ujiji.

The accounts by the two men recreate the growth of their relation-ship. Livingstone tells us less, for there can be no doubt that he was, even at the end, less interested in Stanley as a person than the latter was in him. His descriptions contain many expressions of gratitude, and talk of Stanley's energy, but there is only a glancing reference to his character. In one of his last letters to his daughter Agnes, Livingstone advises her on how to choose a husband, and stresses that she must pick a good-tempered man; he adds: 'Stanley's temper was bad.' It was a fair comment.

The relative indifference of Livingstone towards him is explained by Stanley: 'He had lived in a world which revolved inwardly, out of which he seldom awoke except to attend to immediate practical necessities, then relapsed again into the same happy inner world . . .' As their days together went by, Stanley watched Livingstone with a mounting fascination. In his notebook he shrewdly etched the details which he would pass on to the *Herald* readers, of the explorer's firm but heavy tread, his brown hair streaked with grey, the sharpness of his hazel eyes, the bad state of his teeth. Stanley also noted the poor

Missionary and journalist sit down with a supply of newspapers, carried through the wilds from the coast. This illustration in a London weekly, *The Graphic*, managed to combine self-advertisement with heavy humour

condition of Livingstone's clothes, which had been repeatedly stitched and patched.

Soon the nature of Stanley's comments were to gain in intensity. Around the middle of November the pair made a four-week journey on the lake, during which Stanley was afflicted by a fierce attack of malaria. He lay with a racking headache and pain in a hut he was sharing with Livingstone. His response to the treatment the doctor gave him reveals the direction in which his emotions were moving: 'But though this fever, having enjoyed immunity from it for three months, was more severe than usual, I did not much regret its occurrence, since I became the recipient of the very tender and fatherly kindness of the good man whose companion I now found myself.'

Later, Stanley was to be much more specific. Writing to Livingstone's elder daughter, Agnes, he said: 'I loved him as a son, and would have done for him anything worthy of the most filial.'

A few months after he had finally parted from Stanley, Livingstone expressed his own thoughts in a letter to his daughter Agnes: 'He behaved as a son to a father – truly overflowing in kindness. The good Lord remember and be gracious unto him in life and in death.' He repeated this thought, that Stanley had been like a son, several times in his correspondence.

The softening influence on Stanley is revealed in his diaries. All references to thrashing the porters suddenly vanish. Stanley accepted a rebuke when he was at the point of firing on some belligerent African. The next time, Livingstone did not even need to speak: 'Here, again, my hand was stayed from planting a couple of good shots, as a warning to them in future from molesting strangers, by the mere presence of the Doctor . . .'

One of Livingstone's most quaint pieces of advice on how to win the goodwill of Africans was to address them in the polite, respectful manner of a 'thorough gentleman'. Stanley more often spoke like the sailor he had once been. He was not good at apologising, but Livingstone went as far as to make him shake hands with their cook Ulimengo. This followed a sudden quarrel about some filthy coffee pots. Stanley explains that he was at the time 'half-mad with quinine' – so when the cook dared to sneer he 'clouted him at once'. An affray seemed about to start when Livingstone appeared and parted the contestants. Stanley tells how he allowed himself to be led away to his tent, crying with 'unsatisfied rage and shameful weakness'; by nightfall, the doctor had been so successful as an intermediary that the reporter and the cook apologised to one another.

Such incidents are never mentioned in Livingstone's journals. Instead he was reserved and formal, concentrating on his companion's incessant bouts of malaria: 'Mr Stanley has severe fever, with great pains in the back and loins; an emetic helped him a little . . . Mr Stanley so ill that we carried him in a cot . . .'

After their trip to the northern end of Lake Tanganyika the two men prepared to travel back to Tabora, where Livingstone hoped to find large piles of supplies from Zanzibar awaiting him. It was a dismal journey, hardly a day passing without rain and thunder. Livingstone was troubled by ulcerated feet and his shoes were in pieces, so Stanley bought him a donkey; but at the end of a long march a swarm of bees stung the animal to death: it was 'completely knocked up' noted the doctor, using one of his favourite phrases. He wrote little about his own sufferings in the incident, but Stanley described them vividly: 'He had been dreadfully stung in the head and in the face: the bees had settled in handfuls in his hair; but, after partaking of a cup of warm tea and some food, he was as cheerful as if he had never travelled a mile.'

During the journey the caravan became lost in the forests of Bende, and Stanley decided to lead the way with the aid of Livingstone's compass, despite the doubts of the guides. He stuck to his chosen course for ten days through uninhabited country where food was hard to find and lions roamed around the camp at night. He was too weak with fever some of the time to go out after game for the cooking pot, and Livingstone suffered from bleeding feet. The porters began to complain that they would all starve to death, and Stanley had to urge them on with bold promises that they would soon be out of the forest into a region where food was plentiful.

Livingstone gave him full support and Stanley warned the 'most truculent knaves' that if they goaded him too far he would stop and fight it out with them. He knew the position was desperate; he had to fume and storm when the porters wanted to lie down and abandon hope. But he did not desire to hit anyone at that moment: 'I was too proud of them; but under the circumstances it was dangerous – nay, suicidal – to appear doubtful or dubious of the road.' In the end they came through and Stanley was not only vindicated as a pathfinder but went out and shot two zebra, which gave more than 700 lb of meat to be divided among forty-four men. This delighted Bombay, who the previous night had had a dream in which Stanley was shooting down animals on every side. About his feat in bringing them through the forest, Stanley remarks drily: 'My men praised the compass, they did not praise me.'

In camp in the evenings, Stanley and Livingstone sat together in their tent and talked over the behaviour of Kirk. By this time they were both agreed that amid the relative comfort of Zanzibar he had cared far too little about the straits in which Livingstone found himself.

Livingstone was certainly given grounds to feel discontented with the supply position when he reached Ujiji shortly before Stanley. A half-caste Arab put in charge of a caravan to Livingstone in 1869 had spent fourteen months reaching Ujiji, on the way trading in brandy, soap, opium and gunpowder, to obtain ivory. Then he had 'divined on the Koran' that Livingstone was dead and had sold off almost all the supplies he had not used up. Livingstone had written complaining to Kirk about this well before Stanley arrived, and his tone was sharp (June 26, 1871). The complaint put Kirk in an

Danger in the forest. Entitled 'A Surprise!', this appeared in *How I Found Livingstone*. Richard Burton remarked that the elephant was 'a strange monster, sub-African in length of ear and extra-Indian in length of leg'. He urged Stanley to take more care with illustrations in his books in future

awkward position, since the half-caste had been obtained through Ludha Damji, an immensely wealthy Indian merchant and customs collector with whom the Sultan was deeply in debt. If he fell out with Damji, he might lose his influence with the Sultan.

After Stanley's arrival, the fury is very apparent in all of Livingstone's letters. He wrote a series of bitter accusations to Kirk himself, and reinforced them in messages to friends in Britain. The private recipients often destroyed Livingstone's more outspoken letters, to protect Kirk's name, but in his official capacity Kirk had no option but to forward those he himself received to the Foreign Office. Livingstone was most specific about Kirk's career in a letter to his daughter Agnes: 'He has got by my influence to the top of his ambition – an acting consul and political agent – husband of a wife and two children – and I may go to my grave before he will stir hand and foot for me . . .'

Stanley saw in Kirk the type of insincere and supercilious Briton with whom he could not be at ease. He put him in the same category as those officers in Abyssinia who had sported 'eyeglasses' (monocles) and greeted him with a proud disdain. There was some truth in this view of Kirk, for Bishop William Tozer, head of the Universities' Mission in Zanzibar had written of him: 'He is a great hand at contradicting you flat'. In contrast, Stanley regarded Livingstone, with his Scots burr, as unpretentious and human.

However, there was also another side to Livingstone's nature, as Kirk had warned. The doctor harped obsessively on the weaknesses of his companions on the Zambesi expedition more than six years before. Clearly, he would be hard to keep on friendly terms with during a prolonged journey. But Stanley managed to look beyond Livingstone's cantankerous spells and envied the missionary's spiritual confidence; inside himself there was still that dire insecurity which set loose his fits of rage.

Livingstone was a man of wide knowledge, who liked to quote great stretches of poetry by Longfellow or Whittier from memory as they marched together through the forests. What really filled his mind, however, was the Bible, and he was proud that he had read it through four times in the course of his wanderings around Lake Tanganyika. Although Stanley knew the Bible well from his work-house training, he could not match the doctor's knowledge.

Stanley had now grown so deeply attached to Livingstone that he wanted to coax him back to civilisation. In his journal, the older man noted: 'Mr Stanley used some very strong arguments in favour of my going home, recruiting my strength, getting artificial teeth, and then returning to finish my task.' This was a remarkable switch by one so ambitious as Stanley, now quite deliberately trying to undermine his own scoop. If he did manage to 'bring Livingstone back alive' he clearly would have to play an inferior role.

But despite his repeated efforts, Livingstone would not yield. He must go on, looking for the Nile sources. More ominously, he talked also about his yearning for a quiet grave in the African forest. Nobody would ever disturb it, and he could rest in the same continent where his wife lay buried. In his letters to Agnes, Livingstone argued that he would come home when he had a great success to reveal, for to do otherwise would mean obscurity in some 'unhealthy consulate' for the rest of his life. Stanley sensed that he would be the last white man to see Livingstone. The only course open was to give him all possible aid and hope for the best.

When they at last reached Tabora, Stanley took Livingstone to the solid flat-roofed house he had hired seven months earlier. They set up the Union Jack at one end and the Stars and Stripes at the other. It seemed almost like home, for Livingstone's supplies were waiting – although a large part had been stolen – and the two men could sit down with mail and bundles of newspapers brought up by Arab caravans. It was now February, but Stanley supervised the making of a lavish if belated Christmas dinner; as the rains died away their spirits rose. The two busied themselves in writing up their diaries and reports, and Livingstone kept on until he had completed nearly thirty long letters to relatives and friends.

Stanley filled in the time while Livingstone was writing by sorting out his own goods, in order to leave all he could behind him. He drew up precise lists of his supplies at various stages of his travels, and the cost of paying porters. He gave the doctor nearly 3,000 yards of cloth for bartering and paying tribute, 16 sacks of beads, 350 lbs of wire, clothes, tools, rifles and nearly 4,000 rounds of ammunition.

On Marsh 14, 1872, Livingstone and Stanley parted, with poorly hidden emotions. They had been through many tribulations together; one was staying in Africa, almost certainly to die, the other hurrying back to civilisation. Stanley has described how he left the Tabora house with the doctor beside him: 'The men lifted their voices in a song. I took long looks at Livingstone, to impress his features thoroughly on my memory.' As Livingstone's servants came to shake his hand, he could not stop tears springing from his eyes. As he puts it: 'I betrayed myself!'

A few days after they had parted, Livingstone and his rescuer exchanged final letters by messengers. The doctor's was short, giving a few last instructions and discribing his thankfulness that Stanley's malaria was less severe. He added a postscript: 'I saw your silver tea-strainer last night after I had gone to bed. I have written a note this morning to Mr Murray, 50, Albemarle Street, the publisher – to help you if necessary in sending the journal by book post or otherwise to Agnes. If you call on him you will find him frank and no "eyeglass", though he needs one I believe. A pleasant journey to you.'

Stanley's reply was longer and more effusive. He promised to carry out all Livingstone's instructions, and said he need not have bothered to send on the tea-strainer. He ended on a personal note: 'My dear Doctor, very few amongst men have I found I so much got to love as yourself . . . I am happy in doing you a service, for then I feel I am not quite parted from you. I wish it were a series of services, for then I would feel as if I were with you all the time. I felt very much depressed the whole day – melancholy and lonely. Were it not that I feel a sort of prescience that I shall see you again I should be tempted to return and take one more look and pass a few more hours now. But God's will be done, and England and America expect their people to do their duty . . .' He then added a strictly practical postscript, showing how he had suddenly felt the tug of duty to his employer: 'Do not forget the *Herald* please. The *Herald* will be grateful to me for securing you as a correspondent at the terms agreed upon.'

After sending this off, Stanley spurred his party forward. As they were crossing a flooded river one man fell up to his neck in a deep hole. On his head he was holding a box containing all of Livingstone's journals and letters. Taking out his revolver, Stanley shouted in Swahilli: 'Look out! Drop that box and I'll shoot you.' He described what happened next: 'All the men halted in their work while they gazed at their comrade who was thus imperilled by bullet and flood. The man seemed to regard the pistol with the greatest awe, and after a few desperate efforts succeeded in getting the box safely ashore.'

It was to become a celebrated, or possibly notorious, incident – depicted in a melodramatic fullpage illustration in *How I Found Livingstone*. It well fitted the image of Stanley as a man who stopped at nothing, the product of the new 'blood-and-thunder' American journalism, which taught that action was what the readers paid for.

Averaging fourteen miles a day the caravan reached Bagamoyo in early May. There Stanley was greeted by one of the members of a 'Livingstone Relief Expedition' set up by the Royal Geographical Society. It had been preparing to strike inland, but hurriedly abandoned the idea when the *Herald* man gave his news. A gush of courtesies did not disguise a strong undercurrent of jealousy. Stanley's account of his meetings soon afterwards with Kirk in Zanzibar fails to conceal that he rubbed in his triumph with an overbearing mien which the acting consul must have found hard to bear.

One of the intended leaders of the relief expedition was Livingstone's youngest son, Oswell, and Kirk told him sourly that Stanley would 'make his fortune' out of his father. Oswell wrote to Livingstone and repeated this. In one of his last letters the missionary remarked: 'If so, he is heartily welcome, for it is a great deal more than I could ever make out of myself.'

Kirk was very incensed by the 'ungenerous personal insinuations' of Livingstone's letters. He refused to take over from Stanley – who was eager to be on his way from Zanzibar – the organising of porters to be sent up to join the doctor in Tabora. Kirk suspected that the 'young Yankee' had fanned Livingstone's anger against him.

So Stanley got the men together, relying heavily on the 'faithfuls' who had made the long march with him. Before sending them off by dhow to the mainland he urged them to be loyal to Livingstone: 'You know him; you know he is a good man, and has a kind heart. He is different from me; he will not beat you as I have done. But you know I have rewarded you all – how I have made you rich in cloth and money. You know how, when you behaved yourselves well, I was your friend. I gave you plenty to eat and plenty to wear. When

Safely back after finding Livingstone. This photograph shows Stanley with Kalulu, the slave boy given him by an Arab, and his Palestinian servant Selim. It was taken in Zanzibar. Later, in a fashionable London studio, a better-known series of pictures was posed. But by then, Stanley had removed his beard

you were sick, I looked after you. If I was so good to you, the Great Master will be much more so. He has a pleasant voice and speaks kind. When did you ever see him lift his hand against an offender?'

All the men promised to stick by Livingstone, come what may. They shook hands with Stanley, who then marched them through the streets to the harbour. He wrote in his diary: 'I felt strange and lonely, somehow. My dark friends, who had travelled over so many hundreds of miles, and shared so many dangers with me, were gone, and I was left alone. How many of their friendly faces shall I see again?'

With several members of the aborted British expedition, he arranged to charter a coastal steamer to go to the Seychelles. With luck, they might manage to connect there with a French mailship *en route* from China to Marseilles. A few days before their steamer weighed anchor on May 29, an American sailing ship left for New York by way of the Cape with a cargo of cloves, spices and hides. Stanley had made friends with the skipper, Captain Russell, who had thrown a dinner-party on board for him. Russell said later: 'Mr Stanley was the life of the party, and the stories and anecdotes he told were listened to with breathless attention by all present.' Stanley arranged that Russell should transport a gift to James Gordon Bennett – a brown dog, 'larger than a lion', which looked to be a cross between a St Bernard and some African breed.

Russell was also entrusted with a personal letter (May 18, 1872), in which Stanley said: 'Before I left Zanzibar thirteen months ago I promised to carry out your instructions faithfully unless death prevented me. I now write to inform you that I have redeemed that promise . . . Animated only with the desire to do my duty to the *New York Herald* I halted at nothing – was ever pushing on until my men cried out from sheet fatigue, "Have mercy! . . ." I cannot say that I feel much the worse though I look ten years older . . . I feel pretty tired and worn out, but a few weeks good food will set me all right. Congratulations to you on the successful termination of this arduous enterprise, because the glory is due to the *Herald* – Your ever-ready correspondent, Henry M. Stanley.'

Luck was not on his side when his steamer reached the Seychelles. The French mailship had left twelve hours earlier, and he now had to wait another month for the next vessel to Europe. It was vexing, but the island was beautiful and placid. Stanley and his companions, with whom he maintained a rather fragile amity, rented a house for their stay; they named it 'Livingstone Cottage'.

At last Stanley was able to be on his way again. When his ship reached Suez he paid off Selim Heshmy, who had been with him through many adventures during more than two years, and wrote a warm letter of recommendation to any future employer. He kept with him the self-assured young Kalulu. He had grown warmly attached to Kalulu – and also realised his value as a symbol of his own connection with Livingstone, since the boy had once been a slave.

Stanley could now look forward with mounting excitement to the welcome he would have in Europe. At Aden there had been a cable awaiting him from Bennett: 'You are now as famous as Livingstone, having discovered the discoverer. Accept my thanks and the whole world's.'

15. *Fame and Disaster*

The names of Stanley and Livingstone were first publicly linked – in a tentative fashion – at the end of November, 1871. By then they were already together, but letters sent to London by Kirk on September 22 and 25 relayed only the stale rumours that had taken months to reach Zanzibar from the interior. The letters, to the Foreign Office and the Royal Geographical Society, were a further two months on the high seas. Kirk could only report that Livingstone seemed cut off by the war between the Arabs and Mirambo, the 'black Napoleon' of Central Africa. Kirk then gave an account of 'the American traveller, Mr Stanley', saying that he was believed ill with fever after joining in the war. Kirk left Stanley in a limbo: '. . . I really cannot say where he desires to go; he never disclosed his plans here.' There was, however, a hint that Stanley might try to push on to meet Livingstone. This was briefly reported in the British newspapers, without any mention of Stanley's journalistic interests.

The truth came out in New York just before Christmas and was picked up by the London dailies early in the New Year. Stanley was not just a sporting gentleman with a taste for danger – he was 'after Livingstone'. The Royal Geographical Society was incredulous, then enraged. Who was Stanley? The honorary secretary of the Society, Clements Markham, was able to report having met him in Abyssinia, and the character sketch Markham offered in no way lessened the dismay of fellows and members. The *Herald*'s first published despatch from Stanley ran to 7,000 words, and the paper's readiness to print it at such length proved that this was no half-hearted whim. At the time he sent it down to the American consulate for forwarding to New York, he was still a long way from Ujiji, but he gave his aims without reserve: 'The instructions which I received from you close on two years ago were given with the usual brevity of the *Herald*. They were, "Find out Livingstone, and get what news you can relating to his discoveries." ' It was the second half of these instructions that sounded so intolerable in London; when Livingstone revealed his geographical findings after seven years of travel in Africa, it surely could not be to a sensationalist American newspaper which was notorious for jeering at the British. The *Herald* had not merely lacked the politeness to tell the Society that it was sending off a search party for Livingstone; it had gone to an ultimate point of caddishness by deliberately hiding the fact.

Livingstone had been the most prized member of the RGS for almost twenty years. As early as 1854, his work in Africa had been praised by Sir Roderick Murchison, then president of the Society, as 'the greatest triumph in geographical research which has been effected in our times'. The repute of the RGS had been enhanced by the loyalty of Livingstone to Murchison and his colleagues. So the details of Livingstone's new discoveries must, as before, be first presented to a gathering of the RGS and recorded in *The Times* – never unveiled in James Gordon Bennett's three-cent scandal-sheet.

Here was the crux of what would become a celebrated public feud. On one side, the RGS knew almost nothing about Stanley, and disliked what it knew. On the other, Stanley was ignorant about the RGS, and treated its sense of propriety with a cavalier indifference he would ultimately come to rue.

There were extra nuances: the RGS was not without internal divisions about Livingstone. The attitude of rigidly class-conscious members was expressed by Markham in his private journals. After saying that Livingstone owed his fame mainly to Murchison, he went on to give his own impressions of the explorer: 'His expression was lowering and disagreeable. I did not find that he improved on acquaintance . . . but he knew how to acquire influence over natives . . . he was very ignorant of botany and geology.' In the opinion of Markham it had been the business of the Government, not of the RGS, to sort out what had happened to Livingstone, and save him if need be.

Such views did not find favour, however, with General Sir Henry Rawlinson, who took over as president of the Society on the death of Murchison. After hearing that Livingstone might well be cut off, he resolved to send out a relief expedition – the one which the victorious Stanley was destined to meet preparing to start from Bagamoyo. The despatch from the *Herald*'s impertinent correspondent became a great stimulus to the scheme of Sir Henry and his supporters; they were determined that their expedition must at all costs overtake Stanley and reach Ujiji first. The Society primed the pump for the expedition with £500, and although the Government refused to offer a penny, Sir Henry was in no way discouraged. The expedition leaders were selected; voluntary committees were set up throughout Britain; by the end of January 1872 more than £4,000 had been raised. The haste to foil Stanley is shown by the date on which the expedition and its accoutrements left Britain: February 9. Sir Henry had only announced his project on January 1. But he was still far too late.

This frittering of energy and funds sprang from the sheer lack of communication between Central Africa and London. The time lag was crucial. Nobody could know that Stanley had long since found Livingstone – and was about to leave him – before the RGS relief expedition even set out from London. Early in April the first unconfirmed reports reached Zanzibar of the meeting at Ujiji. By the end of April, Stanley's advance messengers confirmed it all, and the American consul sent up to him, together with wine and other delicacies, a letter which showed how much he enjoyed the victory over the British: 'I think your movements will have great effect upon the Livingstone Expedition. They feel ashamed now, while we Americans are delighted to think how successful you have been.'

A private letter Rawlinson received at the RGS in March from Kirk well conveyed the more jaundiced British view of Stanley's activities. It said: 'I doubt not if in possession of real news of Dr Livingstone he would try to pass it on direct to New York in order that it might first be published in the *Herald*. He used to amuse us here with tales of how he passed on details of the Abyssinian campaign to New York and so outwitted the London correspondents . . .' Kirk's use of the words 'amused' and 'outwitted' give a fair example of his disingenuous style; they were well calculated to inflame Sir Henry's patriotism.

This was the background to the tumult and acrimony of the three months following Stanley's arrival in Europe at the end of July. His own views were put succinctly in a letter to the Reverend Horace Waller, a leading member of the RGS, on July 29 from Paris: 'I have an idea you are prejudiced against me, but I beg you to consider that I could not possibly know whose hostility I might incur by going after Livingstone . . . My success seems to have aroused considerable bitterness in the minds of those from whom I naturally expected a different reception.' Even if Stanley had been a model of decorum, he would have met some irritation from the geographers in Britain and from the Establishment generally.

As early as May, when the first news of Stanley and his coup reached London, Rawlinson had displayed his pique while addressing the RGS in his capacity as President. There was one point upon which he said a little enlightenment was needed – the general belief that Stanley had discovered and relieved Livingstone. In fact, it was the other way around: 'Dr Livingstone, indeed, is in clover, while Mr Stanley is nearly destitute . . . We trust that the expedition sent out by the Society will relieve both Dr Livingstone and Mr Stanley, and enable them to continue the researches upon which they are engaged.'

If this were not enough, several members of the RGS advanced the view that Livingstone had not been found, because he was not lost; he knew precisely where he was. This face-saving argument was popular for a long time despite the simple retort that even though Livingstone knew where he was, nobody in the outside world did; Stanley had found him in the way a mountain rescue team tracks down an injured climber who knows his own whereabouts perfectly well but cannot get to safety. Stanley's answer to the suggestion that the old explorer was 'in clover' was more downright: 'Then why did you send out an expedition to relieve him?'

But where Stanley showed himself in British eyes not merely presumptuous but beyond the pale was in launching his broadsides against Kirk for neglecting Livingstone in his hour of need. It was the issue upon which the majority of the British professional and upper classes – whom he so little understood and instinctively disliked – closed ranks against him. It gave the London newspapers the chance to brand him as boorish and ungentlemanly (the harshest condemnation), while simultaneously denigrating him on several other counts. There is no doubt that Kirk had sent messages ahead to friends in the RGS about his hostile encounters with Stanley in May, but the first public airing of the 'case against the consul' came in a *Herald* summary of July 3, which Bennett's London representative – with a generosity born of triumph – had distributed to all newspapers which asked for a copy.

Stanley's early despatches also contained a slighting reference to Horace Waller: he told how an African, Wekotani, had deserted Livingstone during his travels – and he called Wekotani 'one of the nice honourable fellows' who had been sent to India for education by Waller. This alone was well calculated to put Waller's back up, but Livingstone's regular correspondent and former travelling companion had another reason for joining the ranks against Stanley: Kirk's brother was married to Waller's sister.

The battle intensified a few days after Stanley arrived in Marseilles on July 24. He was interviewed there by the *Daily Telegraph* correspondent, John le Sage, and let fly with all the invective he could muster against Kirk and his sympathisers. One of the most damaging charges was that Livingstone had accused Kirk of failing to help him out of jealousy. Stanley gave direct quotes of a conversation he had had with Livingstone to support this. The *Telegraph* published two long despatches from Le Sage on July 25 and 26. Thus the *Telegraph* had its own scoop, for this was the world's first face-to-face account of the rather mysterious discoverer of Livingstone.

Le Sage allowed himself some journalistic licence, adding two inches to the American's height and saying that his hair turned completely grey in the search. Stanley himself admitted he was startled when he looked in a mirror after his arrival in Zanzibar by the way he had aged, but his hair was only lightly flecked with grey.

There was another personal aspect upon which Le Sage touched in his first report. Livingstone's discoverer was not after all an Englishman – 'or rather a Welshman' – but an American citizen, and there was no truth in recent newspaper reports that his mother kept a public-house at St Asaph. So from the outset, Stanley set himself upon the nerve-wracking path of trying to deny his origins.

The *Telegraph* interviews caused international excitement. Perhaps Stanley was lured into saying more than he meant to by the deceptively stolid look of Le Sage (a brilliant writer who was later knighted and became the *Telegraph*'s editor). Certainly his volubility did not please Bennett, who sent an angry cable with the order 'Stop Talking' as soon as he saw the reports which had been cabled from London to New York. It was hard to obey, for Stanley was eager to tell his story to anyone who would listen.

After a day in Marseilles, he caught the express to Paris. By this time he was learning something about the mixed reactions his success had produced in Britain. Le Sage was able to explain in detail the attitudes of Rawlinson, Markham, Waller and their friends. Stanley could hardly take it in, especially the assertion by Rawlinson published in *The Times* that 'Livingstone had discovered

Stanley'. He wrote later: 'I was then told how men regarded the results of the expedition; but it was not until I arrived in England that I realised it.'

These forebodings were almost forgotten during an exhilarating week in Paris. The American minister, Elihu B. Washburne, brought him together with General William Sherman, who also happened to be in France at the time. 'Do you remember me?' asked Stanley. Sherman said he did not, whereupon Stanley began to quote from memory a high-flown oration lasting several minutes. 'Why, that's a speech I made some years ago to the Sioux Indians,' exclaimed the general. 'Were you there?' The reporter said he was – and what was more, had adapted Sherman's speech to lecture Africans on the journey to Ujiji.

The last night before he left Paris, Stanley was the guest of honour at a banquet in the Hotel Chatham, and sat on Washburne's right hand. It had been arranged by eighty leading Americans in Paris. In proposing the toast, the minister declared that their guest's enterprise 'stood alone in the history of journalism'. The evening was magnificent; splendid wines were served and the chef of the Hotel Chatham had expended all his art upon the menu. It included a special dish: 'Poularde à la Stanley aux truffes.'

When he rose to speak, Stanley was flushed with the wine, and since he had still not recovered his health after twenty-three bouts of malaria, he may have been more in his cups than he realised. He spoke wittily and at length, but with little caution, so that when he turned to the topic of John Kirk and his behaviour there was a certain disquiet among his American audience. Kirk was, after all, the representative of another country, and as if to underline this diplomatic factor, he said that he had just handed over to Lord Lyons, the British ambassador in Paris, Livingstone's official despatches for forwarding to the Foreign Secretary in London. Washburne was unhappily conscious of his situation as Stanley lashed out at the consul in Zanzibar. There was one disastrous sentence: 'I have a mission from Dr Livingstone to describe Kirk as a traitor.' Later, Stanley was to deny that he had ever said this, but too many people had heard him to make that credible.

What had already appeared in the *Telegraph* was harsh enough, and Le Sage was at pains to avoid inflaming the quarrel, saying: 'What I sent was a very modified statement of the information communicated to me.' Now the indignation in London boiled over, for whereas it was one thing to accuse a man of apathy or inefficiency, it was quite another to impugn his honour with a charge of treachery to a national hero. Stanley knew he had gone too far, and wrote in his diary: 'I must endeavour to restrain myself, for though I do think that Kirk has behaved abominably . . . it does not do to run a-tilt at anybody in a mixed assemblage of this kind.'

However, the repercussions were still to come, and the evening at the Hotel Chatham ended on a light-hearted note. Kalulu was brought in, and stood on a chair with a French captain's *kepi* on his head. As the *Telegraph* reported: 'The ebony child displayed a modest assurance and really gentlemanly manners under these trying circumstances. When he went away a great many ladies in the courtyard of the Hotel Chatham kissed him.'

In London, the next day, Stanley braced himself for the fame and the fury. He quickly saw that it was all going to be more exhausting and less pleasant than he had imagined on the way back. He was showered with invitations to dinners and receptions, and pressed to give lectures all over the country. On one day, in the morning mail, came nearly thirty letters from people – many of them distinguished – whose names were completely unknown to him. His life soon became a 'whirl of cabs, soirées, dinners, dress-clothes and gloves.'

There was also the urgent matter of bringing out his book, for various quick-witted publishers were taking advantage of the lax copyright laws of the time to rush out plagiarisations of his despatches and other newspaper reports. Stanley had been anxious to come to terms with Livingstone's publisher, John Murray, but when Murray did not respond quickly enough to his overtures he made a deal with Sampson Low for £1,000 down and half the net profits. The book was a massive undertaking, for he felt he must write to a length commensurate with his subject. Although he had been able to start assembling his material during the month of waiting in the Seychelles and on the passage to Marseilles, much remained to be done and he promised to hand over the text for setting, chapter by chapter, as he had it ready. Galley proofs had to be read and the book's fifty-three illustrations – engraved from Stanley's own sketches – must be checked for accuracy.

It was the war of words against him by fellow-journalists that Stanley found hardest to bear, for he realised in the first week of August that almost all the British papers were trying to belittle his achievement. The *Spectator* voiced a common opinion about the discovery of Livingstone: 'Nor is grandeur wanting, though it be accompanied by something of the comic in this other figure, that of the newspaper correspondent who, in the regular exercise of his profession, moved neither by pity, nor by love of knowledge, nor by desire of adventure, but by an order from Mr Bennett, coolly plunges into an unknown continent to interview a lost geographer . . .'

At the outset, he could hardly believe his eyes when he read suggestions that he had never been to Ujiji and that Livingstone's letters to the *Herald* were fraudulent, for the style did not accord with anything the doctor had written before. Perhaps, it was darkly hinted, the handwriting of the letters should be compared with Stanley's own. The allegation was made worse because he did have a flair for copying handwriting. Doubts were summed up in an editorial in *The Standard:* 'We cannot resist some suspicions and misgivings in connection with his (Stanley's) story. There is something inexplicable and mysterious about its incidents and conclusion.'

The sceptics could not know how deep this knife went into him, that of all men he was least able to handle the charge of being an impostor. They were not able to guess that so much of his life had been made up of fantasy and improvisation. He needed the simple nod of approval for having done something real and noble. Certainly he had helped Livingstone write his letters to Bennett in a colourful style that would suit the *Herald*, but the very fact that Livingstone had been willing to do so was a sign of the goodwill and affection between them. It was unbearable to be accused of inventing a relationship that was so profoundly dear to him. Stanley retorted to his critics: 'Some of you first doubted the truth of my narrative; then suspected that the letters I produced as coming from here were forgeries; then accused me of sensationalism; then quibbled at the facts I published, and snarled at me as if I had committed a crime. With a simple tale – unvarnished, plain, clear, literal truth – you could find fault! What weakness! What puerility!'

Stanley was able to act quickly against the charge of forgery, although he never forgot the slur. The Foreign Office confirmed that Livingstone's despatches appeared authentic. Tom Livingstone, the explorer's eldest son, said the family were agreed that the diary Stanley had handed over was genuine: 'We have not the slightest reason to doubt that this is my father's journal . . .'

Remarkably enough, these affirmations were not entirely successful, and the debate filled the newspapers throughout August; one theory was that Stanley had met a messenger coming down from the interior and had simply expropriated Livingstone's documents, then turned around and gone back to Zanzibar with them. It was scant compensation to be so suddenly famous that he and Kalulu were modelled for Madam Tussaud's and that composers were moved to dedicate tunes to him. Waltzes, polkas and even a banjo march appeared, adorned with his picture, in the music shops. There were some stirring lines in 'Welcome Stanley' by Hubi Newcombe:

> Near and far o'er distant ocean,
> Come the sounds of many a cheer,
> True hearts beat with deep emotion,
> As brave Stanley's tale they hear . . .

Stanley knew that such musical tributes reflected a widespread feeling, for his mail showed he had numerous sympathisers. But he could have done without them. They added to the touch of music-hall frivolity being fixed upon his name. He felt that if his enemies could not prove him a liar, they were determined to make him look a fool. This gave a new edge to his fury, for although he had a laconic wit and could even manage some self-deprecatory fun in his writing, he was not at all good at accepting mockery.

Much of the joking centred on the moment he held most dear. The newspapers had started it, the public quickly followed suit, and now all the world seemed to shout that one unforgettable greeting: 'Doctor Livingstone, I presume.' It soon became the catch-phrase of errand boys and earls. Young men about town would meet one another in Pall Mall with the cry: 'Mr Carruthers, I presume!' The sentence became a stand-by for advertisers, and some jocular acquaintances were rash enough to greet its originator: 'Mr Stanley, I presume!' This witticism fell like a stone with Stanley and he glared angrily.

He often asked himself what else he could have said, and endearingly admitted that he had wanted at Ujiji to give vent to emotion by 'idiotically biting my hand, turning a somersault or slashing at trees . . .' But he was a white man among a crowd of Arabs and Africans and that imposed upon him the need for dignity, so he had done what 'cowardice and false pride' suggested, in greeting Livingstone with Anglo-Saxon restraint.

Had it not been mixed up with all the other tribulations of the moment, the banter about 'Dr Livingstone, I presume' might have been taken with better grace by Stanley. But the Press campaign was too much for him. *The Spectator* had particularly incensed him by picking up from the *New York Nation* a satirical paragraph about Horace Greeley, who was Democratic candidate for the US Presidency in 1872 – and whose newspaper was a rival to the *Herald*. According to this item, Stanley told Livingstone about Greeley's candidacy, and evoked the response: 'I am a simple, guileless, Christian man, but when you tell me Horace Greeley has become a Democratic candidate I'll be damned to all eternity if I believe it. My trunk is all packed to go home, but I shall remain in Africa, for these things may be true after all . . .' The *Spectator* had printed the quotation, and asked whether Stanley ought to be surprised that Britain was incredulous about Livingstone's letters to the *Herald*. The piece attracted attention and provoked some amusement, but it drove Stanley almost berserk. He was not mollified when the *Spectator* apologised and said it had been 'caught napping' by the hoax.

His mood at the time is well revealed by a reply to an unknown sympathiser. The handwriting is jerky and uncontrolled, quite unlike his normally fluent and forceful style. The letter was written on August 25 from the *Herald* office at 46, Fleet Street. It reads:

Dear Sir, Your letter embraces all that I would wish myself to have said. Because even at Zanzibar – on my return from Central Africa – no one knew that Greeley had become candidate for President. But it is all of a piece, first they would sneer at the fact of an American having gone to Central Africa – then they sneered at the idea of his being successful – then when they heard my name they tried to rob me of it – in one paper I was Smith, in another I was Jones, in another Thomas, and now they have changed it to Rowlands.

They would also rob me of my country – and gossip after flying uneasily over the four divisions of British Isles has settled it to be Wales.

My story is called 'sensational' and unreal etc. I assure you that I think after decently burying Livingstone in forgetfulness they hate to be told he is yet alive. What a country!

Yours truly,
Henry M. Stanley

P.S. It is unnecessary to tell you how thankful I am to you – you have guessed my very thought.

As Stanley wrote the name 'Rowlands' his style suddenly changed to a childish sprawl. There are corrections in every paragraph and after starting to write 'Great Britain' he had crossed it out and substituted 'British Isles'.

At this moment, he had the first whiff of Lewis Noe's revelations about their joint desertion from the US Navy, and the Turkish episode, in the *New York Sun*, and knew that all the hurtful details would be picked up with relish by the London papers. Noe's opening letter had appeared on August 24, and the gist was telegraphed to London. By September 13, Stanley was driven to writing a disclaimer to James Gordon Bennett for publication in the *Herald*. In his bid to defend himself he heaped abuse on Noe, and using Livingstone's phrase called him a 'moral idiot'; but there was little he could do to obliterate the facts.

While Stanley was grappling with the Press, he was simultaneously at odds with the mandarins of the Royal Geographical Society. He did not meet Sir Henry Rawlinson at first, for when he arrived in London Rawlinson went to stay in the country. A few days earlier, Sir Henry had declared that he did not see any point in calling a special meeting of the Society to hear Stanley, because nothing Livingstone had sent home was of any interest to geographers.

The snub to Stanley did not pass unnoticed. The *Telegraph*, which praised him without reservation, accused Rawlinson of unworthily revealing 'a certain chagrin'. Markham notes in his journal that a friends told him the Society was going down in public opinion. 'I replied, "Damn public opinion! The fellow has done no geography." ' If Markham had had his way, the Society would have stuck to its guns. 'But Sir Henry Rawlinson was weak and got alarmed.'

However, this process took Rawlinson the best part of a week, and in the meantime Stanley had, on August 3, a five-hour confrontation with Horace Waller. The only account of this event, which took place in the reporter's room at the Langham, is in an eighteen-page letter from Waller to Livingstone. Waller told Livingstone that Stanley 'had a reputation before in Abyssinia and elsewhere, and a pretty strong one too' – an opinion that almost certainly derived from Markham. Yet it was not as a spokesman for the RGS that Waller talked with Stanley, but as a partisan for Kirk. He argued tirelessly that Stanley had maligned Kirk and ruined his career; but it was not, he stressed, because he was related to Kirk that he was resolved to defend him, but only since he knew he was a loyal friend and Christian, who had done his best to aid Livingstone but had been deceived by Indians and Arabs.

It is obvious that Waller, a former stockbroker who had turned to the Church, did not appeal to Stanley, and the antipathy was at once reciprocated. As Waller said later, Stanley was 'a low fellow' who 'twitted him' about being related to Kirk. At one point in his long epistle to Livingstone, Waller gives a vivid account of how he 'caught out' Stanley, who said he had not received a letter from him when, in fact, he had. It is hard to see from the contents of the letter why this was so significant to Waller, and Stanley might have been excused for being muddled at the time by the rush of events and correspondence. But Waller cites it as proof of Stanley's general deceitfulness. 'Most men that I have been associated with would feel awkward in being caught out in a barefaced falsehood, and when I saw the sang froid with which this man quietly shifted his cigar to the other side of his mouth, and the subject, without a word, to something else, I confess, Doctor, I did feel very sorry for you and very sorry for Kirk.'

The controversy was heightened by the appearance in *The Times* of a letter, dated August 2, from Henry Churchill, the erstwhile superior of Kirk in Zanzibar. He was now living in retirement in Maida Vale. While speaking up for Kirk he was bold enough to denounce the distant Livingstone: 'He must not forget . . . that the men he himself selected basely betrayed him and falsely reported his death, whence the source of all his disappointments.' Letters of an almost hysterical tone had been received from Kirk himself. Addressed to a Foreign Office official, they accused Stanley of having opened his mail and of suppressing letters given to him by Livingstone. Kirk also said he was glad that Livingstone – whom he was now calling 'a damned old scoundrel' – would not be likely to come out of Africa for another three years.

In this acrid situation there was almost audible relief when the RGS broke its silence six days after Stanley had landed in Britain. Since the Society held no public functions in the summer, it suggested that he should address a meeting of the geographical section of the British Association. The event would be in Brighton, where the Association was having its annual conference. The public reaction was fervent, for although Stanley's name was on everybody's lips, only a handful of people had seen him. At that time newspapers were not yet able to print photographs, and the only pictures of him to be seen were in shop windows; they had been posed in a West End studio, and showed the intrepid reporter in *safari* clothes, his topee placed jauntily on the back of his head, a revolver at his waist, a double-barrelled gun against his arm and a cigar between his fingers; alongside stood Kalulu with African spear and shield.

If the 3,000 people who crowded into the Brighton concert-hall for the meeting had expected a flamboyant figure, they were disappointed. Stanley's small, rather round form, was dressed in a conservative suit, his face was expressionless, and he seemed dwarfed by Sir Henry Rawlinson, who was escorting him down the aisle. On the way to the platform, he paused beside the front row and was introduced to the two most distinguished guests – the exiled Emperor of France, Napoleon III, and the Empress Eugenie. The last time he had seen Eugenie was at the opening of the Suez Canal; since then, life had changed remarkably for both of them. He gave a slight bow, and went on his way to the rostrum.

Stanley was introduced by Francis (later Sir Francis) Galton, president of the British Association's geographical section. According to the newspapers, which gave most elaborate coverage to the occasion, Stanley seemed totally self-possessed. The *Telegraph* said that he had a 'strong voice, of great compass and considerable flexibility' and had the evident purpose of speaking his mind to everybody without any deference or hesitation. In fact, he records in his diary that he was terrified by the size of the audience. He made three attempts to get into his speech and then decided to abandon a prepared text about his geographical surveys with Livingstone on Lake Tanganyika. He began to speak extemporaneously, likening himself to a troubadour who came to tell of an old man searching for the sources of the Nile.

The professional members of the British Association had never been treated to such a speech before. Stanley was never afraid of hyperbole. He used his hands a lot as he touched upon any points he wanted to emphasise. It was clear now where the inspiration had come from for some of Livingstone's more surprising paragraphs in the *New York Herald*, such as his racy description of the buxom 'black hussies' of Manyema who filed their teeth to points. As the speech ended, Galton said condescendingly that they had not come to hear sensational stories, but to discuss serious facts. It was a slight Stanley did not take to kindly, and ten days later he publicly attacked Galton by name for his 'suavity'.

Following Stanley there were several subsidiary speakers, including Colonel James Grant, who had gone with Speke eight years before to Lake Victoria and the Nile. Grant quite sensibly questioned the accuracy of Livingstone's geographical theories, and when Stanley's chance came to speak again he was excitedly abusive, roughly calling Grant 'a geographer resident in England'. This so irritated Grant that he was to become for some time the sharpest critic inside the RGS of the celebrated reporter-traveller.

The nervous toll the occasion had taken on Stanley showed itself a few hours later when he and Galton were guests at a luncheon given by the Mayor and Corporation of Brighton. In the post-prandial speeches, Galton with a blundering lack of tact asked if Stanley might care to clear up one or two mysteries about himself. Was he a Welshman, or not? Stanley turned on him; such a query, he said, 'could only proceed from idle curiosity'. He wrote in his diary: 'A person like myself, with such a miserable, unfortunate past, cannot possibly find pleasure in speaking before people who have wined and eaten to the full, about his poverty-stricken childhood . . .' The next day his tension revealed itself in even more dramatic form. He was asked to speak at a meeting of the Sussex Medical Society – a formal, dinner-dress function. As Stanley talked he returned to the habit of waving his arms, a style he had acquired while haranguing African porters. Over their brandy, some of the doctors thought this rather droll; they winked and giggled. He saw them, threw a sovereign on the tablecloth in front of him, bowed to the chairman and strode out into the summer night.

As the controversy ground on, he altered the proofs of his book to include ripostes to his enemies. He wrote an emotional preface, which he was to have second thoughts about and delete at the last moment. One paragraph read: 'As you glory in your nationality, and country, permit me to glory in mine. I claim to be an American; nothing can ever force me to deny it. But whether it is my native or adopted country; whether I am a native, or legally naturalised American, is totally foreign to this book and its contents. Be assured I am too proud of my American citizenship ever to disclaim it. When the public call for my biography it will be time enough for me to set about writing an autograph history of my life. I proceeded to Africa to discover Dr Livingstone, not to discover myself . . .'

At the end of August, Stanley received recognition from an unexpected quarter – from Queen Victoria. She sent him a gold and

lapis lazuli snuff-box, adorned with diamonds, rubies, emeralds and the royal cipher. With it was a message praising him for his fearlessness, prudence and zeal. Next there was a letter from Sir Henry Rawlinson, saying that he had been charged with the duty of taking him to meet the Queen at Dunrobin Castle, residence of the Duke of Sutherland. On the way up in the train, Rawlinson gave some well-meant advice on how to behave with royalty – and how Stanley must not, on any account, write a story about what the Queen might say to him.

But the warning was superfluous; not even for James Gordon Bennett would Stanley take such a liberty with 'the lady to whom in my heart of hearts next to God, I worshipped.' Stanley's private record of his visit to Dunrobin Castle is shot through with awe and sentimentality. The audience lasted for ten minutes, then Victoria departed with a 'gracefully gliding movement'.

The cottage where Stanley was born, and (left) his mother at her garden gate

In his capacity as RGS secretary, Clements Markham was driven to an outward acceptance of Stanley because of the Queen's recognition. An invitation to dinner, in company with Richard Burton, came a week after Stanley visited Dunrobin. Moreover, the view was growing inside the Society that Stanley must after all be awarded the highest geographical award, the Victoria gold medal. Leading this movement now was Rawlinson, who was finding the public controversy unbearable. Opponents argued that Stanley's journey to Ujiji was not a true work of exploration; even though he was only the fourth white man to see Lake Tanganyika and had traversed completely unknown terrain west of Tabora, that was all incidental. In Grant's opinion, Stanley should be given money (which would surely have been the most deadly insult of all) or a special medal struck for the occasion. Waller kept up his own campaign, and wrote to H. W. Bates, Markham's assistant: 'Stanley is utterly unworthy of credence and will continue to vilify Kirk to the end . . .'

It was true that Stanley was sticking to his anti-Kirk campaign. After his speech in Brighton he had been invited to lecture in cities all over Britain, and during a tour across Scotland he lambasted Kirk relentlessly. On September 28 he wrote a long and aggressive letter to *The Times*, with which Waller had close contacts and where he could get news items to suit his purposes inserted almost at will. Stanley said that certain criticisms of him in the paper had been 'prompted by one of Dr Kirk's relatives, with whose name I am well acquainted.' In the view of Mark Twain, who liked keeping in with the British ruling classes, Stanley was wrong-headed in still being so bellicose. Writing to his wife Olivia, Twain called it 'puppyism' – 'though indeed he *must* have learnt his puppyism from us.'

As the arguments ground on, and Waller pounded his foe with letters asking him not to attack Kirk in his forthcoming book, Rawlinson saw more and more clearly that the only way to ease the dispute was by at once giving Stanley the Society's gold medal. Rawlinson was so insistent that Grant and Waller were silenced. So the invitations went out for a dinner in St James's, and there on October 31 the medal was handed over. Everybody was on his best behaviour, apologies were offered all around and Sir Henry was the epitome of goodwill. Among the guests, at Stanley's special request, was Mark Twain. Stanley had managed to slip a last-minute postscript into his 700-page *How I Found Livingstone*, which was due out at the start of November, praising the Society and regretting any rough statements he might have made in earlier parts of the book.

Even before the first edition was out, Stanley gave instructions that extensive cuts should be made, excising all references to Kirk and softening several other sections which he now felt were too provocative. The advance orders were so heavy that the publishers could not follow these orders in the second edition, which came hard on the heels of the first, but the changes were made in the third, appearing shortly before Christmas.

After Stanley's troubles with the RGS had run their course, there was a strange sequel. A letter in the family archives shows that even before his book was published, Stanley was eager to return to Africa – in co-operation with the Society, which was trying to restore its name by sending out two more expeditions to Livingstone, one from Zanzibar and another from the mouth of the Congo.

On October 8, Stanley had ended a brief truce with Markham by writing to ridicule the whole idea of sending relief to Livingstone. He said that Markham 'knew as well as he did' that Livingstone did not need any help. He went on: 'If you are a friend of Livingstone, why do you attempt to put a stumbling block in his way? Why can you not wait patiently for his return? . . . I regret very much having

Left to right: General Sir Henry Rawlinson, president of the Royal Geographical Society; Clements Markham, the honorary secretary; and Lieutenant Verney Lovett Cameron. The Society sent Cameron to help Livingstone after being humiliated by the *New York Herald*'s scoop. Stanley offered to go back with Cameron, but was rebuffed

to write to you, but it is for your own good . . .' But very shortly after adopting this provocative tone, he seems to have changed his mind entirely.

The expedition from Zanzibar was to be led by Lieutenant Verney Lovett Cameron, and on October 25 he replied to a letter (not now to be found) from Stanley. Cameron said: 'I regret exceedingly that circumstances have arisen which render me unable to join my expedition to yours. I am very sorry indeed to be unable to avail myself of your experience, pluck and energy, more especially as I am certain we should have pulled together; I hope however that if we meet in Terra Incognita we shall always extend the right hand of fellowship to each other, and if we either want assistance I on my part will guarantee that whatever help I can render you will be given ungrudgingly.' The letter ends by offering congratulations for the award of the Society's gold medal.

There is no knowing how Stanley hoped to finance his expedition. It is unlikely that the *Herald* would have been interested, so soon after supporting the costly march to Ujiji. But far more interesting is his motivation. Had he found, after all, a compelling fascination in the vast spaces of the continent? Did Africa alone seem to offer him the possibility of ceaseless action, and the chance to exercise his newly-demonstrated powers of command? Or was he impelled in his approach to Cameron by a yearning to be once again with Livingstone? As he was to write many years afterwards: 'Somehow these dreams perpetually haunt me. I seem to see through the dim, misty, warm, hazy atmosphere of Africa always the aged face of Livingstone, urging me on in his own kind, fatherly way.'

225

16. Interlude at Newstead Abbey

Stanley made hundreds of acquaintances during his months in Britain in 1872, but it was only Emilia Webb he could regard as a friend against whom no defences were necessary. At a first glance, their relationship was unlikely: Emilia Webb was in her late thirties, had six children, and was married to a wealthy old Etonian whose main preoccupations were hunting and looking after his estates. Emilia Webb had a favourite saying – 'If you do a thing, be sure you do it gracefully.' Whatever might be said for Stanley, gracefulness was not among his virtues.

Yet there was far more to the Webbs than a talent for pursuing upper-class Victorian pleasures. They were friends of Livingstone, and maintained a close interest in African exploration. Livingstone had written to them asking that they should show Stanley all the affection they could; he spoke of the young American with glowing gratitude. Livingstone's letters to the Webbs had been brought back by Stanley among a bundle of correspondence and handed over to the Foreign Office for delivery. The Webbs and their children were at Arrochar on Loch Long, Scotland, when the letters arrived. Their remote house at Arrochar was crowded with shooting guests, and it was not practical to invite the unknown Mr Stanley to stay with them immediately. In any case, he was clearly far too busy in London. But the Webbs studied the newspaper reports about him, and debated whether to go down to hear him speak to the British Association in Brighton. In the end they decided against it – it was a very long way, and there seemed no reason to think he would need support and sympathy.

Two days after the meeting, the daily papers reached Arrochar with their verbatim descriptions of what had been said. The Webbs' eldest daughter, Augusta, leaves an account of her mother's reaction: 'She stood, paper in hand, alternately reading out passages and exclaiming in her indignation. Her blue eyes flashed with anger, and she actually shed tears of compassion for "that poor Stanley", whom neither she nor my father had met . . .' It was several days before

Emilia Webb could regain her equanimity. The formal invitation already sent to Stanley was followed by a more pressing appeal that he should come and stay. He accepted and a date in early October was agreed upon.

From all she heard, Emilia Webb realised that she must invite Stanley alone, without any other guests. She also resolved to devote all her time to him. Her intuition was acute and by comparison William Webb appears as a rather wooden figure – although it was to him that the family owed its connection with Livingstone. He had first met the explorer when he had gone out to Africa on a hunting trip after resigning his commission in the 17th Lancers, and had devotedly maintained the contact for twenty years.

Stanley stayed with the Webbs at Newstead Abbey, their principal home, eleven miles from Nottingham. Surrounded by lakes it was a place of grandeur, and earlier in the century had belonged to Lord Byron, who gives a description of it in 'Don Juan'. Newstead had been considered as a possible home for the young Prince of Wales, but Sandringham was bought instead. Shortly before William Webb acquired it in 1860, a Colonel Wildman, who had made his money out of sugar plantations in Jamaica, added an ugly battlemented structure known as the 'Sussex Tower'. It was in this tower that Livingstone had stayed for several months during his last visit to Britain in 1864, and Emilia Webb put Stanley up in the same high-ceilinged room. He slept in a four-poster bed, with a striped coverlet, that Livingstone had used.

For the first two days of his stay, Stanley recounted his experiences with Livingstone, and startled the Webbs by the details he could remember that the explorer had told him about Newstead. At the outset, the Webbs found Stanley rough, aggressive and suspicious. Emilia Webb called him 'a perfect Ishmaelite, with his hand raised against every man, and feeling every man's hand was raised against him – at any rate in England'. She sensed that she knew how to handle him, and each day she went out walking with him in the grounds of Newstead, or took him for long drives in her pony phaeton. Most of all she encouraged him to speak freely about himself, and in later years he said he had never in his life been so talkative as at Newstead – 'where one was stimulated by that exceptional, most loveable being, Mrs Webb.'

Stanley had only been a few days at Newstead when he poured out to her the secrets of his life, from his very beginnings in Denbigh

Mrs Emilia Webb befriended Stanley when controversy swirled around him in 1872

and St Asaph. He would admit nothing of this in public, but he was softened and relaxed by telling his story to a woman he could trust. Yet Stanley had moments when he was silent and short-tempered. Augusta Webb could never forget his eyes: 'They were like pools of grey fire, but the least provocation turned them into grey lightning . . . They seemed to scorch and shrivel up all he looked at. But his whole personality at this time gave one the impression of overwhelming and concentrated force, a human explosive power that only required a mere chance to turn towards good or evil.'

He showed the least constraint of all when he played with the Webb children, who ranged in age from their teens to six. One afternoon the family made a tour of the estate, looking at work being done on the drains and fences. Their guest was bored, and saw the children were also. Suddenly he led them all off on a chase through the plantations and woods, on what he called 'an exploring expedition in Africa'. He had such a gift for transmitting his own imagining to others that when he told the children that a fallen tree was a crocodile, a big stump a hippopotamus, or a farmer's boy a hostile African warrior, they all believed him. The Webbs found that he was at his best with children, gentle and careful, and able to play with them as one of themselves. He promised that next time he came to stay he would bring with him his famous young servant, Kalulu.

Stanley was able to accept any rebukes from Emilia Webb, and she even dared to give him advice about his manners and the way he dressed. The family noticed how dutifully he obeyed everything she had told him to do. But there was less success when the Webbs decided to invite some neighbours to dine with him. All Stanley's hostility returned, and he glared so incessantly that the visitors left early. Emilia Webb told him: 'I really will never ask people to meet you again. It is hopeless. You are always so very nice when you are with us alone, but directly a strange face appears you are – well, you are a perfect porcupine with all your quills out, and I can do nothing with you.' Everybody laughed, even Stanley, but he knew it was more than a joke.

Emilia Webb often remarked afterwards: 'He has under all his roughness one of the most affectionate natures I have ever met with, and quite the most grateful.' He needed a good woman to marry him – for the right wife could make anything of him. 'Only,' said Emilia Webb, 'she would have to care for him *enough*.'

Stanley was soon to have a painful encounter with Katie Gough-Roberts, the girl who had so nearly become his wife. After his visit to Newstead he went to Wales, where he called on his mother and gave her a gold watch. He also looked in at the St Asaph workhouse, to meet the Governors and again praise 'the education to which he attributed so much of his fame in life'. He may have heard the stories in Denbigh that Katie Gough-Roberts had jilted him after being told by his half-sister Emma, in a fit of jealousy, that he was already secretly married. One of his letters to Katie had been found in a water-butt, and Emma was accused of throwing it there.

A few weeks later, Stanley was in Manchester to give a talk at the Free Trade Hall. It was to be the last of his public lectures before he and Kalulu set sail for New York from Liverpool. Sitting in the best seats were several of his relatives, who had come over from Denbigh especially for the occasion – and also among the audience was Katie Bradshaw and her husband. They now lived near Manchester. Katie had with her the long letter he had written her in March 1869, telling the story of his life; it seems that Stanley had already written to her asking for it back, and she had replied that he must meet her in person if he wanted it. The 'biography', as Katie called it, contained all those painful truths which Stanley had just revealed to Emilia Webb, as well as several blatant pieces of make-believe which he dearly wanted to forget.

During his visit to Denbigh he would certainly have heard of inquiries being made there about his early years. This, he knew, was connected with a forthcoming biography which had been advertised in the *Bookseller* by one of London's less reputable publishers, John Camden Hotten of Piccadilly. It is likely that Stanley also knew that Katie Bradshaw had allowed Hotten to photograph a page of his letter for publication in the book. As if all this were not upsetting enough, a theatrical manager who had hired the Free Trade Hall for the lecture had been approached for help in selling Hotten's book.

After the lecture Stanley went off to the house of the president of the Manchester Chamber of Commerce, with whom he was staying, and Katie followed him. She sent in a visiting card, with a note asking him to see her, but he refused. He sent a man to ask Katie for the 'biography letter'; but she insisted that he must come for it himself. Her former fiancé never appeared at the door, and finally she went away.

The matter stayed clearly in Stanley's mind, and the next day – between making the final preparations for his departure for America and attending a civic banquet – he wrote a letter to *The Times*. In it he ponderously condemns Hotten and all his works. One sentence reads: 'Since this man is so unscrupulous as to use my name unlawfully for a pecuniary purpose, permit me to say that I repudiate John Camden Hotten's assumed connection with me, and anything and everything he may relate concerning me and mine, in any book or books he may publish or have published.' As it turned out, *H. M. Stanley, His Early Life* had a poor sale; the public was becoming sated with the whole Livingstone controversy, and Hotten's notoriety made the contents suspect. But the thought of that bundle of letters being hoarded by Katie Bradshaw in a quiet Manchester suburb continued to nag away in the back of Stanley's mind for many years to come.

17· 'Each Man Has His Own Way'

James Gordon Bennett the elder lived just long enough to see the raffish fame of his *New York Herald* magnified by the discovery of Livingstone. It was an improbable turn of fate, for while both Bennett and Livingstone were Scots of humble origin who had won unparalleled success in their own fields, the world considered them moral opposites. Livingstone was the epitome of self-denial, Bennett the supreme opportunist. When the *Herald*'s founder died in August 1872, the London *Graphic* remarked: 'Mr Bennett had no special prejudice in favour of vice over virtue. He simply regarded himself as a purveyor of commodities. If the public wanted an article he supplied it.' Bennett's early years were not unlike those of Stanley. He had arrived in America in poverty and was saved from starvation by finding a shilling on Boston Common. After several false starts he turned to journalism and began the *Herald* in a cellar, editing it on a plank across two barrels. He lived sparely and died one of the richest men in the United States.

Stanley never saw much of the elder Bennett, who had begun handing the reins to his son in the late 1860's. Yet the death of the almost legendary founder did bring some disadvantages, because James Gordon Bennett Jr was testing his strength. When told a particular member of the editorial staff was indispensable, he asked for a list of the twelve most indispensable men and sacked the lot. Knowing the nature of the younger Bennett, Stanley had been careful to dedicate *How I Found Livingstone* to him, and put a flattering, fullpage engraving of his cadaverous features in front of the introduction. He had even named a group of islands in Lake Tanganyika after the *New York Herald*. Could a loyal employee do more?

But to Bennett there could be only one man on the paper who really mattered: himself. He was jealous, just as the Royal Geographical Society had been. If Stanley had found Livingstone, he had found Stanley: 'Who was he before I discovered him?' So it was characteristic that when the celebrated correspondent reached New York on November 20, to be greeted by the Mayor and huge, cheering crowds, Bennett was not to be seen. Stanley went to the *Herald* building on Broadway and was shown into the proprietor's sombre office. Bennett gave him ten minutes, during which they smoked cigars and exchanged guarded platitudes. They did not meet again before Bennett left at the end of a week for Paris, his favourite haunt.

If Stanley was snubbed by Bennett, he found compensation in the welcome from his newspaper colleagues. A committee to arrange the reception was headed by Colonel Anderson, who when in London had constantly helped Stanley. Anderson took charge of one of the fleet of fast steam yachts used by the *Herald* to meet incoming vessels and collect advance news. The yacht came alongside the steamer well outside the harbour, and by special permission of the port authorities the subject of all the excitement went from one to the other by ladder. The yacht was packed with reporters and geographers, who toasted him in champagne until he stepped ashore.

Across the yacht was a banner, with letters two feet high, reading 'Welcome Home, Stanley!' The words touched him. He felt that America was his home, even though he had not seen it for almost five years. He had found his name here, learnt the crafts of journalism and shaped his identity. It had given him the freedom to follow his dreams of adventure and fame. Now every paper in America was writing about him, and the image they presented was based upon his own mélange of truth and romancing. A typical word-picture said he was a Missourian who worked as a journalist 'more for love than money, as he is a person of means'. He had been a *New York Herald* correspondent in the Civil War, had been set upon by brigands while travelling with his half-brother through Turkey, and among many skills was an expert swordsman. Nobody seemed to question such claims, or to care about the reports of his poor childhood in Wales. Asked if he sang in Welsh, he flatly denied it.

What interested New Yorkers most of all was the battle between the city's newspapers over the Livingstone exploit. The *Herald* did defend him, but relished the controversy stirred up by the *Sun*, who based its claims that Stanley was a fraud upon interviews with Lewis Noe. The final attack by Noe ended by calling Stanley a 'first-class extemporaneous liar'; when Stanley reached the United States he offered no reply and never saw his 'half-brother', who stayed at home in Suffolk County, Long Island, well away from the scenes of jubilation. Stanley also ignored a headline in the *New York Tribune*:

'Impostor. Liar. Murderer.' In his suite in the Fifth Avenue Hotel he waved the worn consul's hat given to him by Livingstone as a keepsake; 'I may be called a forger, but I would like to know if I could forge Dr Livingstone's cap!' To reinforce this, he produced to the journalists filling the suite his valet Kalulu, who did a tribal dance and sang in Swahili. By now, Kalulu was taking every new experience with cool insouciance.

Throughout the first week of his return to America, there was no escape for Stanley from receptions and banquets. As often as he could he made excuses, blaming malaria for 'a serious indisposition which sometimes attacks me in the spleen and liver.' One function he did attend readily was a dinner in his honour by the American Geographical Society, who had sent a delegation bearing formal congratulations out in the *Herald* yacht. He had no dissension with the New York geographers, as with those in London. But he wrote in his diary: 'It is as well that I have a little experience of these public dinners, otherwise I should be ruined in health . . . the wine is well-watered and I never go beyond three dishes.'

Another reason why Stanley begrudged the time spent in being fêted was that he was trying to prepare himself for a series of lectures. He had taken Mark Twain's advice and signed a contract with an American impresario for a long series of platform appearances. If he could hit the right style, he might earn 50,000 dollars.

But the lectures proved what one paper called a 'dismal failure'. At the Steinway Hall he did not draw a full audience on the first night, and by the third night it was all over. The *Sun* quoted the janitor of the Steinway with some relish: 'Stanley's played out; there will be no lecture tonight or any other night, as Mr Stanley's receipts do not meet expenses.' The cause of the debacle is unclear, for whereas some newspapers said he spoke badly and in a low voice, others said that his material was too solemn. Probably Stanley was trying too hard, for he started off with a survey of African exploration from the time of Henry the Navigator, and ended with a peroration about the prospects for evangelism in the Dark Continent.

Christmas time and the first three months of 1873 were spent aimlessly by Stanley, attending dinners and lecturing very occasionally. He re-visited haunts with which he had once been familiar, and spent much time with his newspaper colleagues. One was Felix Lafontaine, a financial journalist whom Stanley called 'my dear old philosopher'. He also saw much of Finlay Anderson and his family.

233

But what Stanley really wanted was to return to normal work, and he awaited a message from Bennett, who was still in France, eating plover's eggs and driving around the countryside in a coach and four. In April the call came, and Stanley first caught a ship to London, where he enrolled Kalulu at the Holbrake School, Wandsworth; it was a rather drab establishment, run by a clergyman, and had been recommended to Stanley by his publisher, Edward Marston. Before Kalulu began his lessons the pair of them went up to stay with the Webbs at Newstead. It was again a successful visit, although Kalulu disappointed his master by failing to live up to the meaning of his name, 'the hare'. In a race against one of the Webb daughters he was hopelessly outdistanced.

In Paris, Stanley found Bennett at the Hotel des Deux Mondes, and the two of them had a disagreeable interview. After Stanley pressed the point, his salary was raised from £400 to £1,000 a year. That hurdle overcome, Bennett told him to go back to Spain, to his old position in charge of the Madrid bureau.

The civil war was still dragging on, and it was almost as though the Livingstone expedition had never happened. Stanley did his best to recapture the spirit of his war reporting in the sixties, but for the moment his career seemed becalmed.

Of most immediate concern was the publication of his second book, much of it written during his months of idleness in the United States. Called *My Kalulu*, it is a long adventure story for boys, set in Central Africa and having for its hero Stanley's ubiquitous servant – his status and nature fondly enhanced; the book has a subtitle: 'Prince, King, and Slave.' It is full of sentiment, leavened with jungle adventures and African folk tales, the narrative often closely following Stanley's own experiences. Although *My Kalulu* ran through several impressions it was not a great success, and he never again attempted fiction.

While Stanley was reflecting upon the contrast between the success of *How I Found Livingstone* and the tepid response to *My Kalulu* he became friendly with a man who really did have the knack of writing boys' books – George A. Henty. In his long career Henty wrote more than seventy successful adventure stories, being unrivalled both in output and in his ability to expound the Victorian faith in Empire, manliness and racial superiority; his influence upon several generations of the British middle class was vast. Stanley had previously met Henty on the Magdala campaign, for apart from

turning out three or four books a year, Henty was a war correspondent for a London daily; Henty's assignments gave him the raw
material for his 'rattling good yarns'.

Together with several other correspondents, Stanley and Henty
were ordered by their papers to sail in November 1873 for the Gold
Coast, where a punitive campaign was being mounted by the British
against the Ashanti people. Stanley was glad to escape from Spain
and go back to Africa; the Gold Coast was on the western side of the
continent, which he had not had the chance to look at before. It
seemed to Stanley that it might be hard to cover the campaign
effectively without private transport, and he had made ready for this
by buying a small Thames pleasure boat powered by a steam engine.
He also hired an engineer to work her. The other correspondents
viewed this as novel, not to say eccentric. But he had rightly judged
the obstacles ahead.

Foremost among these obstacles was General Sir Garnet Wolseley,
an impatient and terrier-like person who was in charge of the
expeditionary force. Wolseley was not one for encouraging journalists
to reveal his strategy ahead of time; if anybody was to tell the British
public how the Gold Coast war was going, it would be Sir Garnet
himself. The appearance of Stanley upon the scene must have made
the general's invariably stiff upper lip even stiffer, for the outflank-
ing of Napier by the *Herald* after Magdala would long be remembered
in army circles. When Stanley told Wolseley he hoped to stay close
to him during the march, he was coldly rebuffed. Throughout the
four months of the campaign, the correspondents were starved of
news, and one report by Stanley was bitterly headed 'Victory over
the Press!' Wolseley made a point of sending official despatches to
London several days before handing out copies to the correspondents
on the spot. The journalists took out their vexation with Sir Garnet
by denouncing the manner in which he ran the campaign.

The Gold Coast turned out to be hot, malarious and tedious.
Stanley looked in vain for action and wrote prolix despatches in
which the words seem to have been dragged out of him. Such spirit
that appears is in the anti-British sentiments peppering his material,
or when he condemns the uselessness of the coastal tribesmen against
the up-country Ashantis; slave-chains might be the answer, he
suggests provocatively. He also spends much space on discussing the
causes of malaria in this 'white man's grave' and blames a shortage
of ozone.

There were weeks of delay while Wolseley awaited the bulk of his forces for the march to Coomassie (now Kumasi). Henty drank vast quantities of claret as a defence against fever, an idea that Stanley did not endorse. However, Henty bore up well; he was a bold, burly man, nine years older than Stanley, and when the correspondents were invited to take a trip down the coast in the *Herald*'s little boat, Henty was the only one to step forward. He later remarked that he had not then seen the vessel, which Stanley had grandly named the *Dauntless* and kept anchored off shore.

Henty's biography, in a chapter called 'A Risky Cruise with H. M. Stanley', tells how the other correspondents warned him that he was the father of a family; he should look after himself, not to mention the interests of his paper. But after a moment of doubt, he decided to chance it. Stanley had, after all, been quite polite in making the offer, so it would be ungentlemanly to refuse.

When they rowed out to the *Dauntless* she was down to the gunwales in the water, having taken two tons of coal on board; as soon as the engine was started, the water washed over the afterdeck. Stanley remained imperturbable, and after a little difficulty while the steam pressure was fixed, they made a successful trip, staying close to the shore and going far enough to interview an officer leading a separate unit of the campaign. Both Henty and Stanley seized the chance to heap extravagant praise on the officer, to the disadvantage of Wolseley. Not surprisingly, Henty made use of the cruise to provide a chapter for his next adventure story, entitled *By Sheer Pluck;* the vessel appears as the *Decoy*, a neat and tidy gunboat, but otherwise the trip is quite accurately recounted. The hero of *By Sheer Pluck* may have been based on a youth called Swinburne who was Stanley's valet and clerk. Henty mentions him briefly, although Stanley never does, either in his published writings or his diaries.

At last the advance on Coomassie began, and it became clear that the Ashanti warriors with their ancient muskets were no match for Wolseley's rifles and rockets. The army also had a Gatling gun, which was useful for striking terror into local chiefs. There were two short battles; the correspondents took part in the fighting, which earned them Wolseley's grudging praise.

Coomassie was duly captured and burnt to the ground. The Ashanti king signed a peace treaty (although troubles were to break out again in the 1890's and another war had to be mounted). Stanley and his colleagues hurried back to the coast to avoid the rainy season and were invited to travel as far as the Cape Verde islands in a British warship. On the way Stanley began to pull together his despatches into a running narrative. This was later to be published, together with his story of the Abyssinia campaign, under the title *Coomassie and Magdala*. In his introduction he says frankly: 'The story of Magdala was written five years ago. The reader will perceive it to be in a much fresher style than the story of Coomassie . . . The story of Coomassie is dull compared with that of Magdala . . .'

When the warship arrived on February 25 at the island of St Vincent, a brief cable gave Stanley the news he must have long been expecting: Livingstone was dead. After the arrival of the men and supplies the reporter sent up from the coast, he had begun a final wandering journey to the south in search of the legendary fountains of Herodotus. His body at last could endure no more, and little more than a year after Stanley had bade him farewell, Livingstone died in a hut near the swampy Lake Bangweulu.

In his notebook, Stanley put down his feelings about Livingstone. The entry is a setpiece of nineteenth-century piety: 'Dear Livingstone! another sacrifice to Africa! His mission, however, must not be allowed to cease; others must go forward and fill the gap. "Close up, boys! Close up! Death must find us everywhere." May I be selected to succeed him in opening up Africa to the shining light of Christianity! My methods, however, will not be Livingstone's. Each man has his own way. His, I think, had its defects, though the old man, personally, has been nearly Christ-like for goodness, patience and self-sacrifice. The selfish wooden-headed world required promptings other than the Gospel, for man is a composite, of spiritual and mundane. But may Livingstone's God be with me as He was with him in all his loneliness, and direct me as He wills. I can only vow to be obedient and not slacken.'

Stanley arrived in London in mid-March. The body of Livingstone, after being dried in the sun by his followers and carried more than 1,500 miles to the coast, had still not arrived in Britain. It was on its way in a steamer due to reach Southampton in a month. Stanley took rooms in the Langham Hotel, and went to the *Herald* office to read the file of stories about Livingstone's death. Any lingering doubts about the truth of the reports fell away, and he composed a five-page letter of condolences (March 18, 1874) to Agnes Livingstone. In contrast to the flowery style of his diary entry, the letter is simple and affecting. One paragraph says: 'How I envy you such a father. The richest inheritance a father can give his children is an honoured name. What man ever left a nobler name than Livingstone?' The letter ends, however, on a much more prosaic note, with the advice that Agnes must make sure that no publisher is given access to Livingstone's journal. It is, he explains, worth at least £10,000.

In the weeks before he was due to go down to Southampton to meet the ship with Livingstone's remains on board, Stanley turned over in his mind the scheme he had hinted at in his diary. He wanted to embark upon a labour of exploration to dwarf all others that Africa had known. He would reduce his critics to silence, or die in the attempt. For the moment he spoke to nobody about what he had in mind.

The ship docked at Southampton on April 15, and Livingstone's coffin was brought ashore to the sound of a twenty-one-gun salute and solemn music by a military band. It was taken by special train to London, and lay in state for two days at the offices of the Royal Geographical Society. The crowds waiting to file past were tearful; as the newspapers said in one sentimental editorial after another, the martyrdom of the great explorer displayed all that was most noble in the national character. Sometimes it was necessary to carry out the civilising mission with bullets and fire, as Sir Garnet Wolseley had just done in the Gold Coast; but Livingstone had achieved it with the Bible in his hand.

The feelings around the coffin in Westminster Abbey may have been more complicated – for although nobody would have dared expressed such a thought, there was irony in the combination of pall-bearers. At the front went Stanley, and beside him was Jacob Wainwright, an African despite his name; the mission-trained Wainwright was a former slave, who had been sent up to Livingstone in May 1872. Another of the pallbearers was Horace Waller – and a fourth was John Kirk, who happened to be in England on leave. The remaining four were former associates of Livingstone, including William Webb of Newstead. Behind them walked Kalulu in a neat grey suit.

As Stanley watched Livingstone's coffin being lowered into place beneath the aisle in Westminster Abbey, he had no doubts about the task he must now undertake. It was his destiny to make the greatest journey of exploration ever attempted in Central Africa – to the great lakes, to the sources of the Nile, then through the heart of the continent and down the Congo to the sea. He went back to his rooms in the Langham Hotel, to start drawing up his plans.

PART THREE

Power and Illusion

18. Servant of the King

When Stanley returned to England at the start of 1878 after his stupendous journey across Africa and down the Congo, the commitment of his life the 'Dark Continent' was absolute. Exactly ten years earlier he had set out for Magdala to report the overthrow of the Emperor Theodore. That campaign was only a remote memory, but it pointed the direction for his career: the 'scoop' that resulted from bribing the Suez telegraph manager consolidated his ties with the *New York Herald*. It caught the attention of Bennett and won Stanley the Livingstone assignment. From then on, there was no turning aside. The Ashanti War, although no more than a journalistic chore, maintained his connection with Africa. Finally came the three-year struggle to complete the work of Livingstone and 'fill in the blank spaces'.

Now he had what he most wanted. The latest expedition earned him recognition as the greatest African explorer. When Stanley spoke, he was listened to with respect. Travellers such as Burton, Baker and Grant had treated him with disdain after his return from finding Livingstone; now they were lavish with their praise. Stanley had settled for ever the debate about the source of the Nile, and demolished the theory put forward in 1872 by Livingstone that the Lualaba joined the Nile – a theory that Stanley himself, out of loyalty, had tended to support. He had proved that the Lualaba was the main upper arm of the Congo (which he vainly tried, again from loyalty, to rename the 'Livingstone River'). Even while he was making his journey across the continent, Stanley had written to a friend asking whether people in Britain and America really believed he was in Africa. He said he was 'labouring to establish a confidence in me in the minds of right-minded people, which my vicious foes robbed me of.' Now there was no longer any suggestion that Stanley was a fraud; he was the new idol of the geographers.

He first addressed them at Burlington House in Piccadilly, pointing out the main features of his travels on a map of Africa hanging behind him. The map had been hurriedly drawn on sheets

With admirers in Paris, after the great journey across Africa. Despite his triumph, Stanley was withdrawn and lonely; he had received the crushing news of Alice Pike's 'betrayal'

of paper sewn together that afternoon by the children of Edwin Arnold, editor of the *Daily Telegraph*. Arnold knew that his long, and often difficult, defence of Stanley at the meetings of the Royal Geographical Society was at last vindicated.

In Washington, the great journey was applauded by a unanimous vote of thanks from both Houses of Congress. The headline in a New York newspaper summed up 1877: 'Three Great Events: Henry M. Stanley's Return, the Pope's Death, and Russia's Triumph.'

When the two-volume *Through the Dark Continent* appeared, it showed a perspective that had been lacking from *How I Found Livingstone*. With such a narrative, popular success was certain, and Stanley displayed once more his flair for sweeping readers along from discovery to discovery and battle to battle. But there was also a seriousness that showed how he meant to be worthy of the gold medals from scores of learned societies and the congratulations of monarchs, presidents and prime ministers around the world. The French statesman Leon Gambetta remarked presciently: 'Not only, sir, have you opened up a new continent to our view, but you have given an impulse to scientific and philanthropic enterprise which will have a material effect on the progress of the world . . . What you have done has influenced governments – proverbially so difficult to be moved – and the impulse you have imparted to them will, I am convinced, go on growing year after year.'

As Stanley changed Africa, so it had changed him. In 1868 he had looked less than his age; now he was grey-haired and drawn. The three-year journey from Zanzibar to Boma, and especially the final, desperate months on the Congo, drained the ebullience and bravado out of him. As he expressed it: 'When a man returns home and finds for the moment nothing to struggle against, the vast resolve, which has sustained him through a long and difficult enterprise, dies away, burning as it sinks in the heart; and thus the greatest successes are often accompanied by a peculiar melancholy.'

The reaction to the sudden lack of a single, clear objective, and the release from the discipline of command, were not the only causes of Stanley's mood. The fickleness of Alice Pike Barney crushed his emotions. The prospect of their reunion had been a spur to his resolve in crossing Africa; as he told her, she was his hope and beacon. But he had lost Alice, just as he had lost Katie Gough-Roberts and Virginia Ambella, and for the moment he shut his mind to the thought of marriage. He was resolved that no woman would find a way behind his defences again.

He told himself that Alice was a 'confirmed flirt', and he bitterly regretted that she had been able to play with his deepest feelings. Defensively, he began to evolve the theory that he was so made he could only achieve 'purely platonic' friendships with the opposite sex. At dinner parties and receptions he was sought out by clever, beautiful women. But that gave him no confidence – he felt they were interested in him as a celebrity, not as a human being. He was admired as 'Stanley Africanus', yet he knew that Africa really meant nothing to all these eager acquaintaintces.

'The heart of Africa is infinitely preferable to the heart of the world's greatest city,' he had written in his journal on the way across Africa. Often the miseries of the journey made such an idea seem absurd, but after being back in London for a few months he knew it was true. The Zanzibaris had constantly enraged him, and yet they were his 'brave lads', who regarded him as their father.

He wanted to return to Africa, to give himself up to action. After the exploration must come the 'regeneration'. This was the ideal he had learnt from Livingstone, and although their methods were so different – as Stanley well realised – the purpose was the same: by the example of the white man the 'African savage' would shake off his sloth, and stimulated by commerce might enter at last the mainstream of progress. He had written, as early as August 1877, about his hopes for the 'redemption of the splendid central basin of the continent by sound and legitimate commerce'. A great field of trade that had now been 'opened to the world, especially to the English, French, Germans and Americans, the English especially . . .'

He argued this case again and again, in the columns of the *Daily Telegraph*, in conversations with members of the Establishment, and from lecture platforms throughout Britain. Twice he badgered the Prince of Wales, who on the second occasion told him amiably that he wore the decorations on his dinner dress in the wrong order, but went no further.

Stanley was both too early and too late – the fervour inspired by the campaign against the slave trade in the sixties had waned, and the Scramble of the eighties had not begun. The British Government wanted no more involvements in Africa, and the formation of the Gold Coast Colony after General Wolseley's drubbing of Ashanti was reluctantly done. Cameron had formally annexed the Congo for Britain, but she would not have it. The merchants of Manchester and Liverpool were content with matters as they stood: British exports to tropical Africa were less than one-hundredth of world exports, and they saw no chance of improving this by pouring in capital. Stanley had the goodwill of Baron Ferdinand de Rothschild,

Baroness Burdett-Coutts and the Duke of Sutherland, but nothing practical followed from it. He wrote gloomily: 'I do not understand Englishmen at all. Either they suspect me of some self-interest, or they do not believe me. My reward has been to be called a mere penny-a-liner. For the relief of Livingstone I was called an impostor; for the crossing of Africa I was called a pirate . . .'

Certainly, despite all the medals bestowed on Stanley, he was not an ideal advocate for a British initiative in the Congo. He was regarded as a typical American, talking like one and writing with all the mannerisms of Broadway. There were still mutterings from liberal quarters about the Bumbiri incident and some of Stanley's more violent encounters on the Congo. As General Gordon remarked to him at the end of a congratulatory letter: 'I will now say good-bye, with the remark and question of, "Why if you had to defend yourself, you said anything about it".'

Stanley did not take seriously enough the influence of his old enemies – especially John Kirk of Zanzibar, whose network of contacts spread widely through the Church and Whitehall. Stanley had declared that he was 'willing to make a thousand apologies' if this would wipe out the memory of his attacks six years before. But it was not in Kirk's nature to view that as a fair amend. After Stanley arrived at Zanzibar at the end of 1877, Kirk made no effort to see him and the two merely exchanged stiff letters about some of Livingstone's former followers who alleged they had been underpaid. The French representative on the island, Gaillard de Ferry, reported to the Quai d'Orsay the accepted view of Stanley among the British on Zanzibar: he was a 'sensation monger of the lowest class', who had merely travelled in Cameron's footsteps.

A chance to even the score was given to Kirk when he received from the British Foreign Secretary, Lord Derby, a question about Stanley's behaviour on the trans-Africa journey. A missionary had been interrogating Zanzibars who were on the expedition, and his findings reached the Anti-Slavery Society, which had passed them on to the Foreign Office. A leading member of the Anti-Slavery Society was Kirk's ubiquitous relative, Horace Waller. With the sanction of Lord Derby, Kirk made his own investigations by inviting the captains on the expedition to his house and offering them money to tell what they knew. With ill-disguised pleasure, Kirk gave his reply on May 1, 1878, and accused Stanley of kicking a man to death, having a black mistress, capturing Africans and selling them as slaves, and attacking villages without provocation. He also accused Pocock of having taken a captured girl as his mistress, and producing a child who was in Zanzibar without any means of support.

In short, declared Kirk, the expedition has been a 'disgrace to humanity' and 'unequalled for the reckless use of the power that modern weapons placed in his hands over natives who never before had heard a gun fired.' On receiving this message, an official at the Foreign Office added a note saying there was no doubt that Stanley's behaviour had in many instances been 'to say the least discreditable'.

It is unlikely that Stanley was ever aware of precisely what charges were made against him in the confidential report to the Foreign Office. But he knew something was being hatched. A watch was being kept on Kirk's activities by Augustus Sparhawk, an American trader with whom Stanley had stayed in Zanzibar. In a letter of July 4, 1878, Sparhawk first told how he had been distributing rings sent out by Stanley for survivors of the expedition. (It was Stanley's idea that the rings would identify his former followers and help them to get work with other expeditions.) He then went on: 'As I wrote you previously, I heard that Kirk was questioning your men about you and the expedition with no good intentions towards you. That reminded me that I had seen Manwa Sera and several others of your best men frequently passing here on their way to Kirk's . . .' Sparhawk learnt that they had been paid if they would talk, but been sent away empty-handed if they 'lied for Bwana Stanley'.

The campaign by Kirk made exceedingly unlikely any British Government encouragement for Stanley's plans in the Congo. The possibility was utterly extinguished when Lord Salisbury replaced Lord Derby as Foreign Secretary in the Spring of 1878. Africa was of not the slightest interest to Salisbury. He had watched sardonically the attempts in 1877–8 to start a British East Africa Company with General Gordon as its administrator. That had all come to nothing, and had wasted a lot of the Foreign Office's time. The idea of trying to 'redeem and uplift' the peoples of the Congo Basin struck Salisbury as perfectly ludicrous, and he looked with aristocratic coolness upon a man of Stanley's type. This indifference was well matched by the Prime Minister, Disraeli. He wrote (October 29, 1878): 'I myself know nothing of Stanley, except from his public acts, which prove him to be a man of matchless energy . . . I myself am ignorant of where Stanley Pool exactly is, but I presume it is somewhere on the Congo . . .'

Scorned in Britain, Stanley found himself involved with a king and a country to whom he had never given a thought when he sent his first exhortations from the mouth of the Congo. He did not even have to court Leopold II of the Belgians – the king came to him. The first approach was in January 1878, at a dinner of the Marseilles Geographical Society, as Stanley was on his way back to Britain from

Leopold II, ambitious and devious ruler of a fragile country

his great journey. Two representatives were sent down from Brussels to find out whether he might be willing to talk to the king; one of them was an American, General Henry S. Sanford, who had been the US minister in Belgium, and then became Leopold's aide and sycophant. Stanley brushed the two aside, saying that he felt too sick and weary. But Leopold persisted. In a note of May 1878, the king said: 'If I like Stanley, I am all for making a contract with this resourceful American, for agreeing to supply him with 100,000 dollars a year over five years to found a settlement on the Congo and from there to branch out as far as possible around this great river.' In June, the tall, spade-bearded king had his first meeting with Stanley. They corresponded for several months. By December 1878 – less than a year after his return – Stanley was committed to going back to the Congo for five years as the administrator of the Comité d'Etudes du Haut-Congo. The journalist was about to become an empire-builder.

For fifteen years Leopold had been the figurehead of the small and fragile Belgian State. He was discontented with his lot; he had close family ties with Britain (the Prince of Wales was his cousin) and while Britain was a small country, it enjoyed the power and wealth of a huge empire. The problem was that the Belgian politicians were totally opposed to any idea of founding colonies. So Leopold must pursue his ambitions in other ways. His father had compared him to a fox, 'subtle and sly.'

After he had been hired by Leopold, Stanley set about organising his new expedition to the Congo with almost frenzied enthusiasm. His first ideas, for a railway from the mouth of the Congo to the Stanley Pool, had to be scrapped – there was not enough money in the royal treasury, and Leopold found no support at all among Belgian industrialists. So he would build a road, and then transport river steamers up it to be launched at the Stanley Pool. He would also build several 'stations' for administration and scientific research. There was no hint at this stage of trading or acquiring territory. The professed aim was simply to study the problems and possibilities of the Congo. Stanley had formed his own idea of Leopold: 'He has been more open with me than he would have been had I appeared as a British subject. Still he has not been so frank as to tell me outright what we are to strive for. Nevertheless it has been pretty evident that under the guise of an International Association he hopes to make a Belgian dependency of the Congo Basin.' But this was looking too far ahead.

The air of mystery which cloaked the royal actions extended far beyond Leopold's talks with Stanley; nothing must leak out to the newspapers about what was planned, and the expedition must reach the mouth of the Congo without any suspicions being aroused. If political troubles forced the king to jettison his scheme, all documents must be burnt. Leopold was afraid of antagonism from his own politicians, and also from France, on whose behalf a Count Savorgnan de Brazza had recently been exploring just north of the Congo.

Stanley readily fell in with this tactic of stealth, and discreetly concentrated upon the details of his plan. First he would go to Zanzibar and recruit a corps of experienced men – including as many as possible of those who had crossed Africa with him. He would send out directly from Europe to the mouth of the Congo a nucleus of white assistants, to await his arrival. With them would go the basic stores for the expedition as well as the flotilla of small steamboats; these could be assembled at once for use in setting up a 'base station' below the cataracts, before being taken to the Pool.

Early in February he took his leave of Leopold and set out from Brussels under the name of 'Monsieur Henri'. A few days earlier he had sent off a chartered steamer, the *Albion*, with instructions that she should wait for him at Suez; the destination was Zanzibar. On board was his secretary, Arthur Swinburne, whom he intended, if necessary, to use as a decoy.

Stanley duly picked up the *Albion* at Suez and reached Zanzibar in April. His unexpected arrival caused astonishment on the island, and to add to the speculation he took several trips up and down the coast. Even the new American consul, William H. Hathorne, was mystified. He wrote to friends in America: 'Mr H. M. Stanley has been hovering between this place and the coast for over a month, and will leave soon for Mombasa. We don't know for what reason he is here, but presume it has some concern with some grand commercial scheme.' The curiosity about Stanley was quickly swamped however by the news that four Indian elephants were about to appear in Zanzibar, *en route* for the African interior, at the instigation of King Leopold and his International Association. There were also three Belgians led by a Captain Popelin, preparing to march inland with no very clear purpose. Zanzibar was awash with rumours. In fact, the elephants and Captain Popelin's team were a manifestation of Leopold's wilder dreams of a string of 'stations' across the African continent, linking up with his main force on the Congo.

All this activity vexed Dr Kirk, notwithstanding the gift of a snuff box from Leopold for his work against the slave trade. The British consul liked the elephants but was most suspicious of Popelin and Stanley. In a letter accompanying the snuff box, the king had blandly said: 'Mr Stanley will profit by his sojourn on the coast to explore some points he has not yet visited, but he will not be able to stay there long, his presence being, I think, required elsewhere.' There was no meeting between Kirk and Stanley, although Sultan Barghash gave Stanley an interview – and immediately told Kirk what had been said at it. Kirk informed the Foreign Office. 'I am told by the Sultan that Mr Stanley at first affected the greatest surprise at finding His Highness still the ruling sovereign of Zanzibar. He had been fully prepared, he said, to find that the English by this time had usurped his place and under the cloak of commercial schemes deprived him of both power and position.'

There is a paradox in this attitude and the eagerness Stanley had shown so shortly before for the British to involve themselves in the Congo. His judgement on large issues could be swayed by his feelings towards people involved. The renewed urge to provoke Kirk may have been stirred up by Augustus Sparhawk's letters about the interrogation of his men; there was no encouragement from Hathorne to cool the feud – like American consuls before him in Zanzibar, he was a bitter enemy of 'Kirkism' and British domination of the Sultan.

Stanley's regard for Sparhawk revealed itself in the decision to hire him for work in the Congo. When the *Albion* sailed at the end of May, Sparhawk was on board with Stanley; so were sixty Zanzibari recruits. Another American, a sailor named Frank Mahoney, had also signed a three-year contract with Stanley in Zanzibar. He was to travel later in the mail steamer, with eight more Zanzibaris under his control, and make his way to the mouth of the Congo as soon as he could. Eleven other whites – five Belgians, two Danes, one Frenchman, two Englishmen and an American – were at that moment secretly setting out from Europe to rendezvous with Stanley at the mouth of the Congo. Eighty tons of stores, in 2,000 packing cases, were also on their way.

The comfortable sense that all was going according to plan suffered a jolt when the *Albion* reached Aden. Stanley was handed a telegram from Brussels saying that a Dutch firm which had been involved in financing the Comité d'Etudes du Haut-Congo had suddenly gone bankrupt. One of its directors had fled to America and another had tried to commit suicide. At Suez, a further cable was waiting, telling Stanley to go to Brussels. He refused, and asked to be met at Gibraltar by a representative of the king. At Gibraltar he was greeted by Colonel Maximilian Strauch, the executive president of the Comité.

Strauch was a precise and rather characterless man wearing pince-nez, and it was he with whom Stanley would have to liaise by correspondence from the Congo. Unfortunately, Strauch had never been to Africa and Stanley felt he lacked any grasp of the problems that must be faced. It had also infuriated Stanley, before he left Brussels, to see openly displayed in Strauch's office a large wallmap marked with the sites of projected stations on the Congo.

The news Strauch gave at Gibraltar was that the organisation in Brussels had been transformed. The king had replaced the bankrupt Dutchmen, and there was no danger of the plan as it stood being abandoned. All the intricacies of the new arrangements were of small concern to Stanley, for his mind was now entirely on what he had to do when he arrived at the Congo. Actions were what would count.

Before they parted, Strauch handed over a list of final instructions, which also covered matters of policy. One statement declared: 'This project is not to create a Belgian colony, but to establish a powerful Negro state.' Stanley responded with a letter accepting the assurance that there was no thought of creating a colony, but saying the other idea – 'a powerful Negro state' – was far more difficult. He added: 'It would be madness for one in my position to attempt it, except so far as one course might follow another in the natural order of things.'

Having discharged this broadside, Stanley sailed out of the Mediterranean and southwards towards the Congo. On August 14, 1879, his ship reached the muddy estuary of the great river. It was just two years and two days since he had last seen it. He wrote to Strauch: 'I am devoured with a wish to set my foot on *terra firma*, and begin the great work.'

19. Five Years for the Free State

Stanley's favourite story about the Congo was how he subdued Chief Ngalyema. The chief was a testing adversary, for he had at his command 1,000 men with muskets, owned a vast store of ivory, and controlled the down-river approaches to the Stanley Pool. The most important station to be set up by King Leopold's expedition would be at the Pool – from there the Congo and its tributaries would give access to a million square miles of Africa. But if Ngalyema stood in the way, the station would have no safe route to the sea, and become a fortress in hostile country.

Like Stanley himself, Ngalyema had risen in the world from an unpromising start. He had been a slave in his youth, but had won his freedom and grown rich by trading in ivory. His wealth had given him the chance to take as his wives the daughters of local chiefs, until he became a chief himself by general consent. Young slaves were the nucleus of his war parties. Ngalyema dressed in silks of yellow, blue and crimson, covered his arms with bracelets of heavy brass, and wore copper rings on his ankles. Stanley weighed him up before they came to grips: 'He was now about thirty-four years old, of well-built form, proud in his bearing, covetous and grasping in disposition, and, like all other lawless barbarians prone to be cruel and sanguinary whenever he might safely vent his evil humour. Superstition had found in him an apt and docile pupil, and fetishism held him as one of its most abject slaves.'

In the past, Stanley might have been disposed to deal with Ngalyema by giving him – to use one of his own expressions – 'a bellyful of lead.' But as the emissary of a committee with avowedly benign intentions, he was in a new relationship with the African chiefs and their people. Formerly he had been only a traveller, paying tribute when he had to, bartering when he could, and fighting if he saw no option. Now he must be the diplomat, negotiating for land to build settlements and make permanent roads.

At the outset, Stanley tried to conquer Ngalyema with gifts. The

252

covetous chief saw a Newfoundland dog with the new expedition, and demanded it. Reluctantly, Stanley handed it over. Then Ngalyema saw and wanted two donkeys, a large mirror, a gold-embroidered coat, jewellery, brass chains, a figured table-cloth, fifteen lengths of cloth and a tin box with a Chubb lock. They were yielded up, and in return Stanley was given Ngalyema's staff of office, decorated with coils of brass wire, as a symbol of their friendship. It was a short lived progress because Ngalyema suddenly sent back the gifts; he had been warned by his followers not to let the white man have a concession of land. This was a provocation, for Stanley and the chief already were blood brothers. The next stage was almost certainly war – unless the expedition gave up all hope of a base at the Pool.

Stanley waited, and learnt one night that Ngalyema was on his way with 200 men bearing guns. The following morning would be decisive. He calculated that the chief would come to the camp with his followers, pretend to enter into friendly negotiations, then try a surprise attack while they were drinking palm wine together. Although Stanley had with him a force of armed Zanzibaris, they were outnumbered. Even assuming he could win, the last thing he wanted was a battle; so he decided on a stratagem. All but twenty of the Zanzibaris were told to hide in the bush, or to crouch behind the tents and huts where Ngalyema and his men would not see them. They were not to move until they were summoned by the sound of a large Chinese gong, which was generally used to wake up the camp in the mornings.

When Ngalyema advanced on the camp, with drums beating and trumpets blowing, Stanley seated himself before his tent and pretended to be reading a book. He had placed the gong prominently in front of him. The twenty Zanzibaris who were not in hiding lounged around the camp, seemingly half asleep. It was a scene designed to make the chief think he had no real opposition to worry about. Ngalyema adopted a truculent manner, and after a brief exchange of trivialities, ordered Stanley to go back the way he had come: 'If you do not promise, this must end in war, and I can no longer be your friend.' He was offered still more gifts, including sixty yards of red baize and a case of gin, but the palaver ended badly. When Stanley said he only wanted a place near the river where 'many white men would come to trade,' Ngalyema strode angrily out of the tent where they had been sitting, with his son behind him. 'Enough!' shouted Ngalyema, 'we do not want any white men amongst us.'

The gong stood by the tent, and Ngalyema suddenly noticed it and paused. 'What is this?' he asked. 'It is a fetish,' said Stanley. 'Strike this, let me hear it,' said Ngalyema imperiously. Stanley answered: 'No, Ngalyema, the sound of the gong will bring trouble. I dare not – it is the war fetish!' Ngalyema would not be put off: 'I must hear it. Beat it now.' He stamped on the ground. With assumed reluctance, Stanley banged the gong until it echoed like thunder, while Ngalyema and his men stood astounded by the noise.

As the gong sounded, Stanley's hidden detachment sprang into the centre of the camp, shrieking and waving their guns. They danced in a frenzy in front of Ngalyema; his men fled in panic, flinging away their muskets as they went. The chief hid himself behind Stanley, threw his arms around his waist and implored to be saved; in turn, the son clung to his father and howled. 'Keep fast hold of me,' shouted Stanley, 'I will defend you, never fear!' At an order all the leaping Zanzibaris fell into line, and the camp was suddenly silent. The guns of Ngalyema's men were strewn around.

This antic took the warlike spirit out of the chief, who had so recently imperilled all of Stanley's plans. His fugitive warriors were persuaded back to the camp, and amid much joking and drinking of palm wine, the white man was given permission to found a town beside Stanley Pool. Although Ngalyema knew he had been fooled by a practical joke, he nervously refused when offered another demonstration on the gong.

It was not quite the end of the bloodless trial of strength, however. After Stanley was established at the Pool, Ngalyema came to visit him and asked to try on his clothes: 'He had seen me wear a black velvet suit (my best suit) on the occasion of a great meeting of chiefs. He tried the velvet coat on, was intensely in love with it at once.' Stanley next let him wear a blue cloak – which had cost eight guineas in London – and Ngalyema was captivated by that as well. He demanded to be given the suit, the cloak and various other articles that took his fancy in the tent; when he was told he had already been given enough, he went off in a rage. Next day Ngalyema was back, and after embracing Stanley, again asked him why he had come to the Congo. When told it was for 'ivory and trade, and friendship' he said he was happy – then pleaded for the velvet suit and the cloak. Once more Stanley declined to hand them over and again the chief went off in a fury. He returned with a detachment of armed slaves, and when Stanley went out to meet him with forty Zanzibaris carrying guns, Ngalyema threw himself on the ground and cried: 'Yes, kill your brother, kill me, I see you are a bad brother!' With much talking, Stanley managed to calm Ngalyema down, but as soon as the chief had walked back among his warriors they clamoured for a battle. At this moment, when fighting looked unavoidable, the chief's son – who had been in camp when the gong summoned up the horde of men – successfully begged his father to go home in peace.

As the days went by, the chief gradually accepted the inevitable: his 'brother' would not move from his camp by the Pool (it was to become Leopoldville, capital of the Congo), so he must make the best terms he could. As an inducement, Stanley gave him the blue cloak that had cost eight guineas, a silk shirt, and a velvet cloak adorned with lace which had been especially run up in the camp. It was enough. To announce there was lasting peace, Ngalyema ordered his warriors to keep up a ceremonial firing of muskets for two days. Then he had one final request: could Stanley order him a coffin from Europe? Ngalyema explained that he wanted it to look like a black tin bath, with handles and lid. Stanley worked out an exact size – 42 inches in diameter at the top and 21 inches deep – and made a drawing, which he sent off to Brussels. He drily explained that Ngalyema would only need it for his funeral, 'when it pleases God,' but was most anxious to have it by him right away. After the delivery of the coffin, there was no more trouble.

Ngalyema had involved Stanley in more delicate dealings than were needed with any other Congo chief; he typified the superficially sophisticated African rulers found near the Atlantic coast. For several centuries, because of the slave trade, such men had been in contact with European goods – even if these were received indirectly through Portuguese half-castes and other middlemen. One of the goods was rum, and every chief downstream from the Stanley Pool insisted upon a bottle before any palaver could start. Writing to his headquarters in Brussels, Stanley said: 'I beg to assure you that if it depended on me I would have no more to do with rum than with poison, but the traders have so supplied the people with rum that without it friendship or trade is impossible on the Lower Congo.' The local people would not work unless they had been given a tot morning and night. So he tried diluting it with water, but this led to discord. Many of the employees preferred to take their wages in rum or gin, which they could later sell at a profit. Stanley soon learnt that the Africans of the Congo were adept at trade to a degree he had never known in East Africa, or had understood on his hurried journey down the river in 1877. He wrote that he had seen a child of eight do more tricks of trading in a day than a European merchant could achieve in a month; it meant that negotiations were exhausting – although the pleasures of success outweighed the frustration.

His writing noticeably comes alive when he describes his meetings with groups of chiefs. Once he held a palaver with thirty tribal leaders, all dressed in cast-off European clothing. Some wore red military uniforms from Britain, others old frock coats, straw hats and necklaces of elephant hair. To greet them he would put on his velvet suit so coveted by Ngalyema, or a cream, high-necked jacket adorned with frogging and embroidered at the cuffs. Although he had always had a reputation for curtness, Stanley felt at ease with Africans and condemned Europeans who 'chilled the native onlooker' with their dignity, and imperious manners: 'Let there enter into those chill, icy eyes, the light of life and joy, of humour, friendship, pleasure, and the communication between man and man is electric in its suddenness.' One of the complaints often made against him by his white assistants was that when he had to adjudicate in a dispute between a European and an African, he always favoured the latter.

One chief named Mata Bwyki (Lord of Many Guns), was nearly eighty years old, but had a voice that could be heard for hundreds of yards. Well over six feet tall, Mata Bwyki dwarfed Stanley; he had 'a large square face and an altogether massive head, out of which his solitary eye seemed to glare with penetrative power.' Stanley made a treaty with Mata Bwyki, and blood brotherhood with his son.

A few weeks later he began negotiations with Siwa-Siwa, who was far less formidable and constantly smiled with boyish delight: 'I admired greatly the loving possessive manner in which his women surrounded me, and cooed their sweetest into each of my ears, without exciting in the least Siwa-Siwa's jealousy, or alarming his susceptibilities.'

The benevolence he showed in his dealings with the Congolese was matched by his treatment of the Zanzibaris, who were the bastions of his work. He chose as his senior captain the veteran Abdullah Susi, who had been with Livingstone on his last journey and had gone to England in 1874 to be presented with a medal by the Royal Geographical Society. Shortly before Stanley hired him, Susi had been regarded as so sunk in drink as to be unemployable. Stanley clearly had other opinions; as it turned out, Susi was reliable and loyal during his service in the Congo. Perhaps he was partly selected because of Stanley's sentimental feelings about him – for it was Susi who had greeted him in English as he had marched into Ujiji in November 1871 for the meeting with Livingstone.

Another of the key recruits was Uledi, who had been coxswain of the *Lady Alice*, and rescued thirteen men from drowning on the trip down the Congo. He had vainly tried to save Frank Pocock. To hire Uledi, Stanley was obliged to get him out of jail – where for some offence he had been committed on the orders of Henri Greffulhe, an official of the French consulate in Zanzibar. What Uledi had done is unknown, but Stanley's letter (May 11, 1879) to Greffulhe is in existence. After praising Uledi for 'sterling qualities, unquestionable fidelity and undisputed courage' – despite a few displays of 'moral turpitude' – Stanley asks how he can help to set him free: 'You may well imagine how it saddens me to hear that this heroic fellow has been arrested, locked up, and ignominiously chained in the Fort of Zanzibar through your orders . . . I should esteem it a great favour if you would kindly explain to me why . . .' Whatever Uledi had done, he obtained his freedom and took him off to the Congo.

But while he felt fatherly towards his Zanzibaris, Stanley heaped scorn upon the Europeans sent to help him. A group of Belgian Army officers became a perpetual irritant, reminding him that he was working for Leopold, although he still nurtured hopes that the Congo might somehow go to the British.

Strauch was the focus of all Stanley's pent-up wrath. He was endlessly calling for quicker progress up the Congo, failed to understand the delays caused by obstinate chiefs, the rough terrain and bad weather; he asked countless questions in a constant flow of letters. Stanley put one argument, again and again – that if Strauch wanted more done, he must supply more men. For preference, he would chose Zanzibaris, not Europeans, who needed too much feeding and coddling. 'My dear Colonel,' says Stanley in his passion, 'when will you believe that this is the hardest-worked expedition that ever came into Africa?' Strauch never seemed convinced that the resources were too small; Stanley did his best to explain how many porters were needed to move supplies, and why lengthening supply lines called for more men. 'My dear Colonel, have you no one at your office who knows what simple arithmetical addition is? and division?' Sometimes Strauch tried to hit back, but he was not equal to such eloquence; Leopold himself had finally to intervene. In a memorandum to Strauch (September 4, 1880), the king ordered: 'It is useless to engage in polemics with Stanley; we must allow him to speak and help him all we can . . .'

Stanley was unrelenting. He pointed out to Strauch that he could not hope to understand the problems, since he had never been to the Congo; twenty years' experience in the Belgian Army was irrelevant. When Strauch accused him of obstinacy, he replied with a counter-charge of injustice and lack of confidence. The very suggestion than Stanley might be anti-Belgian was dismissed as outrageous. It was simply that the pioneer Methodist missionaries who were now appearing on the Lower Congo were better able to run a station that Strauch's protégés: 'Why is it that these English youths, fresh from college and school, succeed where your officers introduced by me with every favourable advantage fail?' The missionaries, in their turn, liked Stanley, praising his 'friendly and gentle treatment' of the Africans.

A Danish recruit to Stanley's pioneering band in the Congo tries riding a hippo. Such frivolities were rare in the struggle to found the Free State. Many of the white men were to die

Although he criticised Belgians, he had unreserved admiration for two Scandinavian sailors in his team – Captain Andersen, a Swede, and Albert Christophersen, a Danish seaman. It was Christophersen most of all who restored Stanley's good-humour amid the stresses of the Congo, by his readiness to run races with the Zanzibaris, or challenge them to boxing matches, and generally make them accept him as a 'guileless friend'. Together Stanley and Christophersen went on a boat journey in May 1882 to explore the Kwa River, north of the Pool, and Stanley's recollection of the trip has an ease and lightness rarely found in his other writings about the period.

One morning Stanley goes ashore at a village and is taken around the fields by a headman. The fields are full of ripe crops, and Stanley is invited to have as much as he can carry: 'I am like a city boy on a rustic outing. I admire everything, eat raw cassava, try the sugar-cane like a barbarian of Inner Africa, eat the groundnuts, which are so fat, so white and so tender. I load my pockets, and finally, pockets and hands being full, think of my cap, and return to the steamer with my gifts of rural produce to exhibit to Albert, who shows his hearty appreciation by driving his white teeth into the cane-stalk, and smiling broadly his full content with the situation – because, for the first time since coming into Africa, we are relieved from stern, severe, and exacting work. We have thrown off memories of anxieties and privations endured together, and are now as happy as schoolboys out on a holiday . . .'

It was Christophersen whom he called to his bedside when he thought he was about to die. The previous twelve months had been punishing to the expedition, with the deaths of twenty Zanzibaris and six Europeans, but Stanley felt no qualms about his own health. Malaria had not bothered him for many months. Then all at once he grew feverish, and had to put off a palaver with a gathering of chiefs. Gradually the fever became more intense, despite heavy doses of quinine, and after six days Stanley grew alarmed. He had his tent moved to a hill overlooking his camp, and took twenty grains of quinine in hydrobromic acid. There was still no sign that the fever was waning, and between moments of delirium Stanley ordered his servant to give him thirty grains. After fourteen days he had the dosage raised to fifty grains, and was now so weak he could hardly lift his arms. One morning Stanley awoke to the feeling that the sickness had reached a climax, and that he was on the point of death. 'Weaker than this, and yet possessing powers of speech and thought,

I doubted whether man could possibly be . . .' Stanley ordered his servant to give him sixty grains of quinine and to call all the people around him before too late, so that he could make his farewells.

As the massive dose of quinine, mixed in Madeira wine, began to overpower Stanley's mind, he heard a rush of feet around the tent. The walls of the tent were rolled up, letting in the sunlight and revealing to Stanley rows of Zanzibaris and a small knot of Europeans. He tried to tell them what they must do when he was dead. 'Again and again I strove strenuously to utter the words that my lips would not frame.' Christophersen came forward and held his hand. 'Look well on me, Albert,' Stanley said at last. 'Do not move. Fasten your eyes on me that I may tell you.' Christophersen stared into his face and clung to his hand, and suddenly Stanley had a realisation that he would not die, after all, 'I am saved!' he cried, and fell unconscious.

For 24 hours, he lay still, and when he awoke he felt hungry. He had soup and demanded more. It took him more than a fortnight to recover enough to walk a few steps. His weight was down to 100 lb. 'Yet the mails on my lap, six months old, contained new tasks that would require an army to accomplish! With a sick man's querulousness I pushed them aside, and dared not look at them lest I should become mad.'

Stanley recovered, and hurried on with his work. He had been told, when he agreed to work for the Cømité, that he should set up three stations on the Congo and launch a steamer at the Pool. He had created five stations, built a wagon road past the cataracts, and launched both a steamer and a sailing boat on the Upper Congo. By the early months of 1882 he had been away from Europe for three years, and believed that under the terms of his revised contract he could now leave and hand over to a successor. It was only ominous that no arrangements about a successor had been made, and no dates fixed for his return. Anxiety was made keener by another attack of fever, which again reduced him to unconsciousness for days on end; it was complicated by gastritis and left him with a dropsical swelling of his legs.

Stanley wrote in his journal: 'I could not disguise from myself that I was not now the hardy, energetic pioneer I once was.' He resolved to go home of his own accord. On the Lower Congo he parted from Christophersen, who was charged with responsibility for escorting a large party of time-expired Zanzibaris to their home. Then by way of Luanda and Lisbon he made his way to Brussels, where he had an interview with Strauch at the end of September, 1882.

It was a shock. Strauch made it plain that the contract was for five years, and Stanley must return to the Congo as soon as possible. In reply, Stanley said that he had already seen a specialist, who warned him that he would be virtually committing suicide to go back. The vast quantities of medicine he had swallowed to beat off malaria had damaged his organs. Strauch was non-committal. The next morning there was a meeting with Leopold, who exclaimed: 'Surely, Mr Stanley, you cannot think of leaving me now, just when I most need you?'

It was indeed the moment when the king needed Stanley most, because his financial commitment to the Congo venture was up from £12,000 a year to £60,000, and it was by no means clear what he would ultimately gain from it. The king had written (December 31, 1881): 'I am desirous to see you purchase all the ivory which is to be found on the Congo . . . I also recommend you to establish barriers and tolls on the road you have opened.' Stanley had done what he could to start up a flow of ivory. He rejected a proposal to charge missionaries for travelling on his road. But by the autumn of 1882, Leopold was absorbed with greater issues than turning a profit on ivory and tolls.

The king's thoughts were centred on France and the actions of its explorer in Central Africa, Count de Brazza. An officer in the French navy, de Brazza was of aristocratic Italian origins and claimed descent from the Emperor Severus; this background made him, like a Catholic convert, most passionate in his loyalties. Less than four months before Stanley arrived back in Europe, de Brazza had returned. He was also worn out in body and spirit; but unlike Stanley he had a precise idea of his objectives. On October 3, 1880, he had signed a treaty with a chief on the north bank of the Stanley Pool, and so acquired formal sovereignty for France in the region. The tricolor had been planted on the Upper Congo, and he was determined that the French Government should ratify his achievement. Leopold saw that if this happened, his secret plans for a vast trading company on the Congo might be worth nothing; if all the Congo Basin became a French colony, there was no telling what controls might be imposed on him.

Early in October, Leopold was told by Ferdinand de Lesseps, president of the Paris Geographical Society, that France was to ratify the de Brazza treaty. Tempers rose in Brussels: the race for the control of the Congo was starting in earnest. Many of Leopold's confidants felt Stanley had advanced too methodically and slowly between 1879 and 1882. Baron Solvyns, the Belgian ambassador in London, went further: 'He ought to have begun by securing the most important point of the Congo, namely Stanley Pool, and one wonders why, as a Californian, he did not think fit to lay his rival low with a rifle shot.' Such criticisms nettled Stanley. If they now wanted speed, he could supply that too.

He agreed to leave towards the end of November for the Congo to push forward with treaty-making and establishing stations in the Upper Congo. This would give him an advantage over de Brazza, who was not returning so soon to Africa. But secrecy was vital. A chartered steamer sailed from Antwerp for Cadiz in Spain, and Stanley revived his tactic of 1879 by travelling there under an assumed name to board it. The ship was loaded with stores and the passengers were a party of new white recruits. Leopold approved of all these schemes, and he did not demur at Stanley's insistence that more of the white recruits should be British; indeed, he applauded the idea – privately deciding that the more British an aspect his 'international' organisation had, the better, since this might fend off the French.

By December 14, 1882, Stanley was once more at the mouth of the Congo. As he went inland he found to his dismay that most of the stations he had so painstakingly set up were in disarray, and tropical vegetation was crowding in. Some white officers had quarrelled among themselves, and others had expended their energies in fights with the Africans. The station at Leopoldville was the worst of all, with grass growing in the roads, gardens overgrown and buildings starting to fall down. He occupied several months in restoring order, then began his treaty-making.

He had constantly asked for an effective deputy to take over the Lower Congo, and wanted General 'Chinese' Gordon. The king feared Gordon was indiscreet, stiff-necked and eccentric, but finally resolved to try him: it was in his favour that he had worked in the Sudan as an administrator. The first step must be to approach the British War Office, and the next to bring Gordon over to Brussels for talks. Gordon was interested, and on January 1, 1884 wrote from Brussels an emotional letter to Stanley: 'His Majesty has asked me to go out and join you in your work which I have gladly assented to, and come from Lisbon on 5th Feb. I will willingly serve with and under you and I hope you will stay on and we will, God helping, kill the slave traders in the haunts . . . No such efficacious means of cutting at root of slave trade ever was presented, as that which God has, I trust, opened out to us through the kind understandings of His Majesty.'

But Gordon never caught the boat from Lisbon. When he went back to Britain to prepare himself for the voyage, he was chosen by the British Government for another appointment. Before the end of January, he was on his way back to the Sudan, where he died, exactly a year later, in the fall of Khartoum to the Mahdists.

The insistence, in the letter to Stanley, on the wiping out of the slave trade, was strangely oracular. Only a few weeks before Gordon wrote, Stanley arrived near the proposed site for his farthest outpost on the Congo, the Stanley Falls. He had last been there at the start of 1877, on his long voyage of exploration to the Atlantic, and been forced to run the gauntlet of suspicious tribes. Now there was an ominous silence, and villages were burnt and abandoned. Large canoes had been deliberately stood on end and rammed into the mud on the verge of the river. Stanley and his colleagues in the steamboat *En Avant* stared in bewilderment, then slowly understood the new forces that had come into the region. The Arabs had arrived from the east.

A few miles farther up the river, Stanley reached the ruins of a large town. It had been burnt, all the palm and banana trees cut down, and acres of crops laid level with the ground. In front of the ruins, on the riverbank, sat 200 people, 'woefully forlorn and cheerless.' Questioned through an interpreter, they said that eight days before they had suddenly been attacked in the night. Most of the men were slaughtered, and many of the women and children carried away up river. Stanley hurried on in the same direction, past twelve villages destroyed by fire, and two days later overtook the perpetrators. Only a few hours before he had pulled out of the water the naked bodies of two women, bound together with cord.

As Stanley looked through his binoculars at the slave-traders hurrying about on the shore, he was seized with a desire for 'immediate and complete vengeance.' But he did nothing: 'I represented no constituted government, nor had I the shadow of authority to assume the role of censor, judge and executioner.' So instead of opening fire, and freeing the slaves, Stanley went ashore and set up a camp. Soon his Zanzibaris were shaking hands and conversing in Swahili with the Manyema mercenaries of Abed bin Salem. In sixteen months of raiding the mercenaries had ravaged nearly 35,000 square miles – an area bigger than Ireland. Stanley was taken around the compound where the slaves were being kept, in a series of long low huts. The Arabs told him there were 2,300 people in the compound, and that five other large slaving expeditions had already returned to Nyangwe. He estimated that in the raid more than 30,000 people had been killed, and more than a hundred villages destroyed.

Stanley re-creates the misery in the slave compound, where the naked prisoners lie around listlessly. They are mainly women and children, and some have been there for months, awaiting their turn to be carried further into captivity. On all sides are the stolen remnants of African village life – pots, drums, basins, baskets, tools, knives, whistles . . . 'My eyes catch the sight of that continual lifting of the hand to ease the neck in the collar, or as it displays a manacle exposed through a muscle being irritated by its weight, or want of fitness. My nerves are offended with the rancid effluvium of the unwashed herds within this human kennel.' He watches the old women being taken out to forage for food, to dig up cassava roots and search for bananas. What is brought back is flung down in front of each group of twenty prisoners, for them to scramble for. Many are half-starved, their bones sticking out and skin hanging in folds.

The advance of the Arab slave-traders beyond the Stanley Falls, on to the wide plateau of the Congo, was to have devastating consequences. Although Stanley does not say so, they had followed in his footsteps. Tippu-Tib had watched him depart into the unknown where nobody dared to venture. When the news came at last that Stanley had survived, the spell guarding the peoples of the plateau was broken.

20. Carving up the Dark Continent

The period when the European nations divided Africa among themselves was viewed with contempt by Stanley. He said it reminded him of the way 'my black followers used to rush with gleaming knives for slaughtered game during our travels'. Yet it was he more than any other explorer who set off what became known as the Scramble. His voyage of discovery down the Congo, and his insistent appeals for some great Power to take control of the region he traversed, compelled attention to Central Africa. In particular, he attracted Leopold, and as his employee began a systematic programme to open up the Congo Basin. It is arguable that only Stanley possessed the experience and will that could have turned the king's vision into reality. Leopold never set foot in tropical Africa; he relied on scheming in Europe. It was Stanley who became known as 'Bula Matari', the Smasher of Rocks, the founder of a state.

When he finally left the Congo in 1884, he had established stations as far inland as the Stanley Falls, nearly 1,000 miles from the Atlantic. More than 400 chiefs had been persuaded to sign treaties giving up their sovereignty. A flotilla of steamers had been launched at the Pool. These were the major achievements, but nothing had ever been too small for his concern: he ordered all the equipment for new stations, down to kettles and frying pans, specifying that frying pans must be exactly nine inches in diameter.

He had started operations in 1879 with twelve whites and sixty-eight Zanzibaris. When he left there were 120 whites and 600 blacks; many were indolent by his standards, but that was not for lack of cajoling and exhortation. He felt he had done well, that Leopold should be pleased; having so few personal attachments, he gave the king a loyalty and trust that was ill-advised. Leopold saw it as his royal prerogative to use people and their loyalties for his ends, until they had served their purpose.

It was one matter to have Stanley in Africa, sweating under the equatorial sun and drowning his fevers in quinine; his irascible letters could be tolerated. He was a far less certain asset in Europe, to a monarch playing for tremendous stakes with a hand almost devoid of trumps. Colonel Strauch, who would never forgive his invective, urged the need to keep him silent. Stanley showed a journalist's knack for capturing attention, and made headlines whenever he spoke in public.

Another man ready to reinforce Leopold's instinct that Stanley had started to become a liability was Sir John Kirk (he had been knighted in 1881). Writing from London, where he was on leave from Zanzibar, he told the king (March 21, 1883): 'Bold explorer as he undoubtedly is, no one here trusts him and unfortunately I know too much of him to be able to say a word in his favour. I have pointed out, however, that the work is so great that there is room enough for a rough pioneer like Stanley and a better class of administrator to manage stations.'

The dilemma facing Leopold was that however much he wished to find a way of keeping Stanley out of Europe during negotiations about the new 'Congo state', he had promised France to recall him. In April, 1884, the king achieved a measure of understanding with the French Foreign Minister, Jules Ferry, about territorial rights. Ferry wrote to de Brazza, who was still in Africa: 'The King of the Belgians has sent me assurances that Stanley's recall is already a settled matter.' Thus without knowing it, Stanley fell an early victim to the intrigues of colonial partition.

It is hardly surprising that he was out of touch with what was going on in the cabinets and embassies of Europe. Since April 1879 he had spent only eight weeks away from Africa. He did not understand the enmity between Britain and France, which sprang in 1882 from the collapse of the Anglo-French liaison in Egypt; the French were looking out for a chance to hit back for what they regarded as a humiliation. In Zanzibar the French were also outflanked, for the British had virtually established colonial rule: a British officer was running the Sultan's army, and in August 1881 the Sultan even asked Britain to take control over the succession to his throne.

When France ratified the de Brazza treaty in the Congo, this was viewed by the British as a threat to their trade. Nine months later, Stanley committed a *gaffe* by writing to a friend in London suggesting that the British should declare a protectorate over the Congo; his letter was read out at a meeting of the British Association. This naturally enraged Leopold, and excited the French, who saw the devious British at work again.

266

Another of Leopold's preoccupations which Stanley did not fully understand was a proposed Anglo-Portuguese treaty to recognise Portugal's claims to the Congo region. It would create a joint commission to supervise traffic on the region and give British firms a tariff advantage; as a side-effect it would effectively wipe out Leopold's assets.

Early in 1883, the king sent a letter to 'dear Bertie', his cousin the Prince of Wales, asking him to make sure that Britain would not allow Portugal to 'rob' Belgium. The Prince of Wales used his influence, and was assured that Portuguese control would only be recognised as far inland as Boma; this reduced Leopold's gloom. A fortnight later the king wrote an article in his own defence which appeared anonymously in *The Times*; it compared his association to the Red Cross, and said it had 'the noble aim of rendering lasting and disinterested services to the cause of progress'.

Thus the king laboured to maintain his image as a philanthropist, and he had wide support in Britain. But it was not merely goodwill that Leopold relied on. Sir John Kirk was keeping him informed about every step in the negotiations with Portugal, by a series of confidential letters to Jules Devaux, the king's chef de cabinet. The letters show Kirk to be keenly anti-Portuguese and anti-French, and he explained (April 19, 1883) how all the drafts of the proposed treaty came under his eye: being in the employ of the Foreign Office, he was constantly called in 'as a sort of African expert'. This gave him 'a good deal of power' to stop anything that 'seemed dangerous', but not a strong position to set the British Government on a new course. However, Leopold could depend on his best efforts.

In another letter, Kirk said that the whole of the official correspondence on the treaty had 'fallen into his hands' and this made it plain that Britain had gone too far to draw back at once. Now the aim must be to make the deal with Portugal abortive. Devaux wrote back on April 16, 1883 and asked whether Kirk might not be able to plant in the 'proper quarter' the idea that Britain should acknowledge the neutrality of the Congolese stations. On May 1, Kirk sent to Brussels a full text of the fourth revise of the treaty. He had copied this out from the Whitehall text, and marked it 'Strictly Private and Confidential'. In a covering letter to Devaux, he said: 'You will understand I have not been idle, for each revise has been under my eye and little by little we are getting your ideas edged in.'

In February 1884, the treaty was signed, but Britain ruled that it could not take effect until other Powers had approved it. The most immediate and dramatic sequel was the action of the United States, which had been subjected to a long propaganda campaign by Belgium. The campaign included the publication of 'laundered' versions of the treaties signed with African chiefs, and exploited Stanley's feats as an American in the Dark Continent. On April 10, 1884, the US Senate passed a resolution authorising President Chester Arthur to recognise the blue and gold flag of the International African Association as that of a friendly government. 'The United States Government have committed a great act of folly', observed an official in the British Foreign Office.

The Portuguese were in retreat, and Leopold was also working on Bismarck to win his support. On June 7, Bismarck told Britain he rejected the Anglo-Portuguese treaty, and that was the end of it.

The next and most daring step for Leopold was to decide on the boundaries of his future state. As soon as Stanley was back in Europe he was called to the king's summer residence at Ostend and presented with a map of Africa and a red pencil. As the king watched, Stanley drew an outline, going far to the north and south of the equator and stretching from the Atlantic to Lake Tanganyika. In the centre lay the frail thread of the Congo stations; on either side were hundreds of thousands of square miles of terrain, largely unexplored and occupied by millions of people who lived in ignorance of Leopold and his grand design. A copy of the map was sent at once to Bismarck: he approved. The French ambassador in Berlin recorded a meeting with Bismarck on August 27, 1884, at which the Chancellor showed him Leopold's map and said: 'I do not know what this Belgian Association is, nor what will become of it, but all the same it will not succeed in establishing itself very seriously, and it is always useful for diverting troublesome rivalries and claims that we could handle less easily ourselves.'

The French were in accord with the boundaries, for secretly Leopold had promised them that if he had to sell up his holdings in the Congo, France would have the first claim to them; it seemed likely that soon Leopold would have to admit that he had taken on too heavy a burden, and in Paris they would be happy to relieve him of it.

Bismarck now had his own ambitions in Africa. Not to be outdone by the British and French empire-builders, Germany had just declared protectorates over Togoland and the Cameroons in West

Africa. A conference of the Powers was clearly needed to decide on ground rules for carving up the continent. Bismarck offered Berlin as the meeting-ground, and in November 1884 the representatives of fourteen nations assembled.

As a monarch, Leopold could not attend, but he kept in touch with every detail of what was happening. What was to be done with Stanley? How could he be stopped from making one of his downright statements which could so easily swing the mood of the conference and snatch triumph from the king's outstretched hands? By an adroit stroke, Stanley was appointed as 'technical adviser' to the delegation of the United States. It happened that one of the two American representatives was the king's lackey, General Sanford. Leopold ordered Stanley to say nothing without asking Sanford first. The greatest explorer of Africa would thus be saved the humiliation of being kept away from the conference, but he would be held on a lead.

As it turned out, Stanley behaved with tact, although some of the onlookers at the conference found him withdrawn and constrained. He was given his chance to address the conference at the very start, and urged that the Congo Free State – as it would soon be called – should be given the biggest possible area and a wide access to the Atlantic. He was questioned by the French, British, American and Netherlands delegates about prospects for the free trade policy for the Congo Basin. He was succinct, and optimistic – too much so, as it was to turn out. But the conference advanced through November and December in a glow of reciprocal euphoria.

More and more countries followed Germany in recognising Leopold's State, and borders were worked out in the Congo region. France was given 257,000 square miles, Portugal 351,000, and Leopold 900,000.

While the conference moved ahead, supervised by Bismarck in his Wilhelmstrasse palace, Stanley went to Cologne, Frankfurt and Wiesbaden to lecture. He had asked the king for permission and was told: 'Speak of the share which the Germans are beginning to take in the manufacture of articles suitable to natives of Africa. Show them that this share will day by day increase, that it will supply work to Germans who are now obliged to go and seek for some in America, and that it will enable them to remain in their own country . . . Do not fear to dwell on this theme, which is of a nature to please M. de Bismarck.' He meekly accepted these orders.

On February 5, 1885, the news came through that Gordon was dead, cut down in Khartoum by the zealots of the Mahdi. Stanley was shocked. Only a year before he had been writing for Gordon to join him in the Congo. But he disagreed with the general's tactics at Khartoum: 'It was optional with Gordon to live or die; he preferred to die; I should have lived, if only to get the better of the Mahdi. With joy of striving, and fierce delight of thwarting, I should have dogged and harassed the Mahdi, like Nemesis, until I had him down.'

When he arrived in London after the end of the Berlin Conference, the storm over Gordon's death was at its peak. The Liberal Government was reeling under the charge that by delay it had killed him. Queen Victoria shared the view: 'That the promises of support were not fulfilled – which I so frequently and constantly pressed on those who asked him to go – is to me *grief inexpressible*! indeed, it has made me ill . . .'

Stanley came forward with the plan for a 'Gordon Association of the Nile', which would set up a confederacy of the peoples in the southern Sudan. They would be reached by way of the Congo and its northern tributary, the Aruwimi. It was appealing in its boldness, but money was lacking; the Gordon Association slipped from view.

The disappointment Stanley felt was briefly overlaid by the publication of his two-volume work, *The Congo and the Founding of its Free State*. It came out in London at the end of July, 1885, and editions in seventeen other languages were to follow. He had produced it with his usual speed. Leopold had warned him to be 'pleasant to all' and took the precaution of reading the proofs, just to make sure. Where Stanley could not praise any of his assistants he ignored them or described their failings anonymously. He indulged his prejudices: a picture of Strauch was given a quarter of a page, whereas Swinburne, the very junior officer who had been Stanley's secretary, was treated to a full page.

The book inevitably lacked the thrills of his earlier sagas of exploration; flashes of his old wit and descriptive skill appear like oases in deserts of leaden prose. Most of the second volume is filled with advice on staying fit in the tropics, and with comments on the behaviour of white men in the Congo; Stanley's statistics show that one in ten of those with him had died and a third had been invalided home.

The most lively part of the whole production is the cover design, showing steamboats, naked cherubs, cacti, pineapples, and scenes of the Stanley Pool. The centre is given over to Leopold, being crowned with a laurel wreath by a buxom, bare-breasted maiden; that was appropriate enough, in view of the king's known fondness for deflowering young girls.

When the book was out, Stanley felt bored and restless. His renewed contract with Leopold lasted until 1888, and he was due back at work. But where? He grew alarmed at reports in Continental newspapers that he was out of favour with Leopold; it was true that he received few letters from the king, and only evasive answers when he wrote to the royal aides. He speculated that Strauch had turned Leopold against him, and in the end wrote direct to the king, that he 'awaited orders' to travel: 'Meanwhile rumour is busy with my name, and with strange caprice reports me having fallen under the ban of your displeasure, and of the Court at Brussels having been long distrustful of me.' The reply came back from an aide: he was not to bother about rumours, and for the moment he was more useful in Europe, where his advice could be sought.

It was some solace to Stanley that he was now regarded with favour by much of the Establishment in Britain. His latest book, with its stress on avoiding bloodshed and spreading civilisation, damped down the complaints against him by missionaries. He was even presented by the British and Foreign Anti-Slavery Society with a large red umbrella for use 'should you go out again to the Congo, as we all sincerely hope you will'.

He wrote again to Leopold and reminded him of a promise made in 1878 that if the Congo project was a success, he would be appointed Director General. The king deflected this challenge, by again extending Stanley's contract and awarding him a Belgian decoration, the Order of Leopold.

Faced with a long stay in Europe, Stanley had given up his rooms in Sackville Street, just off Piccadilly, and taken a flat at 160, New Bond Street. The flat was expensively furnished and was big enough to store all the equipment, including tents and scientific apparatus, that he kept buying for use in Central Africa. This was the nearest thing he had ever had in his life to a permanent home (he was now in his mid-forties), and he was looked after by a housekeeper and a young servant, William Hoffmann. Impressed by his ability to speak German, Stanley had taken on Hoffmann – until then a bagmaker's apprentice – shortly before the Berlin Conference; although Hoffmann was an East Ender, his father came from the Continent.

A constant reminder of Africa in New Bond Street was Baruti, a former slave from the cannibal Basoko tribe. Stanley was hoping to train him to be a personal page. Baruti – whose name meant 'Gunpowder' – was in his fancy a successor to Kalulu, but he was not adapting well to London life. Visitors to the flat saw that Baruti had a tendency to take off his page's uniform and clamber over the furniture. Stanley seemed very tolerant towards his behaviour. The housekeeper was not, because Baruti threatened to throw her baby down the stairs.

Such minor dramas apart, many men might have been utterly content with Stanley's lot. He was on full salary of £1,000 a year from Leopold, with an income from his books, and earned still more from lecturing – which the king no longer objected to. But it was not what he wanted, and a curious lassitude possessed him. He wrote to a friend: 'My mind will not settle for literary work at all . . . The desire for work will come again, I hope, but at present I cannot even walk a mile without fatigue.' This was written from Nice in March 1886, at the start of a tour that would take him to Rome, Naples and the Italian Lakes. He was on a milk diet for his recurring gastric trouble.

Stanley drifted disconsolately into the summer of 1886. All his costly equipment was gathering dust. He remembered with nostalgia his years in the Congo: 'Though altogether solitary, I was never less conscious of solitude . . . My only comfort was my work. To it I ever turned as to a friend. It occupied my days, and I dwelt fondly on it at night. I rose in the morning, welcoming the dawn, only because it assisted me to my labour . . .' Leopold had now kept him in idleness for almost eighteen months.

At that moment he was contacted by Major James B. Pond, a leading American lecture tour manager visiting Britain with Henry Ward Beecher. Pond's account of his encounter with Stanley is to be found in his book of memoirs, entitled *Eccentricities of Genius*. In some ways, Pond and Stanley had much in common: they were almost the same age, and Pond had grown up in the American West; he had left home at fourteen after his father thrashed him, worked as a printer, seen service in the Indian Wars, and called himself 'Major' because it helped him as an impresario. At first he had been doubtful about making an offer to Stanley, recalling the failure of his New York lectures in 1872. But Beecher had pressed the idea on him: 'Get Stanley if you can. He is one of the greatest men we have . . . He is doing good work for civilisation. He is clean.' Pond went to call at the flat in New Bond Street, and found 'a very quiet, unassuming little man with dark hair and penetrating light blue eyes, reticent, but very pleasant.' They went out to lunch at the Café Royal, and in the evening took in a box at the Gaiety Theatre to watch a comedy. They got on well, and agreed terms the next morning. Stanley promised to be in America by November 27.

As the tour opened in Boston, Mark Twain was full of patriotic pride as he introduced the explorer to a crowded hall, and praised his 'indestructible Americanism.' At a time when everyone copied the British, Twain felt it was like 'a breath of fresh air' to stand in the presence of 'an untainted American citizen who has been caressed and complimented by half the crowned heads of Europe . . . He is a product of institutions which exist in no other country on earth – institutions that bring out all that is best and most heroic in a man.'

21. 'I Am Poor, Helpless, Trembling'

Stanley was the great discoverer, but he could never find a steadfast love. It was ten years since the parting from Alice Pike, when she had given her vain promise to wait for him. He still kept her letters, although she had asked him to burn them. She had tried to console him for her failure by saying he could 'easily find a wife all his heart could desire', and would soon forget her. If the wound of this rejection had not gone so deep, he might have taken her advice and quickly bestowed his affections elsewhere. But Stanley hurried back to Africa. He could lose himself there in his work, and give affection on his own terms – to the Zanzibaris, and the sailor Albert Christophersen.

This was self-deception, as he realised when he returned to the cities of Europe. Even while reporting to Leopold about the Congo, he could not hide his feelings; the king wrote drily to Strauch (August 7, 1884) that during the interview Stanley had 'declared he wished to be married'. What Leopold would have found hard to grasp was that he lacked any idea about how to proceed. Alice Pike had lured him into lowering the guard with which he defended his emotions, but it was now rigidly in place again.

Stanley was unable to be at ease with women: he could not shed that stern and distant manner he had adopted to impose his authority on men who were better born and physically bigger. He wrote to a friend in America (August 1, 1884): 'I have lived with men, not women, and it is the man's intense ruggedness, plainness, directness, that I have contracted by sheer force of circumstance . . . I wish to say, my dear friend, that I am absolutely uncomfortable when speaking to a woman, unless she is such a rare one that she will let me hear some common sense. The fact is, I can't talk to women. In their presence I am just as much of a hypocrite as any other man, and it galls me that I must act and be affected, and parody myself . . . It is such a false position that I do not care to put myself into it.'

He even managed to make a joke in the Congo Free State book about his own inadequacies, by remarking that the Zanzibaris were called the 'sons of old Bula Matari'; he felt they were a credit to him – a man who had never been married and was 'one of the most unlikely of men to be married'.

A shrewd picture of how Stanley behaved with women is given by a German writer and painter, Marie von Bunsen, who met him at the Berlin Conference. Her grandfather had been the Prussian minister to the Court of St James's in the 1840's, her grandmother came from Monmouth, and her English was flawless, so Stanley's lack of German was no barrier. The first impression was a disappointment – he seemed less self-assured than she imagined from reading *Through The Dark Continent*; he was short, broad, muscular, with grizzled hair and keen eyes (the whites, she noticed, were rather yellow), but he hardly looked at her and 'sat down uncouthly'. She tried to draw him into conversation, but he would not respond. It was only when she asked him about Africa that he came to life. They discussed the character of Africans, and he said: 'If once they trust a man, if once they know he talks with only a single tongue and invariably keeps his promises, they are capable of affection.' He gave her examples of the affection African mothers showed for their children. At the end of their first meeting, Marie von Bunsen summed him up in her diary as 'one of the tough Conquistador types with the outward habit of a disgruntled farmer and the phraseology and vocabulary of an American journalist.'

They were to meet again a few days later at the American Thanksgiving Day festivities in Berlin. Marie von Bunsen learnt that Stanley had carefully arranged that he should escort her in to dinner. She sat between him and the American ambassador, and decided that he 'talked like a book'. He admitted being still very embittered by the sceptical reception he was given in 1872 on returning from his search for Livingstone. After dinner, he made a short speech, and returned to this theme – saying that tears ran down his cheeks when he realised nobody believed him. As he mentioned the tears, a few people in the Thanksgiving Day audience sniggered. Marie von Bunsen wrote: 'But I realised the element of tragedy and felt a good deal of sympathy for the man.'

She questioned Stanley, following the speech, about his reception by Bismarck and the German Emperor, but he seemed indifferent to favours from the great. As they went into the ballroom, he was surrounded by women who wanted to be introduced to him, but Marie von Bunsen felt that she had captured his attention. General

Sanford was 'very jocose' and came up to her repeatedly, saying 'Why won't you be queen of Africa? You have only to say the word.'

Stanley did not follow up his acquaintance with Marie von Bunsen; he was shy and she was formidable. But, she was – he told another German woman he talked to in Berlin – the only girl he had met 'with the qualities to become his wife'.

Perhaps he was distracted by the crisis involving an Englishwoman who threatened to take him to court. The affair was, and still remains, a mystery. He was so unnerved by it that he planned for a time to leave England for good, and began to look for a place to live in Brussels. Stanley had been given the details in a letter, now lost, from his friend Alexander Bruce. Stanley's reply (December 30, 1884) was marked 'Strictly Confidential', and shows extreme emotion. He says he had cancelled a series of lectures in Britain, and arranged for all his possessions to be moved to the Continent at once. 'I shall at least be able to live without the fear of an absurd and ridiculous scandal instigated by a demented woman.' He pointed out that the public loved scandal, and his old enemies in the Royal Geographical Society, such as Cameron and Markham, would glory in his humiliation. But whatever the source of the drama, Stanley in the end thought better of leaving London.

By the Spring of 1885 he has taken to corresponding with an Austrian woman who had written to him through his publishers. Stanley is clearly tantalised that she will not reveal her name, and addresses her as 'The Unknown Madame or Mademoiselle'. He sends her his photograph, and asks for hers in return – but promises not to try to penetrate her disguise; he will reply through the publishers, who alone keep the secret of her address. His letter (April 11, 1885) is completely frank – perhaps just because of the aura of mystery: 'With women generally I am very shy, for I know nothing of them, though I might be bold enough on paper.' Once he had been 'an enthusiastic soul', but had noticed a strange difference in himself in recent years. 'Now in place of enthusiasm a deeply settled purpose to do whatever I lay my hands to effectively and well has taken possession of me, but the motions and sentiments of my soul lie dormant, and are not wakened.'

This postal flirtation came to nothing, and soon he began writing about the miseries of being single to Alexander Bruce – the husband of Agnes Livingstone. A dull, solid man, Bruce was an ideal confidant and full of sympathetic advice. This included making a visit to Newstead Abbey, to see the Webbs; it was seven years since Stanley had been there, and two daughters were now grown up. Stanley agreed to go, but pleaded for support: 'My timidity is unconquerable. To propose and be refused would be my death, which would not be a politic ending. Were I assisted by a good friend – firm, reliant, like yourself – to push me forward, I might venture. I am rich enough to keep half-a-dozen economically, but not rich enough to deck my bride with Kohinoors . . .'

Stanley went to Newstead, without Bruce, and in May he reported to his friend how hopeless it had been. He had luckily kept himself 'in reserve', having been forewarned by repeated failures: 'I am really glad that I have been the victim of so many miscarriages, because I am uncommonly wise now, and extraordinarily prudent. Except with a practised flirt, I do not think I could be taken in now, and I do not believe flirting is practised in England.' The Webb girls did not flirt with him, and would not look at 'anybody under Lords' with the friendliness he had known when they were children in the 1870's. He only hints at it, but obviously realised with dismay that a tired, middle-aged explorer was of no romantic interest to these two pretty girls, who were being courted before his eyes by 'young gentlemen'.

In the summer of 1885, the timorous search for a wife took a suddenly encouraging turn. Stanley met Dorothy Tennant, society hostess and amateur painter, the grand-daughter of an admiral and friend of Mr Gladstone the Prime Minister. She was thirty-four. The link between them was Edwin Arnold, editor of the *Daily Telegraph*. Arnold was a frequent visitor to the house on the east side of White-hall where Dorothy Tennant lived with her mother; after dinner he could be relied upon, with little prompting, to stand up in front of the assembled guests in the drawing room and read his latest poem. An invitation to dinner on June 24 had been sent to 'dear E.A.' and he was asked if he could bring his friend Stanley with him. The Tennants were eager Liberals, so Gladstone and Joseph Chamberlain were also expected to come. Arnold wrote regretting that he had to dine with the Lord Mayor, but Stanley was willing.

Dorothy Tennant was a tall, handsome woman with auburn hair and heavy eyebrows. She had mixed all her life with the famous, for her mother was tireless in 'collecting social lions' – politicians in particular. Dorothy also had her own circle of friends in the world of art: Sir John Millais had used her as a model in a painting called

Dorothy Tennant, in a portrait by the Pre-Raphaelite artist Watts; it was done several years before Stanley met her

'No!'; it shows a girl reading through a letter she is about to send off, rejecting a proposal of marriage. Considering her usual savoir-faire, it is surprising that Dorothy Tennant seemed in a flutter over the forthcoming dinner party. Perhaps the excitements of the general election campaign then in progress was affecting her; the Liberals were sure to lose – the death of Gordon having been a main element in their undoing – and Gladstone was preparing to move in next door to the Tennants in Richmond Terrace. It was a handsome row of

The photograph of Stanley, taken in London, epitomised the image the world had of him as 'Bula Matari' – The Smasher of Rocks

houses just across Whitehall from Downing Street, so he would be conveniently placed to move back again.

Dolly (as everyone called her) wrote in her diary a list of the guests who were coming, and copied down the letter she had sent to Gladstone, pressing him to accept her mother's formal invitation. She was keen to meet Stanley, because she was in the middle of his new book on the Congo. It would be an 'exceptional' evening, she decided; the entry in her diary ended rather cryptically: 'So much for efforts. I feel astonished at succeeding. Oh God help me. Do help me. What am I to do?' It was no ordinary diary that Dolly kept, because it was addressed to her father. He had been dead for twelve years, but she wrote as though he were still alive. Entries began: 'Now to tell you something particularly interesting . . .' They often ended: 'Goodnight, dearest' or 'Goodnight, my darling.' Dolly was also very close to her mother; they slept in the same room.

The dinner was a success, for all the trepidation. Dolly sat between Gladstone and Stanley, and acted as a buffer for their somewhat acrid exchanges on the Sudan and Africa in general. She was intrigued by the personality of the renowned explorer, and wrote to her father in her diary: 'I felt a friendship immediately. I felt I cared for him. I know he cared back for me . . . Dearest, goodnight.'

Dolly soon decided that she would ask him if she could paint his portrait. It seemed a sure way to foster their relationship. Portraiture was not her normal field, since she specialised in painting urchin boys from the East End, and several of her pictures had been hung in the Royal Academy; she also did buxom nudes in classical settings. But she wrote and explained to Stanley that she had 'succeeded once or twice with portraits', and hoped he would sit for her. There was a confusion at first, because he responded by sending her a package of photographs of himself, but by the start of July she had coaxed him into agreeing: 'I would let you be very comfortable, you shall smoke, and feel just as though you were in your own tent.'

So Stanley became a regular visitor to the Tennant house. It was at the south end of Richmond Terrace, close to the Victoria Embankment, and the double doors at the top of a flight of four stone steps bore the legend 'Knock and ring'. Stanley was led into a small room known as the 'Birdcage', where Dolly did her painting. The whole house recalled a Louis Philippe *salon*, with mirrors framed in baroque gilt, white and gold furniture, and marble-topped tables; in the summer, velvet curtains were pulled across to hide the fireplaces. After the sittings, Stanley sometimes stayed for lunch, to talk with Dolly and her mother, who had lived for twenty years in Paris and met such writers as Flaubert and Alphonse Daudet.

By the middle of July, he was confiding to his friend Alexander Bruce that he had found a woman whom he liked, but doubted whether she would appreciate him 'over and above the conventional Platonism'. His letter (July 18, 1885) shows that he had told Bruce about his thwarted love for Alice Pike and also revealed it to Dorothy

Tennant: 'Strange to say, I had just told her the story of the *Lady Alice* when in came her mother and spoke about Gordon's never marrying, and says she, "I am sure he must have been jilted by some girl in the past of whom no one has heard yet" . . . So very apropos of what I had been saying! My young lady friend and I looked up and our eyes mutually served to say, "What a coincidence." ' Dolly wrote some reflections in her diary: 'I wish Alice had died because then, though separate he could have thought of her with love, and he would not have mistrusted mankind. I felt so sorry for him, not because of this only, but there is a loneliness and disappointment about his life which he will not allow . . .'

From August until November, Dolly and her mother were away from London, mainly staying with titled friends in the country. For a time they were at a small hotel by the sea in Norfolk, and Dolly scarcely hid her boredom when she wrote to Stanley: 'The days speed past hand in hand, nothing distinguished yesterday from today, or today from what tomorrow will be. And it is all pleasant because it is only for a time.' She was missing the social round of London. In his reply, he sternly contrasted his contentment with the beauties of nature, and the need for quiet relaxation, with her pursuit of 'gaieties'.

The end of autumn and the return of the Tennants to Richmond Terrace did away with the need for letter-writing. But Stanley was wracked with uncertainty. Did Dolly really care for him? How could he find out, without risking a rebuff? A month after meeting her, he had written to Alexander Bruce for his advice: 'And do you think I am making any progress in this affair du coeur? I cannot see it . . . If she proposed to me, it might be different, but if I have to propose to her – do you know, I rather think I will not have the courage. And then, there is a mother in this case, and I am rather afraid of her. I think it would be a boon to shy people like myself, if there were no such people as mothers.'

Stanley was so consumed with anxiety that he took the advice of a Baroness von Donop, who said that he should sleep with a piece of wedding cake under his pillow. Then he would dream of his future bride. After carrying out this experiment, he wrote to the baroness (November 19, 1885): 'I have faithfully observed your injunctions, with all the firm belief of childhood in Santa Claus at Christmastime, but alas, I might as well have stuffed my pillow with hop flowers . . . Such a dreamless, uninteresting sleep I do not remember to have passed for months . . .' Stanley wondered if she had not forgotten some part of the instructions, and said his 'utter forlornness' pleaded for her help. But the baroness and her wedding cake left him as perplexed as ever.

Early in January 1886 he made his regular Saturday journey for tea with the Tennants; Dolly presented him with a silver token for his watch-chain. It was inscribed 'Bula Matari tala', followed by Dolly's monogram. 'Tala' is the Swahili word for 'remember'. By this time, Dolly was rhapsodising in her diary about marriage and the way people behaved at fashionable weddings. Although the years were passing, she decided that she still felt young and energetic and 'passionately loving'.

In February there was another dinner-party at which Gladstone was the principal guest; he had now crossed to Downing Street, having been returned to power in the November general election. Stanley was there, sitting beside Mrs Tennant at the far end of the table from Dolly. He did not enjoy the evening, being convulsed with pain from gastritis. He ate nothing, and left for his flat in New Bond Street as soon as the meal was over. A few days later the Tennants went to visit him, and found he was in bed. Dolly was, rather daringly, allowed to see him, and that evening recorded the moment in her diary: 'He wore a kind of brown silk vest with short sleeves, and his arm was bare. He grasped my hand eagerly with all his old vigour, looking so delighted to see me. He looked very brown and copper coloured, enhanced I suppose by the white pillow.'

As he convalesced during a tour of Europe, Stanley wrote Dolly a succession of long travelogues, broken up with moralising. At the end of each one he was sometimes brave enough to say that 'his manhood bade him halt' in case he talked of 'soft things'. By the time he reached Rome, there was a new topic – Gladstone and Home Rule for Ireland; great passions were aroused in Britain by Gladstone's decision to make a pact with Parnell, and the Liberals themselves were divided. Dolly wrote to say she was inclined to oppose Home Rule, for all her faith in Gladstone. Stanley had been seeing the papers from London, and this was his chance to launch into rhetoric, for he had long been critical of Gladstone's Irish policy – an attitude in which Edwin Arnold had influenced him. He praises Dolly for coming belatedly around to his view, and then denounces Gladstone as a 'traitor', 'arch-sophist' and 'mono-maniac'. After four pages of this he switches into a description of Rome, going on for another eight pages. At the end he wonders if writing at such length may have presumed upon her good nature.

By the time he had reached Naples, Stanley was even more aroused by the Home Rule controversy. He devoted almost all his letter to it. On the last page he found time to praise the beauty of an Italian princess and said that Naples was not too hot, as Mrs Tennant said it would be, but too cold. Then he ended with a personal thought: 'Bearing you and yours in mind most faithfully, I seem to have had your company most days, though when I looked upon Pompeii's ancient streets, I felt your absence keenly, because this was a time when interchange of sentiments regarding the awful calamity would have seemed to have increased one's pleasure and interest in the scene . . . Most faithfully yours, Henry M. Stanley.' As love letters, even by Victorian standards, these discourses from Italy were awkward. The attacks on Gladstone may have been his idea of a way to engage her emotions. As he had sadly admitted to his friend Bruce, he did not 'know how to set about it'.

The courtship survived the debate over Gladstone. On his return to London, Stanley continued his visits to Richmond Terrace, and in July went on a cruise around the Scottish Isles with Dolly and her mother. They were invited, together with fifty other people, by William Mackinnon, a shipowner who had various African involvements. Mackinnon was a friend of Leopold and ran the mailship service to Zanzibar.

The cruise was a success. Stanley paid courteous attention to Dolly, who seemed gay and encouraging. When they came ashore at Greenock, he felt that their relationship had progressed, to become a lasting bond. The Tennants stayed on in Scotland to visit friends, while he took the train back to London. There he agonised for a fortnight, before writing a proposal of marriage. Having written it, he kept it for two days, then sent it to Scotland by special messenger.

Gone was the challenging tone of his letters from the Continent. He was humble and uncertain:

My dear Miss Dorothy,

In one of my carefully-treasured notes received from you I read, 'How long it takes people to explore one another.' Eager and interested as I have always been with regard to you, I have been unable to explore with any satisfaction to myself your feelings towards me, and driven by misery and doubt, I have resolved to lay bare my own feelings and ascertain from you, if your goodness will extend so far, whether you can reciprocate them. You have dropped phrases in my hearing which have induced me to think that possibly I did not love in vain; if I have misconstrued them the punishment is mine . . . knowing how woefully ignorant I am of women's ways, I restrained myself, lest by giving expression to the ardour that possessed me, I should unknowingly give offence to one I had learned to esteem, admire and love with all my heart and soul . . . Thus I went to you and came away, visit after visit, always perplexed and doubting, never certain of anything, but that you were the noblest and brightest of your sex and that I loved you . . . You are in need of nothing. I cannot advantage you in anything, therein I am poor, helpless, trembling. I am only rich in love of you, filled with admiration for your royal beauty . . . I have sat and brooded for hours over the possibilities and impossibilities, which confidence alternating with diffidence pictured . . . For all the world I would not wound your feelings, nor offend any delicate susceptibilities. Nevertheless, bear without offence this declaration of mine, and tell me honestly, and candidly, to put an end to this exasperating doubt of mine . . . When I leave you I become miserable and unfit for company, and memory of you obscures all things else . . .

He ended by urging her to tell him quickly what her answer was. If she wished, she need only seal his letter in another envelope and send it back. Then he would know the worst. He signed himself: 'Yours most devotedly, Henry M. Stanley.'

Dolly turned him down. Her letter of rejection does not survive, but Stanley's comments upon it do not suggest that she gave any precise reasons. He believed that his 'base origins' tipped the balance against him; certainly Dolly was very conscious of class.

Stanley was frozen with despair, which soon turned to bitterness. He had been led on – she had been playing with him, just as Leopold constantly played with him. In a letter to Mackinnon, he unleashed his feelings: 'I have been living ever since my book left my hands last year in a fool's paradise. That woman entrapped me with her gush, and her fulsome adulations, her knicknacks inscribed with a "Remember Me", her sweet scented notes written with a certain literary touch which seemed to me to be a cunning compliment to myself . . . on leaving her presence I was buoyed up with some letter or despatch from Brussels which kept me on the stretch of expectation always. "We do not know exactly when we shall need you, but we shall let you know, my dear Mr Stanley, in ample time to prepare." So I lived, constantly hoping, hoping here, and hoping there – and after all both have come to nothing. I look back therefore with regret that nearly sixteen months of my life have been wasted with these artful people.'

22. *The Last Expedition*

'Who is Dr Emin?' This question exercised the British public mind in the autumn of 1886. He was clearly a hero, but a mysterious one. Some people said he was a German, others declared him to be a Turk; his appearance, his age, his habits – all these were unknown. The only certainty, the reason for concern and admiration, was Emin's gallant role on the banks of the Upper Nile. For more than four years nothing had been heard of him. Suddenly it was learnt that he still commanded 4,000 loyal troops in defiance of the Mahdists who had murdered General Gordon. The beleaguered doctor governed Equatoria Province in the Southern Sudan, and although the borders of his domain were vague, there was no doubt that his resistance shone out like a good deed. He was a second Gordon, said *The Times*, and the shameful failure to save Gordon made it even more essential to rescue Emin. Equatoria itself possessed a special significance – as the very place where, ten years earlier, Gordon began his fateful labours to 'uplift the Sudan'.

Missionary opinion was aroused: Equatoria was seen as a citadel of civilisation. It was perhaps slightly confusing, in an age when civilisation was held to be synonymous with Christianity, that all Emin's followers were Muslims; indeed, rumour said that the doctor himself was a devout believer in the Prophet. There was a second obscurity: if Emin and his men were undoubtedly loyal, to whom did they give allegiance? He had been appointed by Gordon on behalf of the Egyptian Government – that was why he bore the honorific title of Emin Bey. But after the fall of Khartoum the administration in Cairo washed its hands of the Sudan; if Emin remained an honest servant of the Khedive, His Highness was a reluctant master.

All these doubts were swept aside in the general excitement. Several letters which Emin had finally got through to Zanzibar were brave without being bombastic. 'We shall hold out until we obtain help, or until we perish,' he had said. Here were unmistakable echoes of Gordon. There was more than martyrdom in his messages, however. In a letter of July 7, 1886, he had asked: 'At the present time, when European powers are racing neck and neck to gain possession of districts in Africa, is it really possible that no one in England should have been enlightened enough to see how easy it would be to occupy the whole of our province, and this too without any cost?' Cut off as he was, the doctor still seemed *au fait* with the Scramble; a practical man, and a lover of England, German or Turk though he might be.

One person upon whom the idea of saving Emin made no impression was Lord Salisbury, the British Prime Minister. He remarked: 'I think the Germans should be placed in possession of our information. It is really their business, if Emin is a German.' He saw no advantage to the Empire, and Lord Wolseley heartily condemned any thought of a military venture into the Sudan. In the view of Downing Street, the revelations about Emin threatened to bring only trouble and expense.

In the face of official stone-walling, the popular fervour might have gradually died away. Any action would need massive funds and skilled organisations: two earlier expeditions had set out for Equatoria in hopes of discovering the fate of the lonely garrison, and both failed to get through. Those most concerned to arouse support for Emin were Charles Allen, secretary of the Anti-Slavery Society, and Robert Felkin, a former missionary in Uganda. They were intelligent idealists, with their own circles of influence, and capable enough to whip up a newspaper campaign – but not really cut out to smash a path to the Upper Nile.

It happened, however, that there were others in Britain ready to face such a challenge; their motives were more complex than those of Allen and Felkin, but they could command the money and the men. Foremost among the 'businesslike group' were Mackinnon, the Scottish shipowner, and Sir John Kirk, who was on leave from Zanzibar pending retirement from the Foreign Service. Also involved was James Hutton, a Manchester merchant. Hutton had at first been sceptical about trying to help Emin: 'You cannot give any hopes of a return,' he wrote to Mackinnon on November 26. His next letter was only slightly more hopeful: 'If the whole matter goes through I will put my name down for £1,000 – but I am not going to contribute this to a mere relief fund which is the duty of the Government.' It was the 'whole matter' which made an expedition worthwhile, and Hutton summed it up in a memorandum called 'Syndicate for establishing British Commerce and influence in East

Africa and for relieving Emin Bey.' It was to be philanthropy plus ten per cent. In Hutton's view, Emin was just an excuse for doing something that had been in prospect for nearly a decade. Only the fears of the Sultan of Zanzibar had stopped the grant of an East African trading concession in 1878 to Mackinnon, Hutton and other speculators. At that time the Arabs were the rivals, but by 1886 the Sultan was a broken reed and it was the Germans who might steal the prize – Bismarck was now after all he could get in Africa.

In November, an Anglo-German agreement was made to divide up the region facing Zanzibar; it left the interior beyond Lake Victoria to be taken by those who acted soonest. In December, the Emin Pasha Relief Committee was founded, with Mackinnon as chairman. In January came first steps for the formation of the Imperial British East Africa Company, with Mackinnon as president; seven of the twelve members of the Emin Pasha Relief Committee became directors of the company.

In Mackinnon's eyes, there was one man fit to relieve Emin, and he was Stanley. Even Kirk saw that. Not only did Stanley possess incomparable experience in Central African travel, but he repeatedly declared his wish to march into the Southern Sudan. He had appealed in vain to King Leopold, and tried to exert extra leverage through the British newspapers. A further recommendation, given the expeditions ulterior motives, was Stanley's proven ability as an empire-builder. It was tiresome that Leopold still had him under contract, but some compromise might be found.

Mackinnon approached Stanley in November 1886 with the idea of an expedition to Emin. Plans were still tentative, but Stanley was eager. A few days later he would sail for America, to start the series of lectures he had agreed on with Major Pond, but told Mackinnon to cable him when everything was ready. He would come back on the first boat; a hopeful clause he had put in his contract with Pond, about obeying a recall order from Leopold, might now prove invaluable.

The message from Mackinnon arrived on December 11, and said: 'Your plan and offer accepted. Authorities approve. Funds provided. Business urgent. Come promptly.' Stanley was in Massachussetts. He cabled Pond: 'Must stop lecturing. Recalled. Sail Wednesday at 4 a.m.' It was then Saturday, and he hurried back to New York, to be received by an anguished Pond. It would hardly have been politic to admit that the message did not come from Leopold at all, so Stanley spread it around that he was bowing to a royal command from Brussels.

Pond took the inevitable bravely, and watched throughout Sunday as Stanley used his office to dictate letters, and interview the makers of firearms. It seems from Pond's memoirs that Stanley contemplated, for a moment, the possibility of leading an undefended party to Equatoria: '. . . Mr Stanley sat down in my office for about two hours, smoking vigorously and uttering not a word. I knew he was undergoing a severe mental struggle . . . As his experience and mine in the Indian country had been somewhat similar, he asked me if I did not think, after all, that if we had pursued wholly peaceful tactics with the Indians our Government would have been more successful with them. He was considering whether it was not best to undertake this mission across Africa with an unarmed company rather than to have the appearance of a body of armed invaders.' It was an astounding proposition, since Emin was known to be so surrounded with enemies that he could not retreat in any direction. Stanley must have realised that this would be his last expedition: perhaps he dreamed of ending his African career with the pacific image of his mentor, David Livingstone. If so, such sentimentality soon evaporated.

Not only did he order fifty of the latest Winchester repeating rifles in America, but after landing in Britain on Christmas Eve began to sign up a team of army officers. They were in marked contrast to the type of man he had taken on earlier expeditions. As usual, the rumours of a new venture led by Stanley produced hundreds of volunteers, and many were non-military, so Stanley's choice under-lined his determination to force a path to Emin. But however different this expedition was going to be in its purpose and methods from anything he had done before, Stanley was seized by a familiar excitement. The prospect of going back to Africa after killing time for so long overlaid his personal frustrations and the knowledge that his health was poor.

Stanley worked at great speed: on January 5 he wrote to Lord Wolseley to ask for the release of two officers, Major Edmund Barttelot and Lieutenant William Stairs. Not only did he spell Wolseley's own name wrongly, but he also misspelt Barttelot's surname and gave him the wrong Christian name; however, Wolseley allowed the two to go – on unpaid leave. Among the others Stanley quickly picked out were Captain Robert Nelson, a cavalry officer, and Lieutenant Rose Troup, who had worked in the Congo as a police supervisor. As a medical assistant he chose William Bonny, who had been a sergeant in the army medical services for many years.

The only non-military members of the expedition accepted in London had each offered £1,000 for the privilege of going with Stanley to save Emin. James Jameson was a wealthy big-game hunter and naturalist, and Arthur Mounteney Jephson was a young gentleman of leisure who had served briefly as a merchant navy officer. Stanley was dubious about both of them, considering that they lacked grit, but the money they held out won the day. Jephson's £1,000 was put up by his cousin, the Countess de Noailles.

Finding the officers had been deceptively easy. The qualities looked for by Stanley and his colleagues on the relief committee were courage, energy and intellect – in that order. Experience in foreign parts was an asset: Nelson, Jameson and Bonny had all spent some years in Africa. The potential second-in-command, Major Barttelot, possessed the special virtue of having served on the Nile with the abortive campaign of 1884 to save Gordon. What seems to have been of small interest to everybody selected was the real point of the expedition. As Barttelot airily put it, Emin was 'some chap who wanted to get out of Africa and couldn't'; to go to his aid meant adventure and better promotion prospects – Barttelot was a major at twenty-seven, came from a titled background, had influential friends in the higher ranks, and might well hope to end up as a general.

Emin was also of secondary importance to Stanley himself, although he admired the shadowy governor for his tenacity. The motives of Stanley were intricate, for he was in a phase of intense bitterness, hidden behind his stiff façade. He seethed at King Leopold's long refusal to use him again in the Congo; this seemed linked by ill-fortune with the latest personal rejection – the turning down of his marriage proposal by Dolly Tennant. In Africa, in leading men through peril, he knew he could succeed. Action could make up for his failure to find happiness in the 'softer emotions', as he called them; and with a triumphant march to Equatoria he could salve the humiliation of the repeated snubs from Leopold. The frame of mind in which he commanded the Emin expedition was quickly summed up by Mounteney Jephson, the despised enthusiast who had bought his way in: 'I had a great argument with Stanley. He seemed to think that the only thing worth doing was to succeed, no matter how, in anything you undertook, and that success was everything . . . Stanley seems to have no sort of patience with anything that does not succeed.'

It is hardly surprising that Stanley insured against failure in a most aggressive style – after his brief flirtation with the idea of taking no guns at all, veering to the other extreme. The fifty Winchester repeaters he had chosen in New York were augmented by more than 500 Remingtons, a Maxim machine-gun, two tons of gunpowder and 150,000 rounds of ammunition. He also ordered tents, medicines, a sectional boat, innumerable accessories, and forty large hampers of delicacies from Fortnum and Mason of Piccadilly. To protect and carry this equipment, he gave instructions that 600 men must be recruited in Zanzibar.

If Stanley failed to reach Emin, it would not be through half-hearted weakness. Early in December, the British Foreign Secretary, Lord Iddesleigh, said that the proposed relief for Emin would be 'purely pacific', but by the middle of the month it was being proclaimed that Stanley was off to Africa 'at the head of an army'.

An operation on this scale was only possible through the backing of the Egyptian Government – although the Egyptians had scant say in the matter. It was decided for them by Sir Evelyn Baring, Britain's administrator in Cairo: they gave £10,000 and the bulk of the ammunition. This meant that Britain need not be directly involved, and would feel under no obligation to save Stanley, as well as Emin, if everything went wrong. The £10,000 matched a like amount raised in Britain, mainly by Mackinnon and his associates. To those who had first drawn attention to Emin's plight, the project soon seemed to be getting out of hand. Robert Felkin wrote in the *Scottish Geographical Magazine*: 'My firm belief is that commercial speculations and philanthropic plans, other than for the aid of Emin Bey, should not be undertaken by any expedition sent to his succour.'

Felkin was probably the only man in Britain who could claim to have seen Emin, having visited him in Equatoria in 1878 – before the advent of the Mahdi; but he was not appointed to the relief committee. Even more alarming to Felkin and his friends was the sudden news that Stanley planned to march to Emin by way of the Congo, instead of going directly from Zanzibar to Lake Victoria, and from there to Lake Albert on the southern border of Emin's territory. This decision meant that the huge expeditionary force would have to go by ship around Africa from Zanzibar to the Congo estuary, then upstream for nearly 1,000 miles before starting a 500-mile trek through the unexplored Ituri rain-forest. Stanley adroitly defended the Congo route, but it was plain enough that he was acting on the orders of Leopold. Was the Emin expedition now merely being used as a cover for extending the Congo Free State to the Nile headwaters? There were further suspicions – that the Belgians were after the huge store of ivory which Emin was rumoured to have accumulated.

Stanley had gone to Brussels as soon as the relief committee confirmed his appointment. Certainly the king was insisting upon the Congo route; he was in no way to refuse, since he had so often advocated it himself in the past, and Leopold still paid his salary. What the British public did not know – and Leopold did not know – was that Mackinnon had told Stanley of the moves to form an Imperial British East Africa Company and invited him to become its first administrator-general. Leopold had wanted Stanley to join Equatoria to the Congo; but Mackinnon made proposals for Emin to come into the British camp. At a later date, Stanley was to say that he had always regarded himself as working for Mackinnon. As if these conflicting roles were not enough, he was also committed to writing a book on the expedition for his publishers, and six British newspapers had made advance payments for the privilege of having despatches from him.

The last ten days in London passed in a bustle of conferences, correspondence and drama. On January 12, Stanley was due to see Lord Iddesleigh at the Foreign Office, but Iddesleigh dropped dead of a heart attack less than three hours before the meeting. The next day, Stanley went to the Guildhall and was made a Freeman of the City of London. On January 14 he was in Belgium for a second meeting with Leopold. On the 18th he went to Sandringham to explain the expedition to the Prince of Wales, and on the following night attended a farewell banquet arranged by Mackinnon. By January 21, he was on his way to Zanzibar.

He was accompanied from London only by William Hoffmann, his personal servant. The officers of the expedition had been sent ahead in other ships, and Baruti, the unruly Congolese boy who had been staying in Stanley's Bond Street flat, was put in charge of the medical assistant, William Bonny. There was a precise timetable to observe, for Stanley was haunted by Gordon's fate and the possibility that he might arrive at Lake Albert to discover that Emin and his forces had been killed by the Mahdists. On February 21, he would reach Zanzibar, and stay there for three days at the most, to make sure that the porters and *askari* had been properly organised. By mid-March the expedition would disembark on the other side of Africa at Banana Point, to start its overland journey to the Stanley Pool. That would take a month, and by mid-June the expedition would be carried – in Leopold's flotilla of river steamers – to Yambuya, a thousand miles up the Congo. From there it might take two or three months to march through the forest to Lake Albert. So by mid-September 1887 at the very latest, he expected to shake Emin by the hand and present him with 100,000 rounds of Remington ammunition on behalf of the Khedive.

Confident that everything would go to plan, Stanley stopped in Egypt in January and went to meet the Egyptian leaders, who had upgraded Emin from bey to pasha. Although they were at first amazed by the thought of the Congo route, he was able to persuade them that it made sense – that their money and munitions were not being thrown away. The Khedive and his prime minister, Nubar Pasha, also provided messages for the Equatoria garrison, offering back-pay to all the men who returned to Egypt, and wishing them good luck and farewell if they chose to stay where they were. This suited Stanley perfectly – he would have the widest scope in his dealings with Emin, when he laid out the secret proposals from Leopold and Mackinnon. It signified nothing that the expedition would march under the Egyptian flag; Stanley had also promised that for old time's sake he would have a man walk in front of him carrying James Gordon Bennett's standard as commodore of the New York Yacht Club.

The brief halt in Egypt was variously successful. Stanley had some clothes made for Emin, on the assumption that he must be in rags. It was awkward not knowing Emin's exact measurements, but having been told that the doctor was very tall and thin, he gave orders to the tailor accordingly.

Egypt settled one important difficulty. In London, a surgeon had agreed to go with the expedition, and then backed out. Stanley was so vexed that he resolved to do without a doctor, but in Alexandria he was approached by Thomas Parke, a young Irish medical officer in the British Army. At first, he turned him down; some intuition later changed his mind. From Shepheard's Hotel in Cairo he sent a telegram to Parke, who delightedly jumped up from his dinner to catch the overnight train from Alexandria.

There was one vital matter Parke had to settle before he left: he was master of the newly-formed Alexandria Hunt and a meeting of the foxhounds had been arranged for the following morning. Who was to lead the hunt in his place? 'In this difficulty I proposed to a brother officer his taking up my responsibilities for the success of the morrow's meet; his modesty at first made him hesitate . . .' Parke began to stress the 'peculiarities of his position'; at that his friend nobly shouldered the burden and the doctor dashed to his train. In the morning, it took Parke and Stanley only thirty minutes to come to terms and sign a contract. The formalities of obtaining unpaid leave from the War Office were soon settled, and within ten days Parke was on his way to Zanzibar. There was just time to play in a cricket match at Suez: 'The game was vigorously contested, and our side, indeed, managed to get beaten, but the result did not depress our spirits.'

In Zanzibar, the diverse forces of the relief expedition were finally marshalled: 620 Zanzibaris, sixty Sudanese recruited in Egypt, twelve Somalis from Aden, and Stanley and his eight white assistants. There was also an unexpected addition to the party – Tippu-Tib, the renowned Arab trader. On the instructions of Leopold, he had been offered the governorship of the Stanley Falls region, as a paid official of the Free State. It was a bizarre appointment, for although Tippu-Tib always denied that he dealt in slaves himself, there was no disputing that his lieutenants did so – and were ravaging the heart of Africa. Yet Leopold had taken over the Congo with the avowed aim of wiping out slavery.

It was mutual weakness that brought Tippu-Tib and the Belgian king together, with Stanley as the intermediary: the Arab was losing his former hold on the region to the west of Lake Tanganyika, for his methods were copied by younger and more ruthless compatriots; on his side, the king had failed to halt the Arab invasion of the Upper Congo, and his officers had been driven out of the Stanley Falls station with heavy losses. Tippu-Tib held no illusions. The Arabs had long since lost the game in Africa, and Leopold would only use him as long as it served his ends. Stanley was equally cynical, recalling his frustration in dealing with Tippu-Tib ten years before, but realising that the Arab might help him find extra porters in the

Congo for the march to Emin. So when the relief expedition left
Zanzibar in one of Mackinnon's ships, Leopold's newest employee
came aboard with an entourage of nearly a hundred, including
thirty-five wives.

The next four months, during which the spearhead of the expedition reached Yambuya on the Aruwimi River, were to give Stanley
and his white associates a variety of shocks and insights. In this time
the seeds of a calamity were sown.

The first shock was that Leopold's flotilla of river steamers were in
a decrepit state. Stanley saw he could not hope to move the whole
expedition and its stores up to Yambuya in one convoy. He had been
assured in Brussels that all Leopold's boats were immediately available to him, as long as they could be given 'without prejudice to the
service of the State'. Three were of no use to the expedition or
the State – one was without an engine, another was damaged and a
third falling to pieces. This proof of inefficiency in the territory he had
laboured so desperately to create dismayed Stanley and added to his
disillusionment with the king. He had heard the forecasts in Britain
that the Free State might collapse, and what he now saw in the
Congo must have strengthened his preference for the Mackinnon
offer to Emin.

He tackled the transport dilemma with typical boldness, by
seizing every vessel on the Congo – not only the State's dubious
steamers, but all the missionary boats. There was also the hull of a
ship belonging to an ivory trading company run by General Sanford;
the hull had just been completed and the engine was still on its way,
so Stanley decided to have a premature launching and tow the hull
behind a steamer. The manager of the company happened to be
Arthur Swinburne, the former servant and secretary to Stanley – who
asserted that Swinburne had offered the hull to him; in the subsequent quarrel between the committee and General Sanford over
compensation, Swinburne argued that if he had tried to refuse to
loan it, Stanley would have simply taken it.

The missionaries had the same impression: the leading Baptist,
Holman Bentley – who was a friend and admirer of Stanley – knew
that he had no alternative but to give up his boat, the *Peace*. Bentley
wrote: 'Had we not done so with good grace he would have taken
her by force. This is no suspicion – we know it.' Before leaving
England, Stanley had applied to Robert Arthington, an eccentric
Yorkshire philanthropist who had given the *Peace* to the Baptists, for

permission to use her if necessary. Arthington refused outright, his letter ending with a demand that he should look to the saving of his soul: '. . . I should like you should "repent and believe in the Gospel" – with real sense, and live in happiness, light and joy – for ever. Here delay for you is more dangerous than delay for Emin.' Stanley dismissed the letter as 'quaint', but was keen that any instructions from Arthington to the missionaries in the Congo should not add to his problems. Major Barttelot made a note in his diary about the negotiations: 'The mail did come in before she was ready, but Stanley had, through the chief of the station, stopped the mail and abstracted all suspicious-looking letters, to be delivered after we had started, and when the next mail came in.'

The sense of decay in the Congo soon lowered Stanley's spirits, and his officers began to see that his quickness of action and laconic humour hid a dark rage. In moments of misfortune this came boiling to the top. The men closest to him took the full force of his temper, and Jameson wrote that he now realised his leader could be 'extremely dangerous'.

Even Mounteney Jephson, whom Stanley had started to like after first thinking him far too effeminate for Africa, was caught up in an alarming quarrel. It started because Jephson and another white officer confiscated from the Zanzibaris a cache of food which had been looted from African villages. The Zanzibaris went to Stanley and protested that they had bought the food – which later turned out to be untrue. While trying to unravel the matter, Stanley went berserk and stamped up and down the deck of the *Peace* in front of 150 Zanzibaris. He suddenly turned on Jephson, who was standing on the river bank, and shouted: 'Goddam son of a sea-cook! You damned ass, you're tired of me, of the expedition, and of my men. Go into the bush, get. I've done with you!' He then addressed the Zanzibaris and told them that if Jephson and the other officers who had annoyed them should give any more orders, they should 'tie them to trees'. Then Stanley turned again to Jephson: 'If you want to fight, God damn you, I'll give you a bellyful. If I were only where you are, I'd go for you. It's lucky for you I am where I am.' Understandably, this scene opened up a gulf between Stanley and his assistants. They agreed among themselves that he was 'not a gentleman'. The cavalry officer, Nelson, wrote in his diary that his commander seemed 'off his chump' and 'an utter brute and a cad'.

Most ominous was the hostility between Stanley and Barttelot,

Stanley's second-in-command on the journey to save Emin was the gallant but unstable major, Edmund Barttelot. Below, the mysterious Governor of Equatoria, a German pretending to be a Turk

who had been so hastily chosen in London as the second-in-command. The antagonism was plain even to the missionaries at the Stanley Pool. The pride of the major, and his lack of flexibility, grated on Stanley, despite an admiration for his energy. For his part, Barttelot resented the threatening manners of a man who was his social inferior and yet tried to keep himself aloof. Worst of all was the clash over the way to handle Africans, for even Barttelot's fellow-officers were shocked by his obsessive racial opinions. The Zanzibaris reacted badly to his attitude and nicknamed him *M'tu Menu* – 'the man who shows his teeth'. Well before the expedition reached the Upper Congo, Barttelot and his leader were at pains to avoid one another. The major wrote in his diary (April 28, 1887): 'Stanley intends leaving me in the rear, I think . . . a bit of spite.'

The grinding advance of the expedition was watched by people in the Congo – both black and white – with mixed feelings. Many of the chiefs with whom Stanley had made treaties on behalf of Leopold came to complain to him about the methods of the Belgians. But some villagers were terrorised by the sudden arrival of his armed men, who denuded every riverside district of food and stole it if they could not barter. The missionaries tried their best to hasten the expedition's progress, although they viewed it with doubt. Holman Bentley wrote: 'The humanitarian aspect does not take me much. I believe it is more for the relief of Emin Pasha's ivory, or possibly there is some other reason at the back of which we know nothing, for it is absurd to think that a man possessed of so much ivory as he has cannot get away if that were indeed his wish.'

The young officials in the service of the Free State and General Sanford's trading concern were simply envious of Stanley's assistants. It was a great privilege to be plunging across Africa to rescue the mysterious Emin. Roger Casement, an Irishman working for Sanford, did everything possible for the expedition, and helped Barttelot to keep his contingent on the move. The major called Casement a 'real good chap' and an 'uncommon nice fellow'. (Many years later, in the First World War, Casement was to be hanged as a traitor by the British.)

Another who did more than help, and managed to join the expedition was Herbert Ward – whom Stanley had recruited for the Congo in 1884. In a letter of recommendation to Leopold, Stanley had described Ward as 'a Clive, a Gordon', and said that he showed more promise than any of 600 volunteers whom he had interviewed up to then. Ward intrigued Stanley because of his background: he had gone to a British public school, but at fifteen ran away to New Zealand, where he had been penniless and lived among the Maoris. For several years he worked as a merchant seaman. But he was more than an adventurer, for he made a serious study of African culture and traditions, which he recorded in notebooks and on sketching pads.

The meeting between Ward and Stanley in the Congo took place while the expedition was still making its way overland, past the lower cataracts. Ward's description of his first sight of it is vivid. At the front marched a tall Sudanese with the flag of the New York Yacht Club. Then came Stanley on a henna-stained mule, with silver-plated trappings that glittered in the sun. Stanley himself wore his usual peaked cap, a frogged jacket, knickerbockers and boots. Behind the mule walked servants in white robes and bright embroidered waistcoats. Next came the Zanzibari and Sudanese soldiers, with their rifles and ammunition. Then appeared a long procession of porters, carrying boxes and bundles; some bore a steel boat, section by section, on poles balanced on their shoulders. Donkeys were laden with sacks of rice and small boys herded goats. One group in the procession which caught Ward's eye were the women in Tippu-Tib's harem, in bright cloths and veils. Perhaps the most dramatic sight of all was Tippu-Tib himself, pacing majestically along in dazzling white robes, and with a decorated sabre over his shoulder. The whole expedition was more than four miles long.

Stanley gave Ward an interview there and then. Dismounting from his donkey he pointed to the ground and said 'take a seat'. He complimented Ward on his appearance: 'Why, you have grown some since I saw you in London in '84.' They quickly came to terms.

Ward was elated to be hired by Stanley, whom he found 'as harsh and rough, sometimes, as any Western State desperado', but also admirable and fascinating: '. . . he has his soft side, if you only know where to find it.' While the expedition made its way up the river to Yambuya, the two lounged on the deck of the *Peace* and talked about their early days in merchant ships. Ward decided that he would follow this grizzled, stocky man anywhere in the world.

To his dismay, he was never given the chance. The news suddenly spread that Stanley had decided to divide up the expedition, leaving Barttelot, Jameson, Ward and two other white officers on the river to bring up the main stores, which were still at Leopoldville through the lack of steamers. They would also care for the Zanzibaris and Sudanese who had fallen ill. Meanwhile, Stanley must hurry across country with an Advance Column to make contact with Emin and give him ammunition. He would take with him the fittest of the Zanzibaris, and four officers.

Barttelot was shattered and angry that he was not to be present at the historic meeting with Emin. Ward had 'never been more keenly disappointed in his life.' Jameson was equally cast down. Stanley did his best to console them: speed was vital to help Emin – who could forget what had happened with Gordon? – and in any case he would be back to collect the Rear Column within four months. Their task on the river was just as important as his own. He shook hands with Barttelot and said: 'I shall find you here in November when I return.' Then he marched eastwards out of the base camp at Yambuya into the dark forest of Ituri.

23. *In the Forest of Death*

An evil presence seemed to lurk like a shadow alongside the Emin Pasha Relief Expedition from the arrival in the Congo in March 1887 until its work was done. Stanley and his white assistants were aware of some malign force, awaiting a chance to wreak disaster. The most sensitive felt this strongly and wrote about it again and again (in the manner of the times, everyone kept up their diaries, regardless of privations). The sharpest impression was made on Mounteney Jephson, who came straight to Africa from acting as a companion to his wealthy relative in the South of France. He found that the waters of the Congo were dark and 'evil-looking'; the jungle made him feel closed in, so that it was almost difficult to breathe – 'of course, it is fancy, but the feeling is nevertheless a strong one'. Even the brooding cranes and kites along the banks added to the sense of nightmare, and the river was like a living thing, arousing a man's fear and hatred: 'The Congo river god is an evil one, I am persuaded.' The naturalist and hunter, James Jameson, felt a 'kind of gloom' over the expedition, and noted how if anyone made a joke that produced a laugh, a 'sudden death overtook this flash of relief.' Dr Tom Parke noted on October 1, 1887: 'The forest is such an utter wilderness – huge gloomy trees and dense thick bush beneath . . . Of all the scenes of desolation for any human being to be left alone in! I could not have fancied it before I came here.' The response of Major Barttelot was more limited, but even he talked of men having 'evil in their hearts' and called the Congo a 'land of treachery and lies'. He had a presentiment of death, but hid it in his letters home behind a wall of jocularity. He told a young nephew: 'I am now living among bloodthirsty savages, who delight in eating the flesh of a white man and drinking his blood while yet warm. Their favourite dish is English boy roasted whole and stuffed with bananas . . .'

Jephson, Jameson, Parke and Barttelot were all at least fifteen years younger than Stanley; they lacked the experience and confidence that made him seem outwardly untouched by their forebodings. Yet his mind could not entirely push aside similar reactions.

The Ituri forest, through which they must march to Lake Albert, he called 'a region accursed for crimes; whoever enters its circle becomes a subject to the divine wrath.' Long acquaintance had brought Stanley to love the might of nature in the tropics, and the Congo had few unknown terrors for him, but he was increasingly preyed upon by the 'dark relentless woods', the 'dead black shadows' of the hills and the 'eternal sound of fury, that ceaseless boom of the cataracts'. Inevitably, the struggle to relieve Emin took on the form of a fight against satanic powers, a Pilgrim's Progress. Afterwards, Stanley was able to write about a 'veritable divinity' guarding him and his officers in the forest – 'I say it with all reverence.'

The white men of the Advance Column might, instead, be regarded as having remarkable luck – not least in that one of them was a resourceful doctor. Stanley himself survived a month-long attack of malaria and gastritis in the Ituri forest: Parke was resigned to his death, but brought him through. The young Canadian, William Stairs, was hit by a poisoned arrow, which lodged half an inch from his heart; Parke sucked out the poison, and more than a year later extracted the arrow-head without anaesthetic. Another officer, Robert Nelson, was abandoned close to death in a forest camp, with fifty-two equally sick Zanzibaris; when he was rescued, seventeen of his charges were dead, five were alive, and the rest had wandered off into the forest. Parke contracted blood-poisoning through treating an epidemic of suppurating ulcers, and had to be cut open in the thigh by a colleague who was also close to death. Jephson was taken prisoner by mutineers, but survived; then he was driven into hysterics by malaria and exhaustion. For weeks on end there was no food but wild roots, lizards, snakes and ants.

The benign influence that narrowly kept the officers of the Advance Column alive did not extend to the Zanzibaris. In the middle of 1887, Stanley left Yambuya with 389 men to find Emin; by the end of 1888, when his appalling journeys through the forest were over, he had lost more than 200. Many of the survivors were maimed, or deeply scarred by ulcers. The fate of the Rear Column was worse: Barttelot and Jameson were to die, and out of 270 non-whites there were only sixty survivors. The total force of more than 700 with which Stanley had arrived in the Congo shrank to 260. Losses among local tribesmen were also severe – nearly seventy Manyema porters died in the forests and an indeterminate number of villagers who came in the path of the expedition were killed for one reason or another.

The relief of Emin was generally held to have been a triumph; if so, it is hard to conceive of a disaster.

Regular news of how completely matters were going awry would have sobered the hopes of an expectant world. But between September 1887 and December 1888 there was only silence about Stanley, broken by rumours of his death. These started before the end of 1887, with a report from a missionary that a steamer had been stranded on a sandbank on the Upper Congo and all its occupants – including Stanley – were massacred. Next came a message from the French consul in Zanzibar, supported by a report in *Le Figaro*, that Stanley had been killed on the Aruwimi. For many months there was only speculation. Emin in his lonely redoubt knew of Stanley's intentions, but a letter he managed to send out to the East Coast said there was no news at all of the would-be saviour.

By the middle of 1888, anxiety was rising in London. Then came a report in a Paris journal that the Belgian government had definite news of Stanley's death. This was expanded by the *Berliner Tageblatt*; even if Stanley was not dead, he was in desperate danger, and in Brussels 'all was consternation'. Next there were rumours from the Sudan of a mysterious 'White Pasha' advancing against the Mahdists, followed by a bold declaration from the Mahdists themselves that they had captured Emin and a traveller who was with him. Finally came renewed stories that Stanley had been massacred on the Aruwimi, and only two porters escaped to tell the tale; the path was 'strewn with human bones'.

By December 1888, there was hardly an editor in Europe who had not offered a snippet of lugubrious news from one source or another in Africa. On December 18, the young explorer Joseph Thomson – who had asked in vain for a place in the expedition – told *The Times* of his conviction that Stanley and all his followers had been annihilated: 'Stanley has met his terrible fate in some such way as this. He started from the Aruwimi, and almost immediately plunged into dense forests, to be made worse by swamps further east. Through such a country his caravan would have to travel in single file, with probably no more than twenty men in sight at one time . . . they would fight at a terrible disadvantage . . . And then the end came. Probably in that last struggle for life not a soul escaped.'

An encounter with cannibals on the march to Equatoria. (An illustration from Stanley's bestseller, *In Darkest Africa*)

But three days after Thomson's letter appeared, a short message was read out to the British Parliament: Stanley was alive, had found Emin at Lake Albert, then marched back through the forest to collect his Rear Column. The House of Commons rose as a man and cheered.

When more facts were known, the sheer complexity of all that had happened hid the extent of the tragedy. Only the *apparent* success was easily grasped. Stanley's own interpretation laid emphasis, naturally enough, on his achievement. At the finish he said he felt like 'a labourer on a Saturday evening returning home with his week's work done, his week's wages in his pocket and glad that tomorrow is a Sabbath . . .' He adroitly turned the horrors into heroics and the desperation into courage. Even his dire errors about the timing of the expedition were hidden in the drama of the tale.

When Stanley had set out for Lake Albert, he expected to arrive in September. He would return by November to the Rear Column at Yambuya, to guide it along the way to the lake. That was his timetable. But he only reached the lake by December, and did not rejoin the Rear Column until August of the following year – by which time it was sunk into chaos.

He had estimated that the distance from Yambuya to the lake was 380 miles in a straight line, but that he might have to travel 550 miles. This was guesswork, because the Ituri rain-forest was one of the last pockets of unknown terrain in Central Africa. In the event, he marched nearly 700 miles to reach Lake Albert, through conditions far worse than he could have thought possible. A force of nearly 400 men needed a large amount of food, and the supplies with which they started were soon exhausted; food was very scarce in the forest, and along part of the route the meagre villages and their gardens had been devastated by slave-raiders.

Stanley tried on his first journey through the forest to keep close to the Aruwimi River, in hopes of moving his force swiftly along it in his steel boat, and in captured canoes. But the river was often more of an obstacle than a help. After going back to collect the Rear Column, and returning once more to Lake Albert, Stanley had marched nearly 2,000 miles through the humid and inhospitable Ituri waste.

Never in his career did Stanley come so close to defeat, or his spirits fall into such a slough of hopelessness. He was even prepared to escape from his nightmare by suicide. He says nothing of it himself, although he admits that at the time (December 1888) 'it became impossible not to regard the darkest view and expect the worst'. He later confided his suicidal intentions to Parke, who gives the most objective record of everything that happened to the expedition. The doctor noted a conversation with Stanley: 'He told me that when the men had remained away eight days collecting food, during his stay at that awful Starvation Camp near the Ituri (before reaching Fort Bodo on his return from Yambuya) – he followed them, bringing his revolver and a full dose of poison, to destroy himself with, in case he could not find them.'

It was a unique lapse. The course of the relief expedition was governed by Stanley's will. He drove through obstacles which Parke believed 'no other living man would have been able to battle with so successfully.' His actions completely dominated those of the three other leading actors in the story – Barttelot, Tippu-Tib and Emin. His relationship with these three was to be decisive for each of them, quite apart from bringing out his own strengths and shortcomings.

The result for Barttelot was tragedy, for he was never able to understand the events that led to his own doom. The commander of the Rear Column was the stuff of which military heroes are made; he had been reared in the traditions of Waterloo and the Charge of the Light Brigade. Left at Yambuya in charge of a mixed contingent of Zanzibaris, Sudanese and Somalis (most of them ailing), forced to negotiate with evasive Arab slave-traders, and baffled by the long silence by Stanley, Barttelot was utterly at a loss. Emissaries were sent out on dangerous missions which achieved nothing. It all became a nightmare. The major was further handicapped by his disagreements with the white men under him, and the intrigues among them. Barttelot particularly distrusted Ward, the clever and unconventional ex-sailor, believing Stanley had left him behind as a 'spy'.

These suspicions were encouraged by William Bonny, whose long career as an army sergeant had taught him how to be ingratiating to superiors; the situation gave scope for the ambitions of Bonny, who secretly resented his inferior status in the expedition – after all, his brother had served as a vice-consul in South America. Bonny, who was in his forties, burned inside at the condescending airs of the young officers around him. Although nobody knew it at the time, he concealed another secret which made him additionally unreliable as Barttelot's confidant – he was addicted to opium, which he pilfered from the medical stores.

It was not long before Barttelot became alarmingly overwrought, and his mind was shrewdly played upon by Bonny. He wrote in his diary (November 24, 1887): 'Bonny and I talked about our probable action in the event of Stanley doing certain things. I expressed myself openly . . .' Five days later he went for a walk outside the camp palisade with Bonny, who said Ward was spreading stories that Barttelot was unpopular with the Arabs. On December 6 there is another entry: 'After dinner, Bonny and I walked again, and referred to our conversation of November 24. I made a determination, never to partake of Stanley's hospitality while out here, as we have a private medicine chest.' Barttelot had come to suspect that Stanley wanted to murder him, and went as far as tasting cyanide of potassium from the medicine chest, so that he could recognise it in a cup of coffee.

306

Barttelot tried to divert his thoughts by reading Pepys's *Diary*. But he could not shut out the moist, malarial air of Yambuya, the stench of the camp, the drumming and shouting of his sick and fractious charges. The Zanzibaris were dying inexorably, from disease and hunger: 'Some of our men have faded away to nothing. It is surprising to me how uprightly and well they walk, though mere skeletons . . .' In such a predicament, discipline called for foresight and sympathy, but Barttelot lacked both. He imposed a regime of heavy flogging for all thefts, and since the ailing men stole food whenever they could find it, it became almost routine for the day to start at Yambuya with the whistling and thud of the lash. The reputation of the major soon spread beyond the camp and made his task of recruiting porters to carry the bulk of the expedition's stores up to Lake Albert almost impossible. When porters were collected, they refused to be under his command, and demanded to be led by one of their own Arab chiefs.

A mission-educated African named John Henry deserted with Barttelot's revolver, was caught, and sentenced to be executed. When the Zanzibaris threatened to leave in a body if the sentence was carried out, John Henry was given 300 lashes and died three days later. A Sudanese was sentenced to 300 lashes, to be given in two instalments, for stealing half a goat. After the first, he was put in chains, but escaped two months later with a rifle; when he was recaptured, Barttelot had him executed by firing squad.

Ward viewed Barttelot's behaviour with the advantage of long experience in Africa, and decided he was 'harsh and inhuman' towards the Zanzibaris, and 'tyrannical' in dealing with the white officers. The disputes between Barttelot and Ward were so bitter that Ward was sent down the Congo and told not to return. The first news to reach the outside world of what was happening to the Rear Column was when two of its members were sent home through illness; they were Lieutenant Troup and Assad Farran, a Syrian interpreter. At Stanley Pool they met a British missionary and he was so taken aback by what he heard that he wrote at some length to a friend in England. The friend showed the letter to another friend, who passed it to a London daily newspaper which printed it on September 19, 1888. The letter bitterly condemned Barttelot, saying that he had done little to save his men from starvation, and was generally incapable of evoking loyalty. 'And his rough treatment of the men, in spite of their sufferings, is considered by Troup and others, to be the worst policy he could have pursued, more than one threat having been uttered by the soldiers, that when they got their commander on the march, they would shoot him.' The missionary had written his letter on July 26, with no means of knowing what was happening more than a 1,000 miles away in the Ituri forest. Seven days earlier, Barttelot had indeed been shot.

In June, Barttelot began his march through the rain forest to find Stanley, but his column was a disorganised rabble. The porters stole stores almost at will, progress was snail-like and the Manyema recruits were rebellious. A Belgian officer, Van Kerckhoven, who saw the Rear Column depart, wrote grimly in his diary: 'I do not believe in its success; its leader has no tact, and no patience with the Negroes.' Van Kerckhoven had arrived at Barttelot's camp unexpectedly in a Free State steamer, making one of the rare patrols on this part of the river. He had been startled that the Rear Column was still stuck near the Congo a year after Stanley had left to find Emin. Van Kerckhoven heard about Barttelot's futile efforts to collect a full quota of Manyema porters from Tippu-Tib, and felt the gloom which shrouded the Rear Column; Barttelot's self-control was cracking up and his actions were no longer those of a rational man. There was scant rapport between Barttelot and Van Kerckhoven, an eccentric figure who had hair down to his shoulders and dressed in pyjamas and an immense white hat with a red band. But the Belgian did all he could to help, and tried to cheer Barttelot up by giving him a parrot, and a bottle of champagne to celebrate Queen Victoria's birthday.

The engineer of the river steamer, J. R. Werner, heard soon after the parting with Barttelot that Tippu-Tib had told the Manyema to shoot their commander if he treated them badly. 'This was such an astonishing statement that I could hardly believe it, but it was confirmed by one of my own men (a Zanzibari), and also by several of Tippu's own men, then on board . . .'

Barttelot's death happened early one morning. One of the Manyema women in the damp was drumming loudly to celebrate a 'festival of the moon' and the noise frayed his nerves. The major went out from his tent and ordered her to stop. He was carrying his pistol and a steel-tipped cane with which he was in the habit of prodding people who upset him. Barttelot and the woman began to argue. A shot was heard and the major fell dead. The bullet had been fired by Sanga, a Manyema chief who was the woman's husband. Sanga was later arrested, tried by Tippu-Tib in his capacity as a Free State official, and executed.

Less than a month after Barttelot's death, his closest friend – the naturalist James Jameson – died of malaria. He might have been remembered as a high-minded martyr in the cause of Emin's relief, except for a macabre incident which shocked Victorian Britain when the news filtered back from the Congo. Jameson had provoked, watched and sketched a cannibal feast. The Syrian interpreter, Assad Farran, made this revelation in a series of blood-curdling statements. According to Farran, he was with Jameson when they reached a village called Riba Riba during a trip to collect porters. Jameson said he was 'very anxious to see the natives eating each other', and urged the local chiefs to arrange it. An Arab agreed, if Jameson would pay six handkerchiefs. Jameson produced the handkerchiefs, and ten minutes later a girl of about eleven was paraded. She was tied to a tree, and stabbed until she died. 'About seven or eight of the natives ran with their knives, which they were sharpening, and began to cut their victim – some cutting the legs, others the arms, and a man with an axe was cutting the head with the breast until all was finished. Some of them went down to the river to wash the meat, while others went to their houses and put the meat in their cooking pots. We were watching them all the time, and Mr Jameson was drawing every act that was going on.'

A fortnight before he died, Jameson wrote his own version, broadly corroborating what Farran described, but denying that he knew the girl would be killed when he paid the Arab the six handkerchiefs. He did not make the sketches while the girl was being cut up, but later that day, in his house in the village. 'The girl never looked for help, for she seemed to know it was her fate, and never stirred hand, foot or head, except when she had to move to the place of execution.'

When Stanley struggled back to find the survivors of the Rear Column on August 19, 1888, Jameson had died only two days earlier. But Stanley could not know about this, because Jameson was on a trip down the Congo when exhaustion and fever killed him. Bonny was the only white man left with the ulcerated, starving Africans who crawled up to welcome Stanley. Catastrophe had brought the despised sergeant to the position of command – a role he was in haste to assert. 'My dear Jameson . . .' he had ventured to write when sending off a letter to explain Barttelot's death.

At first, Stanley was in two minds about Bonny's subtle, self-promoting version of what had gone wrong. In a hurried letter on September 5, 1888, he wrote: 'If I were to enter into details I might perhaps do an injustice to the officers, for I have only Mr Bonny's version. His account furnishes an altogether too terrible a picture to be at once credible . . . In the meantime, if any rumour of these unhappy events have reached England the public will do well to follow my example and suspend judgement . . .' But in a letter to the already-dead Jameson he accused him of being 'demented'.

He certainly did not admit that any faults of his own caused the debacle. Yet he had after all, selected Barttelot, a patently unsuitable man, and by the time he had gauged his failings was still content to leave him in charge at Yambuya. Moreover the orders Stanley gave to Barttelot were ambiguous – suggesting that he should wait where he was for Stanley's return, but also that he might start to march along the Aruwimi when his porters and stores were assembled. If Stanley had been able to return as quickly as he promised, the major's dilemma would not have arisen.

As usual, the most accurate witness is neither Stanley nor Barttelot, but Parke. He wrote: 'Barttelot's last words to me were, that he would not remain a day after the rest of the loads and men came up . . .' Stanley clearly intended the major to follow him if he could, and trees were marked every few yards along the trail as a guide.

The fate of the Rear Column and the burden of guilt were to cause a bitter feud between Stanley and Barttelot's family for more than a decade. The condemnation that was to be heaped upon his dead second-in-command by Stanley was intended to still the questions about his own leadership of the expedition. Any hint of failure or inadequacy was unbearable, about what he had always known must be his farewell effort in Africa. He was leading the expedition at the request of an august British committee, and if he could sustain their faith in him, it would be a final guarantee of his acceptability.

He kept apart from his officers, except for giving them orders, and on the rare moments when he did sit down with them to talk was prone to launch a bombardment of clichés about success and determination. Jephson wrote of Stanley: '. . . He told me that he had been just as impetuous and rash as I am when he was my age, but that time etc. had taught him to curb himself and a whole lot more rubbish. He made himself out to be a St John for gentleness, a Solomon for wisdom, a Job for patience and a model of truth. Whereas I do not suppose a more impatient, a more ungentle, a more untruthful man than Stanley could exist.' Parke noted: 'Mr Stanley called Stairs and myself into his tent last night, and gave us a long lecture – he frequently lectures us – telling us of the great importance of looking well after the men, and getting them into health and good condition. During the discourse he told us that "the path of duty is the way to glory" . . .' But Parke also recognised that many men, having twice struggled through the rain forest and then found the Rear Column 'so completely wrecked' might have been pardoned for giving up and returning to Europe.

If such a thought ever tempted Stanley, he gives no suggestion of it. He turned hurriedly back towards Lake Albert and Emin, and by the end of 1888 was re-united with the main body of the Advance Column. For the third time, he had marched through the Ituri wilderness – although the cost had been terrible.

Desperation forced Stanley to behave during those eighteen months with a ruthlessness he had never shown before. The greatest threat to the survival of the expedition was desertion, for the bulk of the men so hastily recruited for him in Zanzibar proved to be domestic slaves. There was a nucleus of veterans – led by Uledi, the former coxswain of the *Lady Alice* – but too many of the Zanzibaris felt no loyalty at all to Stanley. The outlook was so alarming that he imposed a new sentence for desertion: execution by hanging. The first man to die was a slave named Mabruki, one of a trio who had stolen rifles and fled with them. The three had been captured by an Arab slave trader and returned to camp after being given fifty lashes; the Arab was duly rewarded with a revolver. For the execution, Stanley paraded all the Zanzibaris at dawn and harangued them about the doom that must befall the whole expedition if desertions went on. He then invited the three men to draw pieces of paper from his hand, and Mabruki, after choosing the shortest piece, was told he would die immediately; it would be the turn of his colleagues on the two successive days.

Stanley's début as an executioner was clumsy. A rope was put around Mabruki's neck and then tied to the top of a springy sapling, which had been bent over for the purpose – the idea being to let go of the sapling and send the condemned man hurtling upwards with a broken neck. The technique was reminiscent of ritual sacrifices in the Congo, in which the victims were attached by the necks to small trees, and decapitated with one blow of a sword so that their heads would be catapulted to the far side of the forest clearing. But the tree chosen for Mabruki started to snap as it was pulled down. Parke relates how the rope had to be thrown over a strong branch instead and the two other deserters – who stood by in chains – were ordered to pull Mabruki up.

'When a short interval had elapsed and Mr Stanley asked the question "Is he dead?" I answered, "Yes," and the column immediately filed out of camp . . .' In his account, Stanley makes no mention of the fiasco with the sapling, and does not say that he made the two other condemned men haul up their colleague. He implies that the main vexation of the day was his failure to bring down an elephant which was badly needed for its meat, despite putting five bullets into the animal from a range of fifteen yards.

That night, one of the other condemned men escaped. At dawn Stanley called to his tent a senior Zanzibari named Rashid, to discuss what should be done with the remaining malefactor. There was a long discussion in Swahili, which is reconstructed verbatim, starting 'Well, Rashid, old man . . .' The outcome was that Rashid and the other expedition captains should at the moment of execution suddenly plead for a reprieve, and that Stanley with a show of surprise would grant it; this performance would help to arouse a surge of loyalty among the assembled Zanzibaris. It all went according to plan, and as the noose was taken from the condemned man's neck there were shouts of 'Death to him who leaves Bula Matari! Show the way to the lake!'

Under the pressure of starvation this spirit soon began to wither, and the Zanzibaris began to barter their rifles for corn with the half-caste Arabs who waited like vultures around the expedition. Suspects were tied up and floggings were ordered. Stanley knew the extent of hunger that was destroying his followers – men who looked like grey ghosts, but still had to stagger forward with their 60 lb loads along greasy tracks under the tropical rain. Stanley shot his donkey to give meat, and the men fought over the skin and entrails while the quivering beast was cut in pieces. When they lay down to rest, rats crept out of the undergrowth to gnaw the dead flesh of their legs.

One day Parke removed enough bone from the ravaged feet of the porters 'to fill two soup plates'.

For all that, discipline had to be maintained, and another hanging was carried out. Parke recorded it with a laconic casualness: 'Later on in the day, one of our cooks was hanged for selling his rifle, so I was obliged to cook the dinner, as I am mess-president for this month.' He had formed an opinion of Stanley's methods by this time: 'He is different from any other man. There is no change in his expression or behaviour; he will never be found to sacrifice all in attempting to save one. His policy rather is to sacrifice one and save the remainder.'

It did not occur to Stanley that his behaviour was cruel, even if it was fierce. He took the Victorian view that non-white peoples could only be led by unwavering strength; rebels had been blown from cannons in the Indian Mutiny, and that was the price of disobedience. He was fond of Africans, but did not expect too much – even Uledi had once stolen from him. Stanley was not greatly dismayed when the Congolese boy Baruti, who had lived for years in New Bond Street, deserted and returned to his own tribe. The worst part was that he took with him Stanley's Winchester rifle, two revolvers, bullets, a silver watch, a pedometer, a belt and some money. 'Peace be with him!' wrote Stanley philosophically.

Stanley's understanding shows itself when he writes of the sufferings of Manyema women and children in the forest. He describes how 'a prepossessing lassie' travelling with the expedition went out from the camp to collect herbs, was ambushed by local tribesmen, and struck by poisoned arrows – for which the only treatment was an immediate injection of ammonium. 'Her screams attracted attention, and she was hastily brought in, but even as we were about to inject the ammonium she rolled over, raised her arms, and embraced her young husband in the most touching manner, gave a long sigh, and died.' Another woman covered in pustules 'emitting an almost unbearable stench' was devotedly nursed through her last days by her husband. For Stanley, such behaviour was the saving grace of a people who otherwise enraged and horrified him. As the expedition marched through a village they came across three small children impaled on spears, and two were still alive. Such scenes of savagery were hard to reconcile with the love which the Africans of the forest could also display.

But there was also a markedly different people whom the expedi-

The horrors of the Ituri forest, and the loss of life in the Advance Column, were to shock Europe when the full story was told. This scene is entitled: 'The relief of Nelson and survivors at Starvation Camp'

tion found on the journey to Emin. They were sometimes hostile, but strangely endearing. These were the pigmies, the elusive denizens of the remotest parts of the forest. The first one they saw was a girl of about seventeen, less than three feet tall. Stanley found her figure graceful, her skin smooth and sleek, and her eyes lustrous. 'Absolutely nude, the little demoiselle was quite possessed, as though she were accustomed to be admired, and really enjoyed the inspection.' From time to time, the expedition was able to catch more pigmies, who could be a useful source of information if they knew any recognisable language.

Parke went further and purchased a pigmy girl from an Arab for twelve cups of rice, six cups of corn, and a handful of beans. She became his handmaiden and served him with great devotion. During the march to Lake Albert, Parke lost a stone in weight, whereas his colleagues lost more than twice as much: he decided this was due to the skilled foraging of his pigmy, who would collect fruits, leaves, roots and insects for him to eat. 'Her great difficulty is being unable to conceal these eatables from the ravenous men, who would certainly seize them from her. She wanders off into the forest by day; and

314

generally manages to bring her collection to me, after dark, wrapped in a plantain leaf.' Parke kept her with him for more than a year, during which she nursed him through bouts of malaria. They learnt to talk together in Swahili, and she told him about the customs of her people. But when the expedition reached open country the change in climate made her ill. She could not stand the sunshine, although Parke made a sunshade for her and Stanley provided a pair of scarlet breeches – which she wore upside down with her arms through the legs. In the end, she had to be left with a hospitable tribe. The doctor was sad: 'She was a universal favourite in the caravan, and our parting with her was a very pathetic one . . . this little dwarf always maintained an exalted dignity and superior position among the other women of the caravan, and never once have I known her to be a trouble to anyone . . . her last act at parting was to give me the ivory bangles which she wore in the forest, but which had now dropped from her attenuated arms and ankles.'

Stanley wrote several warm comments upon Parke's unorthodox valet, but he kept up a rigid silence about his own attendant. Never once, in any of his published writings, is there even a glancing reference to William Hoffman, the youth he had taken on in London in 1884. What little can be learnt comes from the diaries of others. Yet Hoffmann was at his master's side from the start of the expedition to the end, and was the only white man – apart from Stanley himself – to make three marches through the Ituri forest. One fact emerges: Hoffmann was viewed with contempt by Stanley's officers. Jephson called him 'the German servant' and never bothers to name him; even the good-natured Parke is bleakly uninformative. Nowhere is a good word to be found for this oddly shadowy figure. According to Hoffmann, Stanley would call him to his tent in the evenings and 'pour out his troubles' about the discontent of the Zanzibaris and the quarrels among the white officers. Stanley would say: 'William, I can't go back. I promised to relieve Emin and I must go on.'

Yet among Stanley's private papers are the minutes of a court-martial of Hoffmann by the white officers – Stanley himself did not take part. The main charge was theft. The minutes show that Hoffmann was dismissed four times during the expedition by Stanley for stealing and lying. Hoffmann not only stole from his employer, but also asked the junior officers for various items he said their leader wanted, then never handed them on.

The first time Hoffmann was dismissed by Stanley was in March 1888, for lying and 'a being filthy in his person'. It is the second misdemeanour, so cryptically phrased, which must contain the reason for the sudden rejection of a boy who had been in his service for nearly four years. It was a time when Stanley had been struck down by gastritis. Jephson notes for February 26 in his diary: 'He hit his German servant across the head with a stick and it has made his arm really bad, for matter has formed among the glands and it will be an affair of many days before it gets well.'

It is possible that 'being filthy in his person' – at a fearful time when appearances could be of no consequence – was an oblique way of charging Hoffmann with cannibalism. He was to admit openly in later years that he had eaten human flesh during the expedition, and said that it 'tasted rather like goat'. The famine conditions in the Ituri forest could well have conquered Hoffmann's qualms, and there was no lack of opportunity for cannibalism. On one occasion a slave was overpowered and eaten by his own comrades only 200 yards from the camp.

By writing letters of repentance, Hoffmann was able to work his way back into Stanley's service. Not only was it impossible to dismiss him effectively in the middle of a forest, but also he was impossible to do without. Hoffmann knew all of his master's personal needs, could look after his clothing, make his bed, supervise the packing before each day's march, and run messages in the camp. The careworn state to which the explorer was reduced made Hoffmann even more valuable; Stanley was sometimes troubled by rheumatism in one knee and had to be carried in a seat made of leather thongs attached to poles. Hoffmann had to massage the knee with liniment.

So only a month after having been struck on the head and dismissed by Stanley, Hoffmann was allowed to go down the escarpment to Lake Albert for the long delayed meeting with Emin. It was night-time, and the two leading figures in the drama were silhouetted against the light of bonfires. Hoffmann watched from the shadows as Stanley hurried forward, raised his cap and seized the Pasha by the hand. The Zanzibaris shouted, danced and fired off their rifles, while Emin's escort stood at attention behind a standard-bearer holding the flag of Egypt. It seemed strange that the man they had come to save was immaculately dressed in a white drill suit, and looked in good health; his neatly-trimmed beard was still black, and his face

unlined. By contrast, Stanley was haggard, and his white hair and moustache made him seem the more frail of the two.

Hoffmann may have wondered if he might be needed as an interpreter, for although Emin wore a fez he was thought to be German. But the Governor spoke perfect English in response to Stanley's greeting: 'I owe you a thousand thanks, Mr Stanley; I really do not know how to express my thanks to you.' The two men sat down on boxes at the entrance to a tent, and were joined by Parke and Jephson, and an Italian captain, Gaetano Casati, who was one of Emin's aides. As the group began an exuberant exchange of news, Hoffmann had one last duty to perform for the evening – helping his master unwrap from clothes in the bottom of a trunk three pint bottles of champagne. Then a toast was drunk on the shore of Lake Albert to His Excellency, Dr Emin Pasha.

It was an exact repetition of Stanley's gesture nearly twenty years earlier, when he had found Dr Livingstone beside Lake Tanganyika.

24. Bringing Back the Trophy

The meeting with Emin was the climax to months of torment in the forest for Stanley and his followers. They soon found it hard to quell a sense of anti-climax. Emin was full of gratitude for the thirty-one cases of Remington bullets, given by Egypt and brought 10,000 miles around Africa to be laid at his feet. But it was hard to know what use he might make of the ammunition, because he was a distinctly unwarlike figure; with his high forehead and steel-rimmed spectacles, he looked to Stanley like 'a professor of jurisprudence'.

Firepower apart, Emin was far better off than his rescuers. They were starving, so he gave them food: aboard his principal steamer, the *Khedive*, the Governor entertained Stanley and his officers – who had come to count themselves lucky to dine off fried locusts and wild berries – to meals of a kind they had not enjoyed for many months. Their clothes were in tatters, so Emin's tailor was told to measure them at once for new suits. A shoemaker was called in, to replace the rough boots the leaders of the expedition had striven to cobble up in the forest. Emin overwhelmed them with kindness, and did not neglect the needs of the Zanzibaris; he was especially attentive to Uledi, whose name he knew from having read of him in *Through the Dark Continent*.

The expedition was supplied with cattle, sheep, grain, vegetables, honey – even soap and gin, both of which were manufactured in the province. There was a carefully-sustained air of calm and normality in Equatoria, and Emin seemed to spend much of his time touring the hundred-mile length of Lake Albert and his private stretch of the Upper Nile; he had two steamers, survivors of the fleet once controlled by Gordon. When on land, the Governor watched over his civil service, which was run by Egyptian clerks. As much time as he could spare was devoted to scientific pursuits, in particular the collecting and stuffing of rare birds and animals. It was all rather perplexing (not to say humiliating), to have broken through to this besieged domain, only to find it so placid and comfortable.

In Stanley's case, the perplexity soon gave way to disillusion.

Emin was different from what he had expected in almost every way. It was said that the doctor was at least six feet tall, but he turned out to be little bigger than Stanley himself; the trousers so dutifully carried from Cairo were six inches too long. The Governor could not help being dreadfully short-sighted – even Stanley could sympathise with that, for his own eyesight, once so keen, was starting to fade. But Emin's peering, hesitant manner matched his irresolute mind.

The worst thing about Emin, in Stanley's view, was that he could in no sense be called 'a fighter'. By this, he meant that Emin did not care to stand up for himself. He compromised. Some months earlier, Stanley had given his own ideas on such matters to Herbert Ward: 'Look after your men. Don't rush into any fighting. Keep peaceful. But mind you, if you have to fight, *fight!*' What was the good of bringing a ton of bullets to a man who did not seem cut out to grit his teeth and stand firm? Stanley had never met anyone quite like Emin, although in some obvious ways they were similar – both used assumed names, denied their origins, and had obscure periods in their early careers. They also shared a love of Africa. After that, any likeness ended: these two were destined to have most delicate dealings with one another, but their characters and styles of decision-taking were utterly at odds.

Stanley was naturally curious to learn about the figure whose life was so shrouded in mystery. It was fairly clear that the doctor was not, as he sometimes claimed, an Arab by birth. His 'rescuer' was gradually able to discover more: Emin had been born at Oppeln, in Prussia, in 1840, and was baptised as Eduard Carl Schnitzer. His father was a wealthy merchant, and Emin had studied at the universities of Breslau, Berlin and Königsberg, qualifying as a doctor when he was twenty-four. Then he spent ten years in the Ottoman Empire, mainly in the service of a prominent Turkish administrator, Ismail Hakki Pasha. After a short visit to Germany after the death of Ismail, the man who now called himself Emin Effendi Hakim went to the Sudan, where he worked his way diligently upwards from medical officer to become Governor of Equatoria.

Stanley was impressed by Emin's intellect and linguistic skill – he was reputed to be master of more than twenty languages. The care with which he kept up his scientific studies was equally astonishing: 'The journals are marvels of neatness – blotless, and the writing microscopically minute, as though he aimed at obtaining a prize for accuracy, economy, neatness and fidelity . . .'

Emin the naturalist. The doctor sent out his staff every day to catch specimens.
But in his flight from a rebellion he was forced to abandon the huge collection of
stuffed birds he had hoped to give to the British Museum

There were some other details that Stanley was unlikely to learn
about Emin – not just that he was a brilliant chess-player and
pianist, but also that his career with Ismail Hakki Pasha had ended
in a considerable scandal. Emin was very close to Ismail's Hungarian
wife, and after his employer's death declared her to be his own wife.
Emin took her home to his family in Prussia, and abandoned her
there with four children and several slave-girls, while he fled to
Africa. For fourteen years, Emin had made no contact with his
family, nor with Ismail's widow. In the meantime he had taken an
Ethiopian wife; she had died, leaving him with a daughter, Ferida.
When Stanley first met Ferida she was six, and 'extremely pretty,
with large, beautiful, black eyes.'

As Stanley fairly observed, Emin had enjoyed a varied life – 'One
that would furnish to quiet home-keeping people much valuable and
enchanting reading matter'. It was also a career that made him a
taxing opponent in debate, for although Emin was evasive, he was
obstinate. When asked about his intentions, he avoided giving any

320

direct reply. It was not his wish to shape events, and for preference he would stay where he was. He was the servant of his people, and must obey their wishes. If it proved impossible to stay in Equatoria, he would go where they wanted to go. Where did they want to go? He could not say. He only knew they did not want to return to Egypt.

This kind of discussion was exasperating to Stanley. He was appalled at the idea of merely transporting to Lake Albert all the supplies his long-suffering Zanzibaris could carry, handing them over to the Pasha, and marching off to Zanzibar. It would be some comfort that he did not have to face cries of 'Too late!' as had the would-be rescuers of Gordon, but he needed some positive rewards for either Leopold or William Mackinnon.

He aimed from the outset to persuade Emin to throw in his lot with the Congo Free State or the British 'sphere of influence' in East Africa (preferably the latter). Stanley could not be frank with his own officers about the propositions he was putting to Emin – as far as they knew, Emin had the simple options of staying put or marching out to the safety of the East African coast. Parke summed it up after the first meeting beside Lake Albert: 'We all hope that Emin Pasha will make up his mind to come out with us; however, Mr Stanley pointedly observed that our object in coming was to bring relief in ammunition, etc., and not to bring him out; as we shall have barely enough men left to enable us to push our way through to Zanzibar, and protect ourselves in the course, without the responsibility and trouble of looking after Emin and all his people.'

The negotiations between Emin and Stanley took place in two stages. At the start, during May 1888, the Pasha was able to talk from apparent strength; the superficial orderliness of his domain hid the true fragility of his position. Stanley was the supplicant – he admitted being afraid that he could not 'appear before Emin with any appearance of success'. To discover what the Pasha's people wanted to do, he decided to send Mounteney Jephson on a tour of the Nile stations, to read out a proclamation. It would urge all the followers of Emin to return to Egypt, where they would be given eight years' back pay. If they stayed in Equatoria, they would be abandoned to their fate. The move was disastrous for Emin – his soldiers definitely did not want to leave Equatoria, where they had harems, slaves and little work; the proclamation was denounced as a fraud. Moreover, Stanley was justified in being worried about the impression he made in Equatoria – his ragged, exhausted band was viewed with contempt.

For many months, Emin maintained a degree of control over his stations near Lake Albert with accounts of the powerful force that was coming to his aid. This had served two purposes: it subdued the rebellious, and encouraged the more loyal to believe that soon they would be made strong enough to hold their ground against the Mahdists and the African warlords along the eastern shore of the lake. The news of Stanley and his modest offering of ammunition spread fast to the northernmost limits of Equatoria, where the garrisons were only tacitly under Emin's command. Stanley's prestige fell even lower when it was discovered that most of the ammunition was old, damaged and useless.

Intrigue and rebellion began at once; disaffection ran like a flame, southwards along the Nile. To make matters worse, the Mahdists made a sortie from the north, so that panic and mutiny were merged. Some of the remaining 2,000 men of the Equatoria army were covert supporters of the Mahdists, and they devised, but abandoned, an outlandish plot to strap Emin down to his bedstead and carry him in triumph to Khartoum.

Mounteney Jephson soon saw the dire extremity into which he was thrown by the order to read Stanley's proclamation to all the garrisons he could reach. The rhetoric fell flat, since Jephson could not speak Arabic and his words had to be interpreted. There was some powerful, if unintentional, irony: '. . . the Khedive and his vizier Nubar Pasha have always kept you in mind though they could not reach you. They have heard from your Pasha, by way of Uganda, how bravely you have held to your posts, and how staunch you have been in your duties as soldiers.' But Jephson stuck to his mission.

There had been a time when Jephson and Stanley were sharply antagonistic to one another, but shared sufferings brought them closer together, and Jephson was determined to show that he had the manliness his leader held to be the supreme virtue. He made a shrewd assessment of the bulk of the Egyptian officers in Equatoria: they were 'lying and treacherous, false and cowardly' – men who had been banished to the furthest corner of the Egyptian empire for a variety of crimes. The Sudanese soldiery, on whom the Egyptians looked down with contempt, were 'infinitely their superiors' in Jephson's opinion.

After Emin and Jephson were taken prisoner by the rebels in

August 1888, the cool courage of Jephson did not desert him. When he talked to a rebel officer he stood no nonsense: 'I rather shut him up, for I told him, I knew him to be a liar and I considered him, in addition, a fool . . .' During the two months' imprisonment, Jephson kept up his diary and had long conversations with Emin, whom he came to admire for his accomplishments, and to pity for his predicament: 'He is now in such a state of nervous exhaustion that he is unable to sleep and his heart gives him a great deal of trouble and anxiety. Unless he goes to a colder climate he says he does not give himself more than three years of life – he is now only forty-eight.'

Jephson decided that if the rebels carried Emin away out of the reach of rescue by Stanley, he would go with him. But this ultimate test of Jephson's bravery was not made, for in the confusion caused by the rebellion and the Mahdist attack, he and Emin were able to escape on foot, towards Lake Albert. Jephson carried Ferida, the doctor's daughter, on his shoulders. It was a heart-rending moment for Emin, not only because his province was in ruins after the five years he had managed to keep it going, but because in the flight he was forced to abandon his collection of stuffed birds. He had meant to give the birds to the British Museum.

By December, Emin and Jephson had made their way to Tunguru at the northern end of Lake Albert; there they waited for the chance to get through safely to Stanley, who was south of the lake. Jephson spent his evenings walking alone in the moonlight: 'It is splendid to stand on the point and facing southwest, down the lake, one sees nothing but water, with a great headland something the shape of Beachy Head, only three times higher, coming down, a great purple mass, sheer into the lake.' He began to understand the love his sad companion felt for the land he now must leave.

Jephson sent messengers with letters to Stanley, reporting on the state of Equatoria as he saw it. He had a reply which irritated him – in particular a section saying, 'Sometimes I fancy you are half Mahdist, or Arabist, then Eminist – I shall be wiser when I see you . . . do not you be drawn into that fatal fascination, which Sudan territory seems to have for all Europeans, of late years, for as soon as they touch its ground they seem to be drawn into a whirlpool . . .' But Jephson's annoyance vanished when he finally arrived back at the expedition's camp. Stanley was at pains to say that he had written the offending letter during an attack of malaria. At their meeting, in front of all the other officers, he stood up, took off his hat and received him with great warmth. Jephson knew that he had passed muster.

The second round of Stanley's talks with Emin now began. The balance of power between the two had dramatically changed, and Emin's failure to stem the rebellion revealed his essential weakness. The arrival of the relief expedition had, however, been a main factor in the collapse of Equatoria, so Stanley had unintentionally set in motion events that allowed him to dictate terms. He now served Emin with an ultimatum: he could be led out of his impasse with any loyal followers who might present themselves at the camp within a month, and join the march to Zanzibar, or stay where he was. If he stayed, Stanley would give him nothing; the thirty-one cases of ammunition already handed over had been seized by the rebels.

By this time, any idea of attaching Equatoria to the Congo, or establishing Emin in Uganda, had been thrown aside. He no longer had a worthwhile following. It was Zanzibar or nothing. On March 26, 1889, Stanley increased the pressure on Emin and gave April 10 as a deadline for starting the march to the coast. He pointed out his duties to the relief committee; every month in Africa cost £400 in wages to the Zanzibaris. He must think also of his young officers, who had been absent from Britain for more than two years – both they and the 200 surviving Zanzibaris were impatient to be away from this remote spot in the centre of the continent. Stanley called in the officers – Jephson, Parke, Stairs and Nelson – and they all said they would not stay a day after April 10. The meeting ended with an appeal from Emin. Would they support him by saying that he had done enough for 'his people'? Parke notes drily: 'We were all unanimous in assuring that we considered that he had done a great deal too much.'

As the day of departure for the coast came nearer, there were several alarums. One morning, Stanley emerged from his tent, blew his whistle furiously and demanded that all able-bodied men should assemble in the centre of the camp. The Zanzibaris were told to bring their guns. Emin's men were also marshalled. With his eyes glaring, Stanley waved his rifle angrily, stamped his feet, and demanded to know of the Egyptians whether they definitely wanted to follow him. Overawed by his display of rage, they meekly said they did, Later he claimed that he had learnt that the Egyptians and Sudanese were plotting to steal arms during the night; he put armed Zanzibaris on patrol after dark, and it was announced that any man roaming about later than ten at night would be shot dead. It was a piece of theatre, designed to reinforce his control. Jephson went to talk to Emin and warned that it was 'not advisable for him to say or even allow himself to think that yesterday's affair was the utmost Stanley could do – he did not yet know the man and what he was capable of.'

When Stanley asked for a final parade of all the men, women and children who were ready to march, it was a pathetic collection. There were fewer than 200 men, and about 400 women and children. Many of the children were in a frail condition, and could never survive the journey. Jephson looked in pity at a soldier with an emaciated baby in his arms: his wife had deserted him. 'There he stood, a forlorn-looking figure in the fast-falling rain, his worldly possessions representing one small basket and a half-starved baby . . .' As Jephson asked routine questions, the man broke into a fit of weeping. 'One's heart ached for him, but what can one do; to stay here is to die and I fear to take to the road means death also to his child – at any rate the poor little baby shall have half my share of milk so long as there is any.'

But not all Emin's people were impoverished, and some brought iron beds, grinding stones, cooking pots, trunks, saddles and tin baths. Stanley made them abandon some of their heavier impedimenta, but it was still necessary to raid the surrounding countryside and impress 500 tribesmen as porters. In all, the caravan would set out on the 1,000-mile march to the sea with 1,500 people; but many would certainly die or desert on the way.

On the evening before the departure there was dancing and athletics, in which Jephson distinguished himself by running faster than any of the Africans. It was a restless night, and as soon as the sun rose above the lake Stanley led the way to the south-east, the column stretching behind him for three miles. Flags waved and bugles sounded, but for all the show of spirit the survivors of the relief expedition had little to console themselves with. The rest of the Remington ammunition – which had been the ostensible *raison d'etre* of all that had been endured – was covertly buried, since there was no point now in carrying it farther.

Within two days the officers who had promised to accompany Emin began to desert. Then a Sudanese soldier named Rehan led away twenty-two companions, and took with him several rifles belonging to Stanley's men. The energetic William Stairs was sent back in pursuit, and returned after four days with Rehan and most of his followers. Stanley was ill at the time with gastritis, and while he lay in his tent a court of officers was convened and sentenced Rehan to death. Stanley was carried out to confirm the verdict. 'Go to God!' he declared, and Rehan was drawn up over a branch. Once again (although Stanley does not mention it) the execution was not cleanly done: the rope broke and Rehan slumped to the ground. Parke took a clinical interest in the condemned man's state of mind during a brief reprieve while the rope was being plaited together to strengthen it: 'I found him utterly indifferent and apathetic; not merely passively or stupidly so, but that he did not seem to mind in the least . . .' When the doctor's examination was complete, Rehan was sent to God in earnest.

After four months' marching, during which there were skirmishes with peoples through whose lands the expedition passed, Stanley came in sight of Lake Victoria. He had last seen it nearly fifteen years before, when he made his circumnavigation in the *Lady Alice* and struggled to convert King Mtesa to Christianity. Now Mtesa was dead, and chaos had followed, but the missionaries whose presence Stanley had demanded were clinging on at the south of the lake. Foremost among these was Alexander Mackay, an aggressive Scot much after Stanley's heart. He was practical and plain-spoken; in his perilous situation he was quite willing to defend the Gospel with his gun. While awaiting news of Stanley he had written (February 24, 1888): 'I guess he will have very much to do . . . quelling insubordination among the Egyptian officers . . . unless Stanley and Emin remove or *hang* some of these, the Sudan Equatorial province will be worth little. No half-and-half measures do in Africa.' Mackay tried his best to restore the dispirited white officers of the expedition, but when Jephson heard a musical box playing 'Auld Lang Syne' in the mission he rushed away to hide his tears.

Eighteen months before Stanley's arrival, the leader of the missionaries, Bishop Parker, had died. His clothes were brought out and auctioned off to the officers, together with those of two other missionaries who were victims of fever. Stanley complained to Mackay that he could not see as well as in the past, and was given the Bishop's gold-rimmed glasses. He was delighted with the first spectacles he had ever worn – 'it seemed to me that my power of vision was increased four-fold'.

Soon after leaving Mackay (who was to die in the following year)

Stanley was joined by a Catholic missionary, Father Auguste Schynse, a Rhinelander who had spent two years in Africa. Even in 1889, the route from Lake Victoria to the coast was still hazardous and Schynse valued the protection of the big relief caravan. He was also fascinated by the motley company Stanley was leading; he remarked that the tribes through which it passed 'could hardly hide their astonishment and fear'. Schynse was soon able to learn the mood of the white officers, who told him that 'a mass of people have died, important resources have been sacrificed, we have spent two and a half miserable years, and what have we got?'

Schynse was intrigued to watch Stanley's direction of the march. It began at dawn with the three blasts on his whistle to order the porters to pick up their loads. 'Mr Stanley lights his short pipe, and armed with a long stick takes the head of the column, followed by a young boy carrying his parasol . . . After an hour or two, Mr Stanley mounts his donkey and the pace becomes more lively. There are no idlers among Stanley's people, even if he should decide to gallop . . .' The march ended before the heat of the day and the leader's tent was at once put up.

Schynse then ventured to talk to him. 'He tells us, detail by detail, various incidents in his adventurous life, and he speaks with such fire, such relish, that one doesn't notice how badly he speaks French . . . Today he is irritated with the Wagogo, who made him pay tribute for passing through their land. "If this had happened at the start of the expedition, I would have given them a bellyful of lead as a tribute", says Stanley.' As soon as the tent was ready, Stanley vanished inside to write up his notes. 'When he returns to Europe, the impatient world won't have long to wait for some interesting reading,' commented Schynse with an element of malice.

Perhaps because he was a countryman, Emin was forthcoming to Schynse, saying: 'Why should a man as cunning as a Scottish merchant suddenly decide to spend large sums of money to send an expedition to find an Egyptian employee, whom he had probably never heard of until then?' By this time, Emin was convinced that Mackinnon wanted merely to exploit him, using Stanley as the instrument. He shrewdly recorded in his journal how Stanley outlined Leopold's proposals, then immediately told him to reject them, before going on to advocate Mackinnon's plan. He was jaundiced with the British. Schynse responded by passing on to Emin the criticisms he heard from the British officers, and when this came out Stanley accused him of being a trouble-maker. Exhaustion made the underlying tensions worse. Stanley was only fit to travel with Zanzibaris, not white men, remarked Emin.

Stanley tried to help Mackinnon's plan by calling on all the important chiefs he passed en route to the coast. Parke complained (August 15, 1889): 'Mr Stanley appears to me to have too much patience with these kings, and queens, and princes: halting an entire caravan of nearly 1,000 people is no trifle, even to please an African monarch.' Later, Stanley unashamedly inflated these visits into treaties, writing down his version of what had been agreed; Britain used them in negotiations with Germany about the final carving up of East Africa.

Near the coast, the expedition found itself making contact with the outposts of German occupation, and Stanley had the novel experience of being interviewed by the Press in Africa – two correspondents were competing to be the first journalist to find him, and he was proud that both were sent by New York dailies. One was from Stanley's own paper, the *New York Herald*, and the other represented the *World*. The winner was the man from the *World*, Thomas Stevens. His name immediately struck a chord with Stanley, since he was the author of a bestseller called *Around the World on a Bicycle*. Stanley had been given several bottles of champagne by the Germans and at once opened one to celebrate the scoop that Stevens had achieved.

Stevens made good use of his time, interviewing ceaselessly. He thought Stanley was in better health than he had expected: 'He looks like a hard, stocky man of the Phil Sheridan or Stonewall Jackson type, and struck one, on first appearance, as good yet for two or three more such expeditions as the relief and rescue of Emin Pasha.' But Stanley admitted that he had nearly died three times in crossing Africa – twice from gastritis and once from eating poisonous fruit. If he made another journey it might well be to die. 'Look at Livingstone,' he said to Stevens.

When he was not talking about 'the blackest nightmare of all my experiences on the Dark Continent' – the journeys through the Ituri forest – he was in a relaxed and whimsical mood. Stevens discovered him to be an 'adept in dry humour', especially when talking about women. Now that he was on his way home, Stanley found his thoughts turning again to the old preoccupation: 'Although I admire the ladies very much indeed, somehow I have never been successful with them . . . They are always greatly interested in my conversation; I'm still a young man; nobody can say I'm not good-looking; and in many other respects I compare favourably with men who have been markedly successful with the ladies; but I have always fallen short of success . . . The young women will never take me seriously. When I talk seriously they won't believe I am sincere. They expect nonsense; moonshine is not in my line, and so in the end I have to take refuge with their mothers or grandmothers.'

This aspect of Stanley aroused Stevens's curiosity; there was more than jocularity in such remarks. He decided that the explorer was chivalrous beyond the age in which he was living, and frightened of women if they were beautiful. 'Mr Stanley thinks a lovely young woman a sort of wingless angel – a superior being who was made for rough man to admire at a respectful distance, but not to be approached too closely without sacrilege.'

After this interlude, Stanley hurried the expedition down to the coast, and reached Bagamoyo on December 4, 1889. As they came in sight of the Indian Ocean, he turned to Emin and said: 'There, Pasha, we are home!' Emin politely replied: 'Yes, thank God!' At that moment a salute roared out from a German battery.

Bagamoyo had much changed from the time when Stanley had first landed there from Zanzibar in 1871 and a French Catholic mission was the sole outpost of European influence. Now it had been converted into a garrison town, and Stanley and Emin rode side by side, on horses supplied by the Germans, to the officers' mess. Emin was in a gay mood, talking to his countrymen and telling them of his experiences in Equatoria. That evening a lavish banquet was presented, for which the diplomatic representatives came over from Zanzibar with British and German naval officers. The food and wine were elaborate. After the meal, speeches were made by Stanley and Emin. In a glow of benevolence the Pasha strolled up and down among the guests, chatting and making jokes. Nobody noticed that he had, after a while, vanished from the room.

Some minutes later, the banquet suddenly ended in gloom. Emin had been found in the street below, his head split open. Stanley raced down the stairs, and saw some of his Zanzibaris crowded around two pools of blood. In the darkness, Emin had fallen over the balcony. He had been hurriedly taken away to the German military hospital, where he was lying unconscious. Stanley went to see him, and found the bed surrounded by doctors. Parke was soon at the bedside, at his own request. Two days later, before crossing over to Zanzibar, Stanley went to the hospital and was able to have a brief, formal talk with Emin, who was out of danger. They were never to meet again.

Parke decided that his presence was unwelcome to the Germans; ill himself with malaria, he went off to the French mission hospital. For several weeks he lived mainly on iced champagne.

In Zanzibar, Stanley was able to survey the cost and achievements of the past three years. He had led 700 people to the Congo, and little more than 200 had come back; of Emin's people, at least half had died on the way to the coast; Equatoria had slipped back into anarchy; a vast sum of money had been spent. And yet, it had somehow been a success beyond anything he had ever done. There was a huge pile of telegrams, all praising him in the most fulsome terms; among the senders were Queen Victoria, Kaiser Wilhelm, the Khedive of Egypt, King Leopold, and the President of the United States.

He could not afford to stay for long in Zanzibar. He bade a last farewell to Uledi, with whom he had been through so much together, and on December 30, 1889, led his surviving white officers aboard a waiting steamer in Zanzibar harbour. Parke had to be carried on a stretcher.

Stanley took a sweeping glance across the island where his fame began. It was from here that he had written to James Gordon Bennett, early in 1871, to promise that he would triumph in his search for Livingstone, or die. He had triumphed, again and again, although others had died – Farquhar, Shaw, Fred Barker, the Pocock brothers, Barttelot, Jameson . . . and hundreds of Zanzibaris. Stanley had survived, to become without question the greatest explorer of his age, but tropical Africa had taken a heavy toll. A correspondent of the *Illustrated London News* who interviewed him in Zanzibar described his 'hollow cheeks and rather fierce expression, which was less the note of hunger than of constant watchfulness.'

The 'Smasher of Rocks' knew the time had come to stop watching and striving; more than anything, he wanted to rest. But first, there was work to be done in Egypt.

25. The Lion of Richmond Terrace

Stanley's visit to Cairo had a double purpose. First he must present to the Egyptian authorities the 246 survivors of the people he had led from Equatoria. Then he must write his book on the expedition; he thought of fifty possible titles, but finally decided to entitle it *In Darkest Africa*, which would suitably echo his bestseller of twelve years earlier, *Through the Dark Continent*. The survivors from Equatoria were soon disposed of – they were taken to an army barracks to await Emin, who was expected in Cairo as soon as his head injuries were healed. The book was a more daunting problem, for Stanley found it hard to focus his mind, which seemed suspended between the horrors of the recent past and the excitements of the immediate future. 'A thousand scenes floated promiscuously through my head, but, when one came to my pen-point, it was a farrago of nonsense . . .'

He originally thought of doing the book in Britain, but quickly realised that he would never find the peace to complete it if he ventured beyond Cairo; all Europe seemed poised to fête him. It was hard enough to work quietly even in Egypt. Stanley and his companions – Parke, Jephson, Stairs, Nelson and Bonny – were taken from Suez to Cairo on January 13, 1890 by special train, and as they stepped down to the platform a big crowd clapped and cheered. With an escort of mounted police, Stanley went by carriage to the Abdeen Palace, where the Khedive bestowed upon him the Grand Cordon of the Imperial Order of Medjidieh. The next night there was a State banquet at the place for sixty guests, and two days later a dinner for nearly 200 people – at which, among other diversions, a Count Zalusky of the Public Debt Commission recited his newly-composed poem in honour of Stanley. There were numerous speeches to be made – although the *Egyptian Gazette* proved rather critical: 'There are divers opinions as to the taste displayed by Mr Stanley . . . Many consider he was not particularly happy or generous in his allusions to Emin Pasha . . .'

Stanley had put up again at Shepheard's Hotel, where he was besieged by well-wishers. Journalists demanded interviews and

Still in his forties, Stanley was prematurely aged by his African experiences. Around him were the officers of the Advance Column. On the left, Dr Thomas Parke, and on the right, A. J. Mounteney-Jephson. Standing: Captain Nelson and Lieutenant Stairs. This picture was taken in Cairo, after the expedition to aid Emin

photographers wanted pictures. It was all hopelessly time-consuming, and there was only one photograph for which Stanley posed with any satisfaction: it showed him with his four Advance Column officers. They were all on good terms now, and the quarrels in the early months of the expedition quite forgotten. In a speech to the Mohammed Aly Club in Alexandria, Parke called Stanley a 'wonderful man', who in his own line was the Napoleon of the age.

On January 23, 1890, Stanley moved out of the centre of Cairo to the Villa Victoria in the Ismailia quarter. It was a quiet, residential hotel with a fountain playing in the middle of a courtyard, and Stanley took a suite of rooms on the ground floor, in the wing farthest from the street. He told all callers: 'I have so many pages to write. I know that if I do not complete this work by a certain time, when other and imperative duties are imposed upon me, I shall never complete it at all . . . let me alone now, for Heaven's sake.' He worked from early morning until midnight, with the help of two secretaries. When telegrams arrived, Stanley's servant Sali bin Othman would push them into the room on the end of a bamboo pole, then run away, followed by shouts of 'I detest telegrams!'

It was not only cables that agitated Stanley; some of the letters he read while forcing himself through *In Darkest Africa* were anything but soothing. A proposition arrived (January 22, 1890) from William Mackinnon – who had just become a baronet – that Stanley should lead an army into Uganda and dictate terms there, then march back to the Congo to crush the Arabs on behalf of Leopold. 'This of course is a suggestion that may be impracticable . . .' said Sir William, as an afterthought. In a letter to an American friend, Stanley admitted: 'I want to rest, for I am very tired. I am not in trim yet, and I fear straining myself too much.'

There were few relaxations, but Stanley did spare the time to pose for a Miss E. M. Merrick, a student of the Royal Academy, who had been commissioned to paint a lifesize portrait for a member of the Royal Geographical Society. Miss Merrick was photographed, palette in hand and a boater jauntily placed on the back of her head, capturing Stanley's likeness in a room at the Villa Victoria. It was said that he 'took great pleasure' in the operation. Perhaps a part of the pleasure was due to the unstinting support he now had from the RGS. Replying to a cable of congratulations from the Society, Stanley said he had tried to keep his promises 'honourably towards all' – a hint that he could not quite forget, even yet, the charges of fraud after his search for Livingstone.

Work on the book advanced erratically. Stanley found that on one day he could not put down more than a hundred words, whereas on another he was writing nine pages an hour. By the end of fifty days he had forced himself to draft 300,000 words, as well as dictating 400 letters and a hundred telegrams. In April he handed the revised manuscript to his British publisher, Edward Marston – who was in Egypt to receive it – and set out for Brussels to meet Leopold.

Just before he did so, the story of the relief expedition was given a final twist. News came from Zanzibar that Emin had decided not to work for the Congo Free State or the Imperial British East African Company; he would not even come to Cairo to meet the Khedive and attend to the interests of his followers; he had signed a contract to serve the Germans in East Africa, and he was preparing to set out towards that very region from which Stanley had so recently saved him. One of the people most astounded to hear this was Surgeon Parke, who had been arranging for Emin to have an operation in Egypt to remove the cataracts from his eyes; the Pasha would now go back to the interior in a state of progressive blindness. Emin's 'defection' to the Germans set the seal of absurdity on the long, costly and arduous expedition.

Few people seemed to grasp this, as the surge of hero-worship spread wider and wider. In Berlin a play, *Stanley and Africa*, hastily turned out by a team named Nathanson and Moszkowski, was playing to packed houses. In Reykjavik, a 'welcome song to the great African explorer, H. M. Stanley' was published with the title 'Aurora Borealis'. In London, mugs and plates bearing likenesses of Stanley and Emin were already appearing in the shops.

When Stanley arrived in Brussels he made a triumphant progress through the packed streets in an open carriage to the palace. Leopold treated him with a new deference. But after a few days, the talks with Leopold went beyond mere courtesies. The king suddenly put forward an idea that far transcended the Emin expedition: Stanley should collect 20,000 Congolese warriors, form them into an army, and march them north along the Nile to capture Khartoum. When he had done it, he could collect £100,000. Leopold would add the Sudan to the Free State. Stanley listened in wonderment, while the king waved his arms around and said that this was the *bonne bouche* he had been saving up for so long. Stanley replied that while he was partial to adventure, he would never try the impossible; merely to organise and train the Congolese into an army would take four years. This rejection was so sharp that the king did not mention his 'titbit' again. With relief, Stanley picked up an ebony and malachite box holding two new honours Leopold had given him and made his way to Britain.

From the moment he stepped ashore at Dover, he was caught up in wild jubilation. The *Spectator* (May 3, 1890), condemned many of the incidents in his reception as 'offensive to good taste', but conceded that his march along the Aruwimi warranted comparison with the journey of Xenophon and the Ten Thousand. Sheet music was rushed out, including a descrptive march, 'Stanley's Rescue', and a song, 'The Victor's Return', with the refrain: 'On, Stanley, on! were the words of yore: On, Stanley, on, let them ring once more . . .' Advertisers were quick to take advantage, one illustration showing Stanley and Emin sitting together in the forest; Stanley is saying: 'Well, Emin, old fellow, this cup of the United Kingdom Tea Company's Delicious Tea makes us forget all our troubles.' Emin replies: 'So it does, old boy.'

Not only commerce seized the chance. When Stanley returned to London after a three-year absence, the evangelist General Booth was forecasting that the Millenium would soon arrive 'by the ultimate triumph of Salvation Army principles.' Noting the hectic promotion for *In Darkest Africa*, General Booth sat down to write *In Darkest England, and the Way Out*. But Stanley was well ahead, and his book went through three big editions before the general's call to salvation appeared. The rights to *In Darkest Africa* had been sold in a dozen countries, and as the first copies came off the presses in England, Oscar Wilde produced an aphorism: 'The difference between journalism and literature is, that journalism is unreadable, and literature is unread.' Whichever category the explorer's lavishly illustrated epic belonged to, it was certainly being read.

Stanley was also being heard. He addressed crowded meetings in London, Edinburgh and Machester. In Newcastle he praised Lord Salisbury for the new Anglo-German agreement on East Africa. God had enlightened the premier, he assured the audience, and the Africans of Uganda would look at their new overlords as their 'fathers and mothers'. It was a year when Africa was making headlines: the Royal Niger Company was having its first general meeting, and the British South Africa of Cecil Rhodes had just begun its occupation of Rhodesia. In the face of such rivalry for attention, a campaign for a Channel Tunnel between Britain and France made little headway and was thrown out by Parliament.

The renown of Stanley was so enormous that everyone expected him to be knighted. His fellow-explorer, Colonel Grant, had openly demanded in *The Times* that some fitting honour should be given him. A party of American friends who had arranged a welcoming dinner in Mayfair were bold enough to name him on the menu as 'Sir H. M. Stanley, GCB'. The honour in fact proposed was slightly different – a Court official came to his flat and asked if a GCMG 'would be acceptable'. Stanley refused, not because he felt he deserved the more elevated GCB, but for a reason he would not disclose. The truth was that he had secretly taken out American citizenship in May 1885 to protect his book royalties from 'pirate publishers'. Any attempt to suddenly jettison this status would leave *In Darkest Africa* at the mercy of the pirates; forced to choose between his royalties and a title, he cryptically declined the latter.

It worried the Queen, who invited him to dinner at Windsor Castle on May 5, and (in contrast to her opinions in 1872) called him 'the wonderful traveller and explorer'. She wrote in her diary: 'Saw Lord Salisbury. We spoke of many things, of Stanley, and what he could do, and of his not wanting to have an order offered to him.'

On the day he saw the Queen, Stanley had his portrait done by a photographer in Regent Street. It shows him standing, hands in pockets, with his check jacket thrown wide open to display a high waistcoat and watch-chain. His white hair is cut close to his head and his face looks reflective and stubborn. Stanley had reasons to ponder, not so much about the knighthood but because he was being bombarded with letters from Dorothy Tennant of Richmond Terrace. She was asking him to visit her, and he was refusing.

It was almost four years since Dolly had turned down Stanley's marriage proposal. She was still a spinster, and now thirty-nine. Neither had in the interim put the other quite out of mind; He guardedly mentioned Dolly to Mounteney Jephson several times in Africa, and she questioned another African traveller, Harry Johnston, about the rumours in 1888 of the expedition's annihilation on the Aruwimi. But Stanley was not an easy man to mollify after his pride was wounded.

Dolly wrote her first letter to him on April 26: 'Dear Mr Stanley, I shall be so deeply glad to see you again, not because you have done such great things, but because you have come back safe, because I feared I might never see your face again.' He did not answer. On May 3 they met at a party, and Dolly grasped his hand and said 'Come to me'. Stanley stiffly said he would, but the next day she waited in vain at Richmond Terrace. Then she wrote him again: '. . . I only want to say goodbye to you, so do not mind coming. I also want to give you back something you gave me . . .' Stanley was resolved not to be inveigled by such tactics, and briefly wrote back refusing to call on her. On May 6 another letter arrived, in which Dolly declared she was saying farewell, but devoted some length to doing so, and ended: 'Well, dear Mr Stanley, goodbye . . . I shall, I promise you, avoid going where we might meet, and if ever you think of me, don't let it be as a poor craven spirit, but as a woman who, though she deserves to suffer, has done so bravely, on the whole. Your sincere friend, Dorothy Tennant.'

At this point Stanley lost the battle, if he really wanted to resist Dolly's blandishments. When the letter arrived he was about to set off to be the guest of the Queen, and he replied with a flourish next day, giving Windsor Castle as his address. His tone was lordly and reproachful, telling Dolly that her cruelty to him was far worse than anything he could have imposed on 'the most degraded pigmy'. Much of the imagery of the letter echoed his recent experiences in Africa. The wound she had inflicted upon him was like a barbed arrow that entered deeper and deeper into his heart; as he 'revolved the weapon within', the wound grew worse. He then described how he had imagined her in 1886, looking outraged at the marriage proposal from a 'base-born churl'. So his love was crushed, like a rose that had been too violently seized. Stanley swept on in this vein, saying that although they were due to meet at a reception that very evening, he hoped it would be 'calmly and as dear friends'. The speed of these exchanges was now defeating the postman, and before this letter was delivered Dolly and Stanley were face to face again in a London drawing room. According to her diary, she told him outright that she would be his wife if he would have her. Stanley went off to compose yet another letter, to shore up his weakening defences. He could not deny that she had a noble heart, but he begged her not to worry herself – he wanted her to be happy, and fulfil her high destiny. If only her nature were steadfast, she could 'aspire to command any fortune'. Now they must both resolve to be good friends, and he would put a painting she had sent him upon his mantelpiece. There was a crucial sentence: 'From a settled indifference, your words have created in me a profound sympathy'.

By return of post, Dolly loosed off an emotional broadside. It started quietly, addressed to 'Dear Mr Stanley', but soon intensified to lay bare all her feelings – telling how she had been praying that he would now accept her, as she had prayed night and morning for three years that he would forgive the rejection of his love. 'Oh, Bula Matari, listen to me. If I made you suffer, I have expiated the wrong done. Remember the difference between us. You were a man, you knew more of life, you had loved before. I was a girl, unacquainted with love . . . When your letter came, I was unprepared, and I felt afraid . . .'

In this long assault on Stanley's affections and pity there was a paragraph with especial power. The inspiration clearly came from the Tennant family's interest in spiritualism – Dolly's brother-in-law, Frederic Myers, was one of the founders of the Society for Psychical Research. The paragraph began by telling Stanley how Dolly had felt a great darkness come over her when he had gone to Central Africa, and she tried to reach out to him. 'I spoke to you, I told you everything when I was alone. I fancied you were kind to me . . . you seemed to tell me that you would always love me, and I must try to deserve your love and make ready morally and spiritually for your coming; and you told me, in my visions, that we should some day be united for ever and ever together. You told me that you too were lonely and sorrowful and I could comfort and help you . . . oh my beloved, you were nearer to me in the depths of Africa.' The letter, dated May 9, ended by asking him to pray for her death, since she could not have his love.

On May 16, a Friday, Dolly was able to tell a friend on *The Times* to announce the engagement. Congratulations poured upon Stanley, and his closest friends were relieved that he had at last found himself a wife; they hoped that he would have the quiet and loving attention that could restore his battered constitution. Dolly soon wrote ecstatically to her long-dead father about all the presents she had already received. It would be a brief engagement, and the wedding was fixed for July 12 in Westminster Abbey.

One of Stanley's anxieties in this moment of bewildering happiness was about coming to terms with Dolly's family. His future mother-in-law, in particular, was a challenge, because Dolly had been constantly at her side since she was widowed twenty years before. Gertrude Tennant, at seventy, retained tireless energy; she had already decided that her daughter would not move out of Richmond Terrace after the marriage. Stanley would come to live with them. The network of the Tennants (who were sometimes confused with a grander, Scottish family of the same name) was considerable, and he was very conscious that he had no relatives to offer on his own side; he told Dolly about his surviving half-brothers in Wales (Emma was dead), but there was no thought of inviting them to the wedding. If Stanley felt deprived in this sense, he had the consolation of being on a pinnacle of popular acclaim, and could number among his friends some of the most distinguished travellers and writers of his time.

Indeed, Frederic Myers was afraid that the fame of the newcomer might dislocate the domestic life of the Tennants. He admitted this frankly in a letter (May 16, 1890) to Stanley, but said that respect for his character made him feel sure that a warm affection would grow between them. In a plain-spoken way, Myers then wrote about his sister-in-law: 'After she is yours I must not criticise her; so now let me say that she has been somewhat over-indulged in life, and that has left her impetuous, and not always wise. But you have learnt to rule gently; and you will find, as you already know as well as I, that whatever there may be over-hasty in her is on the surface only, and that beneath is a power of steady devotion, of cheerful, loving, helpful, intelligent companionship . . .'

A few days before the wedding, Stanley fell ill with a renewed attack of the gastritis that twice had nearly killed him. He lay in agony in his Mayfair rooms, with Dr Parke caring for him with a skill based on the experience in Africa; until the morning of the ceremony, Stanley was in doubt about his capacity to go through it. Dolly rose early for breakfast, also still uncertain as to what would happen – then was handed a telegram to say that the groom had struggled out of bed. The wedding could go ahead. In joyful relief, Dolly put on her dress, of white silk and satin, the seams sewn with pearls. She wore a diamond necklace from Sir William Mackinnon, a locket set with thirty-eight diamonds from Queen Victoria, a bracelet from King Leopold, and a sapphire and diamond bracelet from the groom.

The Abbey was packed, and the principal guests included Gladstone, the Lord Chancellor, the Speaker of the Commons, Lord Northbrook, the Duchess of St Albans, the Duke of Abercorn, Sir Redvers Buller, Prince Malcom Khan, and a contingent of explorers led by Colonel Grant. Five thousand applications for seats in the Abbey had been unsuccessful. The groomsmen were Stanley's companions from the Emin Pasha expedition – Parke, Stairs, Mounteney Jephson, Nelson and Bonny.

During the service, Stanley sat in an armchair. He looked drawn and exhausted. Dolly watched him anxiously; by the end of the service, he was so weak that even with the aid of a stick he could hardly reach the west door of the Abbey. As they went slowly down the aisle, the bride laid her bouquet on the tomb of Livingstone. Dolly was escorted to the carriage by Sir John Millais, and the crowd pressed forward, mistaking him for the groom, and their cheering was so loud 'that he could not make his disclaimer heard'.

When Stanley had been helped into the carriage and it began to move, the excitement grew out of hand. Dolly related the drama to her father in her diary: 'The police struggled in vain to keep back the fighting, shouting, maddened people. I felt so faint and dreaded seeing some horror, some terrible accident. I closed my eyes, and only opened them when I felt the carriage go rather quicker. A reinforcement of mounted police had come to the rescue . . .' It was only a short drive to Richmond Terrace, and the crowds there were still so dense that the couple could hardly reach the front door. Once inside, the groom retired to lie on a sofa, while his bride went out to mingle with the guests in the garden. Among the presents was a gift from Edison, a phonograph machine, thought to be the first in Britain; although Stanley wanted to record a wedding-day message, he was too weak.

Melchett Court, in the New Forest, had been lent for the honeymoon by Louisa, Lady Ashburton, and throughout the reception Parke was anxious to see his patient away to the peace of the countryside. The train from Waterloo to Winchester had a coach reserved for the wedding party, and Parke discreetly took his place in an adjoining compartment; during the journey, the bride gave him progress reports on her husband's condition. Once in the New Forest, Stanley quickly recovered, and after a month at Melchett Court he and Dolly went on a long tour of Switzerland, Italy, France and Belgium. It was a relief to be away from the relentless spotlight in Britain: a fortnight before the wedding the first edition of *In Darkest Africa* had appeared, and although clearly destined to be an international publishing triumph, the book soon was provoking second thoughts about the whole Emin expedition.

Stanley was now so much in the public eye that there was no lack of comments on his character. One of the most hostile came from a fellow-journalist, Frank Harris; when told that Dorothy Tennant was to be wedded to the lion of the season, he declared this was true: 'She is about to marry the king of the beasts.' Another famous Victorian editor, W. H. Stead, was more kind, and called him the 'Sisyphus of Africa'. He added: 'The man has unquestionably great natural gifts – first among which is a great faculty of self-possession. For a Welshman – and Mr Stanley to this day understands his mother tongue, although he speaks it with difficulty – he is wonderfully phlegmatic and self-possessed.'

A review of Stanley's book in *Blackwood's Magazine* paid shrewd attention to his motivation, after complaining that public enthusiasm 'cast a glamour over sober criticism' and made any reviewer diffident about applying ordinary canons of judgement. Marshalling its resolve, *Blackwood's* decided: 'The wondrous success which has attended his career has made him intolerant of failure and perhaps incapable of judging his own contributions towards it. Taking his own narrative and his own exposition of his feelings, we are obliged to recognise a relentlessness – we may almost say a ruthlessness – of purpose underlying his plans, which can scarcely fail to dampen the enthusiasm that his courage, endurance and resource so freely kindle.'

The debate about the explorer's character often centred upon his treatment of Africans. This came in for heavy attack from a socialist writer, D. J. Nicholl, in a widely-read 'Penny Pamphlet' called *Stanley's Exploits, or, Civilising Africa*. The pamphlet opened with an illustration showing Stanley in an attitude of prayer, while behind him an African was hanging from a palm tree. Overhead flew the top-hatted angel of capitalism carrying a wreath to place on the explorer's brow. Nicholl's indignant account was well sprinkled with bloodthirsty quotations, and ended by declaring that the fit punishment for Stanley himself was hanging. 'Let the great thieves and their parasites welcome the sanctimonious pirate who glosses over fire, slaughter and cruelty with the snuffling cant of the mission-hall. We will have none of him. Let him be satisfied with the applause of those who would have crucified Christ and worshipped Barabbas; but, at least, amid their applause he shall hear our hisses.'

It was not all hisses. Harry Johnston, the African traveller, declared that he had never heard a bad word from an African about Stanley, who was 'absolutely uncursed with that odious British pride and snobbishness which seals up the black man's sympathies and confidences.' The verdict of the missionary, Alexander Mackay, was the same; wherever he went, he found that the explorer's treatment of Africans won respect. Antoine Greshoff, the Dutch consul in Brazzaville, began a blunt assessment by branding him as an opportunist, who put a dash of religion into his writing to please the English. He went on: 'But though not a missionary, Stanley has never been on purpose cruel or unjust to the natives, never burnt a town to enrich himself with ivory, never shot a native to show his capacity in good shooting, never shot a native for the mere pleasure of saying to a bystander, "So I do with everyone who does not come at once when I call." '

There was a deluge of satellite books on the Emin expedition – quick plagiarisations, commentaries, and uplifting portrayals for school-children of the white man's pluck among warlike savages. The memoirs and diaries of leading figures involved also hurried off the presses. In Italy, Emin's former lieutenant, Gaetano Casati, brought out an autobiography, in which he summed up his impressions of Stanley: 'Reserved, laconic and not very sociable, he does not awake sympathy; but on closer acquaintance he is found to be very agreeable, from the frankness of his manner, his brilliant conversation, and his gentlemanly courtesy.'

In the autumn of 1890, Stanley returned to America. Major Pond, the lecture tour organiser, was holding him to his promise to take up again where he had broken off in December 1886. On the first night in New York the gross receipts were nearly 18,000 dollars, and the tour proved an unequalled triumph.

The explorer had with him in America a considerable entourage, including his wife and his mother-in-law and several servants. Mounteney Jephson also accompanied his 'old chief'. They were transported from lecture to lecture in a special railway carriage, a 'Pullman palace car' named after the explorer; it had a kitchen, bathroom, three bedrooms, a drawing room with grand piano, and an observation platform. The itinerary arranged by Pond ranged from coast to coast and from Canada to Texas. While they were in the South, Stanley was able to take Dolly on a tour of New Orleans, which he had not seen for more than thirty years. Apart from seeking traces of his adoptive father, he rose early one morning to visit the French market, and drank coffee at a stall owned by a Frenchman named Morel. He learnt that Morel had arrived in New Orleans in 1847. 'Very likely, I must have drunk coffee many a time, as a boy, at his stand!' But many of his former acquaintances in the city complained that he would not see them, and 'hid in his hotel'.

The American tour earned Stanley £12,000 (60,000 dollars), but he worked diligently for it. Pond relates how the party was in Boston on a snowy winter day, and Dolly had been out for a sleigh ride while Stanley stayed indoors preparing for his next lecture. An effort was made to lure the explorer into the snow to relax. Dolly threw her arms around his neck and said: 'Oh, Bula Matari, come and have a ride and breathe the most delicious air under heaven.' Her husband stayed at his desk doggedly, telling Pond that he 'had a duty to do the best he could'.

By the end of April, the Stanleys were back in London, to start a lecture tour of Britain. It lasted for nearly three months and brought in a further £2,000. Dolly did not make the complete circuit and while she was once again enjoying the social round in London a steady flow of letters came to Richmond Terrace from provincial towns and cities. In one of them, Stanley remarked: 'Rest! Ah, my dear! We both need it – I more than you . . . Until then, existence is mere prolonged endurance.'

There were a few compensations, as when he arrived to lecture in Carnarvon, only forty miles from his birthplace; although he still maintained an evasive attitude about his birthplace there was little doubt in the minds of the Welsh that he was a local hero. He agreed to preside at the next Eisteddfod. Eight special trains brought in people from the countryside to hear him at Carnarvon, and for six hours Stanley was either lecturing or being shaken by the hand. The following morning, as he sat in the railway carriage waiting to set out on the next stage of his journey, he ostentatiously opened a copy of the local Welsh-language paper to read a report of his lecture. A shout of delight went up from the platform.

October was to see the start of yet another lecture tour – in Australia and New Zealand. To gather his strength Stanley retreated to Mürren in Switzerland at the end of July. It was a relief, but marred by two unhappy incidents. The first happened as he pursued his great pleasure of walking through the countryside – he slipped in a damp meadow and broke his left ankle; although the bone finally mended without leaving him lame, he was so incapacitated that he could not, on returning to Britain, go to Wales for the Eisteddfod.

The second incident upset Stanley in quite another way. An American correspondent, Aubrey Stanhope of the *New York Herald*, appeared in Mürren to investigate rumours that Stanley's marriage was breaking up. The two men knew one another, through Stanley's long connection with the *Herald*, but this did not save Stanhope from anxiety: the explorer was 'a particularly irascible man, whose health, undermined by hundreds of attacks of ague, rendered him exceedingly irritable'. When Stanhope put his question about the stories of an impending separation and 'domestic infidelity', Stanley was predictably enraged and asked him how he dared ask about such topics. Stanhope clung to his assignment, and after being given a verbal denial, pressed for a signed statement. Having got that, he asked for a signed denial by Dorothy Stanley, who was in the next room. Stanley went to see her, and shortly afterwards handed over a

STANLEY
1893

Dolly's portrait of Stanley, done a few years after their marriage. It was hung in the Royal Academy

message saying, 'I am very much astonished and disgusted with the reports in a New York newspaper that my married life is unhappy and that I am separated from my dear husband.'

With the two documents in his pocket, Stanhope shook hands and 'skidded down the rocky sides of Mürren' with relief. Only a few weeks earlier, Stanley had written to Mackinnon to assure him that the marriage was happy, saying that his early dread that Dolly might prove 'gushing and shallow and a mere society product' was unfounded; she had proved herself a perfect wife – 'gay, sportive, irrepressibly merry', but also quick to show her sympathies.

If there was domestic stress, Stanley hid any sign of it. Dolly and her mother went with him on the long tour of Australia and New Zealand. Shortly after their return, Stanley took a step about which Dolly was insistent: he agreed to give up his American nationality. It was Dolly who wrote to the Home Secretary, Sir Henry Matthews, saying that she was 'extremely anxious' on the subject and had carefully read through the Naturalisation Act to be sure that her husband qualified. She also pointed out how much Stanley had done for the Empire. The reply was cautious. Had Stanley spent a total of five years in Britain since 1872? Dolly consulted the records and was able to produce a total for five years and twenty weeks. So on May 20, 1892, Stanley took the British oath of allegiance.

The following month, the reason for Dolly's urgency was apparent. Stanley wrote in his diary: 'Have consented to contest the constituency of North Lambeth, against Alderman Coldwells, Radical. I accepted because D. is so eager for me to be employed, lest I fly away again to Africa.' The year before, while he was lecturing in the United States, there was a tentative invitation for Stanley to become the Administrator of the Imperial British East Africa Company. He had flexed his muscles with the old eagerness at the idea, and listed his qualifications: 'I can work, and see that others work. I can make roads. I can win loyalty from natives of all kinds – I can make them enthusiastic and devoted. I am impartial – just, yet strict. I am wholly loyal. I can make things grow where none grew before . . .'

While there were his lecture commitments, he could not go back to Africa, but Dolly always saw the threat on the horizon. 'Soon after our marriage, I had thought of Parliament for Stanley,' she wrote.

For a last-minute candidate, North Lambeth was an impossible task. He stood as a Liberal-Unionist (on the Irish question, the right wing of the Liberals had broken from Gladstone), and found himself facing a militant working-class electorate. In the nine days of campaigning left to them the Stanleys were booed and hissed, and fighting broke out several times among the audiences. Stanley wrote bitterly to Pond: '. . . the intolerance they display towards their opponents is wholly unknown in America. When this temper is at the hottest, women go down before the brawny fist like sheep in the shambles, and bald heads often get seriously cracked.'

On his side, Stanley was not conciliatory. A reporter from the *Boston Daily Globe* described him 'glaring fiercely at the mob'. Dolly once burst into tears, jumped up on the platform and shouted: 'When all of you and I are dead and forgotten, the name of Stanley will live.'

As expected, the Radicals won North Lambeth. At once, Dolly declared that her husband must stand again at the next election; meanwhile, she would 'nurse' the constituency for him. Stanley yielded to her zeal, and devoted himself to writing his memoirs. He shut all thoughts of a return to Africa from his mind. The will was going out of him.

26. Stories by the Library Fire

The last years of the nineteenth century ebbed away. In the nostalgia of a premature old age, Stanley relived his journeys through an Africa that was ceasing to exist. The continent he had known was now more orderly and less exciting. It was no longer a place of mystery, where a courageous man could 'fill up the blanks' by discovering rivers, lakes and snow-capped mountains. In that vast interior between the Zambezi and the sources of the Nile, European administrators had replaced the explorers; slave-traders, ivory-hunters – even the most powerful African chiefs – were being forced to bow before this new omnipotence.

Although Stanley paid sober lip-service to sovereignty, his Africa was a place for individualists. Both he and Livingstone had been cast in that mould. More than any other two men, they had caused the wild Africa in which they met in 1871 to be transformed into a patchwork of colonies. The former mill-hand from Blantyre began the imperial process in Central Africa, and the workhouse boy from Denbigh had completed it.

There would never again be anything like the Emin Pasha Expedition. That march from the Atlantic to the Indian Ocean was the grandiose finale to an era. The long columns of porters, trudging through the forests with bundles on their heads, were being replaced by railways and roads. In place of the pioneers came geologists and planters. Even the discovery in 1894 that malaria was not caused by 'miasma' or a shortage of ozone but by the mosquito, made Africa less terrifying and brought about an important change in the psychology of the white men working there.

So when Stanley became an MP in the general election of 1895, he found that he was already an anachronism. Parliament would listen to him, on the rare occasions when he had the chance to speak about Africa, with a polite respect. He made no impact and had to suffer the vexation of hearing long arguments about 'his continent' from men who had never been there. His style of address, based on the dramatic, personal narrative of the lecture platform, would not do in the Commons, so that in trying to adjust he became ponderously boring. He felt that his achievements qualified him to adopt the manner of a statesman, but to the House he seemed an obscure backbencher with close-cropped white hair, a lined, red face and small, thick body. He had been a great explorer, but he was not much of a politician.

He hated his five years as an MP, even though by living in Richmond Terrace he was only two minutes' walk from Westminster and had his North Lambeth constituency just across the Thames. Parliament wearied him and undermined his failing health: '. . . I am too old to change my open-air habits for the asphyxiating atmosphere of the House of Commons.' Even when he was not sitting in his place, listening to endless debates on the Irish question – in which he was little interested – he found himself spending several hours a day on replies to letters asking for his views on affairs of the day. To increase his burdens, there was the social round of the Tennant household. Stanley wrote sadly to his publisher, Edward Marston (March 14, 1896): 'Meantime, domestic and social duties are on the increase, letters multiply . . . I have entered on a wearing life . . . I can truly say I have barely two hours to myself during a week. I sometimes ask myself – to what end? I can add but a grain to the national edifice.'

He had stood again for Parliament merely to fall in with Dolly's wishes. On the night when he was elected, he refused to make a speech to his jubilant supporters but merely bade them goodnight and hurried off to Richmond Terrace with Dolly in a hansom cab. They did not talk to one another during the journey, and when they were home he sat down alone and smoked his pipe.

From the outset, he felt that the whole ritual of parliamentary life 'degraded him somewhat', and did not try to hide this feeling in a diary he kept for Dolly's benefit. He grew even more withdrawn at dinner parties and public functions. Marie von Bunsen, with whom he had been briefly enamoured at the Berlin conference in 1885, saw him at a reception 'standing in the background, flattened against the wall, embittered, like a whipped dog'.

Stanley escaped from London and Parliament as much as he could, visiting quiet seaside resorts and sometimes giving talks to schools. Now and then he was asked to preside or talk at meetings on Africa in London or the provincial cities, but the hero-worship that had surrounded him in the early nineties soon began to fade.

Lady Dickens, a friend living in Cadogan Gardens, wrote that 'he loved having a group of children around him and telling them about his Central African exploits'.

He wrote little, but his books were still being re-issued, and occasionally he would bring himself to provide new introductions, surveying recent events in Africa. In one of his rare articles, Stanley discussed for the *Century Magazine* (February, 1896) the changes that followed his first transcontinental journey. Somewhat aggressively, he made the point three times that in 1876 'there was not a single white man in possession of any portion of the equatorial belt, except at the mouth of the Congo, where a few traders had gathered'.

The autobiography came to a standstill, although Stanley assured his publisher that he would complete it in four months, if he were left alone. However, it was not only time that he needed, because he knew his old fire had deserted him: 'I am now declining in vitality. My hard life in Africa, many fevers, many privations, much physical and mental suffering, bring me close to the period of infirmities.'

A flash of his former dynamism would return when Stanley was able to meet the men he had worked with in Africa. They would reminisce, often breaking into Swahili in their enthusiasm, about adventures shared and horrors overcome. Yet fortune was unkind, for all but one of the young officers who had been with him on the Advance Column to Emin were dead within three years. Nelson and Stairs returned to Africa, and both died there in 1892. Dr Parke had a fatal heart attack in 1893. Even William Mackinnon, main sponsor of the expedition, died in despair after the financial collapse of his schemes in Africa. Stanley had been with Mackinnon in a London club when a message came rejecting the last appeal for government aid to the Imperial British East Africa Company; he watched Mackinnon stand, silent and crushed, staring at the curt letter from Whitehall.

That baneful spirit which seemed to pursue everyone connected with the expedition was not easily assuaged, and claimed Emin himself. In October 1892, he was wandering confusedly in the Ituri rain forest, close to Stanley's route along the Aruwimi, when he stopped at the camp of a slave-trader. Without warning he was seized, thrown to the ground and decapitated with a machete. In contrast to the wave of near-hysteria that had followed his 'rescue' five years earlier, Emin's bizarre end went little noticed in Britain. Stanley wrote in his diary: 'What a strange eventful, story . . .'

As the years passed, Stanley found himself drawn closer to Mounteney Jephson. It was not merely all they had been through together on the Advance Column, but also that he was deeply affected by the younger man's private misfortunes. The Emin expedition had wrecked Jephson's health, so that although he was offered various administrative posts in Africa, he was never well enough to accept them. Finally he was driven to take the lowly-paid job of Queen's Messenger, which meant travelling around Europe from one British embassy to another with diplomatic letters. Through his failure to find a rewarding career, Jephson was denied the hand of a San Francisco girl with whom he was in love. In 1895, Stanley wrote a long and emotional appeal to the wealthy father, Addison Head, asking him to relent and settle some money on the daughter; this was in vain. But he did much to keep up Jephson's spirits – although cannily refusing to lend him £250 in 1895, on the grounds that he had himself been hard hit by losses on American stocks.

In 1896, Stanley turned to Jephson for advice about William Bonny, who was living in squalor on drugs and drink in Pimlico and had resorted to badgering anyone who might give him money. Stanley made loans to Bonny and tried to find work for him, but the former sergeant was still bitter at having been treated as an inferior during the Emin expedition. He declared that he would 'expose' his erstwhile leader and hinted at dire revelations he might one day bring into the light. Stanley wrote gloomily to Jephson, who replied from St Petersburg: 'Bonny so far from being neglected has practically been entirely kept by us for nearly two years.'

In 1899, Bonny died of consumption in an army hospital and shortly before the end was interviewed by the *Daily Mail*. It commented: 'Stanley is said to have made £40,000 out of the book describing his own and Bonny's adventures. Explorers get gold and ivory concessions. What had Bonny done with his share of the plunder? The answer is simple. He never got any plunder.' In one of his last letters to Bonny, Stanley said that life was too short to take 'such trifles' seriously. It was, however, a valid blow, for Stanley had grown rich enough from the continuing sales of *In Darkest Africa* to do what he always wished – buy a place in the country where he could be safe from the dinner-party life of London.

After a long search, he and Dolly selected an ugly, mock-Tudor mansion near Pirbright in Surrey. Called Furze Hill, it was set in its own grounds, and had a small lake, pine woods, and meadows.

The house was decrepit and the grounds neglected, but Stanley summoned up more energy than he had shown for years as he decided to build a new wing on the house and landscape the surroundings. Electric lighting was put in, and the grounds laced with drives and paths. He had one room transformed into a library; although he did not play the game, he converted the huge entrance hall into a billiards room. Towards the end of 1899, the move was made to Furze Hill – which Stanley rather extravagantly called 'the Bride'. Dolly's mother resolutely stayed on in Richmond Terrace, but there was a new member of the family who would be far happier in the country than at Westminster: a son, Denzil, adopted from one of the explorer's relatives in Denbighshire.

A few months before the retirement to Surrey came the honour Dolly had so long wanted. A letter arrived from Lord Salisbury, saying that Queen Victoria had conferred on Stanley the Grand Cross of the Bath. In as far as it attracted attention, the knighthood was welcomed. The *Pall Mall Gazette* thought recognition came 'long after the intrepid African explorer had ceased to expect titular honours'; in memory of old ties, the *Daily Telegraph* praised Stanley fulsomely, as an 'author and orator of distinction', who had more than once shown his debating powers in the Commons. This was followed by another sign of acceptance he had long been denied: proposed by Lord Balfour, he was elected a member of the Athenaeum, most august of all the London clubs.

In his last years, Stanley travelled rarely, although he did make a brief visit to South Africa just before the Boer War, and wrote a series of cursory reports for a weekly magazine. The one show of his old venom appeared when he gave a malicious account of a meeting with President Paul Kruger, the Afrikaans leader.

As the twentieth century began, Stanley's horizons shrank to the hills and woods around Furze Hill. He was delighted when Dolly nicknamed a stream running by the house the Congo and their private lake the Stanley Pool; he called their meadows after the tribal regions of Africa through which he had led his expeditions. Old friends came down from London, taking the train from Waterloo to the nearest station, Brookwood. He proudly showed them all the improvements he was making to the grounds and the house.

He began to take a boyish pleasure in practical jokes. Edward Marston wrote: 'I remember with what enormous glee he pointed out to me an enormous American elk, apparently grazing quietly, at the top of the meadow under the wood. I was quite taken in at the moment, and taken aback too, for I genuinely believed the great animal was alive – it was stuffed! How he enjoyed that bit of deception!' Another of Stanley's games was to hide behind a hidden panel in the library, and when guests were shown in to say in a sepulchral voice, 'Find me!' He was particularly fond of this sport when William Hoffmann, his former valet, came to Furze Hill.

He stubbornly kept in touch with Hoffmann, despite the disapproval of Dolly, and after securing him a job as a junior officer in the Congo Free State took him as a companion and servant on the trip to South Africa. Originally, it was arranged that Dolly and her mother would go, but in the end only Hoffmann went with him. According to Hoffmann's account, he was told by Dolly: 'I am very glad, William, that you are going with my husband. He needs someone to look after him, and he trusts you as he trusts few men.' Dolly certainly did not have this opinion in her heart. She wrote that she 'mistrusted Hoffman through and through . . . he is a weak, untruthful man.'

Hoffmann was emotionally important to Stanley – partly because of his continuing involvement with the Congo; the former valet briefly went back there at the turn of the century. Hoffmann could be relied upon to tell his old master what he wanted to hear about the Congo. Although he played little part in the controversy, Stanley was deeply pained by the mounting campaign against conditions in the Free State.

In public, Stanley remained loyal to Leopold, but his diaries and letters reveal misgivings. He first expressed these to the king himself in September 1896, after reports of women being publicly flogged in the Congo had been given wide publicity by Reuters. He told Leopold that 'a continuance of the atrocities' would increase demands for a change in control of the Free State; it was important that some officer should be arrested, tried and punished to 'show that there was something like Congo justice'.

But the dark news from the Congo did not stop, and Stanley was embarrassed that many of the fiercest condemnations came from British officers he had recruited for Leopold. A Captain Guy Burrows had written a book called *The Land of the Pigmies* in 1897 and Stanley contributed a laudatory preface. In 1903, Burrows wrote another book, *The Curse of Central Africa*, attacking the Free State régime, and this was the subject of a libel action brought by a Belgian officer. Burrows had to pay damages, but *The Times* pointedly said that this did not absolve the Free State. It referred to investi-gations made by the British consul, Roger Casement.

By this time, reformers such as E. D. Morel were relentlessly uncovering what lay behind Leopold's façade of philanthropy, and their work was aided by the appearance in 1902 of Joseph Conrad's haunting novel about the Congo, *Heart of Darkness*. Stanley remained silent, for his strength was slipping away. In the spring of 1903 his repeated attacks of gastritis and fever were compounded by heart trouble. In April he had a stroke that paralysed the left side of his body; his mind was affected and he found it hard to speak. The summer and autumn of 1903 were spent in an invalid chair on the lawn at Furze Hill, but for the winter the Stanleys returned to Richmond Terrace.

In February 1904, there was a wave of shock from Westminster, as the damning Casement Report on the Congo was released by the British Government. Although Stanley was utterly beyond reacting to it, the report seemed to make a mockery of all his greatest feats and tribulations.

He visited Furze Hill in early 1904, but during his stay was attacked by pleurisy. He asked to be taken back to London, and went to Richmond Terrace in an ambulance. At the start of May he was clearly dying. Dolly wrote on May 7: 'My darling is sinking, slowly and painlessly. His dear mind wanders gently at times and his eyes look far away.' He talked of Africa. He repeated: 'I want to go into the woods to be free . . . I have done all my work . . . I want to go home.' Early in the morning of May 10 he died. His last words, on hearing Big Ben strike the hour, were: 'How strange! So that is Time.'

The death of Stanley called forth long, rather equivocal obituaries in the newspapers. *The Times* ended by saying that his founding of the Free State had been 'wonderful in its way', although the results were a disappointment. Perhaps because his name was so closely linked with the Congo, his last and deepest wish was denied. He had wanted his body to rest in Westminster Abbey beside that of Livingstone, but the Dean refused, without giving any reason. Dolly could win no more than a memorial service at the Abbey, and the great explorer was buried in the village church at Pirbright.

There was no epitaph on the large block of Dartmoor granite put over his grave. But Henry Stanley had supplied one in his unfinished *Autobiography*: 'I was not sent into the world to be happy, nor to search for happiness. I was sent for a special work . . .'

27. *The Aftermath*

A barrister in Temple Gardens, London was asked in August 1904 to give an expert opinion on how the publication of a batch of private letters could be stopped. His survey of the problem was elaborately cryptic. The writer of the correspondence and the recipient – identified only by letters of the alphabet – had been engaged to be married about 35 years earlier. X had sent love-letters to Y, and also certain 'notes of his doings in the nature of a diary'. But the engagement was broken off, and X asked for all his correspondence back. He asked in vain. Now X was dead, and Y was in touch with a publisher. The barrister confessed himself perplexed. Litigation might be costly, and would attract attention. He felt that this was an occasion for discreet and persuasive methods.

Two days later a letter was delivered to Mrs Katie Bradshaw, of 3, Seedley Mount, Pendleton, Manchester. It was hardly persuasive. She was told that if she published the letters Henry Stanley had sent to her when she was Katie Gough-Roberts of Denbigh, all right-minded people would regard it as 'a supreme act of treachery'. Ignominy and contempt would descend on her. Stanley had regarded 'up to his last hour' her decision to jilt him while he was looking for Livingstone in 1871 as 'an unspeakable betrayal'. If she gave the bundle of letters now locked in her desk to a publisher, that betrayal would be exposed to the world. She must either destroy the correspondence or present it to Lady Stanley.

Neither of these alternatives appealed to Mrs Bradshaw. Her reply of August 19 made a simple proposition: 'I am willing to treat with you.' Her fortunes had declined since those far-off days when Thomas Gough-Roberts had offered to settle £1,000 on her if Stanley became her husband. During an uneventful life as the wife of a district surveyor in a Manchester suburb she followed Stanley's career, and studied the newspaper reports of his marriage, knighthood and death. She guarded the letters and photographs he had sent her when she was twenty, although several publishers heard of them over the years and made tempting offers. They were all especially interested in the fifteen-page 'autobiography' Stanley wrote on March 22, 1869. There were some curious things in it, such as his account of how he escaped from a prisoner-of-war camp by swimming a river under fire, and how he was made an officer for bravery in the US Navy.

Dolly avoided negotiating directly with Katie Bradshaw, but handed this task to Henry Wellcome, the American-born partner in a pharmaceuticals company. Wellcome had been close to Stanley in his last years, and had visited him regularly at Pirbright in 1903. But he was not an ideal person to 'treat' with a proud woman in reduced circumstances. Wellcome travelled to Manchester to see Katie; he only offended her by offering £10 for all the relics of her romance with Stanley.

Katie was being pressed to publish the letters by Morien Mon Huws, a Welsh journalist who called himself 'Morien, the Bard of Wales'. His motive was not money, but patriotism. When the funeral service for Stanley was held in Westminster Abbey, he had come up to London to attend it. It angered Morien that the great explorer never admitted his origins, although they were common knowledge; England had expropriated the man who should have been the national hero of Wales. There was one place Morien knew of where Stanley had written frankly about his birth: 'I am the illegitimate child of Elizabeth Parry and John Rowland . . .' So Morien kept urging that the letters – and especially the fifteen-page autobiography – should be put in print; he won Katie's husband over to this view, but she could not bring herself to agree.

The lack of progress in dealing with the Bradshaws upset Dolly. Throughout 1905, Wellcome kept writing to discover Katie's intentions. On December 15, 1906, she told him: 'I cannot make up my mind to part with the letters . . . as I have had them so many years.'

At that moment, another ghost emerged from Stanley's past. A letter arrived from Sayville, Long Island. It was signed by Lewis H. Noe, who announced himself as the former travelling companion and shipmate of Stanley. He was willing he said, to tell Dolly everything about the tribulations of the journey in 1866 to Turkey – 'on which we had a peculiar experience'. She would have to be willing to hear the 'good and bad'. Noe was also ready to give her his opinions about the development of Stanley's character, 'from the standpoint of one in whom he confided'. There were also many letters and photographs which Noe had kept for more than forty years. She would understand that he was unable to spare them for less than one hundred dollars.

The letter struck Dolly like an avalanche. She knew almost nothing about Noe, although one angry message from him existed in Stanley's files of correspondence. Written in 1886, just before the Emin Pasha expedition, when Stanley was lecturing in America, it said: 'Do you not feel duty bound to pay over to me a share of the money you obtained from the Turkish courts, for the outrage perpetrated on my person, since you know and remarked at the time that we had no just claims but for this crime only.' There was no evidence that Stanley ever replied.

Dolly consulted Wellcome, and they decided on a concerted effort to silence both Noe and Katie Bradshaw. In the United States, a certain J. C. Smith handed over the hundred dollars demanded by Noe, and came away with a large bundle of photographs and letters. As an afterthought, Noe sent to his hotel a letter Stanley had written for him to his father from the *Minnesota* in 1864. Smith composed a memorandum on Noe's recollections of his time in the navy with Stanley, telling how they deserted together with the aid of a forged letter. To prove this, Noe had written to a retired admiral asking for details from the service records, but the reply urged him not to blacken the reputation of the dead; Noe threw in the admiral's letter as well for the hundred dollars.

Dolly destroyed most of the material Noe supplied. What was left she bundled up and sealed with wax; she included a letter to Denzil – who was now at Eton – to be read when he was grown up: 'You can see what Stanley had to suffer. All the great things he did, and his achievements, are unparalleled in the history of the world. All he did was received with foul abuse and detractions, time after time . . .'

At the end of November, 1907, less than a month after Noe was bought off, Mrs Bradshaw accepted a cheque for £150 and handed over the treasures from her desk. The negotiations with her had been far more delicate. Wellcome despatched to Manchester an agent named George Langston, who posed as a publisher's representative. Langston sent reports on his progress, and one said proudly: 'My identity, except as Mr G. Langston, remains unknown.'

At last, Dolly had the prize in her hands – seventeen letters and the 'autobiography', all dated from 1869–70, together with four early photographs of Stanley and a large portrait in a frame. Dolly read the letters and the life-story, then threw them on the fire.

Langston assured her that nothing was left, no shred of evidence had escaped; Katie chose not to tell him that a copy of the autobiography existed in North Wales.

In a letter to Wellcome (December 8, 1907), Dolly asked to be allowed to pay all Langston's expenses, as well as the £150. She described her relief and thankfulness at being possessed of the papers; never again could they be bandied about from hand to hand. Wellcome had planned so carefully and never lost hope that Mrs Bradshaw would be overcome at last. 'It is such *triumph* – and would have been such a relief to Stanley. I love to think that somehow he knows and approves of the result of all your efforts. So – dear, dear Mr Wellcome, let me at least settle up everything as far as L.s.d. goes.'

She signed herself Dorothy Stanley, even copying the swirling underscore Stanley had used on his signature. But early in that year there had been a change in Dolly's status: she was now married to a Harley Street surgeon, Henry Curtis. He was forty, and sixteen years her junior. But Dolly let it be known that she did not care to be addressed as Mrs Curtis, and went on calling herself Lady Stanley.

Dividing her time between London and the house in Surrey, she slowly edited Stanley's papers, to complete the *Autobiography* for which the publishers had so long waited. She felt confident at last that nobody might emerge from the past to challenge the interpretation that she would present to the world. There was only a faint, nagging anxiety about William Hoffman, who was sunk in penury after his blaze of glory as a junior officer in the Congo Free State. Dolly heard that the Barttelot family was in touch with him. She wrote anxiously to Wellcome: 'They have only to intoxicate him and bribe him, and there is no knowing what he may say . . .' At the end of 1907, Wellcome gave Hoffmann a loan of £14, in return for a bundle of letters and an engraved watch presented at the end of the Emin Pasha expedition. There was some relief when Hoffmann found himself a job as a caretaker in a club near Piccadilly.

Yet it was a source of irritation to Dolly that Hoffmann was one of the three people to whom Stanley had made special bequests in his will, leaving him £300 'as an expression of esteem and admiration for his continued services in Africa.' The other beneficiaries, who received £500 each, were Mounteney Jephson and James Jones – Stanley's only surviving half-brother.

In 1899, on a last visit to St Asaph, Stanley had seen James and driven over to Tremeirchion, to call at Ffynnon Beuno, where more than forty years earlier his Aunt Maria had employed him as a cowherd. He visited the dairy and helped himself out of a large earthenware mug of buttermilk, as he had done when he was a boy.

It was an incident that did not find a place when the edited *Autobiography* finally appeared in 1909. There was no suggestion that Stanley kept in touch with his relatives in Wales until the end of his life. The book had many other omissions and 'Bula Matari' was presented as Dolly wanted – noble, self-sacrificing and uncomplicated. Several copies of the book were produced in a de luxe edition, with heavy, handmade paper and tooled morocco bindings. A copy was sent to the Royal Geographical Society, and in her accompanying letter, Dolly said: 'I always felt Stanley's greatness. He lived up to his ideals most truly. What a glorious joy it will be to see him again, and be with him . . . for ever and ever . . .' Dr Curtis did not have a role in this elysium.

The book generated little enthusiasm. Stanley had been dead for five years, and Edwardian England was losing interest in Africa. Not one of the great travellers of the Victorian heyday was still alive; Stanley's old rivals, de Brazza and Tippu-Tib, survived longer than most, but now even they were gone. Events in Europe, and the mounting rivalry with Germany, compelled public attention.

It was also especially hard for the Edwardians to see Stanley in a simple, heroic posture. His name was still clouded by the shame of his great creation, the Congo Free State. The atrocities Leopold seemed unwilling or unable to stop had given fuel throughout the first decade of the century to the campaign led by E. D. Morel; even the former protégé of Stanley, Herbert Ward – now widely respected as a sculptor – was outspoken in his condemnation of the Free State. By 1908 the British Foreign Secretary, Sir Edward Grey, was admitting that Leopold had forfeited any claim to the Congo, and called the administration there 'monstrous'. At last the pressure became irresistible, and in November 1908 the Free State was taken over by Belgium as a colony. The king was given 50,000,000 francs 'in token of the nation's gratitude'.

As Europe approached the nemesis of 1914, the Congo controversy died away. The 'Dark Continent' was to become a place where the European powers fought their peripheral campaigns, and a fresh generation of black porters carried war supplies to remote tropical battlefronts. By 1918, the African explorers had slipped into an

Alice Pike Barney at 60. By this time she was an accomplished painter and playwright, and a leader of Washington society. She made a portrait in pastels of the long-dead Henry Stanley – as she remembered him, nearly half a century earlier, when they were pledged to be married; the portrait appears on the dust-jacket of this book

obscurity from which another age would retrieve them; harsher symbols of sacrifice and bravery had been evolved in the trenches of Europe.

In October 1925, Dolly died in the room in Richmond Terrace where she had nursed her first husband during his last illness twenty-one years earlier. She was seventy-four, and with her death there were few people left who had been close to Stanley during his years of achievement. James Gordon Bennett died, embittered and lonely, in 1918, having presided over the decline and sale of the *New York Herald*. Even Sir John Kirk was gone, after living quietly in Kent until almost ninety. William Hoffmann still eked out his existence in the East End, sometimes working as a postman, and at others pushing a barrow. Who else had memories?

There was Alice Pike Barney.

The love of Stanley's life, the girl who had jilted him in 1876, was in Washington, D.C. – a patron of the arts and *doyenne* of the capital's painters and playwrights. Alice never forgot Stanley, and long after his death did a remarkable portrait of him in pastels; it was as she remembered him, with arching brows and a mephisto-phelean gaze. But the dust of half a century had settled on the marriage pledge in the Pike mansion at 613 Fifth Avenue; the house itself had long ago been demolished. Stanley's *Autobiography* excluded any mention of their relationship, and Dolly even cut out every reference to the *Lady Alice*.

Alice and Dolly never met, but their common interest in painting and mutual contacts in artistic society kept them both fully aware of the other's existence. Alice had done a much-admired portrait of Bernard Shaw; Dolly knew him well, and he often said that the heroine of his play *Candida* was partly modelled on her.

There was an odd coincidence in their private lives. When Alice's first husband died in the early years of the century, she also was remarried to a man younger than herself. At fifty-four, she became the wife of an artist named Christian Hemmick, who was twenty-six. Hemmick was wealthy in his own right, so to prove he did not want her for her money, Alice divided up the five million dollars left her by Albert Clifford Barney and gave it to her daughters.

The marriage failed, and in 1920 Hemmick was granted a divorce for desertion. Alice re-assumed her former name, and settled in Washington, where she helped welfare schemes among the poor as well as fostering the arts. In her youth, painting was her principal enthusiasm, but in old age the theatre interested her more. She wrote eleven plays and in 1927 won the Drama League of America award with *The Lighthouse*. At her suggestion the government built an outdoor theatre in the Monument Grounds, Washington. She produced plays and pageants, but still found time to paint, to throw parties, and arrange exhibitions for unknown young artists.

Alice dropped dead of a heart attack in Hollywood on October 12, 1931 as she was walking into a concert hall. In its obituary, the *New York Times* described her as a 'playwright, artist, author and music patron'. The Cincinnati *Times-Star* was less restrained, and said: 'Romance and art were the burning passions of Mrs Barney's life. Her romances stretched over many years – from her schooldays to the autumn of her life.' There was no mention of Henry Stanley.

One anecdote savoured by the obituary writers involved a nude statue sculpted by Alice of her daughter Natalie. The statue was set up on the lawn of their house in Washington, and so shocked all who saw it that the police insisted that it must be covered with a tarpaulin.

The affection between mother and daughter was intense, and Alice painted Natalie's portrait again and again. Natalie had inherited the blue eyes and vivid beauty that attracted Stanley, and there was every reason to think she would marry well in Washington. But she had no such wish, and in her early twenties moved to Paris, where she bought a house in Montparnasse. Natalie had first known Paris when she was a child; she went to school in Fontainebleau in the eighties while her mother was studying under Whistler and Carolus-Duran. Now she found the atmosphere of France more agreeable and tolerant.

Natalie became the lover of Colette and the friend of Proust. She wrote an essay, 'The Forbidden Love', which provoked a scandal in Parisian literary circles before the First World War. She pursued her tastes with such a lack of inhibition that François Mauriac called her the 'Pope of Sapphism'. In Radclyffe Hall's novel about lesbianism, *The Well Of Loneliness*, Natalie is one of the leading characters, with the pseudonym Valerie Seymour: 'Her face was humorous, placid and worldly; her eyes very kind, very blue, very lustrous . . . here was no mere libertine in love's garden, but rather a creature born out of her epoch, a pagan chained to an age that was Christian.'

Natalie Barney died in Paris on February 3, 1972, at the age of ninety-six. Her life had begun at the very moment when Stanley was making ready to travel down the Congo in the *Lady Alice*.

POSTSCRIPT

ACKNOWLEDGEMENTS

BIBLIOGRAPHY

SOURCES AND NOTES

INDEX

How I Found Stanley:
A Journey of Biographical Discovery

When I undertook to write Stanley's biography, I knew a number of riddles must be solved if it were to be anything more than the story of a poor boy who rose to fame through fierce determination and skill with his pen. It seemed odd, for a start, that a man so desperate for affection as he clearly was should have remained unmarried until almost fifty. His own explanations of his behaviour towards other people at important moments in his life did not ring true. Was Stanley a homosexual, as several friends (one a psychiatrist) had suggested to me? It seemed too easy an answer.

I wondered about *Lady Alice*, after whom Stanley had named the boat in which he made his voyage of discovery down the Congo River. There was no obvious candidate among the aristocracy of the time to whom he might have wished to pay a compliment. I looked in vain for a clue in his published writings, but it seemed significant that all reference to the name of the boat had been taken out of Stanley's uncompleted autobiography, published by his widow some years after his death.

A first hint as to the identity of Alice came by accident, while I was looking through some back numbers of the *Bulletin* of the Missouri Historical Society to learn more about Stanley's shadowy years in the West at the end of the Civil War. A brief article mentioned a letter given to a Portuguese traveller by Stanley for despatching, at the end of his Congo journey: the fate of the letter was unknown, but the address to which it was sent has survived on a slip of paper in a Lisbon archive. Stanley had been anxious to speed his letter on its way to a Miss Alice Pike, of 613 Fifth Avenue, New York. The article in the *Bulletin* speculated that this must be some girl he had known from his early days in America, and did not connect her with the *Lady Alice*.

I began to address myself to the problem of finding out about a girl who had lived a century ago in New York, in a house long since demolished, and discovering what her relationship with Stanley might have been. At that moment I heard that Gerald Sanger, a retired English newspaper director and father of a friend, had served some years ago as a country magistrate on the same Bench as Major Denzil Stanley, the explorer's adopted son. Sanger had, moreover, been entrusted with a biographical task by Denzil Stanley – to write an account of his father's private life, with the aid of letters and diaries; the aim was to show that the 'Smasher of Rocks' had a softer side to his nature. But Denzil had died and the manuscript was abandoned and forgotten.

When I talked to Sanger it became clear that Henry Stanley had indeed been enamoured of an American girl named Alice Pike. The text of the love-letters still existed. Sanger knew nothing about her family background, but had been told by Denzil that the Pikes came from Cincinnati. I decided Cincinnati was the place to start asking questions, simply because it was smaller than New York.

John Mullane, head of the history department of Cincinnati public library, was able to tell me that Samuel Pike, opera-lover and entrepreneur, had moved from the city to New York in 1866. His home had indeed been in Fifth Avenue – at 49th Street. A check on old street directories proved that this was the site of Number 613 – a spot now occupied by Saks Fifth Avenue. So I now knew who Alice was, and Professor Joseph E. Holliday of Cincinnati University provided me with the results of his research into the career of Samuel Pike. The long-forgotten romance of Henry Stanley began to take shape.

There was a real temptation to be led away into studying the life-stories of Alice and her daughters. Shortly before this book went to press I learnt that Alice wrote her memoirs in 1928, with the aid of William Huntington, an American who now lives in Madrid. She gave instructions that these memoirs should be kept under lock and key in Washington, and only published after both of her daughters were dead. The younger, Laura Dreyfus-Barney, was still alive in Paris at the start of 1974, at the age of ninety-four. Huntingdon has been willing to say that the memoirs contain 'a great deal' about Stanley.

My understanding of Stanley and his tormented private life became clearer through the unstinting help of Richard Stanley, the explorer's grandson. He even managed to uncover from among the papers at Furzehill Place two photographs of Alice and several of her letters. With Richard Stanley's co-operation I was able to sift through the wealth of letters and diaries at Furzehill; the present biography is the first to be published for almost forty years which has the advantage of unrestricted access to the family archives.

One discovery led to another, and I was able to follow up a vague hint in Frank Hird's *Authorized Life* (1935) to discover the truth about Stanley's equally disastrous betrothal to a Welsh girl, Katie Gough-Roberts. In this I was much helped by Lucy M. Jones, a great expert on Stanley's life-long connections with his North Wales birthplace. A cache of papers in the Royal Geographical Society fully explains why so little has ever been known about the man behind the forbidding exterior – Lady Stanley went to all lengths to acquire and destroy the letters her husband addressed to Katie, so that even Denzil seemed totally unaware that his father had nearly been married to a girl from Denbigh.

I was put on the track of Henry Stanley senior by reading a sketchy biography of the explorer written in Berlin in the early 1930's by Jakob Wassermann, a psychological novelist. Although short on facts, Wassermann was often long on intuition, and after describing the New Orleans period he said: 'We are told that Mr Stanley died suddenly in 1861, and that Henry Morton heard of his death long after. We get the impression that before the parting there must have been an estrangement, which the autobiographer shrouds in silence.' These sentences reinforced my own suspicions about the episode, and inquiries in New Orleans showed that there had been a Henry *Hope* Stanley alive there long after the adopted son had 'heard of his death'. It was unimaginable that two Henry Stanleys, both in the cotton business, had lived in New Orleans at the same time; so Henry Hope Stanley was my quarry. Information about him was hard to come by, until I found an article by the late Mary Willis Shuey of Shreveport, Louisiana, in the *Southwest Review* for July, 1940. This made it possible at last to uncover Henry Hope Stanley's origins in Britain. More material was assembled through the help of the Bishop of Louisiana, Dr Iveson B. Noland, Mrs Carroll Buck, and Mrs James Theus of Alexandria, Louisiana.

In piecing together the jigsaw for a biography of a man such as Stanley, who frequently tried to cover up the evidence, the research must be painstaking – and sometimes abortive. It was by slow degrees that I worked out what had happened to Stanley in the five years between his short career as a Civil War soldier and his appearance in Kansas as a reporter for the *Missouri Democrat*. For example, both the explorer and his widow made elaborate efforts to wipe out the memory of his return to Denbigh from Turkey in a make-believe officer's uniform. Diaries had been 'doctored' and all copies of the photograph showing Stanley in the uniform had been retrieved and destroyed; eventually, I discovered one reproduction of the photograph in the *Geographical Review* (New York) for 1918, although the original is no longer to be found.

By contrast, I came upon the diaries of Frank and Edward Pocock in a more dramatic manner. After making some inquiries in the Pococks' home village of Upnor in Kent and tracing one descendant of the family, I was advised to contact a grand-niece in Stow-on-the-Wold, Gloucestershire, a Mrs Jean Brown. She was able to produce a few old newspaper cuttings, a fragment of a letter in Arabic, the bugle Edward Pocock had used to awaken Stanley's caravan, and one or two letters from Stanley to the father of the Pocock brothers.

I had no reason to expect much more, although I was a trifle disappointed that none of the letters written by Frank had survived. Then a few months after my trip to Stow-on-the-Wold a message came from Mrs Brown. Was I still interested in Stanley? If so, I might like to know that her son, while clearing out the attic, had come upon a cardboard box containing some old diaries. She was not certain, but thought they might be diaries kept by Frank and Edward; perhaps I would like to examine them? The simple and poignant record made by the Pococks during their ill-fated venture into Africa had come to light again after being lost for almost a century. The task of transcribing them was formidable, but was done in the most meticulous way by Nicola Harris, formerly of the School of Oriental and African Studies, London. The dogged Frank Pocock, who so nearly reached the Atlantic and safety, has, I believe, been given his due credit at last.

Acknowledgements

In my researches I have been given unstinting support by Rita Christopher of New York, and by Anthony Wilkinson and Sara Lupino-Lane in London. My understanding in various fields was much advanced by discussions and correspondence with Professor Jean Stengers of the Université Libre de Bruxelles, Dr Gerben Hellinga of Bergen-op-Zoom, Holland, Dr Dorothy O. Helly of Hunter College, New York, and Dr Iain Smith of St Antony's College, Oxford. Dorothy Middleton, formerly of the Royal Geographical Society, and D. H. Simpson of the Royal Commonwealth Society, have both helped me with their encyclopaedic knowledge of African exploration. I have greatly profited by the suggestions of Tim Jeal, whose highly-regarded biography of Livingstone appeared in 1973, and by the insights of Harry Rowland Leech of Liverpool, a tireless student of Stanley's family connections. Mr Jem Miller and Dr Andrew Roberts, of London University, made valuable comments on the manuscript.

Much of this book was written in Deya, Majorca, and I am grateful to many of the residents of the village for their help. In particular, I am indebted to Frauke d'Aulignac for her constant encouragement and understanding, and to Patricia Lucca for making available at a crucial stage in my writing a villa which combined solitude with superb scenery. When I unexpectedly found myself homeless, Tony Johnson came to my aid. Others in Deya to whom I am obliged for help in various ways are Ross and Mary Abrams, and George McDowall.

In my efforts to resolve various problems I have harassed many people in Britain, America and elsewhere. To all of them I am grateful for co-operation so readily given. The following list may not be exhaustive, and I apologise in advance to anybody whose name I have overlooked.

Edwin Arnold, *Daily Telegraph*, London; Franklin Balch, Stevenson, Maryland; Paul Betts, *Observer*, London; Vero Bosazza, Parktown, Johannesburg, South Africa; Clare and Morris Broughton, Deya, Majorca; Sir Bernard de Bunsen, London; the Rev. T. J. Bryan, Tremeirchion, Flintshire; Hester Cattley, Kingston, Devon; Laura L. Chace, librarian, Cincinnati Historical Society; Francois Chapon, Bibliotheque Littéraire Jaques Doucet, University of Paris; Dorothy Colvile, West Worthing, Sussex; I. C. Cunningham, assistant keeper, Department of Manuscripts, National Library of Scotland; William Cunningham, Livingstone Memorial, Blantyre; T. M. Dinan, Shipping Editor's Department, Lloyds, London; Jack Dove, borough librarian, Hove, Sussex; Guy Dumur, *Nouvel Observateur*, Paris; Nordis Felland, archivist, American Geographical Society, New York; Janice Fleming, librarian, State Historical Society, Pierre, South Dakota; Charles Flowerree, American Embassy, London; J. Ramsey Fraser, Toronto, Canada; Mary C. Fraser, Kirkhill, Invernesshire; Alys Freeze, head of Western history department, Public Library, Denver, Colorado; E. Gaskell, former librarian, Wellcome Institute of History of Medicine, London; Jack Gee, IPC, Paris; Lewis E. Goodman, Public Library, Dayton, Ohio; Irwin Goodwin,

ACKNOWLEDGEMENTS

Alexandria, Virginia; T. Elwyn Griffiths, county librarian, Caernarvon; John Gordon-Christian, Christ Church, Oxford; J. D. S. Hall, superintendent, Rhodes House Library, Oxford; Elizabeth Hally, London; Jim A. Hart, Department of Journalism. Southern Illinois University; E. D. Hawksley, London; Roxanna Henson, Washington Division, Public Library, Washington; J. M. Holloway, executive secretary, Genealogical and Historical Society, Baton Rouge, Louisiana; Ivor Wynne Jones, Llandudno; Christine Kelly, archivist, Royal Geographical Society; James Lawton, curator of manuscripts, Public Library, Boston, Mass.; Dr Trevor Lloyd, Toronto; Chauncey Loomis, Dartmouth College, New Hampshire; Dr Esmond B. Martin, Roslyn, New York; Jose-Maria Martinez, Museo Maritimo, Barcelona; J. F. A. Mason, librarian, Christ Church, Oxford; N. H. MacMichael, keeper of the muniments, Westminster Abbey; Dr. H. C. G. Matthew, Christ Church, Oxford; Stanley Muir, museums and libraries department, Edinburgh; Y. A. Omar, School of Oriental and African Studies, London; André Ostier, Paris; Gillian Parker, Barnstaple, Devon; Barbara J. Poe, Martin Luther King Memorial Library, Washington; E. Talbot Rice, research assistant, National Army Museum, London; Joseph G. Rosa, Ruislip, Middlesex; Rhona Rawdon, Warminster, Wiltshire; Dr John Roberts, Merton College, Oxford; Lynda C. Roscoe, Smithsonian Institution, Washington; Martin Schmitt, Special Collections, University of Oregon; Joseph W. Snell, assistant archivist, State Historical Society, Topeka, Kansas; Paul Sykes, city librarian, Nottingham; Elizabeth Tindall, reference librarian, Historical Society, St Louis, Missouri; Alma Vaughan, newspaper librarian, State Historical Society, St Louis, Missouri; Geoffrey Veysey, county archivist, Hawarden, Flintshire; Rosina Visram, London; M. Vandewoude, Palace Archives, Brussels; R. C. K. Woodall, Wirral, Cheshire; Ivan Yates, *Observer*, London.

SOURCES OF ILLUSTRATIONS: pp. 23, 179, 225, 242, 297: Royal Geographical Society, London; pp. 22, 149, 205, 344: Richard Stanley, Pirbright, Surrey; p. 247: Mansell Collection, London; p. 278: Tate Gallery, London; p. 359: William Huntingdon, Madrid.

Other illustrations are drawn from Henry Stanley's own works, or from contemporary books and journals.

Bibliography

MANUSCRIPT COLLECTIONS

The Stanley Papers, Furzehill Place, Pirbright, Surrey

This invaluable collection, in the possession of Mr Richard Stanley, the explorer's grandson, contains letters to H.M.S. between 1865 and 1904 from hundreds of correspondents. It also includes copies of much of his own correspondence, as well as journals and notebooks of the African expeditions. Material by Dorothy Stanley also exists here.

The Pocock Diaries

A record of events, 1874–77, kept by Edward and Frank Pocock until their deaths. Despite tantalising gaps, the diaries shed fresh light on Stanley's first trans-continental journey. There are also several previously unknown letters by the explorer. Overlooked for almost a century, the diaries are the property of Mrs Jean Brown, of Stow-on-the-Wold, Gloucestershire.

The Mackinnon Papers, School of Oriental and African Studies, London

This vast collection is essential for any study of the later years of Stanley's active career. It traces the relationships between William Mackinnon, King Leopold and Stanley, as well as the course of British penetration of East Africa. Letters from Stanley relate to the Emin Pasha Relief Expedition.

National Library of Scotland, Edinburgh

The manuscripts department has lately acquired an important set of letters (MS 10705) from Stanley to his friend Alexander Bruce. It also holds the Livingstone material from Blantyre and numerous letters from important nineteenth-century figures concerned with Africa.

Royal Geographical Society, Kensington, London

Many letters from and concerning Stanley and his contemporaries in the world of exploration. Rather surprisingly, the archives hold material about the efforts by Lady Stanley to obtain various 'incriminating' letters after 1904. Also revealing are the unpublished memoirs of Sir Clements Markham.

Palace Archives, Brussels

Correspondence between Stanley and Leopold about the Congo, together with much material by the king's aides. Also, Sir John Kirk's letters to Brussels (Dossier 70).

Sanford Memorial Library, Sanford, Florida, United States

The papers in this collection include nearly thirty letters from Stanley to General Sanford and others. They are important to an understanding of the explorer's attitudes to his work in the Congo, and to his feelings towards Leopold.

BIBLIOGRAPHY

Public Record Office, London
   The Foreign Office papers, in particular the series F.O. 84, are the official record of events in East Africa during Stanley's years of exploring. Other material consulted includes records for North Wales in the 1850's.

British Museum, London
   Material here includes various letters from Livingstone in which Stanley is mentioned, and in Add. MS 37463 the earliest known surviving letter by Stanley (1868).

Rhodes House, Oxford
   Important letters from Horace Waller to Livingstone, describing at length the former's quarrels with Stanley in 1872, are held here. Also the correspondence of the Anti-Slavery Society on East Africa and the Congo.

Wellcome Medical Library, Euston Road, London
   A file of miscellaneous letters from Stanley at various times in his life, some of considerable significance.

The Quentin Keynes Collection, London
   This privately-owned archive includes several letters of the greatest importance from Stanley. There is also much material by Burton and other prominent African explorers.

PUBLISHED MATERIAL

Newspapers and publications selectively studied: *The Times, The Scotsman, Daily Telegraph, Pall Mall Gazette, Standard* (London), *Liverpool Daily Post, Illustrated London News, Graphic, Spectator, New York Herald, New York Tribune, New York Times, New York World, Sun* (New York), *Egyptian Gazette.*

STANLEY'S OWN WORKS

How I Found Livingstone, London and New York, 1872.
My Kalulu, London 1873, New York 1874.
Coomassie and Magdala, London and New York, 1874.
Through the Dark Continent, London and New York, 1878.
The Congo and the Founding of its Free State, London and New York, 1885.
In Darkest Africa, London and New York, 1890.
My Dark Companions and their Strange Stories, London 1893.
My Early Travels and Adventures in America and Asia, London and New York, 1895.
Through South Africa, London and New York, 1898.

EDITED WRITING'S OF STANLEY

The Exploration Diaries, edited by Richard Stanley and Alan Neame, London, 1961.
Unpublished Letters, edited by Albert Maurice, London and Edinburgh, 1957.
Stanley's Despatches to the New York Herald, edited by Norman R. Bennett, Boston, 1970.
The Autobiography of Sir Henry M. Stanley, edited by Dorothy Stanley, London and Boston, 1909.

BIOGRAPHIES AND MEMOIRS OF STANLEY AND HIS CONTEMPORARIES

Anstruther, Ian. *I Presume*, London, 1956.
Ascherson, Neal. *The King Incorporated*, London, 1963.
Barttelot, Walter G. (ed.) *Major Barttelot's Diary on the Congo*, London, 1890.
Brode, Heinrich. *Tippu Tib*, London, 1907.
Brodie, Fawn M. *The Devil Drives: a Life of Sir Richard Burton*, London, 1967.
Cecil, Gwendolen. *Life of Robert, Marquis of Salisbury*, London, 1932.
Chadwick, Owen. *Mackenzie's Grave*, London, 1959.
Coupland, Reginald. *Livingstone's Last Journey*, London, 1945.
Debenham, Frank. *The Way to Ilala*, London, 1955.
Farwell, Byron. *The Man Who Presumed*, London, 1957.
Fenn, G. Manville. *George Alfred Henty*, Edinburgh, 1907.
Frazer, Augusta. *Livingstone and Newstead*, London, 1913.
Johnston, Harry. *The Story of my Life*, London, 1923.
Luck, Ann. *Charles Stokes in Africa*, Nairobi, 1970.
Hird, Frank. *The Authorized Life of H. M. Stanley*, London, 1935.
Hoffmann, Frank. *With Stanley in Africa*, London, 1938.
Inglis, Brian. *Roger Casement*, London, 1973.
Jackson, Peggy. *Meteor out of Africa*, London, 1962.
Jeal, Tim. *Livingstone*, London, 1973.
Jones, Lucy M. and Jones, Ivor Wynne. *H. M. Stanley and Wales*, St Asaph, 1972.
Kaplan, Justin. *Mr Clemens and Mark Twain*, London, 1967.
Luwel, Marcel. *Stanley*, Brussels, 1956.
Marston, Edward. *After Work*, London, 1904.
Nutting, Anthony. *Gordon: Martyr and Misfit*, London, 1966.
Pond, James B. *Eccentricities of Genius*, London, 1900.
Rowlands, Cadwalader. *H. M. Stanley*, London, 1872.
Seaver, George. *David Livingstone*, London, 1957.
Seitz, Don C. *Joseph Pulitzer*, London, 1926.
Seitz, Don C. *The James Gordon Bennetts*, Indianopolis, 1928.
Slatin, Rudolf. *Fire and Sword in the Sudan*, London, 1896.
Strachey, Lytton. *Eminent Victorians*, London, 1918.
Symons, A. J. A. *H. M. Stanley*, London, 1933.
Ward, Sarita. *A Valiant Gentleman*, London, 1928.
Wassermann, Jakob. *H. M. Stanley*, Explorer, London, 1932.
West, Richard. *Brazza of the Congo*, London, 1972.

AFRICAN EXPLORATION AND TRAVEL

Baker, Samuel White. *The Albert Nyanza*, London, 1866.
Burton, Richard. *The Lake Regions of Central Africa*, London, 1860.
Cameron, Verney Lovett. *Across Africa*, London, 1877.
Glave, Edward J. *Six Years of Adventure in Congo-Land* – introduction by H. M. Stanley, London, 1895.
Grant, James. *A Walk across Africa*, London, 1864.
Jephson, A. J. Mounteney. *Emin Pasha and the Rebellion at the Equator*, London, 1890.
Jephson, A. J. Mounteney. *Diary, 1887–1889* – edited by Dorothy Middleton, Cambridge, 1969.
Livingstone, David. *Last Journals* – edited by Horace Waller, London, 1874.

BIBLIOGRAPHY

Parke, Thomas Heazle. *My Personal Experiences in Equatorial Africa*, London, 1891.
Schynse, Auguste. *A travers l'Afrique avec Stanley et Emin Pasha*, Paris, 1890.
Stevens, Thomas. *Scouting for Stanley in East Africa*, London, 1890.
Speke, John H. *Journal of the Discovery of the Source of the Nile*, London, 1863.
Ward, Herbert. *My Life With Stanley's Rear Guard*, London, 1891.
Werner, J. R. *A Visit to Stanley's Rear Guard*, London, 1889.

POLITICAL AND ECONOMIC HISTORY OF AFRICA

Anstey, Roger. *Britain and the Congo in the Nineteenth Century*, Oxford, 1962.
Coupland, Reginald. *East Africa and its Invaders*, Oxford, 1938.
Coupland, Reginald. *The Exploitation of East Africa*, London, 1939.
Duffy, James. *Portuguese Africa*, Cambridge, 1959.
Keltie, J. Scott. *The Partition of Africa*, London, 1893.
Oliver, Roland. *The Missionary Factor in East Africa*, London, 1952.
Gray, Richard, and Birmingham, David. *Pre-Colonial African Trade*, London, 1970.
Gifford, Prosser, and Louis, William Roger. *France and Britain in Africa*, London, 1971.
Ingham, Kenneth. *The Making of Uganda*, London, 1958.
Robinson, Ronald, Gallagher, John, and Denny, Alice. *Africa and the Victorians*, London, 1961.
Sanderson, G. N. *England, Europe and the Upper Nile*, Edinburgh, 1965.
Smith, Ian R. *The Emin Pasha Relief Expedition, 1886–1890*, Oxford, 1972.

MISCELLANEOUS

Conrad, Joseph. *Heart of Darkness*, London, 1902.
Jephson, A. J. Mounteney. *Stories told in an African Forest*, London, 1893.
Jones, Roger. *The Rescue of Emin Pasha*, London, 1972.
Knight, Oliver. *Following the Indian Wars*, Oklahoma, 1960.
Liniger-Goumaz, Max and Hellinga, Gerben, *Henry Morton Stanley Bibliography*, Geneva, 1972.
Marsh, Zoe. *East Africa Through Contemporary Records*, Cambridge, 1961.
Moorehead, Alan. *The White Nile*, London, 1960.
Moorehead, Alan. *The Blue Nile*, London, 1962.
Wauters, A. J. *Stanley's Emin Pasha Expedition*, London, 1890.

OTHER MATERIAL IN PERIODICALS

Bennett, Norman R. 'Stanley and the American Consuls at Zanzibar', Essex Institute *Historical Collections*, 100 – 1964.
Bridges, R. C. 'Europeans and East Africans in the age of Exploration', *Geographical Journal*, London, June 1973.
Helly, Dorothy. 'Informed Opinion on Tropical Africa, 1860–1890', *African Affairs*, London, July, 1969.
Kendall, John S. 'Old New Orleans Houses and some of The People who Lived in Them', *Louisiana Historical Quarterly*, September 1937.
King, Edward. 'An Expedition with Stanley', *Scribner's Monthly*, 1890.
Nicoll, D. J. 'Stanley's Exploits, or, Civilising Africa', *Penny Socialist Pamphlets*, Aberdeen, 1891.

Shuey, Mary Willis. 'Stanley in New Orleans', *Southwest Review*, July 1940.

Simpson, D. H. 'A Bibliography of Emin Pasha', *Uganda Journal*, 1960.

Stead, W. H. 'Mr H. M. Stanley', *Review of Reviews*, January, 1890.

Symington, A. M. 'The New-found World and its Hero', *Blackwood's Magazine*, London, 1890.

Vansina, Jan. 'Long-distance trade routes in Central Africa', *Journal of African History*, 1962.

Sources and Notes

ABBREVIATIONS USED

BOOKS, PERIODICALS AND NEWSPAPERS

AUT   *Autobiography of Henry M. Stanley*, edited by Dorothy Stanley

AL   *H. M. Stanley, the Authorized Life*, by Frank Hird

BD   Stanley's Despatches to the New York Herald, edited by Norman R. Bennett

CFS   *The Congo and the Founding of its Free State*, by H. M. Stanley

CR   *H. M. Stanley, his Early Life*, by Cadwalader Rowlands

DNB   *Dictionary of National Biography*

EAA   *The Exploitation of East Africa*, by Reginald Coupland

ED   *Exploration Diaries of H. M. Stanley*, edited by Richard Stanley and Alan Neame

EPRE   *Emin Pasha Relief Expedition*, by Iain R. Smith

HIFL   *How I Found Livingstone*, by H. M. Stanley

IDA   *In Darkest Africa*, by H. M. Stanley

IP   *I Presume*, by Ian Anstruther

LJ   *Livingstone*, by Tim Jeal

LLJ   *Livingstone's Last Journey*, by Reginald Coupland

MEA   *Mackinnon and East Africa*, by John S. Galbraith

MP   *The Man Who Presumed*, by Byron Farwell

PD   Pocock Diaries (unpublished)

TDC   *Through the Dark Continent*, by H. M. Stanley

UL   *H. M. Stanley, Unpublished Letters*, edited by Albert Maurice

BMHS   *Bulletin of the Missouri Historical Society*

JAH   *Journal of African History*

NYH   *New York Herald*

NYT   *New York Times*

INSTITUTIONS, LIBRARIES AND MANUSCRIPT COLLECTIONS

BM   British Museum, London

MCA   Musée de l'Afrique Centrale, Tervuren, Belgium

PA   Palace Archives, Brussels

PRO   Public Record Office, London

QK   Quentin Keynes Collection, London

RCS   Royal Commonwealth Society, London

RGS   Royal Geographical Society, London

RH   Rhodes House, Oxford

SFA   Stanley Family Archives, Pirbright, Surrey

SOAS   School of Oriental and African Studies, London

Chapter 1: Pledge in Fifth Avenue, Appointment in Africa

PUBLISHED MATERIAL: TDC, BD, AUT, IP. The family background of Alice Pike is given in 'Notes on Samuel N. Pike and his Opera Houses', by Joseph E. Holliday, *Bulletin of the Cincinnati Historical Society*, July 1967. A rather bland account of the *Daily Telegraph*'s early years is in Lord Burnham, *Peterborough Court* (1955). Newspaper cuttings: *NYT*, June 22, 1878, quoting the *Freeman's Journal*, Dublin; *NYH*, July 17, 1874. Author's interviews and correspondence: Professor Joseph E. Holliday; Mrs Jean Brown on the Pococks.

UNPUBLISHED MATERIAL: letters and diaries quoted are in SFA.

NOTES

There was an exploring tradition in the Pocock family. An uncle of the brothers, Francis Pocock, died in 1845 on the ill-fated Franklin Expedition to the Arctic.

The Langham Hotel is defunct. Its building is now used by the BBC.

A Court House fire in 1884 destroyed official records in Cincinnati, where Alice Pike was born; it is virtually certain that her birth occurred in January 1857, although in later life she claimed 1860 as the date.

Chapter 2: To the Great Lakes

PUBLISHED MATERIAL: TDC, ED, BD, EAA. The scanty knowledge in 1875 outside Africa about the Victoria and other lakes can be gauged from books written in the previous decade by Speke, Grant and Baker.

UNPUBLISHED MATERIAL: Letters of Stanley and Alice Pike are in SFA. The comments of the Pococks are in PD. Stanley's letter to Agnes Livingstone, dated September 24, 1874, is in the Quentin Keynes Collection.

NOTES

The view that Stanley had been duped by Mtesa is forcefully expressed in Charles Chaille-Long, *Central Africa: Naked Truths of Naked People* (1876), p. 106 *et seq.*

A letter to Edward Levy-Lawson, August 15, 1875, from Stanley, defends the Bumbiri slaughter by saying the warriors would not heed any 'overtures of peace or amity' (letter in MCA). A useful contemporary account of the affair is in Ch. 47, 'The Stanley Episode', of J. Ewing Ritchie's *The Pictorial Life of David Livingstone* (1877).

For ease of reference, quotations from Stanley's despatches are generally the *NYH* versions, collected in BD. The versions in the *Daily Telegraph* have only minor differences, caused by sub-editing.

Chapter 3: The Cauldron of Slavery

PUBLISHED MATERIAL: TDC, BD, ED, EAA. The account by Tippu-Tib of his meeting with Stanley is in *Maisha yo Hamed bin Muhammed el Murjebi yaani Tippu Tip* (1966). A discussion of Stanley's effect upon trading in Nyangwe appears in Jan Vansina, 'Long Distance Trade Routes in Central Africa' (*JAH*, Vol. 3, no. 3, 1962, pp. 375-390).

UNPUBLISHED MATERIAL: letters quoted are in SFA and PD.

NOTES

Stanley was acquainted with the legends of the Mountains of the Moon from Henry Cary's translation (1847) of Herodotus, Book 2, Euterpe, pp. 87–93.

An account of the debate over the Congo-Nile watershed is in LJ, *passim.*

While Stanley was in Nyangwe, Alice Pike gave birth to her first child, Natalie – on October 31, 1876 (Probate Court records, Montgomery County, Ohio).

Chapter 4: Down the Congo to the Sea

PUBLISHED MATERIAL: TDC, BD, ED, CFS. Numerous published accounts confirm the existence of slavery in the Congo – e.g., Herbert Ward, *Five Years with the Congo Cannibals* (1890). An account of the development of Congolese society in pre-colonial times is in Isaria Kimambo, *Aspects of Central African History,* ed. Terence Ranger (1968). Newspaper cuttings: a satirical account of Stanley's journey is in *NYT,* April 18, 1878. Also, New York *Sun,* February 12, 1878, has a report headlined 'The African Manslayer'.

UNPUBLISHED MATERIAL: letters and diary entries are found in SFA and PD.

NOTES

A Portuguese missionary is reputed to have reached the Stanley Pool overland in the seventeenth century. Otherwise, there is no record of any European having penetrated beyond the Lower Congo rapids. The port of Boma had a notorious reputation as a slave-trading centre until the middle of the nineteenth century.

The original of Stanley's letter of August 4, 1877 is in QK; it does not differ from the published version. Confirmation that the account in TDC accurately gives the experiences of Stanley and his men is provided by W. Holman Bentley, a Baptist missionary, in his *Pioneering on the Congo* (1900), vol. 1, p. 396. Bentley interrogated Robert Feruzi and others, and found that their recollections always tallied with Stanley's record.

Stanley's attempt to send a letter to Alice Pike in August 1877 is recounted in Douglas L. Wheeler, 'On the Trail of a New Henry M. Stanley Letter' in *BMHS,* April 1962.

The reception in Paris is described in Edward Marston, *After Work* (1904), and *NYH,* February 3, 1878.

Alice's wedding is reported in *NYH,* January 13, 1876. A portrait, showing her in her wedding dress, is in the President Monroe Foundation, Fredericksburg, Virginia.

Chapter 5: The Workhouse Rebel

PUBLISHED MATERIAL: AUT, AL, CR, DNB, IP, MP. Especially valuable on the childhood is Lucy M. Jones and Ivor Wynne Jones, *H. M. Stanley and Wales* (1972). There are numerous works on the area where he grew up; useful is the official guide to St Asaph and environs published by the Rural District Council. Newspaper cuttings: *Denbigh Free Press,* February 9, 1889; *Rhyl Gazette,* May 5, 1971. *The Times,* May 11 and 17, 1904; Author's interviews and correspondence: Rhona Rawdon and Harry Leech on the Rowlands family; A. G. Veysey on the Vaughan Horne legend; Lucy M. Jones and Ivor Wynne Jones on various key points; the Rev. T. J. Bryan on Stanley's baptism; Arthur Pennant on Ffynnon Beuno.

UNPUBLISHED MATERIAL: most letters quoted are in SFA; data on the Denbigh background also exists in Wellcome Papers, RGS.

NOTES

The Parry pedigree can be found in *H. M. Stanley and Wales;* a Rowlands family tree was kindly drawn up for the author by Mrs Rawdon. The name Rowlands sometimes drops the s, and is the anglicized form of the Welsh Rollant – the spelling Rollins also occurs.

A copy of the certificate awarded to Francis is in PRO file NM12/16140. The word-picture of Stanley as a youth by Hughes is quoted in CR, p. 52. The letter to his uncle is in AL, p. 24, and a photographed copy is in *AUT*, 2nd edition, facing p. 56.

An inconclusive file of copy letters on the Vaughan Horne legend is in the County Archives, Hawarden, Flintshire.

St Beuno was an early Christian evangelist who drank at the well on a journey through Wales; a monastery had previously been on the site of the house, which dates from the fifteenth century.

Stanley stayed with his relatives in Liverpool at 22, Sherrif Street; but in *AUT* he gives 22 Roscommon Street – a more affluent road.

Chapter 6: New Life in the Deep South

PUBLISHED MATERIAL: AUT, IP, CR. A biography by Jakob Wassermann, *Bula Matari* (Berlin, 1932) makes an inspired guess about the quarrel between Henry Hope Stanley (HHS) and his 'son'. Mary Willis Shuey identifies HHS in an article in *Southwest Review* of Dallas, Texas, for July 1940. Newspaper cuttings: the Stanley home in New Orleans is described in the *Times Picayune*, February 25, 1973, together with some speculation about HHS. The cutting quoting 'a lady of undoubted veracity' exists in SFA, marked 1891, and by-lined 'States reporter'. Author's interviews and correspondence: Harry Leech, Gerald Sanger, and Katie Theus.

UNPUBLISHED MATERIAL: letters quoted are in SFA.

NOTES

Selina Brooks, mother of HHS, died on July 7, 1873 in Southport, Lancs. One of the executors was 'Henry Hope Stanley of Arcola, Louisiana, USA, merchant'; the other was his half-brother, James Howard Brooks.

From his letter in SFA, it appears that Schumacher worked for a Dr Russel in New Orleans, and that Stanley was disliked by Russel.

'Stanley Hall' in Arcola was destroyed by fire in 1929.

I am indebted to Dr Gerben Hellinga for establishing the flaws in Stanley's own chronology of events in New Orleans.

Chapter 7: From Dixie to the Federal Fleet

PUBLISHED MATERIAL: AUT, MP, CR. The second version of Stanley's 'shipwreck off Spain' appears in Thomas George, *The Birth, Boyhood and Younger*

Days of Henry M. Stanley (1895) – spurious apart from this one account. Author's interviews and correspondence: Lucy M. Jones on Stanley's first return to Wales. H. Leech on probable visit to Stockport. Lloyds of London and Mariners Museum, Newport News, Virginia, on the *Jehu*, and her journeys in the 1860's.

NOTES

Letter from James A. Slate, March 23, 1891, exists in SFA. Charles Wilkes, uncle of Stanley's friend at Fort Douglas, was made an admiral after removing from a British ship the Confederate emissaries to Europe.

The story of Emma's receiving a letter announcing the death of John Rowlands appears in *Review of Reviews*, January 1890, p. 24. The career and personality of Stegman, who entered Stanley's life in 1864, are illuminated by his records from the U.S. Army (National Archives).

The role of Maggie Mitchell in *Fanchon* is described in T. Alston Brown, *A History of the New York Stage* (1903), vol. 1, pp. 198–9. On November 16, 1864, the *NYT* advertised a 'farewell benefit' to Maggie Mitchell in *Fanchon*.

The British census, 1861, shows the Brooks-Stanley family in Cheadle.

Attorney Thomas Irwin Hughes is detailed in *Lains Brooklyn Directory*, 1862–66.

Chapter 8: The Vagabond Freelance

PUBLISHED MATERIAL: AUT, AL, CR. There is a special debt to BD: this draws together much contemporary material about the 'Noe controversy' and the abortive Turkish venture. For the *Missouri Democrat* and Stanley's earliest connection with it, Jim A. Hart, *History of the St Louis Globe-Democrat* (1962). Much information on journalism beyond the Missouri in the 1860's is in Robert Taft, *Artists and Illustrators of the Old West, 1850–1900* (1953). For a popular account of early mining in Colorado, Caroline Bancroft, *Historic Central City* (Boulder, Colorado, n.d.). Newspaper cuttings: Stanley's time in Central City – *Denver Republican*, June 17, 1890, Denver *Daily News*, May 17, 1891, *Rocky Mountain Herald*, Sept. 7, 1872; the explorer's own version of his exploit at Fort Fisher: CR and *Abergele and Pensarn Visitor*, Wales, December 20, 1930; the description of Miss Noe is in the *NYH*, August 29, 1872 (not included in BD); Stanley's immediate account of the Turkish affair: *Levant Herald*, October 17, 1866. Author's interviews and correspondence: Jim A. Hart, and Miss Elizabeth Tindall, Missouri Historical Society, on the newspaper background; Paul Hogarth on the character of Colorado in Stanley's time; Alys Freeze on memories of Stanley in the West.

NOTES

The first quotation from Noe comes from an interview by J. C. Smith, agent for Henry Wellcome and Lady Stanley, in October 1907 (in SFA); other quotations date from 1872 and are generally to be found in the appendices to BD.

The desertion date is mentioned in MP and confirmed by US naval records, although Noe was rebuffed when he sought documentary proof.

Horace Greeley visited Central City as early as June, 1859, for the *New York Tribune* with William N. Byers, editor of the *Rocky Mountain News*.

The homosexual rape is confirmed in a letter Cook-Stanley, undated, in SFA: 'The two are sentenced for the act of sodomy according to the criminal code.'

Stanley's assertion that his father was a lawyer may have been inspired by working for 'Lyons law office' (J. C. Smith to Henry Wellcome, November 3, 1907, quoting Noe); Cook also said (*Chicago Times*, August 31, 1872) that Stanley had worked in a law office but found it 'too musty'. In later writings, Stanley refers sarcastically to the behaviour of New York lawyers.

Chapter 9: Wronged Children of the Soil

PUBLISHED MATERIAL: AUT, CR, BD. Quotations and background on Stanley with the Hancock expedition and the Peace Commission come mainly from the following: H. M. Stanley, *My Early Travels and Adventures in America and Asia* (1895); Oliver Knight, *Following the Indian Wars* (1960); Jim A. Hart, *op. cit.* A valuable compilation of writings by Stanley for the *Missouri Democrat*, from the newspaper's files, has been done by Douglas L. Wheeler, for the *BMHS* (April, 1961). A more detailed extract from the coverage of the Medicine Lodge Peace Councils is in *Kansas Historical Quarterly*, vol. 33, Autumn 1967. Theodore R. Davis's descriptions of Stanley on the Hancock expedition are reproduced in *The Westerners Brand Book, 1945–46*, privately published in Chicago. The Pulitzer shooting affray is in Don C. Seitz, *Joseph Pulitzer* (1926). Newspaper cuttings: *NYH*, September 26, 1872; *Denbigh Free Press*, February 9, 1889; and May 24, 1904; *Daily Tribune*, Jefferson City, July 4, 1890. Author's interviews and correspondence: Miss Lucy M. Jones, A. G. Veysey, Harry Leech and others on the visit to Wales.

UNPUBLISHED MATERIAL: letters quoted are in SFA.

NOTES

Reproduction of Denbigh Castle book entry is in CR, facing p. 108. The *Ticonderoga* had been the Federal flagship at the Fort Fisher battle. The move by the Morris family to Davis Street, Liverpool is confirmed by Noe, New York *Sun*, August 29, 1872.

A description of Stanley's visit to the workhouse in CR, pp. 70–75. Stanley's last greeting to Noe was from the Red Sea, January 1, 1969.

Douglas L. Wheeler, *op. cit.*, draws attention to the phrase 'wronged children of the soil'.

Details on William Fayel – who died, 1910, in the Old Folks' Home, Magnolia Avenue, St Louis – appear in W. A. Kelsoe, *St Louis Reference Record*, p. 77.

Chapter 10: A Coup in Abyssinia

PUBLISHED MATERIAL: AUT, AL, CR. For an account of the *New York Herald* and its owners, Don C. Seitz, *The James Gordon Bennetts* (1928). Stanley's record of the Magdala campaign: Coomassie and Magdala (1874); the best popular version is in Alan Moorehead, *The Blue Nile* (1962). Newspaper cuttings: *The Graphic*, June 29, 1872.

NOTES

Statistics for the Magdala expedition, from official sources, are at the end of *Coommassie and Magdala*.

A description of Stanley, the 'active little Yankee', just after his Abyssinian coup, is in J. Macgregor, *Rob Roy on the Jordan* (1869).

Chapter 11: Two Loves Lost

PUBLISHED MATERIAL: AUT, AL, BD, CR, HIFL. Stanley's first experiences in Paris: Edwin Swift Balch, 'American Explorers in Africa', *Geographical Review*, vol. 5, June 1918. The letter to Katie Gough-Roberts is reprinted in Jones and Jones, *op. cit.*, pp. 20–24. A vivid account of Stanley's performance in Spain is given by Edward King in *Scribner's Monthly*, no. 5, 1872, pp. 105–112. The bulk of Stanley's despatches on his Asian journey, 1869–70, are in *My Early Travels and Adventures* (1895). Author's interviews and correspondence: Franklin Balch and Nordis Felland, American Geographical Society, on Edwin Swift Balch, Harry Leech and Lucy M. Jones on the Gough-Roberts family.

UNPUBLISHED MATERIAL: Documentation for the engagement to Katie is in RGS archives, Stanley, 13-1/2. Letters from Ambella family, including two from Virginia, in SFA.

NOTES

Shortly after the Abyssinia campaign, Stanley was nearly drowned while swimming off Alexandria. He was saved by a Reuters man, Edward Virnard, who 25 years later demanded compensation from him (correspondence in SFA).

The father of Edwin Balch first met Stanley in Cairo in February 1869, and recorded in his diary that the reporter had 'been sent to Aden en route to Zanzibar to meet Dr Livingstone', but had returned on learning that he was still in Central Africa.

On September 14, 1868, Stanley wrote to His Excellency Heke Kyan Bey, of Cairo, asking him for a reference to present to the Ambella family (BM Add MSS 37463).

The Denbigh church register gives the baptism of Catherine Maria Gough-Roberts as January 25, 1849. Her marriage to Urban Rufus Bradshaw, 22, architect, was in Denbigh on September 22, 1870.

It is recorded by Seitz, *op. cit.* that Bennett thought of sending another *NYH* man, De Benneville Randolph Keim, to find Livingstone, but could not contact him quickly enough and resorted to Stanley. For details of Keim: District of Columbia *Biographical Record*, 1908.

Chapter 12: Friends and Foes in Zanzibar

PUBLISHED MATERIAL: HIFL, BD, LLJ, EEA, LJ, IP, MEA. The first journey by white travellers to Lake Tanganyika is related in Richard Burton, *The Lake Regions of Central Africa* (1860). Relations between the Zanzibar consuls are made plain in Norman Bennett, 'American in Zanzibar: 1865–1915', *Tanganyika Notes and Records* (March 1963). A notably pro-Kirk position is taken in LLJ and EEA. Author's interviews and correspondence: Derek H. Simpson, librarian, RCS, on Stanley's African colleagues; Tim Jeal on Livingstone's reputation after 1866; Vero Bosazza on Kirk. Unpublished material is in SFA and RGS archives.

NOTES

In letters to Stanley (SFA), Captain Francis Webb referred bitterly to 'Kirkism'.

The quarrels between France and Britain over Zanzibar are detailed in EEA, p. 35 *et seq.*

Kirk's letter to Livingstone about Barghash is dated October 20, 1870 (NLS). The explanation of Stanley's break with Katie Gough-Roberts is in a letter to Henry Wellcome from Morien Mons Huws (August 18, 1904) in RGS archives, HMS, 13/1.

Chapter 13: Blazing a Trail to Ujiji

PUBLISHED MATERIAL: HIFL, BD, LLJ. An account of the searches for Livingstone is given by P. A. Cole-King in *Livingstone, Man of Africa* (1973). Racial attitudes and the behaviour of explorers are discussed in H. A. C. Cairns, *Prelude to Imperialism* (1965), and in Roland Oliver, *The Missionary Factor in East Africa* (1952). Author's interviews and correspondence: Abdullah Sud, Ujiji, on Arabs on Lake Tanganyika; David Martin, Dar es Salaam, on racial attitudes. Unpublished material: SFA.

NOTES

Livingstone's malaria remedy is quoted in Owen Chadwick, *Mackenzie's Grave* (1959).

It is difficult even today to reach Ujiji by road.

The account of Stanley's arrival is based on his NYH despatch (August 10, 1872), which differs slightly from the version in HIFL.

Chapter 14: 'Doctor Livingstone, I Presume?'

PUBLISHED MATERIAL: HIFL, AL, IP, BD, LJ, LLJ, EAA. The development of the British position in East Africa is discussed in Ronald Robinson, John Gallagher, Alice Denny, *Africa and the Victorians* (1961). Livingstone's diary comments on Stanley are in *Last Journals*, edited by Horace Waller (1874). Author's interviews and correspondence: Dorothy Helly on Kirk and Waller; Tim Jeal on Livingstone's attitudes to Stanley; Rosina Visram on Livingstone's behaviour towards his followers; Stanley Muir on William Farquhar's origins; Vero Bosazza on Stanley-Kirk dispute.

UNPUBLISHED MATERIAL: letters in PRO, NLS, BM and QK.

NOTES

There is a long-standing argument as to whether the Ujiji meeting was on November 10, 1871, or slightly earlier.

Livingstone was not told by Stanley that he was Welsh. It is mentioned contemptuously in a letter Waller-Livingstone (November 25, 1872) but Livingstone did not live to read it.

Livingstone's views on Stanley's bad temper are in BM Add MSS 50184, f. 58.

The Kirk-Livingstone dispute is revealed in PRO, FO 84/1357 – Kirk to FO, May 9, 1872; Livingstone first castigated Kirk in a letter to Agnes, November 18, 1871. Kirk's letter to Rawlinson on the prospect that Stanley might reach Ujiji is in RGS archives, and dated January 15, 1872. Stanley's remark about the Africans' admiration for the compass is in a letter to James Gordon Bennett, May 18, 1872, in MCA.

The patriotic fervour in the RGS over the search for Livingstone is exemplified by *The Times*, January 10, 1872, reporting Sir Bartle Frere as saying that it would be 'disgraceful to them as Englishmen' if they did not send an expedition.

Chapter 15: Fame and Disaster

PUBLISHED MATERIAL: AUT, HIFL, IP, CR, LLJ. John Camden Hotten, *The Finding of Dr Livingstone* (1872), recounts the return of Stanley to Europe. Augusta Fraser, *Livingstone at Newstead* (1913), ch. 12, gives reactions to Stanley's treatment in Brighton. Newspaper cuttings: *Daily Telegraph*, July 3, 1872; *The Times*, August 15, 1872; various British newspapers, August-November, 1872.

UNPUBLISHED MATERIAL: Letter Stanley-Agnes Livingstone, August 3, 1872, in QK, argues case against Kirk. Waller Papers, in RH, Afr. s. 16, contain important letters to Livingstone. Memoirs and notes by Sir Clements Markham, in RGS archives, are forthright on both Stanley and Livingstone.

NOTES

The reasons why the RGS 'felt a sense of ownership in Livingstone' are clearly set out in LJ, p. 94 *et seq.*

An interesting letter from John Smith Moffat, Mrs Livingstone's brother, to Stanley, dated August 16, 1872, is in SFA. It derides the 'childish' behaviour of RGS members.

A congratulatory letter from Mark Twain to Stanley, dated September 1, 1872, is in SFA. Their paths first crossed in St Louis in 1867: Justin Kaplan, *Mr Clemens and Mark Twain* (1967).

Cameron's letter of Stanley, October 25, 1872, is in SFA. The whereabouts of Cameron's diaries and correspondence is unknown today. Stanley's letter of August 25, 1872, is in QK.

Chapter 16: Interlude at Newstead Abbey

This chapter is largely based upon Augusta Fraser, *op. cit.*

NOTES

The Webb family papers, which would throw much more light on Stanley's attitudes at this crucial moment in his life, cannot be traced. They were known to be, earlier in this century, at Pepper Arden, Northallerton, Yorkshire.

Stanley's threat to sue his critics for libel was reported in Liverpool *Daily Albion*, October 2, 1872. His letter condemning Hotten and the latter's rejoinder appear in *The Times*, November 12 and 13, 1872.

Chapter 17: 'Each Man has His Own Way'

PUBLISHED MATERIAL: AUT, TDC, IP, AL, LJ. G. Manville Fenn, *George Alfred Henty: The Story of an Active Life* (1907), refers to Stanley in the Ashanti campaign. Frank Harris, *My Life and Loves* (1925), vol. 2, ch. 1, quotes Wolseley on Stanley's role in the fighting at Ashanti. Newspaper cuttings: New York *Tribune*, November 21, 1872; *Christian World*, April 27, 1874.

UNPUBLISHED MATERIAL: Stanley's letter of condolence to Agnes Livingstone (March 18, 1874) is in NLS, Harryhausen Collection.

NOTES

Winwood Reade, a friend and colleague of Stanley on the Ashanti campaign, acquired notoriety for his atheistical views; he died, 1875, aged 37, from the effects of the campaign (DNB).

Chapter 18: Servant of the King

PUBLISHED MATERIAL: AUT, AL, MEA, CFS, UL. The career of Edwin Arnold is in Brooks Wright, *Interpreter of Buddhism to the West* (1957). A perceptive study of Leopold II is Neal Ascherson, *The King Incorporated* (1963). Roger Anstey, *Britain and the Congo in the Nineteenth Century* (1962) sets the background to Stanley's initiative. Norman R. Bennett, 'Stanley and the American Consuls at Zanzibar', in Essex Institute Historical Collections, no. 100 (1964), describes the explorer's visit to Zanzibar in 1879. Newspaper cuttings: NYH, April 5, 1878, notes the stimulus to missionary endeavour derived from Stanley's discoveries.
UNPUBLISHED MATERIAL: Documents in SFA, RGS, PRO.

NOTES

Kirk's indictment of Stanley is in PRO, 84/1514, no. 61 of 1878. Farler's original letter is in RH, MSS British s.22/G2; it is far less sweeping than Kirk's commentary. See also, United Society for the Propagation of the Gospel archives, Box AI, 6A, no. 423. Sparhawk's letter of July 4, 1878 is in SFA.

Sir Samuel Baker, writing to Arnold, January 20, 1878, warmly defends Stanley against his critics – letter in RGS archives.

Chapter 19: Five Years for the Free State

PUBLISHED MATERIAL: CFS, UL. A good account of Stanley's rivalry with the French is in Richard West, *Brazza of the Congo* (1972). Leopold's intrigues are discussed in 'King Leopold and Anglo-French Rivalry, 1882–84' by Jean Stengers, in *France and Britain in Africa* (1971). Also: Stengers, *Leopold II et la fixation des frontières du Congo*, in *Le Flambeau*, nos. 3–4, 1963. Conditions in the Congo in the early 1880's are described by Harry Johnston, *The Story of my Life* (1923).
UNPUBLISHED MATERIAL: Correspondence in PA and SFA.

NOTES

Stanley had an open confrontation with Count de Brazza in Paris in October 1882, and came off worst.

A copy of Stanley's letter to Greffulhe, May 11, 1879, and the original of Gordon's letter to Stanley, are in SFA. Braconnier's comments on Stanley are quoted in *Review of Reviews*, January 1890.

This period in the Congo, when he was not a traveller but effectively a resident, make Stanley's *rapport* with Africans much more apparent. The subject will be examined in detail in Donald Simpson's forthcoming *Dark Companions*.

Chapter 20: Carving Up the Dark Continent

PUBLISHED MATERIAL: AUT, CFS, MEA. Among the numerous studies of imperialism in Africa, the following are most relevant: J. Scott Keltie, *The*

Partition of Africa (1895); Margery Perham, *Lugard: The Years of Adventure* (1956); James Duffy, *Portugal in Africa* (1962); Robinson, Gallagher and Denny, *op. cit.*; documents on the Berlin Conference are collected at the end of CFS. On Stanley's journey to America, 1886: J. B. Pond, *Eccentricities of Genius* (1901). On the death of Gordon: Lytton Strachey, *Eminent Victorians* (1918).

UNPUBLISHED MATERIAL: Kirk's letters to Brussels are in PA, dossier 70.

NOTES

By 1882, Kirk had emerged as *doyen* of the Africanists in London. His circle is discussed by Dorothy Helly in ' "Informed" Opinion on Tropical Africa in Great Britain, 1860–1890', *African Affairs*, July, 1969.

The turbulent Congolese boy Baruti, whose name appropriately meant 'gunpowder', had been given to Stanley by Sir Francis de Winton, his successor in the Congo.

Chapter 21: 'I am Poor, Helpless, Trembling'

PUBLISHED MATERIAL: AUT, AL, CFS. Marie von Bunsen, *The World I Used to Know* (1930), for the encounter in Berlin. Julian B. Arnold, *Giants in Dressing Gowns* (1942) has a description of Dorothy Tennant. Author's correspondence and interviews: Sir Bernard de Bunsen on Marie von Bunsen; Richard Stanley and Gerald Sanger on Dorothy Tennant; John Gordon-Christian on Dorothy's involvement with the Pre-Raphaelites.

UNPUBLISHED MATERIAL: Dorothy's diaries and Stanley's correspondence with her are in SFA. Letters to Alexander Bruce are in NLS, MS 10705. The letter to Baroness von Donop is in the Wellcome Medical Library archives. The letter of April 11, 1885, to an anonymous Austrian woman, is in the National Library of Wales. Stanley-Mackinnon, September 23, 1886, is in Mackinnon Papers, SOAS, Box 55, F218.

NOTES

The Tennant house in Richmond Terrace has been empty and threatened with demolition since 1972.

Charles Tennant (1796–1873), was Tory MP for St Albans in 1830. He was an author and landowner, with estates in Glamorgan.

Chapter 22: The Last Expedition

PUBLISHED MATERIAL: AUT, IDA, EPRE, MEA, EAA. For the accounts by Stanley's officers of what happened on the Emin Pasha expedition, the following are especially valuable: Thomas Parke, *My Personal Experience in Equatorial Africa* (1891); Walter G. Barttelot (ed.), *Major Barttelot's Diary on the Congo* (1890); Dorothy Middleton (ed.), A. J. Mounteney Jephson, *Diary, 1887–89* (1969). Pond, *op. cit.* on the dash from New York to London. W. Holman Bentley, *op. cit.*, on activities at Stanley Pool. Herbert Ward's description of the expedition is in *My Life with Stanley's Rear Guard* (1891). Newspaper cuttings: the EPRE and implications of the march were exhaustively reported and discussed in *The Times* and other journals, 1886–90. Author's interviews and correspondence: Iain R. Smith, Dorothy Middleton and Donald Simpson.

UNPUBLISHED MATERIAL: Mackinnon Papers, SOAS; Stanley's view of Ward is in letter to King Leopold, September 4, 1884, PA, Dossier 102.

NOTES

Robert W. Felkin, whose articles advocated the relief of Emin, had been a missionary in troubled Uganda; Mtesa had once put a rope around his neck to hang him (*Scottish Geographical Magazine*, April 1886).

Leopold had told Stanley to 'buy over' Tippu Tib, taking advantage of his reputed lack of funds. Great secrecy was used, and the Arab was referred to as 'Number One' in correspondence (PA).

Stanley's letter to Wolseley is in Wolseley Papers, Hove public library.

Chapter 23: In the Forest of Death

PUBLISHED MATERIAL: IDA, EPRE, AL. The fears for the safety of the expedition is related in A. J. Wauters, *Stanley's Emin Pasha Expedition* (1890). Other material is in the diaries of Parke, Jephson, Barttelot and Jameson (*Story of the Rear Column*, 1890).

UNPUBLISHED MATERIAL: diaries of Nelson are in the possession of Dr Esmond B. Martin, New York. Bonny's logbook of his time with the Rear Column are in SFA, with other correspondence on the EPRE.

NOTES

Jameson's involvement in cannibalism was fully discussed in Chapter 6 of the official report of the Emin Pasha Relief Committee (pp. 68–99). Proofs of the report were prepared, but through internal dissension it was never printed (Copy in Mackinnon Papers, SOAS).

Tippu Tib's version of events in 1887–88 is in his autobiography (1966 edition, *op. cit.*). He is highly critical of Stanley. Valuable details about Barttelot's death are in Tippu Tib's letter to his brother, Mahomed Masood, December 21, 1888 (translation in F6, Mackinnon Papers).

Chapter 24: Bringing Back the Trophy

PUBLISHED MATERIAL: IDA, EPRE, and diaries. A. J. Mounteney Jephson's record of his time with Emin is in *Emin Pasha and the Rebellion at the Equator* (1890). Final stages of the journey were recorded in Auguste Schynse, *A travers l'Afrique avec Stanley et Emin Pasha* (1890), and Thomas Stevens, *Scouting for Stanley in East Africa* (1890). A succinct account of the 1888 disturbances around Lake Victoria is in Kenneth Ingham, *The Making of Uganda* (1958).

UNPUBLISHED MATERIAL: Correspondence in SFA and Mackinnon Papers.

NOTES

The warmth of feeling between Stanley and the missionary Mackay is demonstrated by a letter of September 29, 1889, from the latter (in SFA).

Stanley's pleasure at having Bishop Parker's spectacles is mentioned in a letter of March 12, 1896 to the bishop's brother (in possession of Miss Gillian Parker).

The court-martial of Hoffman took place on the final stage of the expedition. The record, six pages of questions and answers, is in SFA.

Chapter 25: The Lion of Richmond Terrace

PUBLISHED MATERIAL: IDA, EPRE, AUT. A defence of Emin – and criticism of Stanley – by the German adventurer Carl Peters is in the *Contemporary Review*, November 1890, pp. 634–38. A rejoinder by Mounteney Jephson is in the *Fortnightly Review*, January 1891. Newspaper cuttings: Most complete account of Stanley's activities in Cairo are in *Egyptian Gazette*, January 15, 1890 *et seq.* The Rear Column controversy: NYH (London edition), October 26, 1890, *The Times*, November 8, 1890, *Pall Mall Gazette*, November 10, 1890, and others. Author's interviews and correspondence: Donald Simpson on the reception for Stanley in London; J. A. F. Mason, Librarian at Christ Church, Oxford, on the history of Stanley's knighthood.

UNPUBLISHED MATERIAL: Correspondence in SFA, NLS, RGS and Mackinnon Papers.

NOTES

The doubts Stanley felt immediately after the expedition are revealed in letters from Cairo to Sir Francis de Winton, March 5, 1890 (in SFA), and Mrs French Sheldon, February 6, 1890 (in RGS). The relations of Jameson had already complained to De Winton about Stanley's attitude (letter from Andrew Jameson, February 24, 1890 (in SFA)); on May 4 the widow, Ethel Jameson, wrote bitterly to Stanley. The explorer James Grant summed up the Rear Column controversy as 'a disgusting affair' in a letter to Blackwood, November 24, 1890 (NLS, MS 4551).

Aubrey Stanhope's account of his visit to Mürren, to investigate relations between the Stanleys is in *On the Track of the Great* (1914), pp. 151–55.

Chapter 26: Stories by the Library Fire

PUBLISHED MATERIAL: AUT, AL. A convincing description of Stanley in his last years is in Edward Marston, *After Work* (1904). Also: Sir Henry Lucy, *More Passages by the Way* (1912). The campaign to reform conditions in the Congo is examined in Brian Inglis, *Roger Casement* (1973).

UNPUBLISHED MATERIAL: correspondence in SFA and RGS.

NOTES

Stanley's letter to Marston, March 14, 1896, is in MCA archives.

A long exchange of letters between Stanley and Mounteney Jephson covering the period 1891–1904 is in SFA; in one Jephson describes a visit to Emin's daughter in Germany. Other letters show that Stanley, writing through a missionary, maintained a correspondence with Africans in Uganda until the turn of the century.

Chapter 27: The Aftermath

PUBLISHED MATERIAL: Ascherson, *op. cit.* for the final years of King Leopold. A compilation on Alice Pike Barney, reproducing her paintings and giving a brief biography, was published by the Smithsonian Institution, 1957; *American Art*

Annual, 1931, contains an obituary. Newspaper cuttings: Obituary of Dorothy Stanley: *The Times*, October 6, 1926. Author's interviews and correspondence: on Alice Pike Barney – William Huntingdon, Joseph E. Holliday, Jack Gee, John Mullane; on Natalie Barney – Jean Stengers, Derek Patmore, Francois Chapon; on Katie Gough-Roberts – Harry Leech and Lucy M. Jones; on Morien Mon Huws – Ivor Wynne Jones.

UNPUBLISHED MATERIAL: letters and diaries in SFA, RGS.

NOTES

Denzil, the adopted son of the explorer, was sent to Eton and Sandhurst. He became a regular army officer, served in Mesopotamia, and retired with the rank of major.

Alice Pike Barney was buried in Dayton, Ohio. Her gravestone bears only the epitaph 'The Talented One'.

Henry Curtis, second husband of Dorothy Stanley, spent his last years in the Inner Temple, London, and died there in 1944.

Natalie Barney was the model for one of Hemingway's characters in *The Sun Also Rises*.

The descendants of Louis Noe are still living in Suffolk county, Long Island.

Indexes

The Indexes to this book were compiled by the Rev. S. B.-R. Poole

Index of Persons

393

Index of Places

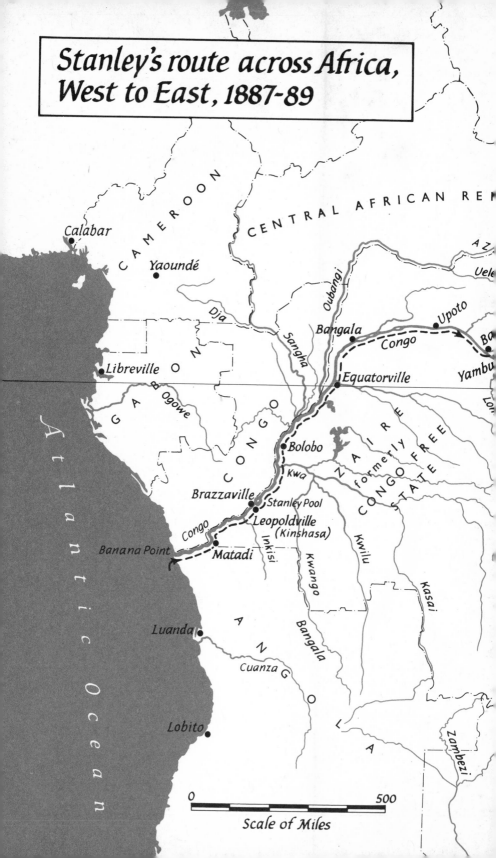

Stanley's route across Africa, West to East, 1887-89

CAMEROON

Calabar

Yaoundé

CENTRAL AFRICAN REP

AZ

Uele

Oubangi

Bangala

Upoto

Congo

Ba

Libreville

Equatorville

Yambu

GABON

Dja

Sangha

Ogowe

Lo

ZAIRE

CONGO

formerly

Bolobo

CONGO FREE

STATE

Kwa

Brazzaville

Stanley Pool

Leopoldville
(Kinshasa)

Kwilu

Banana Point

Congo

Inkisi

Matadi

Kwango

Kasai

Atlantic Ocean

Luanda

A

N

G

Bangala

Cuanza

Lobito

O

L

A

Zambezi

0   500

Scale of Miles